The Fatal Friendship

Ned Kelly, Aaron Sherritt & Joe Byrne

IAN JONES

The Fatal Friendship

Ned Kelly, Aaron Sherritt & Joe Byrne

Lothian
BOOKS

Thomas C. Lothian Pty Ltd
132 Albert Road, South Melbourne, 3205
www.lothian.com.au

First published 1992
as *The Friendship that Destroyed Ned Kelly*
This revised edition published 2003

National Library of Australia
Cataloguing-in-Publication data:

Jones, Ian.
     The fatal friendship: Ned Kelly, Aaron Sherritt and Joe Byrne.

     Revised ed.
     Bibliography.
     Includes index.

     ISBN 0 7344 0543 X.

     1. Kelly, Ned, 1854–1880. 2. Sherritt, Aaron, 1855–1880. 3. Byrne, Joe,
     1856–1880.
     4. Bushrangers—Australia—Biography. I. Jones, Ian. Friendship that destroyed
     Ned Kelly: Joe Byrne & Aaron Sherritt. II. Title.

364.1552092

Index for the original edition by Susan Liepa revised by Russell Brooks.
Cover and text design by Dennis Ogden
Typeset by Ogden Art & Design
Illustration layout for the original edition by Tom Kurema revised by Dennis Ogden
Inside cover illustration by John Ward
Printed by Griffin Press

CONTENTS

Preface and Acknowledgements

On the night of 26 June 1880 outlaw Joe Byrne, lieutenant of the Kelly Gang of bushrangers, shot his lifelong friend Aaron Sherritt, declaring to the dying man's mother-in-law and pregnant bride, 'The bastard will never put me away again.'

Sherritt died an informer's death, in a house bought by police money, wearing clothes given to him by a detective, with four constables dithering impotently in the next room. Even his funeral and his widow's crepe were paid for by the police. Everything confirmed his guilt.

Aaron Sherritt is the classic traitor of Australian folklore. His name has a splendid ring of villainy to it and his best-known portrait shows an avaricious, almost cruel face, with sensual lips, cold eyes, and dark hair glossed back from a devilish widow's peak.

But the 'portrait' is a contemporary press engraving which distorts Aaron's features in conscious or unconscious homage to the traitor role in which he was already cast. In marked contrast, an original photograph records a striking, open face, with broad mouth ready to smile and bright, calm eyes. It is the face of a likeable rogue. In it you seek, without conviction, the man who betrayed his best friend for blood money.

Joe Byrne's avenging role completed, he rode off to his own death only thirty-five hours later. He fell in battle with police, clad in plough-steel armour, as he raised a glass of whiskey in a last, defiant toast, 'Many more years in the bush for the Kelly Gang!'

It was an end worthy of the outlaw legend he had helped to create and as preposterous as much else in the twenty-three year life of this opium-addicted bush poet who spoke Chinese, wooed barmaids, rode a magnificent grey mare, outwitted watching police to visit his widowed mother and was 'the idol of the girls of the district'.

When some photographers won a bizarre photo session with Joe's stiff-ened corpse hung on a cell door, they recorded a sadly handsome boy, the youth and gentleness of his face accentuated, rather than camouflaged, by a downy moustache and beard. Here is the poet, the lover, not the hard-riding outlaw, the killer.

In the end both the despised traitor and the swashbuckling outlaw seem equally miscast. In essence, they were. Each was playing a role he had stumbled into. Yet each responded to the demands of his particular audience, so successfully that masque and reality interfused, to become almost indistinguishable.

Joe's killing of Aaron was seen, for nearly ninety years, as simple retribution for betrayal. Since I first challenged this view in 1967, most Kelly writers have taken a less black-and-white view of Aaron's motivations—though clearly reluctant to abandon completely the image of a traitor driven by greed.

Their reluctance is understandable. If Aaron was not a traitor, his death at the hands of his friend becomes an unlikely mystery—unlikely because everything about it seems so clear-cut, even down to Joe's statement of motive, almost before his victim was dead.

'The bastard will never put me away again!'

There can be no doubt that Joe believed Aaron had betrayed him. That much, at least, is clear. But his reasons for holding that belief are far more cloudy, far more complex.

This book is an investigation of that mystery.

Much of the truth lay buried in the Minutes of Evidence of a Royal Commission which inquired into the conduct of the Victoria Police during the Kelly Outbreak—more than 17,000 questions and answers, appendices, tables, supplementary returns and reports. Other vital clues were scattered through eight cheese boxes of documents stored in the basement of the old Melbourne Public Library—the Kelly Papers—now largely available on microfilm at the Victoria Public Record Office but still awaiting exhaustive cataloguing. Court records, newspaper reports, government documents and publications, private papers and printed works of incredible range also contributed. Yet all this material created only a partial picture of the remarkable chain of events which destroyed Aaron Sherritt, Joe Byrne, Ned Kelly and nine other lives.

Crucial pieces of the puzzle and much of its eventual solution were provided by those most fallible and perishable of historical sources—human memory and the landscape in which these people lived and died.

I owe a special debt to my wife, Bronwyn, for her enormous research contribution in helping to fill gaps and tie loose ends accumulated in the preceding 30 years of sporadic investigation. Many of the people involved in that process have died. Below, I do not distinguish them as 'late' because, to me, they are all a part of the intricate pattern of lives linking Aaron and Joe with the present day.

Max Brown, Ned Kelly's biographer, first made Joe and Aaron live for me. Des Zwar introduced me to his native Beechworth and the last contemporaries of the pair—George Collier, George Stilley and Ernie Manton. Historian and Burke Museum curator, Roy Harvey, guided me into Beechworth's past and, with his wife May, accompanied me on several investigations of obscure sites. Bill Knowles, whose mother and grandfather play a part in the story, shared with me his encyclopaedic knowledge of the Woolshed Valley and the people who had lived in it. Almost blind from a bungled cataract operation, he navigated the bush with uncanny skill, still able to identify every location and landmark, and to lead me within a few feet of virtually invisible features he had not seen for twenty, sometimes fifty years.

Members of the Byrne and Sherritt families, some still scarred by the tragedy of the Trouble, trusted me with memories of 'the old people'. In life and death, I have respected their privacy. Mounted policeman Jim Clifford introduced me to his former colleague, Tom Lloyd jr, whose memories of stories told him by his father have been of seminal value. In 1964 an old school friend, Don Woodford, told me that Elly Byrne, Joe's sister, was still alive. At Albury's Mercy Hospital, with the help of Mother M. Hugh and her nuns, I had three long and precious interviews with 93-year-old Elly before her death later that year.

Among the people whose help and hospitality I have enjoyed during my field work are Lin and Ray Zwar, Louise Earp, Clive and Alan Robinson, Pat and Jim White, Wilma and Ted Wells, Jack Walsh, Hubert Warner, Greg Forrest, Jack Healey, Margaret and Brian Gladstone, Esmai and Ken Wortman, Ken Embling, Gwen and Charlie Griffiths, Paddy Griffiths, Len and Dulcie Griffiths, Colin Crawford, Ivy Johnson, Rene Knowles, Bernie Clancey, Richenda and David Martin, Bill Short and Laura and George Fraser.

Long-serving Beechworth Shire Secretary, Graeme Gray, was generous in his support and Beechworth Clerk of Courts, Don Hammond, gave me free access to the court and mining records then stored in the court house.

Veteran Kelly scholars Keith McMenomy and John McQuilton have been open-handed with their material as have the next 'generation' of researchers, the incomparable Dagmar Balcarek, Alan Nixon, Noel O'Shea, Rob Ogilvie, Graham Jones, Judy Bassett, Kevin Passey and Gary Dean. Other valued help is acknowledged in the notes.

Paul Gorry of Dublin energetically pursued several leads on the Irish origins of the Byrnes and Sherritts. Aaron's grand niece, Allie Trezise, conducted her own research on a recent visit to Ireland and contributed further insights.

The staff of the Public Record Office of Victoria at Laverton and in Melbourne have been unfailingly helpful. My special thanks to Chris Diver and to Harry Nunn for his guidance when the state's archives were still tucked away in the bowels of the Public Library.

Sgt Hugh Bell of Victoria Police Public Relations and former detective, Jim Puls, gave valued help and advice. Present members of the Victoria Police Historical Unit have cheerfully dealt with a number of queries.

Frances Freeman and Catherine Herrick of the Ministry of Education Historical Service were extremely helpful and introduced me to educational researchers, L. J. Pryor and Max Waugh, both of whom freely shared their knowledge and resources.

My longtime friend and colleague, Veda Currie, typed the manuscript.

Keith Harrison enabled me to examine Ned Kelly's and Joe Byrne's Jerilderie Letter. I cannot adequately express my gratitude.

My son Darren, companion on innumerable adventures among the haunts of Joe and Aaron, has provided most of the modern photographs.

Finally, a dedication to Tony Doogood, Australian television pioneer and Kelly enthusiast. In 1960, scarcely a month before he was fatally injured in a riding accident, Tony joined me on a three-day ride through the Wombat Ranges. Camped in the shadow of Toombullup's long ridge, we yarned about the enigma of Joe and Aaron. Tony urged me to write a book.

Preface to the revised edition

This edition includes a number of corrections and some new material in text, notes and illustrations.

I am grateful to Dennis Ogden for designing yet another book for me and assisting in its production under considerable time pressure; to my wife, Bronwyn, for ongoing research support; to my editor, eagle-eyed Amy Thomas; to my daughter, Elizabeth, who integrated the corrections and revisions; and to Russell Brooks for revising the index.

Among the people who have supported my continuing fieldwork are Lorraine Lucas, Jan and Alan Robinson, Roger Smitheram, Adrian Bartsh, Jan and Peter Powles, Pat and Jim White, the Lloyd family, Brendon Kelson, the Sonneman clan, Mick and Barry Spencer, Brendan Pearse, Matt Shore and my son Darren.

Finally, I acknowledge an enormous debt to the late Wilma Wells, niece of Aaron Sherritt, who was so much more than a source of family tradition. She was a dear friend who enriched my time in the Beechworth district for forty years. Through her trust and generosity, many vital strands of the story were preserved.

October 2002

CHAPTER 1

The Byrnes and Sherritts

1833–64

The roots of this story lie in Ireland, a country that has seldom recognised a middle ground between loyalty and betrayal. Here two families had their beginnings. The Byrnes sprang from Catholic, nationalistic stock—a peasant family deeply scarred by the ongoing war against English rule. The Sherritts, descended from French Huguenots who had fled Catholic persecution, were Anglo-Irish farmers, four-square for the Crown and the Established Church, strongly anti-Catholic.

A generation later, in a different country, two young men, Joe Byrne and Aaron Sherritt, clashed tragically. It is easy to imagine that family origins played their part in the final tragedy—too easy. In fact, the militantly opposed Orange and Green allegiances of the two families create a new mystery. It was the strength of the boys' friendship—defying their Irish origins—not any enmity, which lay behind the tragedy.

Joe Byrne was named after his grandfather—an Irish rebel transported to Australia for life. Old Joe came from County Carlow. Here, and in the neighbouring counties of Wicklow and Wexford, the Viking name Byrne (from *bjorn*—bear) was very common and the Christian name Joseph popular. Our Joseph Byrne lived in the parish of St Mullins at the southern tip of Carlow—a rough triangle of woods, bogs and farmland bordered to the east by the Black Stairs Mountains and to the west by the River Barrow. Joe was a 'farm servant' and shepherd, a hard-working young man supporting a wife, Catherine, four sons and a daughter.

Joe had been born only two years after the 1798 rebellion and grew up in its heartland on stories of the atrocities committed by the British rulers of Ireland in crushing this tragic uprising—the picketings, half-hangings, pitch-cappings. Among the heroes of the rebellion were Garrett Byrne, leader of the Wicklow rebels, and Miles Byrne of Wexford. After the rebel defeat at the Battle of Vinegar Hill, Michael Dwyer waged his legendary five-year guerilla war against the English, despite a five hundred guinea reward on his head.

Michael Dwyer's mother was a Byrne, and his cousin, Hugh Byrne, was a loyal lieutenant. Both were eventually forced to surrender and exiled to Australia for life, leaving behind them a legacy of defiance and hope—and an imperishable idea of outlaw heroes who were friends to ordinary folk and enemies to their oppressors. Small wonder that, as a young man, Joe was ready to swear his loyalty to the rebel cause. He joined the Whiteboys, a secret society of activists who have been called 'the ancestors of today's Provisional IRA'.

Each year the folk of St Mullins parish had to pay £600 in tithes to a wealthy landowner who then paid the Church of Ireland curate a meagre £32. As a fighter against such abuses, in what came to be called the Tithe War, Joe was betrayed, arrested and tried at Wexford on 30 July 1833, for the definitive Whiteboy crime, 'Unlawful Oaths'. He was found guilty and sentenced to transportation for life. Three Carlow men (including another Byrne), sentenced with him to transportation for life, were found guilty of less typical crimes but may have been fellow Whiteboys.

After seven months in prison and on a crowded brig that had carried him north to Dublin Harbour, Joe was put aboard the convict transport *James Laing* which sailed for New South Wales on 16 February 1834 with a cargo of 200 convicts. Catherine Byrne was left grieving in Carlow with her five children. The eldest was only eight, the youngest a baby. And Patrick, who would pass on Joe's name and perhaps more of his legacy, was only two. Joe would never see his wife and daughter again and the young sons would be men before he was reunited with them.

The *James Laing* unloaded its convicts in Sydney on 29 June 1834, after a voyage of 133 days. The convict system in New South Wales had by then shed some of its early harshness and assignment to a decent master offered many men and women a better life than they might have found in the old countries. Yet there were still atrocities and the old hands kept alive stories of Emu Plains and 'cursed Toongabbie'—hell camps of Sydney's western fringe—immortalised by Frank the Poet or some other convict bard in the ballad 'Moreton Bay'.

As a transported rebel, Joe quickly learnt the fate of other Irishmen who had struck out at British rule in this new land. Only thirty years before, some 200 Irish convicts, most of them 1798 rebels, had broken out of the Castle Hill prison farm to gather supporters, plant a 'Tree of Liberty' at Government House, Parramatta, and march on Sydney. In what came to be called the Battle of Vinegar Hill, a couple of dozen British redcoats smashed the rebel force with ugly efficiency. Seventeen rebels were shot and bayoneted, eight were hanged, nine received 200 to 500 lashes and 34 were sent to the hellish coal mines at Newcastle.

Three years later another rising was aborted when seven Irishmen were arrested and tried—among them Michael Dwyer and Hugh Byrne, Joe's childhood heroes. Five, including Dwyer and Byrne, were acquitted; the other two received 1,000 lashes; all were scattered through the colony.

Joe disappeared into the system, probably working as a shepherd in the Maneroo district—today's Monaro—and carefully keeping his peace. After nine years he appeared in the Braidwood district where he was granted a ticket-of-leave in 1843, first step to freedom. Soon after, he was working for Luke Hyland, who ran a hotel and sheep property at Long Swamp in a high-land valley near Bungendore. Hyland, the son of an Irish convict who had been transported for life, was successful and respected. Whatever bitterness Joe felt against the system that had taken him from his family, however deeply his inborn hatred of English rule had been intensified by his ten years as a convict, here was living proof that a man's origins need be no handicap in this new land.

In the intervening years, Joe's wife had died, his daughter, Mary, was probably married. Ireland had become a sad and terrible place, wracked by the potato famine. When Joe was granted a conditional pardon in November 1848, he had already arranged to bring his four sons to Australia under the bounty migrant scheme.

In mid-1849, 18-year-old Patrick Byrne set off on the great adventure with his three brothers, 22-year-old John, 20-year-old James and 16-year-old Michael. They made the voyage on a ship that fitted the dream, a former East Indiaman with the stirring name *Success*. Aboard were 33 families, eleven single girls and fourteen single men, all rejoining convict fathers. Among the few passengers without convict parents in Australia were two 21-year-old girls, Mary Wall and Jane Treehey. By the end of the voyage John Byrne had lost his heart to Mary, James was courting Jane. Both couples would soon marry.

Joe probably met his sons in Sydney on Tuesday, 18 December 1849. He was now nearly 50, trying to recognise in these four young men the children and babies of sixteen years before. They travelled with him back to the Monaro to celebrate an alien Christmas among the twisted, high country gums and sun-bleached grazing lands.

The Byrne brothers were shaping lives for themselves in the district when the discovery of gold near Bathurst in 1851 changed everything. While James was a married sheep farmer, already settled near his father, the other three showed more of a buccaneering spirit and would head off to find the crock of gold at the foot of the rainbow. Old Joe never forgave his three sons for what he seemed to regard as desertion. 'His beloved James' and James's two daughters would be the sole beneficiaries of his will.

While the three Byrne boys hesitated between plough and gold miner's pick, in neighbouring Victoria newly discovered goldfields were drawing diggers by the tens of thousands. While a few won wealth, most struggled for a living, and a government licence fee, brutally enforced by a hated police force, became the catalyst for rebellion. Spearheaded by Irishmen, the rebels of Ballarat hoisted a magnificent Southern Cross flag and swore on it 'to fight to defend our rights and liberties'. They built a crude stockade on the Eureka lead and some of them drew up a Declaration of Independence which proclaimed the Republic of Victoria. On 3 December 1854 redcoats and goldfields police cut them to pieces in a brief, dawn battle. At least 22 diggers were killed or died of wounds, about half of them Irish.

When thirteen Eureka prisoners stood trial for treason, Melbourne juries refused to convict them. Already, a Commission had recommended scrapping the odious licence fee and replacing it with a £1 annual Miner's Right which would entitle the holder to a living space of land and a vote. Within a year of the rebellion, Victoria had a new constitution (which England had been dithering over for years). Its first parliament instituted universal manhood suffrage and the secret ballot.

Australia's first Irish rebellion at Castle Hill fifty years before had won nothing, not even an acknowledgement of its simplistic ideology. This second Irish rebellion had been crushed with equal brutality but already had emerged as a pyrrhic British victory. Perhaps the next Irish-led rebellion would find better fortune.

In July 1855 at the Catholic Church of St Peter and St Paul in Goulburn gold digger Patrick Byrne married a local girl, Galway-born Margret White, a slim, brown-haired 21-year old with a strong, open face and the palest of blue eyes. She had prominent teeth which flashed brightly in a smile but, in repose, gave her face a determined set. Patrick was 24, strongly built with powerful hands, a gentleness in his blue or grey eyes, and probably a touch of red in his hair and beard.

Margret signed her name in the register with a strong, angular hand. Patrick was illiterate but had learned to write his Christian name. The priest allowed him the dignity of tracing out his 'Patrick' then wrote for him 'Byrnes'—a more common form which Margret would continue to use long after Patrick had learnt to write and to spell his name correctly. (The half-signature was unacceptable for the certificate lodged with the government. Patrick had to sign with a mark, as an illiterate.)

Patrick failed to strike it rich and the following year he and Margret headed south to Victoria, accompanied by or soon to be followed by John and Mary Byrne with three young sons, and bachelor Michael. Paddy and Margret's 250-mile journey ended in north-eastern Victoria near Beechworth, a raw, booming gold town that sat on a sway-backed, granite plateau, 1,800 feet above sea level, reigning over the camps and towns of the Ovens goldfield and their 40,000 diggers.

Gold had first been found in Spring Creek that looped across the end of the plateau and plunged down in a series of cataracts to become Reid's Creek. Here, the town called Reid's Creek grew up by a goldfield. Then the creek leapt down more cascades and a superb waterfall to become Reedy Creek, flowing westward through a rolling valley called the Woolshed—named after a building that stood near the district's first strike and whose timbers had been used to shore up the first shaft. The gold town Woolshed sprawled here, a place of uncountable, nomadic population, but close to 4,000. Built of canvas, sawn timber, saplings, split log and bark, its two-mile span on both sides of the creek, joined by the Sunbury Bridge, bustled with 150 businesses to serve the miners—ten hotels, seventeen restaurants, two breweries, several ginger beer and cordial factories, even a professor of music.

It was probably here, in a tent or flimsy shack, that Margret Byrne bore a son in November 1856. Paddy was determined to proclaim his pride in the father he had scarcely known by naming his son after him, even though John and Mary Byrne had called a son Joseph only two years earlier. Before the end of the following year, when little Joe was only ten months old, Margret became pregnant again. A second son was born in June 1858 and they called him John. He lived only 25 days and died after a three-hour attack of convulsions. Paddy took the tiny body up to Beechworth the following day and arranged a lonely, mid-winter burial in the town's new cemetery. The fact that infant death was commonplace in such a community made the tragedy no easier to bear. When little Joe was three, Margret had a daughter they called Catherine after Paddy's dead mother.

By now Paddy and Margret had ended their odyssey. Past Woolshed the valley formed a wide basin between two striking hills. To the north of the creek was a broad, granite dome called Sugarloaf. To the south Native Dog Peak brooded over the valley like an Aboriginal sphinx—a face of rutted granite to the east, a shaggy mane of native pine and hill gum over rock shoulders, with a timbered spine and flanks sloping away to the west. Opposite these hindquarters, the village of Sebastopol had sprung up beside another diggings. Here, Reedy Creek made a sweeping horseshoe bend to the south around the low hill and flat on which the settlement stood. Paddy and Margret settled at the bottom of this bend on the far bank of the creek. John and Mary Byrne made their home nearby.

Paddy's Miner's Right entitled him to an eighth of an acre of land for a house and garden, half the size of a modern Australian house block. Like most diggers, he cleared at least twice as much from the apple gum scrub and built his hut hard by the creek on the rim of a shallow gully which carried a tiny stream down from a deep-cut gap in the thickly wooded southern range.

A willow tree was planted to shade the hut from the fierce afternoon sun of summer and Margret established a garden of old country flowers including a patch of blue and white flag irises and some rose bushes. They planted fruit trees and cultivated a patch of potatoes, the whole garden enclosed by a low fence of split palings.

Paddy didn't take out a gold claim himself but probably worked with a friend called Phillip Riley who staked a claim for eight men below the Byrne hut in 1861. By the following year, when Riley took out a second claim beside the hut, Paddy had abandoned gold mining to become a bullock driver. The hubbub of a working gold claim was no place to have a baby and Margret's second surviving son was delivered at the nearby town of Chiltern on 17 March 1862, St Patrick's Day. If Paddy ever doubted that he should name a son after himself, the saintly birth date left no choice. Young Patrick joined Joe and Kate.

Already Joe promised to be tall and strong, a handsome boy with blue eyes and sandy fair hair. Only one thing marred his good looks—a slight imperfection of his upper lip. One man described it as 'short', another said, 'he had a double lip'. Most people noticed nothing unusual but young Joe became acutely sensitive about the defect. In the outlaw years a policeman would report, 'It was almost certain he never had his likeness taken, he was always opposed to it from a schoolboy.' He was wrong in one respect. As an adult, Joe did pose for one portrait—but only after he had been able to grow a moustache and carefully brush it down to hide his lip.

Meanwhile, with little Paddy and Kate, he learnt the expanding world of house and yard, then the riches of the valley. It was a superb place to spend childhood. There was always the creek behind the house with its yabbies and tortoises, its changing levels, courses and moods. Swollen by rain and melted snow, it swept past in a broad, sinuous torrent. More often, two wide channels looped around an island of white gravel below the Byrne clearing. In rainless summers the creek almost disappeared and broad gravel beds became hunting grounds for coloured pebbles, crystals, rough sapphires, zircons, garnets, agates, topaz, china shards and waterworn glass. Paddy had rigged a swing in the willow on the creek bank and there were always a hundred games to play, strange animals and birds to watch in the dense scrub beyond the Byrne fence, traffic to enjoy on the back Eldorado road that ran across the slope just above the front gate.

These were happy years but the golden days were passing. In 1862 and 1863 the diggers slowly drifted off to booming Eldorado a few miles westward, and elsewhere, following the trail of gold that was easier to win. Houses were abandoned to rot, leaving fireplaces like lonely altars; gardens wasted until only some fruit trees and a few stubborn irises remained to show where people had lived and dreamt. Then, in 1864, the Chinese started moving into the Woolshed in larger numbers, often making a living from worked ground abandoned by impatient Europeans. The next year drought blighted the district and more white diggers moved on.

Across the creek, the township of Sebastopol was melting away to a few scattered buildings. Closest, on a low rise opposite the Byrnes, was the Diedrich house with its acacia trees and oleander bushes. Just beyond was the exciting little world of Sebastopol's main Chinese camp, a few shops and a collection of huts. There was a smaller Chinese camp only a few hundred yards west of the Byrnes—eight or nine huts in the scrub by the back Eldorado road, built of stringybark saplings with thatched roofs of creek rushes. Here lived some twenty Chinese miners who worked with butcher Ah Shing on a sluicing claim served by a nearby dam and a race that cut across the Byrne clearing, channelling water more than a mile-and-a-half from beyond the Sunbury Bridge.

As the race silted up and was cleared out through the years, it came to form a high bank between a new Byrne homestead built further back from the creek and Margret's flower garden by the old creekside hut. The race also provided a handy source of water for the garden—a simple example of coexistence. The Chinese race crossed the Byrne land: the Byrnes used some of the Chinese water. In this atmosphere the Byrne children grew up to accept the gentle, industrious Cantonese as neighbours, with their coolie hats, dungarees and sandals made of pieces of plank fitted with leather thongs. Children brightened the monastic lives of the Chinese miners and Joe spent more and more time among them. They shared their food with him and called him Ah Joe. Gradually, he learned to understand the cadences of Cantonese and, eventually, could speak the language.

John, leader of the Byrne brothers, also stayed on at Sebastopol. He and Paddy were now carriers and probably worked together, carting goods for the remaining townspeople, the few, bigger gold claims, and sometimes selling firewood.

Paddy and Margret had made staunch friends in the dwindling communities of the valley. A second daughter, Mary, was born. Paddy had already learnt colonial ways and built a verandah on the new house. He and Margret could sit and look up to the flanks of the range, ragged with dark native pine and granite outcrops among the hill gums, catching the last light of each day. Just beyond this superb escarpment was a rolling tableland where another young Irish family, the Sherritts had settled. In this family too, a first-born son grew tall and strong.

Back in 1853 County Cavan in Ulster had seen a springtime romance between a schoolgirl and a young policeman. The girl was 15-year-old Agnes Anne Nesbitt (who liked to be called Anne), a small, attractive lass who attended a Church of Ireland girls school. Her father, Hugh Nesbitt, was a farmer. The policeman was 1st sub-constable John Sherritt of the Irish Constabulary (later the Royal Irish Constabulary), stationed at the district headquarters in the market town of Cootehill. John, an Orangeman, was a

Leitrim farmer's son, an olive-skinned 25-year-old, 5ft 8¼ins (above average for the time and place), powerfully built, with dark hair, sidewhiskers and 'laughing eyes'—a dashing figure in his dark blue uniform and cockaded shako.

According to family tradition, the pair eloped. While this isn't strictly correct, there were some curious hints of secrecy about their marriage in the Church of England and Ireland chapel at Knockbride, only six miles south of Cootehill, on Tuesday, 7 June 1853.

Unlike most couples, they didn't supply precise addresses, merely 'Knockbride Parish'. Anne (who did not give her full name of Agnes Anne) claimed she was a year older, John that he was three years younger. More significantly, John told the Reverend Mr Popham that he was a farmer, though this was his fourth year in the Constabulary. Hugh Nesbitt's signature as a witness could suggest parental approval, tolerance or perhaps insistence.

There is no reference to a marriage in John's Constabulary record and his police career limped on for another four months. He had received punishment in May (probably a fine). In August he was demoted to 2nd sub-constable and on 4 October he resigned 'to emigrate'. The next day another punishment was recorded. For hot-headed John Sherritt this seems to have been the final straw.

Under a cloud of official and, probably, parental disapproval, John and Anne travelled sixty miles to Dublin and caught a ship across the Irish Channel to Liverpool. From there, on Monday, 27 February 1854, they sailed on the *Matoaka* as assisted immigrants to gold rush Victoria, their passage subsidised by a payment of £40 5s to be made by the Victorian government on their safe arrival. Even though the colony urgently needed police, John avoided any link with the Constabulary and described himself as 'agricultural labourer'—confirming the fugitive nature of the couple's departure.

The *Matoaka* was a vessel of 1,323 tons which could carry its 403 passengers fairly comfortably. It was well managed and there were no deaths on the voyage of slightly less than three months. Most of the passengers were Irish Catholic, so the Orangeman and his bride kept very much to themselves—no hardship for two young people in love on what was virtually a honeymoon voyage.

On Friday, 26 May 1854, the *Matoaka* dropped anchor in Hobsons Bay off Williamstown and the Sherritts travelled up the River Yarra to Melbourne by paddle steamer. They found themselves in a handsome, brand-new English city with tarred streets, churches and inns abounding, already past the mad circus days of the gold rush and its population explosion.

If John had planned to become a gold digger, the cool winds of autumnal and economic change deterred him. Within a week, he and Anne had found work—six months employment with Captain John Harrison at the rate of £75 a year, not princely wages but, with bed and rations included, more than enough to give them a good start in this challenging new land.

The Sherritts worked at Prahran, a developing suburb a few miles to the south-east, probably on a dairy farm owned or leased by their employer. Harrison was an extraordinary man—a former sea captain and squatter who had been prominent in several radical movements and now championed the cause of Victorian gold diggers, on the verge of revolt against their exploitation by a squatter-dominated government. When the Eureka rebels were crushed by police and British troops on 3 December 1854, Harrison was a prominent figure in a massive protest against this bloody act of suppression.

John and Anne Sherritt might have attended a mass meeting of some 10,000 citizens in Melbourne's Swanston Street on Thursday, 7 December, when Captain Harrison shared the platform with speakers who included the co-founder of the city, the ageing John Pascoe Fawkner.

Harrison declared that 'he preferred the word citizen to subject as the former sounded more of freedom'. He concluded, 'Victoria would never go ahead or prosper till it was released from the thralldom of Downing Street, but our object can be effected by constitutional means, and without bloodshed.'

Whatever their regard for Harrison as an employer, the ex-constable and his wife may have felt that all this had an uncomfortable tang of treason about it. Their initial six months with Harrison had just expired, and they had a pressing reason to look to their future: Anne was pregnant and in August 1855 their first surviving child, Aaron, named after John's brother, was born.

Soon after the birth, perhaps advised by Captain Harrison, John headed off with his wife and baby son to the Ovens goldfields. On the gruelling 170-mile journey, they joined a new breed of pilgrims, no longer dazzled by the dream of fortunes easily won with pick and shovel. As one shrewd observer put it, 'Towards the middle of 1855...out of ten emigrants, nine were speculating in something or other—tool handles or lemonade at a penny a glass, and the tenth, stripped of all resources, kept to his pick, but with what ill grace!'

Outside Beechworth John and Anne settled at Reid's Creek, a gold mining township that had sprung up at the foot of the widening gorge where the golden creek tumbled down from the plateau to enter the Woolshed Valley— only a couple of miles from the mining camp where Joe Byrne would be born the following year.

John took out a Miner's Right to gain ground for a house and garden, but probably never worked full-time as a digger. The rush had already rolled further down the valley and to other creeks in the district. Only three years before Reid's Creek had been a violent pesthole which boasted fifteen murders in its first six months; now it was becoming a quiet backwater which could muster only ten businesses in 1857 beside the Woolshed's 150.

John found work with a Woolshed dairy farmer, delivering and selling milk with a horse and cart through the valley's camps and townships. Anne was already pregnant again and Aaron was barely eleven months old when a sister, Elizabeth, was born in July 1856.

The next year Anne's 20-year-old brother, Robert Nesbitt, immigrated to Victoria in time to greet his nephew, John James, to be called Jack, born in March 1858—the third Sherritt child in four years. By 1860, when a third son, William George arrived, John had established his own dairy farm, grazing his cows on rented land.

For a farmer, three sons were a rich blessing, with the promise of several more in the years ahead. But in what John came to see as a cruel twist of fate, Anne's next six babies were to be girls—Anne Jane (1862), Julia Frances (1864), Esther (1867), Mary (1869), Maria (1872) and Martha (1875).

The Sherritts attended Beechworth's Christ Church (enduring the Reverend Bennett's notorious hour-long sermons) and when Aaron was five or six, John and Anne sent him off to the new Reid's Creek Church of England school. The teacher there, Mrs Eliza Jane Scott, proved totally ineffectual and Aaron would grow up virtually illiterate.

Even after the school had been running for some six years, an inspector would damn it as 'a mere infant school and that of the most juvenile kind'. Mrs Scott tried to teach reading by inviting the children up, one at a time, to read from a book she held. The rest sat idle, prompting the inspector's scathing judgement, 'Mrs Scott has no idea of giving youngsters any employment. More than once a child asked for a slate and pencil; her answer was, "No, certainly not." Children are very quiet, but it must be a great penance having nothing to do.'

In these years before compulsory education, attendance at school was a matter of choice—for children or parents. Aaron chose, more often than not, to avoid the boredom of Eliza Scott's classes. And, once he could sign his name, and read and write at a rudimentary level, his parents don't seem to have worried about his missing school. He was a tall, strong lad with native wit and shrewdness, well equipped to help his father on the farm. Here he would gain a more practical education.

By 1864 the Sherritts had left Reid's Creek and moved to the rolling table-land which ran along the southern rim of the Woolshed valley, behind Native Dog Peak. Here, John grazed his cows on land rented from Dr George Mackay, a former ship's surgeon, who had taken up the 50,000-acre Tarrawingee run in 1853.

It was harsh country, thinly forested and ribbed with granite, bitterly cold in winter, hot and dusty in summer, drained by Sheepstation Creek which wound down to Reedy Creek just below the Woolshed falls.

About two-and-a-half miles above Reid's Creek, up near the headwaters of Sheepstation, John found a low knoll close by the creek, screened by a ridge to the west and foldings of the gully to the south. Here, he cleared bush for a homesite and small garden, as sanctioned by his miner's right.

He left one tree, an ancient red box crowning the rise, where horses could be tethered in shade.

From the felled trees, John split slabs and stripped bark to build a hut which, in time, became the kitchen to a homestead that grew through the years to accommodate the growing family. On the gentle slope between the hut and the creek, Anne planted a small grove of cherry plum trees for jam and sauce and some lilac bushes for a breath of old country beauty. She raised fowls and sometimes sold a basket of eggs in Beechworth to eke out the family income. She often had to walk into town—an eight-mile round trip with a steady climb across Dodd's Hill, over patches of bare rock. To preserve her one pair of boots, she used to walk barefoot and carry them around her neck until she reached the town's outskirts. Yet only once was she heard to complain. A daughter remembered her, in that one, dark moment, saying, 'I wish I'd never left my mother.' But most of the time, she found pleasure enough in her husband and children and was a devoted wife and mother though, steadily, the youth and gentleness drained from her face. A daughter-in-law would recall her as 'determined-looking'.

John took well enough to the harshness of bush life. He would be described as 'the usual sort of bushman you meet…pretty active…pretends to know a good deal'.

Increasingly, this tough, kindly man presented a taciturn, often belligerent face to the world. One day a strapping young fellow turned up to work for John, only to be told, 'You're too small. I'm looking for a big, bony, bloody Irishman that can carry a twelve-stone man on his back all day.' In old age he affected deafness as a barrier against people he didn't want to be troubled with or things he didn't want to hear.

In years to come John found some argument with the new vicar, W. Corbett Howard, and stopped attending the Church of England. After a ten-year absence, John temporarily healed the breach in 1879 for the baptism of three children. In the interim he conducted prayers and Bible readings in the home. The family recalled a winter night when they were gathered around the big fireplace for one of John's readings. A glowing hot coal fell out on the hearth and, on an impulse, young Willie rolled it against his father's boot. John continued reading until he'd finished the passage, then, without even closing the Bible, unleashed a mighty swipe that knocked Willie head over heels. Willie's 'joke' was taken as indicating a slight 'strangeness' about the lad. A friend was to say, 'They were smart, the Sherritts, all of them—all except Bill. He just seemed to miss out.'

The two older brothers, Aaron and Jack, showed early signs of strength and toughness beyond the ordinary. The three-year gap in the boys' ages made Aaron the dominant figure but, year by year, the physical gap between them closed, and Jack began to compete with his brother—as a runner and jumper, as a horseman, as a fighter. Both were pushed to extend themselves. Willie, two years younger than Jack, five years younger than Aaron, tried hard to be like them but he would grow up smaller and mentally and physically slower than the two older Sherritt boys, admiring them both, but adoring Aaron.

The girls too, were a spirited brood. Bessie, the eldest, was like her mother, a hard working and responsible child, growing tall and slim. Julia, with her curly hair, was to be the beauty of the family, while Anne Jane was the most striking of the girls—a willowy tomboy with her father's 'laughing eyes', an intensely vivacious youngster who, like all the girls, became a superb horsewoman.

The Sherritt children looked back on happy childhoods, with all the drudgery of dairy farming and tending fowls and pigs, as a background against which special, simple things stood out brightly—like Anne taking them on picnics with 'a treacle-tin billy filled with hard-boiled eggs'.

Aaron, growing tall and straight, every inch his father's son, was greatly loved. He grew up with a special confidence in himself: a readiness to be different.

There is one last glimpse of Aaron when he still attended the Reid's Creek school. A family called Robinson took over a fellmongery further down Sheepstation Creek near a rock formation called the Three Sisters. One morning Aaron was walking to school with young Will Robinson when they noticed two stringybark saplings that had sprung up on either side of the track. The two lads tied the top branches together and through the years, the saplings grew into a living arch, two trunks with a single canopy. Long after Aaron was dead, long after the Reid's Creek school was closed, Robinsons and Sherritts passing along the track saw the archway and remembered those days of the long lost 1860s, those days before the Trouble.

CHAPTER 2

The Careless Years

1862–75

In the Woolshed valley below the tableland the Byrne children led happy lives in passing sunshine. As Joe was approaching school age, it seemed that he would have to travel to Beechworth or Eldorado to receive a Catholic education. Then, as though it was meant to be, on 27 January 1862, soon after his fifth birthday, a Catholic school opened only a mile-and-a-half away at Woolshed. It stood on a scrubby rise above the Sunbury Bridge—whitewashed weatherboard with a shingle roof, brick chimney, two double windows on each side, and raised on blocks with steps up to a door that faced the creek.

On Sundays, Mass was said here, affirming to the Irish of the valley that the faith of their fathers would be equally reinforced during the school week by teacher John Egan.

One of Margret Byrne's daughters recalled, 'Mum always believed in education. She always said you couldn't get into anything without education.' So Joe trudged off to school with his older Byrne cousins—Uncle John's sons, James, Joseph and Michael—all dressed up like little men in long trousers, waistcoats, jackets and hats.

Each morning the boys crossed Reedy Creek by the footbridge near the Byrne house, cut up past Sebastopol to the main road, and followed its dusty, white windings up the valley, past brooding Sugarloaf and the scattered settlement of Devil's Elbow, along to Woolshed township, where the road dipped down to the Sunbury Bridge and the Catholic school. Here, with the under-sevens, Joe sat on the bare, board floor, learnt simple rhymes, and started to copy the letters of the alphabet with slate pencil on a wood-framed slate.

Joe's education—which played a significant role in his outlaw life—had a blighted beginning. The little school, basically funded by the Church, was caught up in the dying throes of the Denominational School Board and the birth of the Board of Education. Two months after opening his school, poor

Egan was plaintively asking the old Board if he was to receive a salary. Before the end of the year a new head teacher, James Doherty, was complaining to the new Board about not being paid. Next year, after missing three weeks of second term due to an eye injury, Doherty resigned and Beechworth priest Father William Tierney appointed the school's third teacher in nine months, Cornelius O'Donoghue—'Dunahoo' to the folk of the valley—a man who would become a staunch friend to the Byrne family. A century later he was still remembered with love by Joe's sister, Elly.

'Old Mr O'Donoghue—you couldn't beat him. One of the nicest men God ever put on earth. I think he had a little whisker. He was very kind to us and taught us everything he could at school. He was a good teacher.'

'Old' Mr O'Donoghue was only 18, a County Kerry farmer's son, newly arrived from Ireland, when he first faced Joe and the other pupils of the Woolshed school in August 1863. Quite unqualified but anxious to become a good teacher, he attacked the job with great energy and would devote the next twenty years of his life to the children of the valley, teaching at least one Byrne child all that time.

Only two months after the young Irishman's arrival, there was dramatic news for him and his pupils. The 'bush telegraph' reported—probably at Sunday Mass in the school building—that a newly appointed inspector of the Board of Education was working through the district and would probably be at the Woolshed the next day, Monday, 19 October. In a bid to help O'Donoghue earn a higher salary through the 'payment by results' system, parents herded every available child off to school, despite flooded creeks and roads turned to quagmires by spring rain. Fifty-one children—some eleven more than usual—packed the 32 by 17-foot schoolroom that morning and O'Donoghue had to give up his teacher's platform to First Class.

The morning passed and tense expectation stretched to relief: obviously, the inspector had been cut off by floods. Then, just after lunch, Inspector G. Wilson Brown came riding down the rutted, hoof-churned road, a soberly dressed figure of nemesis. He swung up the school's low hill and tethered his horse near the door. Then he climbed the steps and entered the hushed room.

Brown was only 31, but a Bachelor of Arts from Cambridge, a thoroughly British young gentleman who would carve a comfortable place for himself in the colony's establishment. Glancing around the over-crowded schoolroom, already suspicious that his arrival had been expected, he took a notebook from his pocket and began a cool and meticulous assessment of teacher, pupils, premises and equipment. Not surprisingly, he found the school 'under standard'. The building was unlined: there were no toilets: the teenage teacher was disorganised and inexperienced: most of his pupils lacked even basic learning skills. And the big turn-up of children highlighted the school's lack of furniture—no desks, one rough table, and only four eight-foot benches.

The punctilious little notes made by Mr Brown that spring afternoon give history its first glimpse of Joe Byrne—a handsome six-year-old reading a passage from the Irish National Schools Second Book, to gain a pass in reading. Of fourteen fellow pupils in Second Class, thirteen passed reading but, with all the others, Joe failed in writing and arithmetic. Brown noted, '2nd Class begin to write letters and figures on slates but do nothing in the way of numbers.' All would repeat the class the following year. When Inspector Brown returned in March 1864 he again could find little to commend, except O'Donoghue's discipline, which he considered 'very fair'.

Teacher and pupils worked strenuously through autumn and winter and, when the Inspector returned in October, there was a spectacular improvement in almost all aspects of the school. This time, Joe passed in all subjects—reading, writing, arithmetic, grammar and geography—to become equal best in his class, tying with 8-year-old Mary Anne Maddern, daughter of his parents' great friends, Anne and Daniel. In years to come, many judgemental eyes would study Joe's writing which by now satisfied Mr Brown. Perhaps coincidentally, Joe came to adopt a quirk of Brown's handwriting—a curving upsweep at the ends of words which ended with certain letters.

Cornelius O'Donoghue was eager to accept Brown's criticism and advice and, in his turn, the inspector developed considerable respect for this energetic, kindly, disorganised young Irishman who would devote all but the last few months of his life to teaching. And the inspector continued to approve of young Joe. In three out of four visits over the next two years, Brown would place Joe as first, equal first, and second in his class.

At home Margret Byrne's influence was significant. Evening activity in the Byrne house, as described by Joe's youngest sister, probably varied little from ten years before when Joe was at school.

'We used to have tea and we'd wash up and we'd go out and have a game...then it would get dark and we'd come in and we'd sew, and we'd write—anything that was in another book—and copy it out, like a verse, a poem, like that. Mother used to like us to do that. And we'd often take it and read it to her and she'd think it was nice. Sometimes we made up little verses and we'd take them to her and she'd laugh. Anything really—"One, two, knock on the door; three, four, something else...".'

Young Joe developed a flair for writing simple verses and parodies that clearly delighted his mother and was to win grudging acknowledgement from a senior policeman leading the pursuit of the Kelly Gang, who commented, 'He was, for a bushman, rather clever with his pen.' And again, 'He was very fond of writing, and a bit of a poet.'

From far off, the schoolhouse was a tiny white cube on its rise among the cluster of grey huts along the creek—dwarfed by the untouched ranges that echoed the chanting of rhymes and tables. Year by year the grey huts grew fewer but the chanting grew louder as the remaining families bloomed in biennial fidelity to partner and Church. While the population of the Woolshed halved, school attendance doubled from 30 to 60.

On a forgotten day, a new face appeared in the schoolhouse—a friend of Joe's and a year older—a tall lad with dark brown hair and lurking mischief in his face, untidy of dress, almost unlettered. And a Protestant. He was Aaron Sherritt.

How Joe and Aaron met remains a mystery. But, for a time, and probably irregularly, Protestant Aaron rode the three miles down from the tableland to escape Eliza Scott's boring, babyish lessons and join his friend in the valley's Catholic school. It's easy to imagine O'Donoghue's disapproval but, after all, under the new Act, this was a Common School and advertised as such by a sign erected in 1864. There were other Protestants here, including the bright Wallace boys, and Aaron's presence was tolerated—even though it soon became clear that Joe and Aaron made an unholy pair.

'They were good cobbers and scoundrels with it,' said a schoolmate.

Trips to the new slab toilet might become an expedition to the creek; or playtime could signal pitched orange and green battles; end of school, a home-going raid on Anton Wick's little orchard just over the bridge. Like almost everyone else, O'Donoghue probably worried that Aaron was a bad influence on Joe and did nothing to discourage his long and frequent absences.

One of O'Donoghue's more senior pupils, James Wallace, was also drawn to Aaron, beginning a strange and fateful relationship. Wallace had been born in Melbourne, son of Scots migrants. His father, 'an experienced seaman', was an inexperienced gold miner and drifted from field to field, trailing his wife and, eventually, seven sons, six of whom would become school teachers. Young James Wallace, foreshadowing a lifelong interest in the paranormal, dabbled in hypnotism ('mesmerism' as it was then called) and Aaron agreed to become a subject for his schoolyard experiments. Wallace was later to say that Aaron was 'guarded and cunning' but easily won his confidence and, perhaps, some level of dependence for the rest of his short life.

Joe achieved something of the same power over Aaron, winning, with charm and a keener intellect, the fierce loyalty of a boy who was already physically remarkable, a runner and fighter, impervious to discomfort and cold, bold horseman, expert bushman.

For Joe, Aaron supplied a hardening influence, giving his friend some of the physical toughness nurtured in his sons by John Sherritt. Without such influence, Joe's brother Paddy, while more physically powerful, would grow up a gentler man, in the mould of their father.

Together, Joe and Aaron explored the creek, the valley and the ranges, finding places where huge boulders and slabs of granite were piled together like houses of cards to form caves and shelters blackened by Aboriginal fires, their floors deep with ancient charcoal. They chased the wild goats and newly arrived rabbits that swarmed on the ranges, enjoyed the black walla-bies hurtling across the slopes in low, plummeting bounds, and watched giant wedgetail eagles gliding over the ridges and gullies in search of prey.

Soon they came to explore Byrnes Gully that cut up into the range in front of the Byrne homestead—right up to the tableland where the Sherritt farm lay. It was a journey of bewildering mood changes.

Up beyond the Byrne cowyard and the back road to Eldorado, the gully fanned to peaceful slopes below the thickly timbered ravine of Byrnes Gap. A tiny creek of unusually opalescent water ran down a gutter of pinkish rocks and sand, winding among stringybark and native pine that grew, free of undergrowth, from a carpet of fallen gum leaves. In a glade by a bend of the little stream, a natural granite throne with a moss-padded seat offered rest and rich food for imagination.

Above, Byrnes Gully narrowed and the serenity of the creek was lost in a chaos of boulders and tree carcasses that had torn loose from the steepen-ing sides, steeper and wilder, until the way was blocked by a black rock face with a little waterfall.

To the left was a cliff-like slope studded with boulders and tenacious trees; up to the right emerged a huge, dark tor called London Rock. At its base, reached by a narrow, cliff-face track from the head of the waterfall, was a small, triangular cave, just big enough for two, with a chimney-like vent that ran up and back, into the heart of the rock. For young Joe and Aaron, it was a hiding place, a vantage point commanding the approach up the gully. A cool, dark, secret grotto that breathed the peace of centuries and the protective might of the tor.

Many years later, in a fugitive winter, Joe the outlaw would write to his boyhood friend, 'Meet me under London, you know.' Perhaps as he waited in the cave, gun close to hand, he recalled all those lost times when they had met or sheltered here, hidden from imaginary enemies, and feeling affinity with the hunted as they watched wedgetail eagles patrolling the slopes. Joe and Aaron must have dreamt of the horses that could master this haunting terrain.

In years to come, a senior policeman would watch incredulously as Aaron rode down the 'nearly perpendicular' side of Byrnes Gully opposite London Rock. Later, when the officer described the descent, one of his subordinates, a seasoned bushman, would scarcely believe him. As an outlaw, Joe would regularly ride into the Woolshed 'down the steepest part of Wall's Gully'—a sheer, granite slope in the hills behind the Woolshed school. It was a safe route because no one believed a horseman could negotiate it.

For now, Byrnes Gully was a devil's playground for young Joe and Aaron, an adventurous short-cut between their homes, a private realm they shared with the goats, black wallabies, and eagles.

In 1946 writer Max Brown spoke to the few Beechworth people who could remember the pair. His picture of the young Joe comes from them: '...a quiet, intelligent, lithe youngster, clean and tidy in his habits, a little old-fashioned and grave in his ways'. By comparison, Aaron was 'a shiftless character, with no other ambition than to follow his whims and ride fine horses. Yet he had a vitality and wayward Irish charm which Joe found attractive.' Brown quotes a Beechworth girl who knew Joe well. After describing him as 'a nice, quiet boy, not flash', she went on to say, 'He got in with Sherritt and that was when the trouble began.'

Intriguingly, Anne Sherritt said of Aaron, 'My son was an innocent fellow, and easily led astray.' A loving mother's assessment of her son, especially soon after his death, may be less than objective, yet other evidence suggests that Joe and Aaron's characters and the dynamics of their relationship were easily misread by people outside their circle.

Joe's sister Elly would have laughed at any suggestion that Joe was 'quiet'. She said of him, 'That was "The Demon", the one we used to call "The Demon"...he was always doing things the other boys wouldn't do. He climbed the trees and took the fruit or anything out of anyone's garden. You know, anything like that.'

And one of Joe's school mates, Annie Wick, recalled, 'He was a wild boy...good looking but wild.'

Sister and friend knew another side of the apparently quiet Joe, a side which could flare into violent anger. One day while he was yarding horses, a sister let some escape. Joe rushed up 'foaming with rage', grabbed her by the hair and hit her across the face with a bridle. This was recalled when Joe had shot down his best friend, the memory lit by those gun flashes. An acquaintance in the years before his outlawry needed no such stimulus to describe him as 'a dangerous man'. Like others at the time who called him 'Bullet Eyes', he saw a coldness, a threat in Joe's remarkable blue eyes and, though locked away in prison for six years, he feared to name Joe to the police.

Much of Joe's apparent reticence may have sprung from ingrained sensitivity over his imperfect upper lip, which also might have contributed to his tearaway and potentially violent behaviour. As for him being drawn to Aaron, evidence suggests the reverse. Aaron, we recall, started his education at Reid's Creek Church of England School but left it to attend the more distant Woolshed Catholic School where Joe was a pupil, travelling six miles each day, up and down the tortuous bridle track through Maddern's Gap. Certainly, Joe was the more diligent student, growing up to be, at least 'a bit of a poet', while Aaron could scarcely sign his name. Yet, of the two, Aaron proved to be the steadier worker, with some ability to tackle a daunting job and follow it through. Joe would remain the grasshopper, flicking from place to place through the brief summer of his life. With his good looks, unassertive charm, and sober clothes, Joe always carried with him an illusion of respectability, while Aaron's often eccentric mix of bush and town clothing advertised the larrikin streak which both boys shared but which Joe managed to conceal.

In 1866, when Joe was nine, Paddy Byrne developed heart disease. The trauma of his father's first heart attack may have been reflected in Joe's school work. On 13 May 1866 this boy who was usually first or second in his class, came last, with a pass only in reading.

Paddy gave up the trade of carrier and again worked as a miner for a time before setting up as a dairyman. There were two more children, Dennis born in 1866 (Joe and his clever classmate, Mary Anne Maddern, were sponsors at the baptism) and Margaret in 1869.

In September of 1869 Joe the old rebel died at Tarago, on the Monaro, independent to the last. Although 69 and struck by 'paralysis' (probably a stroke) a month before, he had continued to live on his farm, refusing to burden 'his beloved James' and his family at nearby Boro.

There is no way of knowing whether young Joe ever met his grandfather. If not, old Joe's legacy was just as surely handed on when the Byrne boys held their wake in the Woolshed valley for how could they honour the old man without honouring what he had believed in? To see Ireland a nation and her people freed from English rule—in whatever corner of the world they found themselves. If 12-year-old Joe wore a black armband to school in the manner of the times, he honoured much more than a dead grandfather.

This year, 1869, our last glimpse of Joe's schooldays is as the sole pupil in Fifth Class, the 'big boy' of the school, working without a timetable, helping O'Donoghue teach the junior classes, yet passing only in spelling, writing and arithmetic, and failing four subjects including reading.

Was it once again the impact of his father's illness on Joe's schoolwork? Certainly, by the following year, 1870, Paddy's heart condition had deteriorated so much that he was admitted to the Ovens and District Hospital in Beechworth. It meant the end of Joe's schooling. He was only 13.

The family visited Paddy, parading through the hospital's classic white granite portico into the echoing wards. The new resident surgeon, kindly Antoine Moussé, may have offered Margret some hope, but Paddy died on 7 November. He was buried in the Beechworth Cemetery the following day, without benefit of clergy.

Uncle John Byrne was there at the graveside with Joe to offer a prayer for gentle, hardworking Paddy, old before his time and dead at 39, to leave 36-year-old Margret a daunting legacy. She was six months pregnant, with six children and a dairy farm to manage.

At first, Joe seems to have given his mother what support he was capable of. During the last months of this lonely pregnancy, he slept with her in the double bed across the back of the living room. As Margret's time approached, Mrs Ellen Barry, a stout, red-headed Woolshed woman who had delivered little Margaret two years before, shared the bed with the young widow and her son, to await the onset of labour.

A daughter was born on 7 February 1871 and christened Ellen. Schoolmaster Cornelius O'Donoghue and his bride, Ellen, were sponsors at the baptism. Only five days after the birth Margret went up to Beechworth herself to register Elly, symbolising the independence and determination with which she approached widowhood. That spirit would be captured by Elly when she spoke of her mother running the dairy farm.

'People came to the house to buy milk and butter. Mother never took a pannikin of milk out of the house to say, "Will you buy this?" We never had to beg money. We always had enough.'

Within five years Margret would have 'fourteen or fifteen' cattle grazing on the Woolshed Common, about a thousand acres of Crown land administered by a committee which charged an annual fee of 4s per animal and provided a herdsman.

Helped by the children, Margret rounded up her cows for morning and evening milking, sieved some of the milk into big dishes to set the cream, then skimmed it off to churn butter, a product the Irish dairy farmers of the district had long been famous for. Her dairy farm was remembered as 'well conducted and clean'. As well as the cows, she had some goats, fowls and a flock of geese which provided many a Christmas dinner for Beechworth folk and would prove useful watch-dogs in years to come.

Everyone expected that Joe would soon be a bread winner for the family. Certainly, soon after his father's death, he got a job as cart boy at Dodd Brothers Tannery, not far from the Sherritt farm. He drove the tannery cart on errands to and from Beechworth and was remembered as an intelligent boy, popular with the men. But he soon drifted off to begin a round of occasional itinerant work which occupied the next four years. At some early stage he worked at Thologolong Station on the Upper Murray, probably 'picking up' in the shearing shed. He would have turned his hand to fencing, wood cutting, gold mining, some shearing, and is said to have once worked in a Chinese store. In 1872, when he gave evidence at the inquest into the death of a Chinese acquaintance, Joe described himself as 'labourer'.

Already, a love of horses had come to play a key role in Joe's life—as in Aaron's. Horses were essential in this broad country where a man might regularly travel a thousand miles for seasonal work. Back in Ireland the horse had been a symbol of wealth and power. Englishmen, landlords, officials and soldiers looked down on the Irish peasantry from horseback. In this new land, every man could sit a horse, eye to eye with the squatter, the trooper, the boss. Small wonder that in parts of Australia riding a fine horse with a saddle and bridle to set it off proud came to be treated as a right—a mark of freedom.

Beechworth storekeeper Paddy Allen commented, 'No one had ought to leave a saddle loose in those parts—a saddle or a horse. There were folks there that would never think of taking anything else who couldn't see a horse or a saddle wanting someone to look after it. Strange the fancy they had for horses.'

It would be some years before Joe and Aaron could afford mounts to match their ability and ambitions, and they soon had reputations as 'borrowers' of horses. Their schoolmate Annie Wick remembered, 'If they wanted your horse, they'd take it at night, ride to Eldorado, gallop all the way, and it'd be back in your paddock next day, all knocked up.'

The Beechworth girl who had found Joe 'a nice, quiet boy' showed surprising tolerance of his careless ways. 'He spent most of his time roaming about the Woolshed. He would come without warning in the evening, and we would have to make up a bed for him. My father would say: "Whose horse have you got today, Joe?" and Joe would reply briefly.'

But boyhood years were passing. While borrowing horses seemed harmless enough, the charge of Unlawful Use was only a legal nicety away and could quickly blur into theft.

Through the 1860s and 1870s, the opening of the colony's land for settlement by small farmers was slowly progressed through a series of Land Acts. Under the Act of 1865, John Sherritt applied for 'a licence to occupy' 16 acres of land surrounding his home, including a quarter of a mile of Sheepstation Creek. But because the creek was gold-bearing, the application was shufffled for two years in a bureaucratic limbo between the Lands and Mines departments. Meanwhile, without security of tenure, John fenced the allotment and built, beside his homestead and separate kitchen, a dairy, stockyard, barn and hay shed. He cultivated the balance of the land to grow hay and wheat.

Eventually, with a strip one chain wide along each side of the creek reserved for mining, John received his licence for the remaining 12 acres in March 1867. He paid £4 a year in rent for three years, then, as permitted by the Act, applied to buy the land. The purchase, at £1 an acre, was not completed until July 1872, after more departmental shuttlecock. By then John had bought an adjoining five acres of hayfield to the west and was renting, on licence, another five acres to the south, which he now applied to buy. The purchase of this last field would not be completed for almost twenty years as the tragedy of the Trouble, natural disaster and bitter conflict intervened.

Two Irish Catholic families, the Keltys and Murphys, settled on Sheepstation near the Sherritts, to begin a sporadic but long-running feud with the Orangeman and his family. John bore his Protestantism like a banner, and his 'laughing eyes' could easily lose their laughter. Perhaps unwisely, he attended a wake in the Woolshed, one of those Celtic rituals where grief, nostalgia and hard drinking dissolved whatever restraint the mourners normally displayed. When neighbour James Kelty called John Sherritt 'a dirty Orangeman', a fight started. John subsequently admitted to his family that he hit Kelty with a chair. Kelty claimed that John 'got the worst of it'.

Soon after this, Anne Sherritt took nine-year-old Dan Kelty to court after he hit her with a stick. The case was dismissed.

Early in 1870, John was taking a drayload of wheat to Beechworth when he ran in with James Kelty also heading to town with a horse and dray. Later, each man alleged unprovoked assault by the other. Only one thing is certain: John beat Kelty senseless and reported the clash to the Beechworth police. Two constables went back with John and found Kelty lying face down at the roadside with two black eyes and head injuries. He was taken to hospital and John found himself facing an assault charge, which eventually became 'wounding with intent to do some grievous bodily harm'.

After legal preliminaries, John appeared in court in August. On the same list the famous bushranger Harry Power was to receive fifteen years imprisonment. Power's apprentice, a teenage boy called Ned Kelly, had earlier been released in distant Kyneton, due to lack of evidence. John Sherritt's case was remanded to the General Sessions in October but the jury was unable to agree and John was again remanded to the General Sessions in February. Bail was refused and the ex-constable spent three-and-a-half months in Beechworth Gaol. Fifteen-year-old Aaron became the man of the family, helping his mother run the farm and dairy.

On 3 February 1871, a year after the fight with Kelty, John was brought from prison to face Judge Smyth in one of the most farcical courtroom scenes ever witnessed in the colony. His Honour was incoherent and, later in the sitting, needed 'temporary restraint'. Two theories were put forward: 'alcoholic excess' or 'aberration of intellect' due to sunstroke.

Despite an attempt by the Crown Prosecutor to adjourn proceedings, His Honour insisted on continuing and John was placed in the dock. Without explanation, the Prosecutor entered a *nolle prosequi*—a suspension of prosecution against John Sherritt—which had the effect of a good behaviour bond. John was released to his jubilant family as a stunned court was left to cope with Judge Smyth's 'illness'.

John resumed his struggle with the land, the seasons and officialdom, and, for two years, seemed to win. Then bushfire destroyed the Sherritt farm—house, hayfields, fences and outbuildings—miraculously without loss of life. Some of the children escaped by taking refuge at the Three Sisters. For the next fifteen years John and his family would battle to recover from this crippling blow—and those to follow. John was eventually to acquire an additional 73 acres and enjoy all too briefly a period of comparative prosperity before another fire destroyed the farm.

By now Joe and Aaron's lives had settled into a strange dualism. Their homes were primitive—mediaeval by European standards—yet a short ride

Aaron Sherritt, more soberly dressed than usual, in everyday working gear—lanky moleskins, rough riding boots, two shirts, and pork pie hat. For his visit to town he has buttoned his waistcoat and donned a sash. The Bray portrait probably dates from 1875 to '76, before Aaron grew the small chin beard he wore during the Kelly outlawry. The photo captures Aaron's whimsicality and the deceptive, 'light-looking' quality of his physique. He was six feet and weighed 12 or 13 stone.
(*Burke Museum, Beechworth*)

A 1911 Sydney *Sun* reproduction of a lost original photo of
Aaron which was the basis for the two portraits on page 36.
The handsome boots may be a pair he received as payment
for some cattle he stole from one of storekeeper Paddy
Allen's debtors. He leans on the same studio prop
(reversed) used for Joe's portrait. Prints of this photo were
supplied by police to the press at the time of Aaron's
murder and enterprising *Sketcher* artist, Thomas
Carrington, used Aaron's 'flash bushman' clothing and pose
for his cobbled-together 'portrait' of Ned Kelly, [lower right].
(*Keith McMenomy*)

It is ironic that Aaron Sherritt, supposed
betrayer of the Kelly Gang, should be one of
only two men ever photographed wearing
their chinstraps 'Greta-fashion', badge of
the Kelly sympathiser. Even more ironically,
this photo—reproduced in Superintendent
Hare's book—may have been taken for
police purposes, like a matching study of
Aaron's brother, Jack.

Hard to believe that this urbane figure is Joe Byrne, posed in James Bray's Beechworth studio—the only portrait taken during his life. The photo can be dated to early 1877 when Joe was 20, just before he started growing the beard he wore throughout his outlawry. The slightly flared riding pants and high-heeled boots betray the bush larrikin so effectively disguised by Joe's typically respectable town clothes.

Ned Kelly, as Joe and Aaron may first have seen him—unofficial boxing champion of the district at 19, ready to take on the world. This photo, by Melbourne photographer Chidley, captures something of Ned's extraordinary physical quality and, more effectively than any other portrait, suggests the charismatic impact of the man.

Part of Beechworth's Chinese village at Spring Creek in the 1860s. Joe and Aaron were familiar figures here. Joe spoke Chinese and was an opium addict, Aaron took out a gold claim with Chinese diggers. (*Burke Museum, Beechworth*)

took them to Beechworth which, by the early 1870s, had developed as a sophisticated and modern town. Founded on the wealth of the gold rushes and without the debris of preceding centuries to clutter its development, Beechworth had already achieved standards which many European cities would not match until the twentieth century.

Its two main streets, Ford Street and Camp Street, marked a bold cross on the plateau, lined with prosperous shops and business premises. At the intersection, a handsome, white granite post office with Italianate colonnade and tower had just been completed. Imposing, two-storey banks faced one another from rival corners and twenty hotels—from modest little pubs to the palatial new Commercial in Ford Street—honoured the free-spending, heavy drinking gold diggers.

Straddling its ridge, folded by gum and pine-clad hills, Beechworth had the healthy, hybrid air of an Indian hill station. Shop awnings formed friezes of deep shade along both sides of the main street, branding it as frontier, while at its head, on the town's highest hill, Christ Church's battlemented tower of white granite was splendidly English and mediaeval. At the far end of the street, on a lower hill, the granite fortress of the gaol marked the opposite pole of British authority, sustained by an honour guard of public buildings—telegraph office, courthouse, survey office, police station and sub-treasury—handsomely colonial with their white flag poles and picket fences.

Joe and Aaron's generation had taken their first steps in gold-mining camp and boom town but before they were out of their teens they found themselves living on the fringes of a highly developed urban community—a town which had grown to service the huge population of the Ovens goldfield with a flour mill, soap factory, iron foundries, sawmills, breweries, coach builders, a hospital, asylum, old people's home, library, museum, parks, swimming baths and racecourse. The very respectability of Beechworth, on which the civic fathers so prided themselves, was living proof that the Roaring Days had passed. Increasingly, and with diminishing success, the community would try to become its own reason for existence.

For a time, Joe and Aaron were accepted and acceptable figures in the streets of Beechworth—Joe with his 'peculiar swagger', Aaron with his 'remarkable' walk, or turning heads with their latest horse, tight-reined to make it prance along the white-metalled streets.

They would buy a pie at Dunlop's Scotch Pie Shop opposite the Post Office, or a piece of fried fish (fresh daily on arrival of the Chiltern coach) from Cortissos's fish shop, and eat it while they hung around Gray & Co.'s saleyards, 'window shopping' for horses and cattle, smoking pipes packed with tobacco they'd bought at young William Foster's tobacconist shop, with its painted wooden cigar-store Indian sloping out over the doorway like a figurehead.

The lads often visited the shop of Beechworth pioneer James Ingram—a newsagent, stationer and bookseller next to the post office—chatting with him in a Dickensian back room. Ingram, a small, fiercely eyebrowed and bearded Scot, found Joe 'a nice, well-behaved lad'. His thoughts on Aaron aren't recorded. But Richard Warren, son of a local newspaper proprietor, recalled him, 'Flash as Lucifer, dressed up to kill!…Anyone seeing him coming down Ford Street would ask, "Who the hell's this—some advance agent for the circus?"'

Joe and Aaron were equally familiar figures in Beechworth's Chinese village above Spring Creek—much bigger than the Woolshed camps and a far more elaborate re-creation of an old land in the new—houses, stores, theatres, temples washed with raw, vital colour, putting out elaborate signs and banners to advertise, honour the Joss, or merely decorate.

In the Woolshed camps, and probably here, Joe and Aaron were known as Ah Joe and—because the Chinese couldn't say 'Aaron'—Ah Jim. Aaron too, may have spoken some Cantonese. At seventeen, he had taken out a claim on Sheepstation Creek with two Chinese miners, Ah Loy and Ah Fook (joined soon after by Ah Kim and Ah How with Aaron's brother Jack).

One of Joe's friends in the Spring Creek village was the extraordinary Nam Sing. Born in Canton in 1835, he had come to Australia at nineteen and opened a store in the Beechworth Chinese camp. He called it Sun Quong Goon—Great New Beginning—and later established a hotel with the same name. He was soon a wealthy man and a noted philanthropist, highly respected in Beechworth's European community. He lived with an English woman, Annie Cohen, raised a family and in 1871 was baptised William at Christ Church. Yet he remained with his people, living on the edge of the Chinese village in a large house with a huge flower garden beside it. Sitting on Nam Sing's broad verandah, sipping jasmine tea and looking out across jubilant camellias to the colourful sprawl of the Chinese village, Joe could easily forget that he was the son of a Woolshed dairywoman, perhaps even that he was European.

Down in the Woolshed, from childhood, Joe had seen the Chinese smoking opium—twisting a bud of sticky, dark opium gum on to a needle, heating it over a flower-shaped, terracotta lamp, then transferring it to a broad opium pipe. He watched smokers sink into a waking dream of celestial beauty and envied their visions. As naturally as any other youth experimenting with tobacco, Joe experimented with opium and became an addict. Perhaps Aaron joined him in this adventure too. If he did, no one attached much significance to it. England had fostered the opium trade in China and the colony of Victoria looked on the vice with smug, European superiority. The Official Post Office Directory matter-of-factly listed the Chinese village's opium dealers.

In the years to come a policeman would call Joe 'half a Chinaman', clearly seeing it as a pejorative term. Joe would not have been offended, least of all after the Prince of Wales Birthday Carnival of 1873.

Organised on an ambitious scale to raise money for the town's institutions, it featured a spectacular procession of 3,000 performers, led by a re-enactment of Henry VIII's entourage at the Field of the Cloth of Gold. But all the sumptuous costumes, all the pomp, all the jollity, were overshadowed by the Chinese. Some 250 strong, they paraded through the streets to the music of four bands—gongs, cymbals, drums and wind instruments— arrayed in costumes of breathtaking splendour and variety, representing leading figures of the Dragon Emperor's court and their retainers. Nam Sing and other leading merchants and businessmen had imported the costumes and props from China at their own expense and for this one day the 3,000 people of Beechworth and their 7,000 visitors saw Chinese miners, carpenters, gardeners, confectioners, storekeepers, labourers, nightmen and billiard markers awesomely transformed. The *Ovens and Murray Advertiser* admitted, 'We have been forced to recognise a civilization different no doubt from ours, but in many respects higher.'

Beechworth had never seen anything like that carnival, and would never see its like again. The costumes and props would be dusted off the following year and paraded on other special occasions but they were dying echoes of the town's golden age.

The year 1873 had seen the railway from Melbourne to the New South Wales border pass through Wangaratta, 25 miles to the west. Beechworth was no longer on the main route to Sydney. Like other by-passed towns, it would start to die.

This was hard to recognise in the slow-fading euphoria of the carnival which occupied the next seven issues of the *Advertiser*. Joe relished it all— more than most. On his visits to the Burke Museum and Library, he saw that some of the ancient weapons and a suit of Chinese armour had been placed in the collection. He seems to have looked at the armour with more than passing interest and remembered its design—the cylindrical breast and back plates, the apron, the shoulder pieces.

The pattern would be followed in the Kelly Gang's armour. And the Chinese connection would impact on Joe's outlaw life in other ways. His need for opium would help trace his movements as a member of the Kelly Gang. His familiarity with the language would win valuable Chinese allies throughout the north-east, including gold buyers to handle a stolen ingot. Chinese rockets would signal the aborted beginning of a revolution. But for the present, Joe's intimacy with the Chinese was no more than an engaging eccentricity; a measure of his 'brightness' and the elusive, chameleon quality to be glimpsed so often in this contradictory life.

In September 1873 Joe succeeded in exhausting the patience of Anton

Wick, the German miner and market gardener who lived opposite the Woolshed school. Wick, a dour, hard-working man, had lost his lovely wife Margret three years before and was bringing up four children. He and Margret Byrne were close friends and marriage did not seem out of the question. Joe put an end to that.

One Saturday morning, Wick released a black horse from his paddock. Although it never usually strayed, it didn't return until Tuesday evening— sweaty and saddle-sore. Ten-year-old Bill Wick had been hunting for his father's horse on the Saturday when he saw it being ridden by Joe as he and farmer Ned Kennedy headed out of Kennedy's small paddock in Byrnes Gully. Joe gave young Bill a 'coo-ee' as he passed.

Summonsed by Wick, Joe made his first appearance in the Beechworth's superb white granite court house. Margret Byrne engaged solicitor William Zincke, a small puckish man with flowing grey locks, who played the cello in the local string ensemble. Zincke could do little more than question Bill Wick's identification of his father's horse. Magistrate Butler was unimpressed. 'His worship said he had not the slightest doubt that defendant had ridden the horse, and he warned him that if he continued this style of riding it would lead him at length to horse stealing. The defendant had better remember that he rendered himself liable to three months' imprisonment without the option of a fine.' The threat hung for a moment. 'But in this case he would inflict a fine, warning him against appearing again on such a charge.'

Joe was fined 20s, with 1s 6d costs, to face three days' imprisonment unless he paid immediately. On top of the fine and costs, there was a guinea fee for Mr Zincke. It all added up to a week's wages, a hard enough blow for the Byrne family.

Just short of his seventeenth birthday 'respectable' Joe had run foul of the law. Two days before, 'shiftless' Aaron had embarked on a project which would occupy all but a few months of the rest of his life—and profoundly influence its course.

Since he was fourteen or fifteen, Aaron had been running cattle with his father's herd, adding an 'A' to John's brand of 'S' and half-circle. Now, as he turned eighteen, he prepared to take up his own selection.

About a mile from the Sherritt farm, on the highest corner of the table-land between Byrnes Gully and the Woolshed, a creek took its rise in a spring and formed a small ti-tree swamp with wattle trees and fishbone fern around its edges. This fed a broad, shallow gully thickly timbered with stringybark, box and apple gums, running south to a low spur, which turned it eastwards, down towards Sheepstation.

At 9 a.m. on Saturday, 20 September 1873, Aaron placed posts or piles of stones with notices on them to mark out a broad tract of land down the western slope of the gully, including a good stretch of the creek below the little swamp. Two weeks later he engaged surveyor Henry Davidson to produce a plan and description of the block. Davidson surveyed a western boundary parallel to the rim of Byrnes Gully, a northern border just back from the granite-studded edge of the Woolshed escarpment, with eastern and southern limits dipping to the corner nearest Sheepstation.

Davidson recorded a boundary of 140 chains and 21 links, enclosing 106 3/4 acres. In a single bold throw, Aaron had selected a paddock that would stand out on survey maps in vivid contrast to the nearby Sherritt selection which was growing, through the years, block by block, like a cluster of paving stones. It was the act of a man who had come to terms with the broad strokes demanded by this new land and rejected the slow-dying habits of the old. And it was the act of a man who didn't shrink from hard work.

The survey cost Aaron five guineas. The following month, when he'd been able to pay for it, he took the plan along to the Beechworth Survey Office and made formal application. Three months later he appeared before the Land Board sitting at Tarrawingee and was recommended for approval. Aaron now began a five-year battle to develop, pay for and retain his precious allotment. He must pay £5 7s each six months, the money accepted only if he could satisfy the Land Act's requirements that he was adequately cultivating, 'improving' and living on the block. Holding his big paddock on sufferance, Aaron launched into a year of back-breaking work.

Even though his licence didn't come through until June that year, 1874, Aaron started work immediately on clearing timber, building a house, and erecting 1 3/4 miles of fencing. Helped by Joe, his father and brothers, he felled trees, split and morticed fence posts, dug them in at nine or ten-foot intervals, and ran three sapling rails between them. When this seemed to be taking too long and the job was only half done, he switched to a type of chock-and-log fencing—post and a top rail with small trunks and large branches criss-crossed and stacked between the posts.

In the lowest corner of the block, on a gentle rise above the creek, he built a ten-by-twelve foot hut with slab walls, bark roof and small, stone fireplace. Although he continued to live most of the time with his parents, this hut became, for the purposes of the Land Act, his dwelling. A few years from now it would be called 'a squalid den, the sole-furniture of which consisted of a large bunk, a rough table, and a stool'. But it was all Aaron needed, eloquent of a man with little care for physical comfort.

On Monday, 27 July, while he was looking for a strayed mare, Aaron called at the Kelty farm and saw young Dan Kelty sharpening a knife.

'What for?' he asked.

'I'm going to kill two or three bloody billygoats for the pigs.' The 'billygoats' turned out to be a small mob of sheep.

Aaron was helping to gut a skinned sheep when he saw the lad kill a second sheep which carried the red dagger brand of the Mackay family who still rented grazing land to the Sherritts. Aaron told Dan that these were Mackay weaners, warned him he'd be caught and left.

The following Saturday Aaron appeared in court as a police witness against Dan and his father, James Kelty, in a prosecution which ended two months later with James being given four years hard labour and Daniel receiving three years in a reformatory school.

Aaron had been drawn in to the Sherritt–Kelty feud.

During their hard winter work on the selection Aaron and Joe welcomed the odd visit to Beechworth. One of Aaron's haunts was the Imperial Hotel in High Street, a single-storey, timber pub built out from the steep downhill slope above Spring Creek. The Imperial proclaimed the allegiance of publican Edward Rogers with a bust of Queen Victoria on its sign.

Rogers was a livewire with a keen eye for publicity and special events to entertain his patrons—wrestling bouts, games of cricket and athletic contests on the lush creek-side flat below his pub. Joe and Aaron may have been here on Saturday, 8 August 1874, when Beechworth witnessed a remarkable and probably impromptu boxing match between two young men called Ned Kelly and Isaiah 'Wild' Wright. Kelly, working as an axeman at a sawmill in nearby ranges, had recently completed a prison sentence. He had been seen riding a horse stolen by Wright. Even though obviously unaware that the horse was stolen, he was given three years hard labour for Receiving (and a brutal pistol-whipping from a trooper) while Wright got off with a surprisingly light year-and-a-half sentence for Illegal Use.

Probably to settle this old score, they staged a bare-knuckle fight. Wright was a strapping 25-year old, over six feet, weighing about 13 stone. Kelly was only nineteen, about an inch shorter and more than a stone lighter. Quaintly decked out in silk shorts worn over long-sleeved, long-legged underwear, he was nevertheless a commanding figure, lean, fierce-eyed, with a long, first beard hiding his youth.

The two fighters 'toed the scratch' and the fight began, to the brutal old London Prize Ring rules which dictated that a round would last until a man was felled or blood drawn. The bout dragged on through twenty gruelling rounds of indeterminate length until Wright was beaten, to concede, 'He gave me the hiding of my life,' even though he later became a professional boxer. In his twentieth year Ned Kelly had become a sort of heavyweight boxing champion of the district. A man to reckon with.

The first six months' rental for Aaron's selection fell due on 1 December 1874. Always a slow payer, he was balancing his own needs (and probably Joe's) with those of his family, when disaster struck, in the shape of the Kelty feud. Aaron had a fight with John Kelty over some Sherritt goats that strayed on to Kelty land. Taken to court for assault, Aaron was fined £1 plus costs with a crippling £25 bond to keep the peace for six months.

Aaron couldn't meet his rental payment until April 1875. By then, another payment was due in only two months.

An unknown hand filled in the statement of improvements form (and even signed it for Aaron), claiming 75 chains of fence in the 'post and rail: split stuff' category, at one guinea a chain, and 75 chains of chock-and-log at £1 a chain—heavily inflating the length of fencing, the value of the chock-and-log, and up-grading his sapling rails. Giving the 'dimensions' of his hut as 'bark' and the 'material' as 'slab', Aaron valued it at £10, making total improvements of £163 15s. He described his land as 'hevelly timberd' and 'not fit for cultivation', being used for 'grazing cattle'.

Despite partly exaggerating the value of his improvements, he had done well. The big block was adequately fenced and could carry his cattle and some of his father's. Another payment of £5 7s was due in two months, but that was a long time off. Sixty sunrises and sunsets. An age.

Tilted to catch the first rays of the sun, his paddock was a place of optimism, where he could indulge his simple dream for the future. In a rare moment of intimacy, he told a senior policeman, 'I should like to have a few mares and an entire horse, and get a nice farm.' Then he confessed, 'Do you think if you got me the best mares you could buy, and the best entire horse you could purchase, that I could withstand the temptation of taking my neighbour's horses and selling them? No, I could not, no more than fly.' That irresistible temptation was shared by Joe. They would soon indulge it to the full.

It was no chance that Aaron's selection was placed between his parents' home and the Byrne homestead. He and Joe had found a secret place in Byrnes Gully—a remarkable, grassy, gently sloping bench, high on the sheer eastern side, about a hundred yards long by fifty wide, with a natural entrance at the northern end and almost no other point of escape. Screened by dense timber, rock outcrops and precipitous slopes rising in a wall to the east and dropping to a precipice to the west, it was inaccessible and almost invisible until you were standing in it.

The boys ran a wing fence of post and wire down from the north-western corner of the selection, almost to the bed of Byrnes Gully, cutting diagonally across the slope near the bench. From above or below, it was now possible to drive horses along the fence to a point near the access, then swing them straight across the slope into the bench, where a few stretches of dog-leg fence between rock outcrops and trees could easily hold them secure. Along the high, eastern edge, a natural terrace was buttressed by big boulders that seeped water. This could be collected in shallow drinking troughs scooped out at their bases with an old shovel the boys kept hidden under a rock just below the entrance.

If Joe and Aaron hid any stolen horses in the secret yardsite that year,

Aaron seems to have made little money from them. June 1875 came and went, bringing the bone-piercing tableland winter, and the rent on his land was unpaid.

Aaron earned some money from one of Beechworth's less popular 'characters', an old rogue called John Phelan who was the town's pound keeper, Inspector of Nuisances and dog catcher. Aaron broke a colt for him in July and went on to do some rather unusual work. It involved taking horses from their owners' paddocks and putting them in a holding area from which they were subsequently impounded by Phelan using false names. Phelan could then collect a proportion of the pound fee paid by the owner. Or, once passed through the pound books, unclaimed animals could be 'sold' to non-existent buyers at bargain prices then re-sold elsewhere at a profit, with apparently legal documentation of ownership. It was a system of 'laundering' stolen stock that may have inspired a more ambitious scheme to be practised by a major horse-stealing gang which included Joe and Aaron.

Meanwhile, Aaron's old weakness for 'borrowing' horses was about to land him in trouble. At the beginning of September a good-looking chestnut appeared in the Sherritt paddock at Sheepstation. The Sherritts' hostile neighbours, the Keltys and Murphys, later told police that they had seen Aaron and Jack riding the horse. On 4 November, Jack went to the police fairly aglow with public spirit, and claimed that he had put the animal in the Sherritt paddock for safekeeping after seeing young John Murphy riding it. The chestnut's owner, who was offering a reward for its recovery, was unimpressed by this tale, particularly as he found his horse lame and sore-backed. He laid a complaint against Murphy and the Sherritt boys.

On 25 November 1875, charged with Unlawfully Taking and Using, Aaron and Jack faced a forbidding, three-man bench—police magistrate Robert Pitcairn and two justices of the peace. Uncomfortably, the charge against John Murphy was dropped and he became a prosecution witness, supported by members of the Kelty family, telling how they had seen Aaron riding the horse through nearby bush and Jack riding it towards Beechworth.

The boys were defended by William Zincke. He made no attempt to refute the prosecution evidence but claimed that the horse had been ridden by boys of all three families. 'The animal strayed into their neighbourhood and they all used it, as it was quiet and easily caught, to catch their own horses.' Answering the charge against Aaron, Zincke told the court, 'A feud has long existed between the families, and this case has been got up to feed it. It will be hard to make my client the scapegoat.'

The bench did not agree. The fact that the horse had been reported to the police nearly two months after its appearance at Sheepstation clearly suggested to them that Jack's public spiritedness was prompted by a desire to collect the reward. Unfortunately, Zincke had failed to notice that the reward was not advertised until a week after Jack's appearance at the police station.

Perhaps unluckily, Aaron was found guilty. Echoing the warning given to Joe two years before, magistrate Pitcairn told him, 'You have been found guilty of a misdemeanour which renders you liable to twelve months' imprisonment.' Aaron's heart must have sunk. 'We will, however, merely inflict a fine of one pound, but if ever you are again brought up we shall send you to prison without the option of a fine.' Jack was fined £1 on the same charge and both boys paid the same day.

Aaron had been lucky, with the sentence, at least. His relief didn't last long. Back in October, he had been seen driving another chestnut—an unbroken filly that had disappeared from its owner's well-fenced paddock at Whorouly and was subsequently found in John Phelan's pound, 12 miles away. Only four days after his previous court appearance, Aaron found himself facing a glowering Pitcairn on another charge of Unlawfully Taking and Using. John Phelan had been summonsed for Illegal Impounding and False Entry over the same incident, and Aaron's case was adjourned for a week.

So on Tuesday, 6 December, he had to wait through Phelan's trial as the convoluted story emerged of the filly vanishing from its paddock, seen while being driven along a road by Aaron and a lad, then being found in the Beechworth pound with an entry in the pound book signed 'D. McAulay'.

Luckily for Phelan the charge of False Entry specified an alleged sale to 'Duncan McAulay' (a lad who worked for Phelan) yet, as Mr Zincke pointed out, the pound book had no such entry, the name being written as 'D. McAulay'. Pitcairn examined the summons, pronounced Zincke's objection as 'fatal', and dismissed the case.

Phelan's trial was proceeding on a charge of falsely impounding six head of cattle when the case was adjourned by Pitcairn, who described it as 'one of the most serious that has been brought before me'.

Phelan and Aaron were due in court on Thursday, only two days off. Incredibly, on the intervening day, Joe was drawn into the imbroglio. He rode up to the pound, probably with Aaron, and Phelan recognised Joe's saddle as one of his that had disappeared about three months before. He said nothing to Joe then but, later that day in Beechworth, gave him in charge to a constable for having stolen the saddle.

Next morning Joe, Aaron and Phelan prepared for their day in court. Joe's case was in progress when the ubiquitous Zincke applied for an adjournment 'as he had just heard of some important evidence in favour of the defendant'. Joe was given a week's grace.

The last charge against Phelan—the Illegal Impounding of cattle—was quickly disposed of when it emerged that they had been impounded by Phelan at a landowner's request.

Pitcairn summed up against Phelan, pointing out that the pound books were kept 'in a very peculiar manner' and that, while he had seen no evidence of 'actual dishonesty', he marked his 'sense of the gravity of such irregularities on the part of a person holding public office' by fining Phelan a total of £15.

Now Aaron again faced Pitcairn on the charge of Illegally Using. The court was hearing the same old evidence of the missing filly being driven by him and later appearing in the pound when Pitcairn interrupted, 'I cannot see that there is any evidence whatever of illegally using. There may be a presumption that there was illegal impounding on the part of the defendant.'

Now it was the police prosecutor, Sergeant Baber, who came to Aaron's rescue. 'Yes, your worship, if the defendant had followed up the driving by impounding, but he did not do so. The filly was actually impounded by another person four days afterwards.'

Oddly irritated by the unusual spectacle of the magistrate and prosecutor effectively defending his client, Zincke objected to the police 'arguing cases'. Sergeant Baber misunderstood the objection and thought Zincke was saying that the case should not have been tried. Pitcairn was equally confused by Zincke's extraordinary outburst and defended the police presentation and conduct of the case. 'There is not a syllable to be said against them,' he declared. 'On the contrary, I think they should not have been subjected to some very injudicious remarks.'

For a moment it seemed that Zincke may have snatched defeat from the jaws of victory but Pitcairn went on to discharge Aaron, with another stern reprimand. 'I warn you that I am determined to put down the practices going on in your neighbourhood, and if you come before me again on a similar charge, and are found guilty, I shall give you twelve months' imprisonment!'

Aaron's luck hadn't yet run out, a fact clearly acknowledged two days later in an *Advertiser* editorial which speculated on a jury's reaction to the evidence. 'We feel convinced that twelve of his peers would have considered that young Sherritt took—we shall not say stole—the horse from Whorouly for the purpose of placing it in Mr Phelan's paddock with his knowledge and a foregone conclusion that the horse was to be impounded.'

Joe made his second appearance in court on Thursday, 16 December, on the charge of stealing Phelan's saddle. Mr Zincke produced a mysterious lad called Daniel Sherritt, (probably Duncan's brother, Daniel McAulay, misnamed by a reporter), who swore that he had been riding a horse of Phelan's with the saddle in question, when the horse threw him and galloped off.

Zincke claimed that Joe had subsequently found the saddle in the bush 'and very ignorantly and improperly retained it, instead of endeavouring to find the owner'.

Pitcairn took a lenient view and discharged Joe, though warning him 'of the danger he ran in picking up unconsidered trifles and unlawfully turning them to his own use'.

Joe and Aaron had good cause to celebrate and, two days later, they were offered the perfect opportunity. The Grand United Circus Company was performing in Beechworth and on Saturday night presented as its farewell attraction, 'Dick Turpin's Ride to York or The Life and Death of Bonnie Black Bess—characters by the entire strength of the company'.

If Joe had never before encountered the highwayman hero (an unlikely possibility, especially since Dick Turpin's Ride was a popular circus draw-card in 1870s Victoria), the Grand United Circus Company gave him the chance to see all that was expected of such a figure—to be handsome, splendidly dressed, a fine shot, stylish horseman, a terror to rich travellers, but a friend to the poor, always courteous to women and, above all, courageous unto death.

The year before, novelist Thomas Hardy described an identical performance whose action began with Turpin galloping ahead of the Chief Constable and his men to clear a toll gate. Hardy noted the 'nice sense of dramatic contrast between our hero, who coolly leaps the gate, and halting justice in the form of his enemies, who must need pull up cumberously and wait to be let through'.

The lesson of the performance and its reception was clear. That the criminal who conducted himself within the highwayman code could be a hero in the eyes of ordinary, law-abiding folk—even citizens of a respectable town like Beechworth. If the idea momentarily disturbed some of Beechworth's more thoughtful citizens, it was easily dismissed. The days of England's highwaymen were long past and, as everyone knew, the last of Australia's bushrangers had been run down years before.

CHAPTER 3

Day of Reckoning

1875–6

J oe and Aaron were now men—a formidable pair. Approaching his adult height of 5ft 10ins, Joe was tall for the times, well built and strikingly good-looking, with his light, coppery hair, remarkable blue eyes and 'sandy' skin. He tended to wear his hat with the brim turned down to avoid sunburn, dressed simply and well, in both bush and town, with jackets and slightly flared riding pants.

Aaron was almost six feet, of a slim, loose build that made him appear 'light looking' and 'a slip of a lad', even though he weighed 12 or 13 stone. He had John's hazel 'laughing eyes', a long jaw, broad, mocking mouth and straight, dark brown hair growing down in a widow's peak. A couple of moles punctuated smooth cheeks that tanned easily, and he wore a hat with a pork-pied crown well back on his head. Winter and summer, he favoured shirt sleeves and waistcoat ahead of the jacket worn by most bush horsemen against the wide temperature variation met in the ranges. An unworn jacket had to be carried on the saddle, rolled or folded, so it was usually worn. Because Aaron was almost impervious to cold, he needed no jacket—except for 'best', when he might also don a short peaked collar and broad-knotted tie, with strapped riding breeches tucked into spurred, high boots, or rolled outside them.

Aaron was by now a dangerous bare-knuckle fighter and later boasted 'that he could lick any man in the police force'. The only policeman known to take up the challenge, a Constable Jim Dixon, received a beating.

So they strutted into adult life, Aaron with his brash self-confidence, Joe with his reticent charm, Aaron flash, Joe sober, each in his own way dangerous. But never to each other. They were mates.

Through the years the Byrne and Sherritt families had grown very close. Margret and Anne were firm friends—firm enough for their friendship to endure, in some form, through the tragedies ahead. In spite of the religious differences between them, they must have delighted to see their children, all attractive, intelligent youngsters, drawn together.

By now, Aaron was 'travelling with' 15-year-old Kate Byrne and it was generally assumed that they would marry. At about the same time, Joe and 19-year-old Elizabeth Sherritt were considered sweethearts and would soon be unofficially engaged. Within a few years Paddy Byrne and Anne Jane Sherritt would be spoken of as lovers about to announce their engagement.

Of course, there were shadows. Money remained a constant problem for both families. Aaron continued to do what he could to help his beleaguered parents and Elizabeth worked as a dressmaker in Beechworth. Jack would soon become a fencing contractor.

Paddy Byrne, now 13, used to come home from school and hawk firewood around the Woolshed in his father's old blue, red-wheeled cart. Kate got a job as general servant with James and Margaret Feely at the Black Springs Hotel, on the main road just outside Beechworth, and lived there during the week. Joe still had no steady job. He helped Aaron on the selection and scraped together enough money to dress well, to maintain his facade of respectability. In his town clothes he could easily pass as a well-to-do young squatter, while his mother ran her dairy farm, milked and churned, cooked, washed and sewed.

In these last months of 1875 people talked about the end of the good old days and muttered about changing times and the coming of the branch railway to Beechworth, which called up some old Irish demons. Many believed that smoke from steam engines had blighted Ireland's potatoes and caused the famine. Now, in this new land, there were attempts to de-rail trains and sabotage the railway. It was as though, unable to prevent the past slipping away, some folk were trying to hold off the future.

The autumn of 1876 threatened chill times for the folk of the Woolshed valley—falling gold yield, lower prices for crops and produce, a dwindling market as people drifted away from the district. Margret Byrne, in this sixth year of widowhood, faced a harder winter than most. Michael, second of the Byrne brothers, had just died; John, the clan leader, had left the Woolshed to return to New South Wales.

By now Joe spent all his time with Aaron, contributing nothing to support the family. His mother would say bitterly, 'He has not lived with me for some time…he has not come to my place regularly, lately.'

Then, unexpectedly, on Friday, 19 May, Joe turned up at the Byrne homestead and stayed the night. He may have been moved by his mother's coolness to him, by the obvious and increasing hardship of the household, by the efforts of Paddy and Kate to earn money, or perhaps by the grave, blue eyes of 5-year-old Elly, studying this stranger at the candlelit dinner-table. Many years later she would say, 'I can't remember Joe at all. I know the name of course, the name and that we had a brother named Joe…I can't

Incredibly, these contemporary press portraits of Aaron were engraved from the same photograph (see insert between pages 22 and 23). They suggest both the enigmatic quality of the man and the degree to which his character has been distorted through the years. He was neither as innocently fresh-faced as the *Illustrated News* version at left, nor as coldly calculating as the *Sketcher* offering. Yet he was both naïve and cunning.

remember his face, but I can remember him not coming home. I remember them saying he was good looking...'

Something made a profound impact on Joe that night and at last he decided to help his family—in a way that would reverberate through all their lives.

Next day, Saturday, Joe and Aaron rode to the Eldorado common, a few miles down the creek, and brought back a young, white cow. Between four and five in the afternoon, Joe called at the Batchelors, the Byrnes' nextdoor neighbours, and spoke to Jane Batchelor, she of the stern face and trim waist. He told her, 'I've got a calf down a hole on Limeburners Flat', and borrowed two knives and a steel.

Just below Byrnes Gap, only a few hundred yards from the Byrne house, was Ned Kennedy's now-abandoned farm. As the sun dipped below the western ridge, Joe and Aaron put the cow from Eldorado in the old milking yard and Aaron slit its throat. The cow gave one sharp bellow that echoed in the cool-shadowed gully. Nine-year-old Denny Byrne had been watching and Joe sent him to tell his mother that they were butchering a beast. Denny headed off, driving a bullock and some goats down the slope. He carried news of something far better than roast dinners in the offing. Joe was a member of the family again.

But the cow's death call had been heard by Sandy Doig as he crossed the foot of the gully on his way home from a Sebastopol mine. Sandy, a stocky, redheaded Scot, known as a busybody and gossip, lived up to his reputation by making a 300-yard uphill detour to the derelict farm. He saw the two lads in the yard with the cow, now 'bled and dead'. Aaron held the knife and, as Sandy approached, he quickly cut two small pieces from the cow's hide.

'Do you call yourself a butcher?' Sandy called.

He didn't hear the reply but Aaron made his meaning very clear: he sliced out the cow's tongue. Sandy decided it was high time to leave but first noted a description of the dead animal. 'The cow looked a dirty white in colour. The horns were very fine, and a little turned in. The tip was off the right ear and I thought there were one or two cuts in the other ear, but that was in the dirt.' Assuming that he had seen Aaron cut out the brand, Sandy concluded 'that the beast was not their own', and determined to report the incident to the Beechworth police. As he left, Joe was sharpening the second knife.

That evening Joe and Aaron took down to Mrs Byrne the head and heart of the cow and half the carcass—a forequarter and hindquarter. They stayed the night and rode up to Sheepstation on Sunday morning, to deliver half the hide and a third quarter of beef to John Sherritt, now frequently in court for non-payment of debts.

The former policeman seems to have known that there was something suspicious about this beef. He also seems to have been aware that there had been a specific reason to cut two small patches out of the hide, because he now sliced off some strips and gave them to Aaron—ostensibly to tie bark on the roof of his hut but actually to make the tell-tale holes in the cowhide less obvious.

Sandy Doig, in his Sunday best, had by now paid a visit to the Beechworth police station. Constable Twomey rode down to the Byrne home and, when Joe and Aaron failed to return, stayed there overnight.

Next morning the Byrne geese honked a warning as a second mounted policeman rode up to the homestead—a smallish man who cut a dashing, almost balletic figure in skin-tight white breeches, 'V' cut boots and short blue tunic, a man whose devious influence would scar the lives of all the Byrnes and Sherritts and bring about the deaths of two of them. Constable Michael Edward Ward was a stock inspector for the North Ovens Shire—a 31-year-old Irishman who had been in the force for seven years, at Beechworth for six. He was darkly good-looking, with grey eyes, brown hair, tightly sculptured beard and a reputation for tampering with schoolgirls.

Ward had established that a cow very like the one seen by Sandy Doig had been stolen on Saturday from the Eldorado common. With Constable Twomey, he now collected the meat, head and heart from Mrs Byrne and found half the hide up at the old milking yard.

Next morning Ward and Constable Mullane went to Sheepstation Creek where John Sherritt produced his share of the meat and hide. The two troopers then rode up to Aaron's hut where they found their two suspects. Ward asked them about the meat the police had recovered.

'It is my own,' Aaron said calmly. 'It was a beast from Barambogie that knocked up coming home, and I put it in Kennedy's yard and killed it.'

Asked about a brand, Aaron said that the animal carried his own 'A' off rump, 'S' and half circle off-side, and was earmarked with two holes punched in one of the ears. When Ward pressed him about the earmark, Aaron had to admit that he had no other cattle marked in this way.

Questioned about the hide, Aaron showed the police the strips cut off by his father, now tying down some bark on his roof. Ward retrieved these, then took Joe and Aaron back to the Sherritt house and fitted all the pieces of the hide together.

'Point out the brands,' he said.

'That's your business,' Aaron countered.

'No, it's your business!' snapped Mullane. 'To show us where the brands are and how you came possessed of the meat. Or I must take you with me.'

Aaron shrugged. 'If the hide was shaved, I might show you the brands.'

During this exchange with Mullane, Ward had been watching Joe. He was less hard-edged than his formidable mate. Less in control. And a year younger.

'Were you with Sherritt on Saturday?'

'Yes.'

'What time did you go to Barambogie for the beast?'

'After dinner, about two o'clock.'

Ward must have almost smiled as he asked, 'When did you go to Mrs Batchelor's for the knife and steel?'

Joe didn't answer. Barambogie was about eight miles away—a round trip of 16 miles. He had been at Batchelors between four and five. He and Aaron could not have covered 16 miles in two to three hours, driving a cow for half the distance. But they could have made the short trip to Eldorado and back.

Joe and Aaron were placed under arrest and taken back to Beechworth with the cowhide jigsaw and beef quarter. That same day they appeared before police magistrate Robert Pitcairn, each charged with, 'Having in his possession part of the carcass of a certain heiffer stolen from Richard Maddern herdsman of the Eldorado Common for the lawful possession of which he cannot satisfactorily account on the 23 inst at Sheepstation Creek'. Pitcairn remanded the lads for a week, on bail of £50, a daunting sum which each family managed to raise from loyal friends.

Despite the tortured prose of Ward's charge, his case seemed almost watertight. It was now just a matter of having the hide pieces and head identified by the owner of the cow. The owner was Kate Byrne's employer,

James Feely of the Black Springs Hotel. Ward claimed, many years later, 'We couldn't get Foley [*sic*] to identify the beast, however. He said, "I've got hundreds of head of cattle and if I do what you ask, they won't leave me one."' This explanation, like every other aspect of Ward's version, seems to be pure fiction.

Five years later a Royal Commission would be told that Ward had seduced Kate Byrne. Given the extraordinary immorality and deviousness of the man, it is tempting to link Kate's submission to the collapse of Ward's case. Kate loved both Joe and Aaron, had turned sixteen only a month before, was living away from home, and Ward's investigation of a case involving both her brother and her employer gave him access to her. She was in every way a vulnerable target for the raunchy constable. Perhaps Ward got her compliance with promises of freedom for the two lads?

The fact remains that one week later Ward's charge was withdrawn and the trial proceeded on three new charges laid against Joe and Aaron, this time by Constable Mullane—killing Feely's cow with intent to steal the carcass (this too was immediately withdrawn): having in their possession the carcass of 'a certain cow for the lawful possession of which they cannot satisfactorily account'; and unlawfully cutting the brand from the skin of 'a certain cow'.

In reporting the case, the *Ovens and Murray Advertiser* would head its item: 'Cattle stealing', though conceding that 'three charges amounting to cattle stealing were withdrawn by the police'.

Aaron was defended by Frederick Brown, the long-reigning shire president, and Joe by puckish Mr Zincke. Sergeant Henry Baber prosecuted, first calling Sandy Doig, who described the encounter at the old milking yard and went on to say, 'I told Mr Ward.'

Mr Zincke obviously knew of Sandy's reputation. 'Who did you tell besides?'

Sandy responded like the proverbial red-headed Scot, 'Your worship, am I to answer all this man's impertinent questions?'

It was one of the few points scored by the defence, but won only a few chuckles. Jane Batchelor told how Joe borrowed the knives for a 'calf down a hole', and Margret Byrne recounted what she knew of the business, with thinly veiled bitterness towards Joe, so thinly veiled that, at the end of her evidence, Pitcairn asked, 'Is your son good to you?'

'I cannot say,' she replied, a comment which, in its total coldness, was probably more damaging to the boys than all the circumstantial evidence brought before the court.

As Constable Ward was describing the crucial exchange in which he asked Joe the time he left for Barambogie, Mr Zincke interjected to ask if Ward had cautioned the lads that anything they said might be used in evidence against them. He had. Zincke's question was a desperate attempt to neutralise a key piece of evidence. Instead, it highlighted the incriminating nature of Joe's reply.

Ward was commended by the bench for his 'energy and sagacity'. His investigation had been a sound piece of bush detective work which Pitcairn would draw to the inspector's attention, probably assisting Ward's appointment as detective in eight months time.

When John Sherritt took the stand, Pitcairn cautioned him that he need not answer any question which might 'criminate' him. It was a timely warning. The ex-constable did everything he could to bear out Aaron's story, claiming that his son was indeed the owner of a white cow that had strayed and subsequently been seen at Barambogie. He himself had gone there to look for the cow on three occasions. He also described how he had cut the strips from the hide.

With near-sarcasm, Pitcairn asked if he was in his son's employment. Did he receive payment for looking after his cows? Old John's reply was a striking contrast to the tone of Margret Byrne's evidence.

'It was all the same for me to look after the cow if my son was doing something else. We are not separated.'

John Sherritt's loyalty to Aaron earned only a sharp warning from the magistrate. 'I advise the witness to avoid in future tampering with the hides of slaughtered cattle.' Unchastened, John Sherritt stepped down and rejoined Anne in the pew-like benches as Robert Pitcairn summed up.

'I do not think there is sufficient evidence to sustain the destruction of brands, as no brands are proved to have been in existence. But I certainly convict the prisoners on the other charge. And, as this is not their first appearance in court...', he read out a list of fines and convictions, 'I give each of them the heaviest punishment the law allows, namely, six months with hard labour in Beechworth Gaol.'

In the hushed recoil from these words, the court was adjourned and Joe and Aaron were led off to the the white granite fortress at the end of the street.

The Sherritts returned home, grieving. Margret Byrne headed back to the Woolshed with a trace of guilt in the bitterness she had not attempted to hide. She refused to speak of the incident until years later. Then she told young Elly a strange, secret fairytale in which the seed of guilt germinated. And the day before Elly died she shared the secret.

> I'm going to tell you something I've never told anyone before and I don't care if you put it in the paper. My mother went out and she got a calf—or it might have been a full-grown cow—and she took it home and she killed it and my brother did two years in gaol for that.
>
> My brother came home and she saw him and told him where she had got the cow. The policemen must have come down to see and they must have found that the cow was killed. They were going to arrest her and my brother said he

had killed the cow. They arrested him and tried him and he went to gaol for killing the cow. And he did—I always thought it was two years.

And my brother swore in court that he killed the cow, to save my mother.

When Margret Byrne told Elly this fable, any old bitterness must have been replaced by a fierce pride in her son, a pride which she felt some compulsion to justify, if not in Elly's eyes then in her own.

Inside the gaol, Joe and Aaron stripped off their town clothes and stood naked to be measured and examined. The prison recordist noted Joe as 5ft 9 1/2, with blue eyes, light brown hair and a scar on his left shin. Aaron was recorded as 5ft 10ins (nearly two inches less than his actual height) with hazel eyes, dark brown hair and a mole on each cheek. The recordist scanned their features, saw nothing remarkable and noted their noses, mouths and chins as 'medium'. Joe's upper lip, that disproportionate scar on his self-image, passed unnoticed.

Joe and Aaron went to the bath yard, then received their prison clothes— grey woollen jackets and moleskin trousers, good, stout garments for the coming winter. Now past that first naked vulnerability, it was easier to approach the prison term with bravado, ready to win their way with their fists or with the confidence born of that readiness. Anyway they'd be free before December to pick up their summer lives, leaving the convict months behind them.

CHAPTER 4

'These Two Strapping Lads'

1876–7

Beechworth Gaol in winter was, literally, a chilling place, a classic Victorian prison with two-storey cell blocks meeting at a central hall, 'The Circle', where a warder sat by a pot-bellied stove, looking down both wings. Raw granite walls were whitewashed to shoulder height, heavy boots rang on steel stairways and galleries, massive, iron-studded doors echoed a cold doom as they slammed shut and bolts drove home.

From the gaol's highest windows, Aaron could see his selection on the uptilted corner of the tableland, even pick out the dying crowns of ring-barked trees. Perhaps it gave him some comfort. He couldn't have known how close he was to losing that precious land.

On 29 June, the boys' old enemy, Constable Mullane wrote to Inspector Brooke Smith, pointing out that Aaron had taken up a selection, and commenting, 'It can hardly be considered that Sherritt is complying with the regulations of the Land Act while undergoing sentence in H.M. Gaol.'

The note was endorsed by Sergeant Baber, 'This offender had a very narrow escape from being Committed for trial on Cattle Stealing the identity of the beast was so much destroyed that it prevented any person setting up a claim of ownership.'

On the inspector's behalf, the report was sent to Melbourne, to the Chief Commissioner, Captain Frederick Charles Standish, who, on 3 July, added his own cold endorsement, 'for the information of the Secretary for Lands'.

While each man in the chain of police command lent his weight to the attempt to take Aaron's land from him, John Sherritt was fighting for him to keep it.

Aaron had arranged that his brother Jack should live on the block, look after the cattle, and keep up the fencing. This was not enough.

On 1 June, two days after entering gaol, Aaron had been a year overdue with his rent. Somehow, old John raised the necessary £10 14s and took it to the Beechworth sub treasury on 13 July. But the receiver of revenue refused to accept the payment until Aaron had made his statement of improvements. In vain, John protested that his son couldn't provide the statement because he was in gaol. The Land Act demanded its pound of paperwork.

John turned for help to P. F. Murphy, broker and commission agent of Spring Creek. That same day Murphy wrote a delightful letter to the Lands Department in his old-fashioned style (he still used an 'f' in writing double 's') stating the facts of the case and cannily basing his plea on the plight of old John, 'a hard working industrious man having a family of ten Children to Support Solely depending on him and the small returns of a poor farm of land held by him'. Murphy implied, probably accurately, that Aaron was helping to support 'his much afflicted parents'.

The homespun appeal of Murphy's plea for the payment to be accepted undoubtedly helped neutralise both the police approach to the Secretary for Lands and the normal bureaucratic demands for Aaron to satisfy the letter of the land law. Good Mr Wimble of the Lands Department was a benevolent man who showed considerable feeling for the rural battlers the land legislation was supposed to help. On 20 July he scanned Murphy's letter with the police report attached and scrawled a simple 'Accept'. Two months later, when asked if he wished to take action in light of the police representation, he replied, 'Not at present.' Aaron's land was saved, paid up to 1 June 1876.

Unaware of this drama, Aaron had his own urgent concerns. He had left some horses in the secret yard in Byrnes Gully—a pair of foals which were probably stolen—and a blue filly which Jack wouldn't find in the course of his work on the selection. Somehow, Aaron had to get word to his brother.

On a visit to the prison library, Joe or Aaron secretly tore the title page and fly leaf from a volume of *Wilson's Tales of the Borders and of Scotland*. Then, with a secreted pencil, Joe wrote a letter for his mate. It was addressed:

> For Johnny Sherritt Esquire,
> Sheepstation Creek, Reid's Creek P.O.
> Near Beechworth.

The letter began:

> Jack I wish you would fetch a pound of tobacco to me you can send it in easy give it to the chap that is working in the garden a tall thin chap.

A passage later destroyed by folding described where Jack could find the horses. The letter continued:

> I don't ask you to do all this for nothing. If you secure them two foals and have them and the blue filly for me when I get out I will make you a present of the best [indecipherable] I have got.

You must be careful of these few pieces of paper it is very hard to get them for this is wrote on the sly and posted out of the gaol.

We must now conclude by sending kind love to all.

We remain your most affectionate brother

Aaron Sherritt and

Joseph Byrne (well known)

The 'tall thin chap' was a trusted prisoner who quickly demonstrated how he had won that trust. He took the letter straight to Constable Mullane, who followed the directions and recovered the two foals. Curiously, no charge was laid against Aaron for their theft. Mullane then posted the letter and it duly reached Jack, who presumably went to retrieve the horses only to find that they were already gone. Aaron, on his release, would reasonably doubt Jack's story and suspect that he had taken the foals for himself. Certainly, about this time, a rift developed between them, a rift which would have tragic consequences.

Apart from this incident, Joe and Aaron's six months in prison are a blank. They probably spent most of their time in the prison quarry and the stonebreaking yard where convicts broke up road metal. During those six months they got to know many criminals, that much is certain. Who were those criminals and what influence, if any, did they have on Joe and Aaron's futures?

Detective Ward has the answer: '[In Beechworth Gaol] they met some notorious New South Wales criminals—and also Ned and Jim Kelly. There is no doubt that it was while the three [*sic*] of them were serving their sentences that they arranged the systematic scheme of stock-lifting and sale that they subsequently put into operation.'

Ward's lack of doubt in the matter shouldn't carry too much weight. He was certainly wrong about Ned Kelly. The man who would become a bushranging legend—close friend and idol to both Joe and Aaron—wasn't in Beechworth or any other gaol at this time, and hadn't been for more than two years. He was foreman of a sawmill supplying timber for the branch railway then being built from Wangaratta to Beechworth.

Ned Kelly's brother Jim had received a five-year sentence for cattle stealing at Beechworth back in 1873 and, even though he was released early, his sentence overlapped Joe and Aaron's by three months; but he was released from Pentridge Prison outside Melbourne and wasn't in Beechworth during their time. Ned Kelly's former boxing opponent and later friend, Wild Wright, had been sentenced to three years for Receiving at Beechworth in 1874. He, too, was released from Pentridge, in May 1877, and had left Beechworth before Joe and Aaron arrived.

Dan Kelly, Ned's younger brother, was tried at Beechworth during Joe and Aaron's time for stealing a saddle. Able to produce witnesses to its purchase, and a receipt, he was acquitted. And Steve Hart, Dan's mate, who would become a member of the Kelly Gang, served twelve months in Beechworth Gaol for illegal use of horses but arrived there eight months after Joe and Aaron had been released.

Even Joe's sister, Elly, believed that he had met other members of the Kelly Gang during his imprisonment. Her story of what happened on his release points to the truth.

According to Elly, 14-year-old Paddy was sent up to meet Joe on the day of his release but, embarrassed to be seen standing at the gaol gate, waited just around the corner. Meanwhile, Joe emerged to find no one there. After a long wait, 'these other fellows' who had been in gaol with him—some of the Kelly boys or their associates—came out and asked him the shortest way to their home. 'They must have decided then,' said Elly 'that they'd take up robbery or whatever they did.'

The story—like Margret's fable of stealing the cow—places blame for Joe's actions with another member of the family. It tries to excuse the fact that he did not come home after his release and, during this absence, met the Kelly family.

The most likely explanation for Joe's failure to return home is that on his release in November 1876 he went back to Sheepstation with Aaron—avoiding an awkward reunion with his mother who had openly displayed her bitterness to him at the trial. And, at Sheepstation, Joe could have met Ned Kelly's sister Kate.

One of Beechworth's many vivid characters was the coaching magnate, American-born Hiram Crawford, a handsome man in the Buffalo Bill mould, who had made a fortune from the Crawford & Co. coach line, and built Melbourne's Eastern Arcade. Crawford had a teenage daughter, Emma, a high spirited girl who was a friend of Kate Kelly 'all her young life'. When Emma returned home to Beechworth on holidays from a young ladies' academy in Melbourne, Kate often came to stay with her, and the two girls—both superb horsewomen—spent much of their time riding. Crawford had large paddocks adjoining the Sherritt farm; Emma knew Aaron (she would eventually buy his selection from him) and, about this time, Aaron became smitten with Kate Kelly.

Kate was small, with beautiful, near-black hair, 'dark, piercing eyes', and a quiet, reserved manner, in sharp contrast to her fondness for riding astride—an outlandish thing for a girl at that time. Kate was not yet fourteen but, in a time when many girls married at fifteen, she was far from a child in Aaron's eyes, and tempted him to waver in fidelity to his childhood sweetheart, Kate Byrne.

A few hours riding down from the Beechworth hills and over the Oxley flats, crossing the Ovens and King rivers and Fifteen Mile Creek, took Joe and Aaron to the Kelly homestead below the Bald Hills. Here they would have met Kate's mother, the redoubtable matriarch, Ellen Kelly (now Ellen

King after her second marriage to a young Californian, George King) and her large family. And here they might have met Kate's brother, Ned Kelly, the charismatic young bushman who had defeated Wild Wright in that gruelling bare-knuckle fight in Beechworth, back in 1874.

Ned stood two inches taller than Joe, eye-to-eye with Aaron and a year older—a powerful, raw-boned man with stern, dark eyebrows, piercing hazel eyes and a dark, reddish beard. A man born to command notice and to compel allegiance or hostility. From Joe and Aaron he won immediate allegiance.

A senior police officer would report, 'Sherritt had a most exalted opinion of Ned Kelly, and said he did not believe there was another man like him in the colony. He said, "He is about the only man I ever was afraid of in my life, and I certainly give him the best in everything."'

On another occasion, Aaron told the same officer, 'Ned Kelly would beat me into fits...I look upon Ned Kelly as an extraordinary man; there is no man in the world like him, he is superhuman...I look upon him as invulnerable, you can do nothing with him.'

From a man of Aaron's remarkable toughness, this testimonial tells us much about Ned Kelly. It also tells us much about Aaron. Like Wild Wright, he in no way resented Ned Kelly's physical superiority. Wild Wright tested himself against Ned before accepting him as the better man. Perhaps Aaron too pitted himself against Ned. Or perhaps he knew there was no point, because, in some curious way, he wanted to believe in a man who could best him in everything. Certainly, like Wild Wright, he gave Ned his complete loyalty. And Ned Kelly, in his turn, showed his belief in Aaron. Even after Joe had come to accept that his lifelong mate had betrayed the Gang, Ned Kelly was reluctant to believe it and, after his capture, asked a policeman if he had tortured Aaron. Only this could make Aaron's betrayal credible to him.

Joe's reaction to Ned Kelly was as immediate and as vivid as Aaron's. Three years later he wrote, 'I was advised to turn traitor but said that I would die at Ned's side first.' Joe gave his total loyalty to Ned, devoted the remaining three and a half years of his life to him, and did, in fact, die at his side in battle.

The chemistry of human relationships often defies analysis. Apart from his Irish charm and keenness of mind, Joe must have seemed a kindred spirit to Ned. Joe, too, dressed soberly with the occasional touch of bush flashness. He, too, was the eldest son of a widow, one of seven children. His family, too, had been scarred by the transportation system. He, too, was a Catholic. Like Ned, Joe had served time—for the crime which had sent Ned's father 'Red' Kelly, to gaol just before his death, possession of stolen meat.

Ned would describe Joe as 'my best friend' and, as a member of the Kelly Gang, his 'best man...as cool and firm as steel'. In Ned's eyes, Joe's flaws of character would not emerge or, if they did, they became irrelevant, outweighed by his unswerving devotion.

The three young men made a formidable alliance—fine bushmen, consummate rough-riding horsemen, all athletic, all handy with their fists.

Joe and Aaron also met Ned's younger brothers, Jim and Dan. Jim was a strapping young buck of 17, already hardened by four and a half years of prison labour and much in Ned's mould—promising to be equally good-looking and even taller.

Dan was a slim, sallow 15-year-old with crow-black hair, living in the shadow of his older, bigger brothers, and reminded of his physical inadequacy by having to wear their cast-off clothing. Small wonder that Dan tried too hard to assert himself, swaggering around with the Greta Mob—a local band of bush larrikins (including Dan's mate, jockey Steve Hart) who wore bright sashes around their waists and jammed their hats low over their eyes with the chinstrap under their noses, to ride flashly and furiously around the district, a bikie gang of that time and place.

Dan seems to have hit it off well enough with Joe and was almost always in his company during the outlaw years, apparently accepting Joe's senior role in the Gang; but he always showed distrust of Aaron and would be there at his death, apparently enjoying the event.

Ned Kelly was now foreman of a sawmill at nearby Burkes Holes Farm. After completion of the Wangaratta–Beechworth railway that July, the mill owners had gained a contract for the main Gippsland line. Ned's leading hand was moving to Gippsland with the mill plant and half the men; Ned was to follow with the rest of the team. Joe and Aaron met two of these men, Oakley and Peter Martin, and probably joined them on an expedition into the Wombat Ranges with Ned and his brothers.

From the head of Fifteen Mile Creek, a trail struck into a tangle of thickly timbered ridges near the headwaters of Ryans Creek—a wild domain of soaring white gum and stringybark, broken by dark thickets of wattle, with swamp gum, fern and sword grass along the gullies. It was a misty place in winter, sodden with rain and snow, where trunks and branches grew shaggy, glowing green moss, and wet wood bloomed with orange lichen. Now, in early summer, the bush was dry and honey-smelling, stirred by breezes blowing across the last snow of the Alps.

Ned's old bushranger mate Harry Power had once worked as a digger in these ranges and may have shown the young Ned a stronghold that would have caught any boy's imagination: a basin high in the ranges, screened by steep, folding hills, with a dilapidated log hut on a rise by a small alluvial stream called Bullock Creek. There had been a minor gold rush to these gullies in the 1860s but the diggers had moved on and their huts and workings were slowly being reclaimed by the bush. The little party started to repair the Bullock Creek hut, re-establish the mine, and clear and fence some adjoining land on the creek flat as a horse paddock. Ned's idea was apparently to get Dan and Jim started on a project that would keep them out of the way, out of trouble, and provide a livelihood.

Aaron couldn't have stayed long because of his selection, and Joe had to confront his mother and family. His eventual return home seems to have gone well. His brothers and sisters all adored him, while Margret Byrne's guilt over her behaviour at the trial probably helped their reconciliation. And, after all, Christmas was near. Times were harder, but one of the Byrne geese would provide a yuletide feast and they could put the shadows of the year behind them.

During the festive days of early summer, Aaron worked hard on the selection, with help from Joe and, on their way through the district, Ned Kelly and the Martin brothers. In the huge store of forensic trivia soon to be gathered, it would be recorded that the Martins were seen at 'Mother Byrnes' before heading for Gippsland. They left without Ned Kelly. That year Ned was drawn into the squatter–selector land war by clashing with James Whitty, a dour and implacable grazier who led the King Valley squatters against the battling cocky farmers of the district. It was a fight Ned Kelly chose not to turn his back on. In a fateful decision, he gave up the sawmill job for the heady pleasures of horse stealing—encouraged and helped by his American stepfather, George King, himself an expert in the craft.

Joe and Aaron would soon join Ned. For the moment, they worked with axe, cross-cut saw, broad-axe and adze to improve the selection's chock-and-log fences. They sprawled smoking in restless gum shade when the noon sun shimmered on silvery grass, their eyes narrowed over mugs of scalding tea, and rode together through the wild statuary of Byrnes Gully.

The idyll was brief. On 10 January, Aaron's father sent him into town with a drayload of hay for sale to Dennett's stables. As Aaron was driving down Ford Street, the leader of the tandem pair refused to pull. A constable noticed a piece of sacking under the horse's collar and, when he investigated, found that both the animal's shoulders were 'completely stripped of skin to the flesh'. The collar's leather was worn through to the straw stuffing. Aaron was arrested, the dray and horses seized. Next day he appeared in court charged with 'cruelly torturing a horse'. Old John did what he could to accept responsibility but earned only a tongue lashing from magistrate Pitcairn. 'It is no wonder your family bears the character it does when such practices are encouraged by the father himself.'

Aaron was fined £5, in default, seven days imprisonment. He paid the fine that day. Meanwhile, the load of hay had been soaked by a brief downpour and had dropped in value from £4 to 10s. With a guinea fee to Frederick Brown for defending him, it had been an expensive day's work and another setback for the again overdue payment on his selection. Worse trouble was at hand.

On Saturday, 13 January, only two days after the trial, Anne Sherritt and 16-year-old Willie came with Aaron on a visit to the Byrne house. In late afternoon, while Anne and Margret chatted on the verandah, enjoying the long, blue shadows after the heat of the day, Willie went off with Joe and Aaron. It was shaping to be a harsh summer and, despite the rain three days before, Reedy Creek was still a single, narrow channel snaking through gravel beds broken by dwindling pools of dead, black water. By comparison, the tawny waters of the nearby dam seemed cool and inviting, so Joe and Aaron stripped off and went for a swim.

A single Chinese hut—much closer to the Byrne homestead than the back road camp—lay on the far side of the dam, past a vegetable garden. As one of the Chinese, Ah On, came to fetch water for the garden, words were exchanged and he went back to the hut. Joe and Aaron quickly dressed and, according to Ah On and his two mates, started to pelt stones at the Chinese hut. According to Willie Sherritt, Ah On and one of his hut mates, Ah Seong, came to the dam with bamboos and started slashing at Joe and Aaron. Chased by Ah On, Aaron ran to the nearby footbridge, then snatched up a branch and hurled it at his pursuer. Struck on the side of the head, Ah On fell to the ground.

The Chinese claimed that they produced bamboos only after Joe and Aaron had bombarded the hut and Aaron had hit Ah On in the temple with a stone. They had then chased Joe and Aaron away before Ah On collapsed from his injury.

Margret Byrne, Anne Sherritt and 12-year-old Mary Byrne claimed to have seen the later stages of the incident as the irate Chinese pursued the boys, hitting them with bamboos, before Aaron caught up the stick and threw it at Ah On, who, they said, showed no sign of injury until then.

Next evening Ah On was operated on at the Beechworth hospital. Five fragments of bone were removed from the zygomatic arch, between the ear and cheek bone. His injury was considered 'dangerous' and 'permanent'. The incident was reported to the police and Senior Constable Mullane rode down to the Chinese hut to recover the stone allegedly thrown by Aaron, 'a rugged piece of rock, the size of a small fist'. It was stained with blood.

Warrants were issued for 'unlawfully and maliciously inflicting grievous bodily harm' and Mullane arrested Joe the same day at Sheepstation Creek. Joe told the trooper, 'I've nothing to say. I didn't do it and didn't see it done…we were bathing in the dam; when we got out the Chinese hunted us with bamboos; I ran one way, and Aaron ran the other, and I saw nothing at all of it.' Joe appeared before Frederick Brown as justice of the peace and was remanded to the police court on 13 February.

Meanwhile, on 5 February, Aaron was arrested while bark-stripping in the hills between Eldorado and Chiltern. He told a trooper from Eldorado, 'I admit the charge; he ran after me and struck me first, and then I struck him with the stick.' Aaron did not mention Joe.

On Tuesday, 13 February 1877, the two lads appeared before magistrate Robert Pitcairn who had sent them to prison eight months before. Sergeant Baber again prosecuted. Frederick Brown now donned another hat to defend Aaron while Zincke defended Joe.

The allegedly unprovoked attack by Joe and Aaron and the wounding with the stone were described by the three Chinese. Doctor Fox gave his opinion that the stone produced in court had caused Ah On's injuries, a view hotly debated by the defence, who called Margret Byrne, Anne Sherritt, Willie Sherritt and Mary Byrne—all of whom described the Chinese chasing Joe and Aaron and beating them with bamboos before Aaron retaliated by throwing a piece of branch. Anne Sherritt told the court, 'There is blood at the place the Chinaman was struck, at the bridge, still.'

Pitcairn committed the boys to trial at the Court of General Sessions on 28 February, allowing each of them bail of £50.

Although the General Sessions trial before Judge Hackett was almost a re-run of the Petty Sessions inquiry which had been given detailed coverage in the *Advertiser*, the paper stated, 'the case appears so important that we repeat it in full'.

Much the same evidence was presented—with some additional detail from the defence. Willie told the court that 'both prisoners were bleeding on the arms from the blows the Chinese gave them with the bamboos. Ah On was hammering my brother all the time he was running after him.' Aaron laughed at this, attracting the sarcastic ire of the *Advertiser*, who thought him to be amused 'that he should have been so terribly wounded and still live to be tried by his country'. The reporter also noted that Mary Byrne told the same story as Willie, 'and repeated it word for word twice to the Crown Prosecutor just as if she had learnt it as a lesson'.

After a second day of testimony the jury retired for two hours and ten minutes to return the 'extraordinary' verdict that, while Joe was not guilty, Aaron was 'guilty of a common assault committed in self defence'.

Joe was discharged but the judge said that he must ask for 'at least a reasonable verdict' in Aaron's case. The jury retired for a few minutes more and Aaron, too, was found not guilty. The judge told him, 'You have had a very narrow escape. I caution you against throwing stones again as it is a low and blackguard practice,' showing that, unlike the jury, he accepted the Chinese story.

The *Advertiser* weighed down heavily against the boys and their families, devoting an entire editorial to the case and the occasional failings of juries in reaching 'very extraordinary, not to say absurd conclusions'.

The editorial concluded, 'There is undoubtedly a ludicrous side to a trial which results in a verdict of "Guilty of an assault committed in self defence" but there is also a very serious aspect of this particular case, owing to the character, the career, and the proclivities of the defendants. We would just remind these two strapping lads of the fate of SMITH and BRADY, who commenced life like them, and ended it on the gallows.' James Smith and Thomas Brady were minor, latter-day bushrangers who killed a publican and were executed at Beechworth in 1873.

The *Advertiser* recorded another case heard in the Beechworth Court on the first day of Joe and Aaron's trial—a charge of stealing a saddle. The defendant was Dan Kelly. It was virtually a carbon copy of the case heard against him in the Petty Sessions hearing while Joe and Aaron were in prison. Dan produced a receipt for purchase of the saddle and witnesses to the transaction—his cousin Jack Lloyd, his brother-in-law William Skillion, and his brother Ned Kelly. Ned further told the court that he knew the man who had sold Dan the saddle and had tried to find him 'for the purpose of this trial'. Dan was found not guilty. For a few hours on that last day of summer, the beautiful, white granite court building held Ned and Dan Kelly, Joe Byrne and Aaron Sherritt. It was their first documented encounter. It represented yet another curious harmony with Ned's life: he too had been charged with assault on a Chinese; he too had been discharged.

After Joe and Aaron's acquittal the next afternoon, they may have celebrated with Ned and Dan—perhaps into the evening when fireworks burst and blazed in the cooling sky to mark an 'illuminated' exhibition of tightrope prowess by the Canadian Blondin, with a rollicking brass band to make it even more of an occasion.

A chill in the mountain air was a reminder that summer was passing. The long, dry spell was broken: Reedy Creek had washed away the stagnant pools, and the greening hills would offer good riding and better feed to lure 'these two strapping lads' and their newfound friends into adventure.

After Joe's trouble over the 'borrowing' of Anton Wick's horse, relations between Margret and Wick had become strained. The widower and the widow, both hard workers, devoted to their families, became friends again and in the custom of the time, they 'exchanged portraits'—studio photographs of themselves or family members. Wick gave Margret a *carte-de-visite* of his daughter Annie, who had been Joe's classmate. And, at last, Margret Byrne managed to persuade Joe to go and have his portrait taken at James Bray's studio in Camp Street, Beechworth. He had succeeded in cultivating a downy moustache to hide his upper lip. This photograph is the only image of Joe ever made while he was alive; our one glimpse of the 'quiet' and 'respectable' young man.

For the portrait, Joe wore his usual town clothes—waistcoat, jacket, slightly flared riding pants—and leant on one of Bray's studio props, a cabriole-legged table fitted with an ornate bureau top to bring it up to elbow height. The impact of the photo is of a surprisingly urbane, mature figure, hair carefully brushed, long sideburns trimmed close, the moustache gaining maximum shadow effect from Bray's skylight. But Joe's eyes achieve a strange quality: the left eye is wide, piercing, alert; the right is half-hooded by the lid, with a strange dullness and deadness to it. Perhaps a trick of the light or the moment, a flick of the eyelid half-frozen by Bray's shutter. Or perhaps the camera captured a curious discrepancy found in descriptions of Joe's eyes. To one man they were 'full and remarkable', to another 'shifty looking'. They earned Joe the nickname 'Bullet Eyes' and call to mind that uncharacteristic assessment of him as 'dangerous'.

In some curious, even coincidental way, Bray's lens may have suggested one of the many contradictions of the man. His photo certainly records another. Joe stands with one leg relaxed across the other shin, boot resting on its toe to display a high, undercut heel, a bush larrikin touch at odds with the guise of the sober, young townsman.

Margret Byrne proudly gave Anton Wick a one-shilling *carte-de-visite* print of the photo—this frozen moment, a last gesture to Joe's respectable Beechworth life.

CHAPTER 5

The Coming of the Trouble

1877–8

During 1877 Joe and Aaron worked with Ned Kelly and others on what Detective Ward described as 'a systematic scheme of stock-lifting and sale' and which Ned drily called, 'wholesale and retail horse and cattle dealing'.

Aaron claimed that, 'he, Joe Byrne and Ned Kelly used to steal horses wholesale...they made raids on horses from about Wagga to Albury, took them on a back track to Melbourne, and on their return would pick up a number of horses in Victoria and take them over to Wagga or Albury for sale.'

As soon as the horses were 'lifted', their brands were altered. 'Supposing a horse was branded H on the near shoulder, they would turn the H into HB (conjoined) by getting a pair of tweezers, pulling out the hairs to make a B, and then prick the skin with a needle dipped in iodine. This burns up the skin, and for about a month afterwards it looks like an old brand; new brands were also put on in this fashion and they would never be detected.'

Ned and his mates then obtained papers 'proving' ownership of the horses with their altered brands. This was the cleverest part of the scam. According to Aaron, 'one of the party used to act as the master, and the others as his servants' with a second member of the group playing 'a stranger who wanted to purchase the mob of horses'.

Superintendent Frank Hare, who recorded Aaron's account of the scheme, admitted that Ned and Joe were 'fine, good-looking and well-dressed men'. Almost certainly, one played the owner, the other a would-be purchaser.

After lifting a mob of horses in New South Wales and changing their brands, the gang would drive them down across the Murray River into Victoria. Aaron explained how they would then 'make for some squatter's station where they were unknown, ask permission to put their horses into his stockyard, on the pretence that they had met a stranger who wanted to purchase the mob of horses...At last they would agree to a price, and then would ask the squatter to allow them to go into his office to draw up a receipt, in which all the brands would be entered...After the receipts had been drawn up the squatter would be asked to witness it, and the supposed buyers would start off towards Melbourne, and the seller appeared to return back to New South Wales.'

For the charade at the station, the 'servants' were probably split between 'buyer' and 'seller'. After the sale, the seller and his men would circle back to rejoin their mates and take the mob along the 'back track' to Melbourne, now with apparently legal documentation of ownership.

In the long Indian summer of that year, the gang would have ridden behind their prizes like men of some ancient raiding party, sitting their horses with careless grace, full of success and easy laughter, every moment of every day sharply spiced with the threat of discovery and pursuit; Ned and Joe in their gentlemen's tweeds, Aaron and the others in their mole-skins and sashes, flash shirts and bush hats, stockwhips looped over their shoulders, smoking their pipes, yarning away the miles to 'Marvellous Melbourne'.

In the colony's capital, they had the choice of dozens of establishments eager for the custom of young gentlemen selling fine horseflesh. Perhaps they took their mob into the bustling heart of the city, haltered against the clamour of traffic, and climbed the western hill of Bourke Street to the imposing facade of Kirk's Bazaar—mecca of the colony's horse dealers. Under lofty skylights, buyers and sellers strolled, yarned and haggled by a block-long tan track where horses with numbers on their rumps were paraded by Kirk riders carefully showing off good points.

The sale made, the gang could relax with money in their pockets.

Perhaps after a night at a hotel, they rode out along Elizabeth Street to what had been the Beechworth Road and was now the Sydney Road, heading north, skirting most of the ranges until they came in sight of the Strathbogies. Then the horses stepped more briskly, knowing that there would soon be hard and fast riding to gather another mob, and after that, superb mountain tracks north across the Murray to another sale town.

It was a wonderful adventure, a heady, addictive brew of long riding, comradeship and fine horses, with some money to show for it all. Joe was won over and returned home less and less. Before the year was through, he would be living with Ned Kelly and his family. For Aaron, there was always the selection pulling him back to Beechworth and 'his much-afflicted parents'.

Three times that year, John Sherritt was in court for non-payment of debts. When Willie was found guilty of ill-treating a harness horse, he, like Aaron, was fined £5 or, in default, seven days' hard labour. The family couldn't pay and 17-year-old Willie had to go to gaol for a week's stone breaking. In this climate, meeting the rental on Aaron's land took second place to the needs of the family. Another June came and went with his

Believed to be Joe's father, Paddy Byrne, photographed in Melbourne when he was about 36, some three years before Paddy's death. The unusual jacket and waistcoat may be connected with his trade of carrier which probably took him to the city.

Identified in police files as a portrait of Aaron Sherritt, this is almost certainly his brother, Jack, wearing his chinstrap Kelly-style. The photo was circulated to police in case Jack accompanied the Gang on a bank robbery in the course of his work as a police agent. (Aaron was also photographed with his chinstrap under his nose, probably on the same occasion as Jack and for the same reason.) (*Victoria Police Historical Unit*)

Margret Byrne, Joe's mother, was about 45 when she posed for this Bray portrait, her fashionable dress undoubtedly bought with proceeds of the Euroa or Jerilderie robberies. She sits at the same studio table used for Joe's portrait, minus its bureau top.

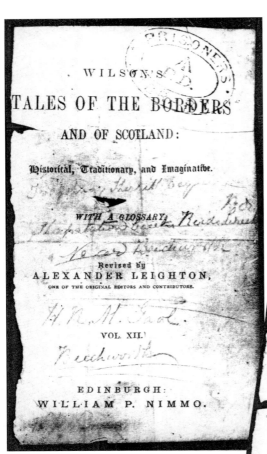

Part of the letter smuggled out of Beechworth Gaol by Joe and Aaron during their 1876 prison term. For the text, see pages 43–44. (*Victoria Public Record Office*)

Beechworth solicitor William Zincke defended Joe and Aaron on several occasions, was involved in the defence of Mrs Kelly, and also appeared for Kelly sympathisers. In 1880, when he was a member of the Victorian Parliament, it was announced that he would defend Ned Kelly at his trial for murder. However, he refused to work with the controversial and high-profile David Gaunson. (*Burke Museum, Beechworth*)

Superintendent Nicolson described Aaron riding down this sheer eastern flank of Byrnes Gully. Descending steep slopes on horseback was a stock-in-trade of the Kelly Gang, guaranteed to shake off the most intrepid pursuer.

Johnny Byrne, who built this superb hut at Tolmie, was a distant relative of Joe. While visiting here on 25 October 1878, Ned Kelly, and probably Joe, found the tracks of police horses heading towards nearby Stringybark Creek, scene of a tragic gunfight the following day.

The last of the Byrnes, Joe's sister Elly, photographed in 1964 at the age of 93, in the Mercy Hospital Albury only two months before her death. To the end, she spoke of her outlaw brother with clarity, pride and a sense of fatalism.

Kate Kelly poses for a studio portrait in her best riding costume. Aaron was briefly infatuated with Kate and wooed her again unsuccessfully during the Gang's outlawry. Kate's older sister, Maggie, discouraged the liaison.

A few pieces of wood and scattered rocks from the fireplace mark the site of Aaron's hut in 1961. This photo looks west towards the rim of the tableland above Byrnes Gully.

year's rent still owed. Another £10 14s. Another reason to rejoin Ned and Joe and the others to earn some easy money.

The Kelly–King horse-stealing trade continued unabated through the winter of 1877, with a serious setback in June when Ned's brother Jim and a mate were convicted of stealing a couple of horses at Wagga. It was an amateurish effort, exacerbated by pugnacious young Jim hitting an arresting trooper. Jim wasn't part of his brother's highly organised gang, but his sentence of three years hard labour was a blow to Ned and the Kelly family.

Meanwhile, in the heart of winter, Ned at last struck at his old enemy, James Whitty, leading light of the King Valley squatters. The full gang— Ned, Joe, Aaron, George King, Wild Wright, Big Mick Woodyard, and a lad with a string of aliases called Billy Cook—swooped over the ridges from the Fifteen Mile Creek down to Myrrhee and gully-raked eleven horses from the lush winter paddocks of Whitty and three neighbours, his nephew James Whitty, John Farrell and John Jeffery. Whitty lost six horses, mainly fillies and mares, James junior missed a gelding, Farrell contributed three fine draughthorses, Jeffery another superb draught. Total value of the eleven horses was £170.

With four draughts, and at least one mare heavily in foal, the gang drove the mob at a steady pace across the ridges and up the northward valleys to the settlement of Howlong on the Murray River. The 'culls' were left in a paddock owned by a German called Petersen, while the pick of the mob, with their brands altered, were sold to two prosperous Barnawatha winegrowers, Gustav and William Baumgarten, and a man called Samuel Kennedy, described by Ned as 'strangers to me and I believe honest men'. Another local, Thomas Studders, was involved in the transaction.

On the expedition, Ned used the name Thompson, and Joe was called Billy King—adopting the Christian name of Billy Cook (who, on this exploit, called himself John Mack) and the surname of Ned's stepfather, George King. It would be seven months before the police traced their way through the maze of names to Ned Kelly. It would take a hundred years to identify Billy King as Joe.

The money was divided up and the members of the gang went their way. George King—who had given Ned's mother her last pregnancy before leaving on the Whitty raid—disappeared. Wild Wright rode back to Mansfield, was charged with assault almost immediately, and was serving a month in the Jamieson lock-up when Whitty offered a £2 reward for his arrest. Billy Cook and Big Mick Woodyard became early suspects, soon to be arrested. Ned and Joe brazened it out around Greta and the King Valley while Aaron returned to Beechworth and his money troubles.

In November, on information provided by Petersen at Howlong, the police moved on Woodyard and Cook but also on men who weren't part of the gang—the Baumgartens, Kennedy and Studders.

Two young men *believed to be* Dan Kelly and his cousin Jack Lloyd had been seen driving horses *believed to be* some of those stolen on the Whitty raid. Six months later warrants would be issued for their arrest on charges of stealing Whitty's horses, triggering forces that would destroy twelve lives. Joe, to be one of the victims, was about to play a central role in the genesis of the Trouble.

Key figure was a 21-year-old trooper, Alex Fitzpatrick, a former friend of Ned Kelly and suitor of Kate Kelly, dangerous allegiances when police budgets were threatened by a shaky economy and political crisis. To safeguard his job, Fitzpatrick decided to exploit his intimacy with the notorious Kellys.

On 17 September, soon after the Whitty raid, Ned visited Benalla without Joe, became drunk and, after riding his horse across a footpath, was arrested by his 'friend' Fitzpatrick. Ned—who didn't drink heavily and was never seen drunk on any other occasion—suspected his grog had been hocussed. The next morning, when Fitzpatrick tried to handcuff him on the way to court, Ned's suspicions seemed confirmed. He broke away into a bootmaker's shop and, in the course of a wild brawl, knocked Fitzpatrick unconscious and beat off three other police and the bootmaker, who were trying to subdue him. He eventually allowed a respected justice of the peace, William Magennis, to handcuff him and take him to the court. Ned was fined £4 for resisting arrest and assaulting police, five shillings for damage to Fitzpatrick's uniform, and a risible one shilling for his drunkenness.

In spite of this event, only a month later Ned let Fitzpatrick persuade him that Dan and two of his cousins, Tom and Jack Lloyd, should surrender to the police over an out-of-hand prank at a Winton store—a good indication that nothing too serious had happened—but the lads were given three months and Tom subsequently received another four months for assault.

Ned had little time to brood over the incident. The following month the police made the first of their arrests over the Whitty raid. Without haste, Ned advertised his horses for sale and sold some in Benalla. Then, in late summer, he and Joe rolled their swags and rode away, driving the rest of the horses across the Murray for sale in New South Wales. On the proceeds, they could enjoy the halcyon days of early autumn, vagabonding through the Riverina and the Murrumbidgee valley to visit Joe's ailing uncle John and his family at Wagga, then follow friendly ranges that led down across the border or provided safe passage to the Monaro where Dan sometimes sheared and where old Joe first breathed the freedom of the new land. Ned and Joe's mateship was sealed in long days of riding and yarning.

Nearly ninety years later Elly Byrne spoke of that friendship as she sat fingering her rosary. 'Joe was Ned Kelly's best friend the same as this,' she gestured with the precious beads, 'is my best friend. When I want something, I pray with it. It was like that with Joe and Ned Kelly.'

By now, Ned was riding a superb, bright bay mare he called Mirth. Yet it was Joe's mount, a magnificent grey mare he had graced with the name Music, which would pass into legend as 'Ned Kelly's celebrated grey mare'—a symbol of two lives inseparably bound until death and, perhaps, of Joe's unrecognised contribution to the Kelly legend.

As summer passed into the autumn of 1878 Ned and Joe received word of a warrant eventually issued on 15 March for Ned's arrest over 'the Whitty larceny'. They had also heard of police raids on the Kelly homestead—of the Kelly girls being manhandled by troopers, of milk, eggs, flour and meat tipped out onto the floor, and of wild threats made against Ned.

It was clear provocation to bring Ned back home into a police trap. One of the police involved was Ned's erstwhile friend Trooper Fitzpatrick, another was Joe's old enemy, Detective Ward. Ned and Joe swung their horses' heads to the south, back towards the Kelly homestead at the foot of the Bald Hills.

The warrant for Dan Kelly and Jack Lloyd was sworn on 5 April and listed in the *Police Gazette* of 10 April. On 15 April Constable Fitzpatrick, who was in trouble with his sergeant, saw the item while waiting to take temporary charge of the Greta police station. He had seen Dan three days before and made a bid to win his way back into favour by telling the sergeant that he would try to pick Dan up.

Fortified by some brandy and lemonade at a Winton store, Fitzpatrick rode towards Greta along the old Beechworth Road below the Bald Hills and, close to sunset, came in sight of the Kelly homestead. He detoured a couple of hundred yards to see if Dan was home, but found only Mrs Kelly with her two-day-old daughter, Alice King, and some of the younger children. Hearing sounds of woodcutting some way off, Fitzpatrick investigated. It was only the Kellys' neighbour, Bill Williamson, splitting fence rails in the dying daylight.

As the trooper headed back to the road, he saw two horsemen entering the slip panel near the homestead. By the time he reached the yards, only one man was there, holding a horse by its bridle, another by its mane. A third horse was nearby, saddled, with its bridle removed. Peering down through the dusk at the man holding the horses, Fitzpatrick thought he recognised Ned Kelly's brother-in-law, Bill Skillion (real name Skilling or Skillen, but called Skillion by police, press and even Joe Byrne). Fitzpatrick was wrong. It was not Skillion, but Joe Byrne, whom he had never met.

Fitzpatrick nodded at the saddled horse. 'Who's riding it?'

'I don't know.'

The trooper examined the horse and turned to Joe. 'It's Dan Kelly's mare. Where is he?'

There was no point in Joe lying. 'Up at the house, I suppose.'

Fitzpatrick rode his troop horse over near the back door. 'Dan!'

The door opened and Dan stood there, in his shirt sleeves, a knife and fork in his hand. Fitzpatrick dismounted. 'I'm going to arrest you on a charge of horse stealing, Dan.'

The slim, almost 17-year-old, was very calm, probably confident that he was innocent. 'Very well. I suppose you'll let me have something to eat, I've been riding all day.'

Things were going well. Fitzpatrick was happy enough to wait. 'All right.'

He followed Dan inside, leaving Joe in the yard. It was a peaceful scene, the newly built slab hut glowing with lamp light in the autumn dusk, the smell of woodsmoke and cooking and horses in the cool air...and Joe, his pulse racing, about to be drawn into the mysterious fracas that spawned the Kelly Outbreak.

About five minutes after Fitzpatrick entered the Kelly homestead, violence erupted.

Fitzpatrick claimed that, after Mrs Kelly had roundly abused him, he saw Joe, whom he believed to be Skillion, passing the back door leading a horse. A moment later, he claimed, Ned Kelly appeared in the doorway with a revolver and fired but missed. Mrs Kelly then struck him over the helmet with a fire shovel and a second shot from Ned struck his raised wrist. In a struggle for the revolver it went off a third time. Meanwhile, 'Skillion' had come through the back door, armed with a revolver and Bill Williamson emerged from the bedroom, also armed with a revolver.

Up to now, the story is unlikely—especially Ned's readiness to fire into a room where his mother, brother and sisters were, and his missing with his first shot at point-blank range when, six months later, he would display lethal marksmanship. But the story now becomes unbelievable. Fitzpatrick has Ned turn angrily on 'Skillion'.

'You bugger! Why didn't you tell me who was here! If I had known it was Fitzpatrick, I wouldn't have fired a bloody shot!'

Deeply remorseful at having wounded his dear friend, Ned wants to remove the bullet with a rusty razor, but Fitzpatrick digs it out with his own penknife. Ned then urges the trooper to 'say you were arresting Dan when two men rushed from behind a tree and fired. Describe them as two big men, one like me, and they will think it is my brother Jem. Say that was the man who stole Jackson and Frost's horses...which he sold to Kennedy on the other side of the Murray.'

Quite apart from the fact that Ned Kelly never tried to blame others for his own crimes—even in the case of murder and, least of all, his own brother—Ned would have known that Jim was serving three years hard labour in New South Wales, a fact which had clearly escaped Fitzpatrick's attention.

The Kelly version was quite different. Ned claimed that Mrs Kelly told Fitzpatrick,

Dan need not go without a warrant unless he liked and that the trooper had no business on her premises without some authority besides his own word. The trooper pulled out his revolver and said he would blow her brains out if she interfered in the arrest she told him it was a good job for him Ned was not there or he would ram his revolver down his throat—Dan looked out and said Ned is coming now, the trooper being off his guard looked out and when Dan got his attention drawn he dropped the knife and fork which showed he had no murderous intent and slapped Heenan's hug [a wrestling hold] on him took his revolver and kept him there until Skillion and Ryan came with horses which Dan sold that night. The trooper left and invented some scheme to say that he got shot which any man can see is false...

While later 'Kelly' versions set out to explain how Fitzpatrick received a minor wrist injury, the fact that Ned's account ignores the wound is curiously persuasive, and coalesces with Fitzpatrick's need to identify his own penknife as the instrument which enlarged his alleged bullet wound.

Ned's version doesn't tell the whole truth. It is often said that he claimed to be hundreds of miles away at the time of the 'row'. Actually, in his earliest direct account of the incident, he describes the arrest and arraignment of his mother, Skillion and Williamson, and says, 'I knew nothing of *this transaction* until very close on the trial I being then over 400 miles from Greta.' [My italics]

The statement is ambiguous, but consistent with him being present, though leaving before the arrests were made.

At the trial Ned's cousin, Joe Ryan, produced a receipt showing that, on the day of the Fitzpatrick incident, he had bought a horse from Ned for £17. The sale took place near Greta. Even if the receipt was a fake, it shows that, at this stage, the Kellys were not concerned to prove that Ned was hundreds of miles away on 15 April.

Six months later Ned Kelly casually admitted that he was present during or immediately after the fracas. ('I almost swore after letting him [Fitzpatrick] go that I would never let another go.') But only after his capture and near-death would it be alleged that he admitted to shooting at Fitzpatrick. ('Yes, it was I that fired at him.')

Bill Williamson, after his imprisonment, told the police a number of tales about the incident. He told them that Ned had shot Fitzpatrick, perhaps because that is what they wanted to hear and he was looking for remission of his sentence.

There was no comparable reason to implicate Joe Byrne and in fact Williamson specifically avoided doing so. Identifying Joe as Billy King ('but that is not his proper name'), he told police 'he ["Billy King"] was in Kelly's house when Constable Fitzpatrick was fired at; he wanted the Kellys not to let Fitzpatrick get away alive, and said that, in place of being shot in the arm, he should be shot through the heart; he is a man that would fire on any one that would attempt to arrest him; he is a dangerous man.'

Williamson failed to tell the police that this was the man Fitzpatrick had mistaken for Skillion. It wasn't until 1928 that he admitted, 'I blame myself for Skillion being arrested as he was mistaken for Burns [*sic*]. I pulled Burns back in the dark when he was going into Fitzpatrick's presence at the Kelly homestead after the brawl. Had I let Burns go forward, Skillion would not have been in trouble.'

Williamson and Fitzpatrick are unsatisfactory witnesses. Like all the protagonists, each had his own reason to distort the truth. But out of the violent shadows of that chaotic evening, two things seem to emerge. Ned Kelly, whether or not he shot Fitzpatrick, was present. And his mate, Joe Byrne, whether or not he urged the killing of the trooper, was also there.

It is clear, too, that Joe could not have had a revolver at this stage; otherwise the weapon would have been in evidence six months later when he and his mates bailed up a heavily armed police party and went on to hold up a bank.

Ned Kelly *may* have had a revolver at the time of the incident, but it seems unlikely that it produced the constable's wound, certainly not as alleged by Fitzpatrick.

A doctor giving Crown evidence readily accepted the contribution of Fitzpatrick's penknife to the injury while apparently reluctant to state definitely that a bullet had been involved. His reticence may have led the *Ovens and Murray Advertiser* to make the extraordinary editorial comment, 'We believe the story told by Constable Fitzpatrick though, no doubt, he did colour the part of it relating to the wound a little.' Even the acting commissioner of police later admitted that Fitzpatrick was 'a liar'.

Any attempt at detailed reconstruction of the events of 15 April is built on sand but, carefully choosing the firmest historical ground, it seems that Ned and Joe were in the district engaged in horse dealing. Joe and Dan arrived at the homestead while Fitzpatrick was talking to Williamson. Ned was not far behind them. Alerted by Joe and/or Williamson that Fitzpatrick was in the house with Dan, Ned burst in to precipitate or interrupt the 'row' or 'brawl' which everyone admits took place.

Whatever really happened, it was enough to make Ned, Joe and Dan fugitives. They rode off, obviously never considering that the police would strike at Williamson, the patently innocent Skillion and Mrs Kelly with her new-born baby. But these three became the law's victims.

The first rock of the avalanche was rolling down the hill.

CHAPTER 6

A Respectable-looking Murderer

April–November 1878

Back in the Beechworth ranges, money remained Aaron's greatest problem. The new year of 1878 was only three days old when he faced the court over a debt of £3 18s. He escaped with a guinea fee to Mr Zincke. But, on 18 April, the very day the *Advertiser* published the first news of the Fitzpatrick incident, John Sherritt was summonsed to court over a debt of £10 14s. Aaron's rental money for the selection, almost two years overdue, may have settled the debt.

Soon after this, he was drawn into the Trouble. Ned seems to have headed back to New South Wales immediately after the Fitzpatrick row. Joe may have gone with him or he may have retreated with Dan to the old stronghold on Bullock Creek in the Wombat Ranges.

The court appearances and remands of the three Fitzpatrick case prisoners would occupy the next six months, with the trial proper taking place at Beechworth's spring assizes in October. Money would be needed for the protracted defence—to be earned from the Kelly gold workings where Joe and Aaron's lifelong familiarity with sluicing techniques helped develop the old mine 'with tools and sluice bores and everything requisite for the work' into a project which could earn 'good wages'.

A willing team of helpers—Joe, Aaron, Tom and Jack Lloyd, Wild Wright, Dan's mate Steve Hart (after his release from Beechworth Gaol in June) and other relatives and friends from the Greta Mob—also established an ambitious scheme to raise money by distilling pot whiskey. Twenty acres were cleared for cultivation, to produce a crop of barley and mangold-wurzel (a type of beet) to make the mash. A primitive still was set up—a large, cast-iron pot and a 'worm'—a job for which a relative of Joe's, Johnny Byrne, a skilled blacksmith who lived nearby, beyond the steep Toombullup ridge, could provide expert help.

As the trial approached, Aaron played an extraordinary and strangely neglected role in the Kelly cause—a role which would foreshadow his activities over the next two years.

By June Fitzpatrick was back on duty after suffering an infection of his wrist wound. He was now stationed at Beechworth, where he carried out normal police duties. In the course of these duties he met Aaron—or, perhaps more accurately, Aaron went out of his way to meet Fitzpatrick, claiming, said the trooper, 'that he could lead me to the Kellys in a very short time'. Aaron explained that he was trusting the information to Fitzpatrick because he had a 'down' on Senior Constable Mullane and Detective Ward.

Fitzpatrick mentioned the offer while out on a search party with Senior Detective Kennedy. The detective obviously knew Aaron. 'Oh, we will put that down as worthless,' he scoffed. While Fitzpatrick saw this as a missed chance to catch the Kellys, there is little doubt that Aaron's approach represented an attempt to lure Fitzpatrick into a trap. His capture would remove the chief witness against Mrs Kelly, Skillion and Williamson, and place a valuable hostage in the hands of the Kellys.

Fitzpatrick probably had a narrow escape but neither he nor Detective Kennedy mentioned the incident until 1881. If they had, Aaron's subsequent dealings with the police—including an attempt to lure another key policeman into a trap—may have attracted greater suspicion. As it was, while many in the force remained as dubious as Kennedy, more influential officers believed in Aaron, or professed to believe in him, as readily as Fitzpatrick had done.

Whatever its planned outcome, the scheme to decoy Fitzpatrick failed and the momentous spring of 1878 heralded the October assizes in Beechworth.

Ned Kelly, Joe and Dan were in the ranges near Beechworth as the Fitzpatrick trial was about to begin. Joe and Aaron's old ally, Mr Zincke, was instructing the defence. Presiding was Sir Redmond Barry, a senior judge of the British Empire.

The main thrust of the defence would be to prove that Skillion was not at the Kelly homestead during the incident, thereby discrediting Fitzpatrick's testimony. It was obviously considered too dangerous to call Joe as a witness. Apart from the danger of him simply replacing Skillion as one of the accused, two of the Whitty case defendants, William Baumgarten and Samuel Kennedy, had been remanded to this assize. Billy Cook and Mick Woodyard had already received eight years and two years hard labour respectively.

So Frank Harty, a Winton farmer, and Ned's cousin, Joe Ryan, swore that Skillion was with them, four miles from the Kelly homestead, at the time of Fitzpatrick's attempt to arrest Dan, and that he did not leave until 7.40 p.m. The Crown simply argued that, because the evidence did not agree with Fitzpatrick's, the two witnesses had obviously committed perjury.

After a two-hour retirement, the jury found Mrs Kelly, Skillion and Williamson guilty. Three days later they were sentenced—Mrs Kelly to three years hard labour, the two men to six years hard labour.

It was a bitter blow. Ned, Dan, Joe and probably Aaron rode to the Bullock Creek stronghold and hurled themselves into the gold sluicing and the whiskey project, which Ned saw as 'the quickest means to obtain money to procure a new trial for my mother'.

While the boys were working at their digging, sluicing, scrub-clearing, ringbarking, fencing and cultivating, they also found time to fortify the log hut, armouring its most vulnerable point, the door, with iron from a ship's ballast tank—another job for Johnny Byrne. They then drew small charcoal targets on surrounding trees and practised their marksmanship with Ned's 'rifle'—a queer old carbine sawn off at butt and barrel and held together with waxed string—and Dan's shotgun—'a common, single-barrelled fowling piece, a cheap gun, common bore'.

Later it would be claimed that Joe was armed with 'a very old fashioned gun, with a very large bore, more than an ordinary large bore' and that Steve Hart probably had a double-barrelled shotgun. Later when Ned and his mates needed every weapon they could find, neither of these guns was to be seen. Almost certainly, they never existed, and the Kelly armament at Bullock Creek consisted only of Ned's quaint old carbine and Dan's cheap shotgun. Ned probably also carried a pocket revolver.

The lads' defence measures were well advised. Two police parties were preparing to comb nearby ranges in a pincer movement—one party striking south from Greta, another heading north from Mansfield. Both parties were plainclothed and heavily armed, believing that they were seeking two men involved in the attempted murder of a policeman.

There had been recent, well-publicised cases of trigger-happy New South Wales police killing suspects and there is persuasive evidence that the Victoria police about to ride in search of Ned and Dan Kelly were equally likely to shoot first. As one later admitted, 'If he [Ned Kelly] resisted with firearms, I would shoot him. If he was charged with murder and, after being called, ran away, I would shoot him.' Another went further. 'If I come across Ned Kelly I'll shoot him like a dog.'

The two police parties started out early on Friday, 25 October. The Mansfield party was led by Sergeant Kennedy, with constables Lonigan, Scanlon and McIntyre. Lonigan was an old enemy of Ned's from the bootshop brawl in Benalla. Each man wore a revolver and the party also carried a Spencer repeating rifle borrowed from a gold escort, and a double-barrelled shotgun loaned by the Mansfield vicar.

Riding up into the Wombat Ranges, Lonigan and McIntyre saw a tiger snake sunning itself and raced to get in a fatal blow. McIntyre won, and crowed, 'First blood, Lonigan!', an admission that he expected other blood to be shed. The party's equipment included unusually long straps, designed to be looped around a pair of bodies so they could be slung, straight, on either side of a pack horse. Bodies draped over a horse, in the time-honoured way of Westerns, stiffened into impractical shapes.

The four police passed near Johnny Byrne's hut, crossed Holland's Creek and Toombullup ridge, and by 2 p.m. had ridden down the gully of Stringybark Creek to the burnt-out remains of a prospector's hut in a clearing littered with fallen timber. It was a cheerless place, with clumps of black-plumed speargrass, screens of dead wattle, and huge white gum trunks against the gully gloom. As previously planned, Kennedy halted and pitched a tent here, without knowing that the clearing was less than a mile from the Kelly hut on Bullock Creek.

In late afternoon, believing that they were a good ten miles from likely Kelly haunts, Constable McIntyre went out to try and shoot some kangaroos.

Earlier that day Ned and possibly Joe had ridden south across Toombullup to visit Johnny Byrne's hut and nearby discovered tracks heading deeper into the ranges, tracks of horses shod with government-issue shoes. On the way home Ned saw what he believed to be a different set of police tracks making for the old hut site on Stringybark Creek. The boys did not sleep that night, obviously fearing police attack.

About six next morning, Sergeant Kennedy and Constable Scanlon rode off 'on patrol' but not before the four-man party and its armament had been studied by one or more of the Kellys, watching from the cover of the bush.

It was now Saturday, and of all the cousins and mates who could have been at the Bullock Creek stronghold that day, only Joe Byrne and Steve Hart were with Ned and Dan to take part in a council of war. If the runes had fallen differently, Aaron would have been there to stand by Ned and Joe; but something had taken him back to Sheepstation, and Ned, Dan, Joe and Steve laid their plans in the sunny irony of that spring day while great ramparts of cloud were massing above the southern ridges.

Ned Kelly records, 'We came to the conclusion our doom was sealed unless we could take their firearms. As we had nothing but a gun and a rifle if they came on us at our work or camp, we had no chance only to die like dogs. As we thought our country was woven with police, and we might have a chance of fighting them if we had firearms.'

At the police camp, the morning and afternoon passed in breadmaking and boredom. As the sun settled below the ridges and the sky threatened rain, Lonigan and McIntyre built up the fire to guide Kennedy and Scanlon back to camp. McIntyre was making a billy of tea when a cry cut through the storm-waiting stillness of the clearing.

'Bail up! Hold up your hands!'

The two police whirled and saw four men emerging from the clumps of speargrass about forty yards across the clearing. McIntyre claimed that all four had guns, but Joe and Steve were almost certainly unarmed. McIntyre's shotgun was against a tree, his revolver in the tent. He stood, helpless, holding a fork to stir the tea, then dropped it, and extended his arms.

But Lonigan had his revolver slung, bush-fashion, across his kidneys. A moment of transfigured time stretched, and Lonigan moved.

In McIntyre's words, 'he put his hands to his revolver, at the same time slipping down for cover behind the log on which he had been sitting. Lonigan had his head above the level of the log and was about to use his revolver when he was shot through the head [my italics].'

Lonigan leapt to his feet, and fell with a cry of 'Oh, Christ! I'm shot...'

At a range of forty yards, Ned had shot him through the right eye with a ball from his sawn-off, tied-together carbine. As the echoes scattered, Ned and his mates ran forward and Lonigan was 'struggling and plunging along the ground'.

Ned had started to question McIntyre before Lonigan stopped breathing. He was shocked to discover the identity of the man he had just killed. He had mistaken him for Constable Strahan of the Greta party. Ned established that the other two police were away from camp, secured the police shotgun and two revolvers, then emptied the shot from the two shotgun cartridges and reloaded each with a bullet.

Dan seemed close to hysteria, smiling nervily and even laughing. Joe and Steve were clearly shaken by Lonigan's ugly death but Joe pulled himself together quickly.

As McIntyre adjusted himself to his plight, he studied the four lads, able to identify Ned and Dan from photos and family resemblance. For some time Joe and Steve would remain 'two men whose names are unknown'. McIntyre recalled Joe as about 21, 5 ft 9 ins tall, of 'slight build' and 'thin', with 'very fair complexion, fair moustache and long beard on chin, very fine like first growth'.

Even in this nightmarish situation, Joe made a favourable impression. In McIntyre's first description, he noted Joe's 'mild expression of features'. Later he called him 'respectable looking' and subsequently said, 'he had not the villainous expression of the others'. Much later he wrote, 'Joe Byrne was a nervous man, thoroughly under the control of Ned Kelly. Apart from Kelly's bad example and bad influence he would have been a fairly reputable citizen.'

His appearance aside, Joe seems to have won McIntyre's approval by showing the unfortunate policeman some consideration. McIntyre deposed, 'Byrne, having the tea that I had made, handed me a pannikin and said, "Here, mate, have some tea!" And, again, Byrne said to to me "Do you smoke, mate?" I said "Yes." And he said "Well, fill your pipe and have a smoke."'

When McIntyre packed his pipe, Joe and Ned asked for some tobacco and the three smoked as Ned continued to question the trooper about Kennedy and Scanlon. Ned asked McIntyre to get them to surrender on their return, telling him, 'We don't want their lives, only their horses and firearms.' The trooper believed this to be true. After about half an hour they heard horses approaching.

Dan and Joe fell back to the sword grass, Ned crouched behind one of the fallen trees by the fire, and Steve took cover in the tent. Ned had his carbine and the police shotgun, Dan his old gun, while Joe and Steve were apparently now armed with the police Webleys, short-barrelled .45s, dangerous only at fairly close range.

The two police appeared at the far end of the clearing, about a hundred yards away, horses at a slow walk, Sergeant Kennedy ten or twelve yards in front of Scanlon, who had the Spencer repeating rifle slung muzzle-down across his back.

When they were about forty yards off, McIntyre moved forward to meet them and said loudly, 'Oh, Sergeant, you had better dismount and surrender, for you are surrounded.'

Obviously thinking that this was a practical joke, organised by a bored McIntyre and Lonigan, Kennedy smiled and reached for his holster.

Ned Kelly rose from behind the log, calling, 'Bail up! Hold up your hands!' Dan and Joe advanced from the speargrass, Steve from the tent.

As Kennedy struggled to unbutton his holster flap, Scanlon tried to wheel his horse, then swung the still-unslung rifle across his body and fired. Before he could operate the lever to re-load, Ned shot him. Scanlon fell forward on his horse's neck and rolled off.

Ned dropped the carbine and caught up the police shotgun. Meanwhile, Kennedy had dismounted on the off-side of his horse and opened fire with his revolver, across the rump, as Ned and his mates advanced. One of his bullets would graze Dan's shoulder, another snicked through Ned's beard.

McIntyre now saw that Scanlon was on the ground, trying to unsling his rifle. Though unaware that the trooper had already been shot by Ned, McIntyre accurately described the actions of a badly wounded man.

'He fell upon his knees in dismounting—he caught at his rifle as if to take it off his shoulder out of the strap—and endeavoured to get upon his feet. He again fell upon his hands and knees and in that position was shot under the right arm.'

McIntyre thought that Ned had fired the fatal shot, but, after seeing Scanlon fall from his horse, Ned had switched his attention to Kennedy. McIntyre said that four shots were fired as Scanlon was hit. One of those shots was fired by Joe, who was on Scanlon's right, as the trooper knelt, supported on his left hand, his right hand lifting the Spencer to try to clear the sling from his neck. In that vulnerable moment, with Scanlon's side exposed to him, Joe took careful aim with his unfamiliar weapon, squeezed the trigger, felt the kick and bounce of the shot in his hand, and saw the policeman pitch over on to his back. Whether or not it was his bullet that killed Scanlon, respectable-looking Joe was a murderer.

Kennedy's frightened horse pulled away from him and, as the sergeant took cover behind a tree, McIntyre swung into the saddle, missed the off-side stirrup, then hurled himself on to the horse's neck and galloped off into the bush, to the north, away from Mansfield.

Kennedy now waged a lone and losing fight, described by Ned.

'Kennedy kept firing from behind the tree...my brother advanced from the spring. Kennedy fired at him and ran...I followed him he got behind another tree and fired at me again...I shot him in the armpit and he dropped his revolver and ran I fired again with the gun as he slewed around to surrender I did not know he had dropped his revolver the bullet passed through the right side of his chest he could not live or I would have let him go...'

Wounded in the head, chest and side, the sergeant lay in a clutter of fallen bark at the foot of a huge, white gum. The four young men gathered around him, bark crackling awkwardly under their boots in the hushed and deepening dusk, Ned trying to make Kennedy comfortable, Dan fetching water from the creek, Joe and Steve watching, helpless.

Ned talked to Kennedy at some length, conscious all the time of McIntyre riding for help. Kennedy spoke of his wife and five children, often mentioning an infant son who had recently died. According to one account, the dying sergeant forgave Ned, prayed God would do the same and, with his failing strength and wit, scribbled a last note to his wife. Eventually, in near-darkness, Ned could wait no longer at Kennedy's side. Yet he couldn't leave the dying man to continue this pointless agony, helpless prey to wildcats, dingoes and ants drawn by blood and torn flesh. Ned held the muzzle of the vicar's shotgun to Kennedy's heart and fired a last shot. A last volley of echoes died. Then he fetched a police rain cloak from the camp and draped it over the sergeant's body. He later told Aaron that this was a gesture of respect for 'the bravest man he had ever heard of'.

Back at the police camp, whether or not he had yet realised it, Joe was a member of a Gang—four men inseparably bound by complicity in murder. As they checked the tent and the pockets of the dead men for their fugitive needs—money, watches, ammunition, blankets, capes, food—Joe slipped a ring from Scanlon's finger and placed it on his own, 'a plain English gold ring set with an oval-shaped opaque stone', a topaz. One tries to read in this strange, chilling act an acceptance of his role as the policeman's killer. If this becomes comprehensible as some barbaric warrior rite, it is harder to explain why he then took a ring from Lonigan's finger, 'a gold ring with a large white seal' and placed it on a finger of the other hand.

To many, Joe was the member of the Gang least credible as a killer. In these actions, he shows his readiness to brand himself in that role: an unequivocal acceptance of guilt.

They fired the police tent before they headed back to Bullock Creek with the four police horses, the flames briefly lighting the empty clearing and the bodies of Lonigan and Scanlon before the darkness closed in and the distant thunder of a coming storm rumbled closer.

On Monday morning, only two days after the Stringybark Creek battle, eight shots were fired on the hill above Aaron's selection. He investigated to find Joe and the other three members of what was now the Kelly Gang—Dan wounded, all of them soaked through, after driving the four police horses and two pack horses ahead of them in a grim 60-mile journey from Bullock Creek.

Before anything was said, Aaron would have noticed the crown brands on some of the horses, the police firearms, and perhaps sensed the indefinable and eventually fatal gulf that had suddenly opened between him and these four—even between him and Joe. The terrible blood rite of Stringybark bound them and, not having been part of it, he could never truly belong, only listen with still breath and drumming heart to words that told him of the three police deaths.

He heard how Tom Lloyd had arrived at the stronghold in time to guard them during a few hours exhausted sleep on Saturday night. They had then ridden to Greta through rain-swept bush, changed into dry clothes and set out yesterday, Sunday, with their ten horses, across the soggy Oxley Flats. In the early hours of this morning Joe had bought a bottle of brandy at Moon's Pioneer Hotel, beside the first of nine bridges across the Ovens River and its skein of anabranches which had merged to a single, half-mile-wide stream. Unable to reach the far bank, they were forced some eight miles upstream to a crossing below Taylor's Gap, where they were seen and recognised by Constable Bracken, before swinging back to the east to pick up their well-known northward route. In the foothills of the Beechworth ranges, they bought some oats and several boxes of sardines at Coulson's store beside the railway in 'new' Everton, before crossing the line under Blind Creek Bridge and climbing up here to the tableland.

Aaron brought them food and guarded them while they slept—in a cave just beyond the long spine of Native Dog Peak—a structure of huge boulders forming two lofty chambers, one leading up into the other. A native pine trunk barbed with branch stumps, provided a ladder to the rock dome of the roof and its soaring view of the Woolshed, blurred with scrims of passing rain.

It was a place for boyhood dreams of outlawry: this was cold, adult reality. Ned and Joe carrying dead men's guns, with dead men's watches ticking away the minutes and hours of lives that, until now, had been careless of days and weeks.

From here they could see the Byrne house with its plume of smoke below Reedy Creek's horseshoe of trees. Joe slipped down the slope to face a brief and agonising reunion with his mother, to watch the pleasure of his arrival drain from her face as she heard whatever he could bring himself to say. Then he probably crossed the footbridge to the main Chinese camp and bought some opium before climbing back to the cave and Aaron and the other three fugitives.

The Gang were driving their mob of horses along the old horse-stealing route across the Murray to New South Wales. Every small creek was swollen with rain, big creeks and rivers were already running bankers, low-lying ground was forming swamps. When they set off again, late that day or early the next, Aaron probably scouted for them, at least part of the way, riding ahead to find the driest route while still avoiding settlements and roads where they might be recognised by police or public now alerted to the Stringybark murders.

Poor Constable McIntyre, after abandoning Sergeant Kennedy's exhausted horse, had spent a few dark, haunted hours in a wombat hole, then struggled through the bush carrying his boots so he couldn't be tracked. He reached Mansfield on Sunday afternoon (ironically, in a buggy provided by Johnny Byrne's father and driven by his brother) and, at eight on Monday morning, the first news of Lonigan and Scanlon's deaths was stuttered out in morse code to telegraph offices all over the colony, scrawled on telegram forms, and raced to police stations and newspapers. That day, Monday, 28 October, the government announced a reward of £800 for the Gang: £200 for each of the Kellys and the 'two men, names unknown'. Search parties recovered the bodies of Lonigan and Scanlon and, days later, Kennedy.

McIntyre's paranoia set the tone for the early stages of the police pursuit. A trooper riding from Mansfield to Benalla imagined that the Kellys were after him and, like McIntyre, abandoned both his horse and his boots. Detective Ward was ordered to the King Valley but, armed only with a pocket revolver, flatly refused to go until he was properly armed, then managed to be marooned by floods for a couple of days before resuming a cold trail. A sub-officer with news of a fresh sighting chose to follow stale information which kept him out of danger. A senior officer who seemed a little too close on the heels of the Gang ordered his men back to their base.

There were dogged police pursuers as well—parties led by Detective Kennedy, Sergeant Harkin, and Superintendent Nicolson—pushing north behind the four fugitives as they entered the Murray Valley and faced disaster. The river had broken its banks to form huge lakes and broad, new flood courses which must be crossed before the turbid main stream could be reached.

On Wednesday morning beside a lagoon at Murray Flats the Gang met a farmer called Gideon Margery who gave them some bread, cheese and wine. Nearby, they lit a fire in a hollow log and eventually told Margery who they were. Even at a time like this, Ned said, 'that he intended calling on a man called Whitty about some horse stealing case'.

Early that afternoon they appeared at the home of William Baumgarten, now serving a prison sentence over Whitty's horses. Here, they made camp until sunset. Mrs Baumgarten bore the Kellys no love and had just watched them ride off into the lagoons when a police party came up. Alerted by her, the police spurred their horses in pursuit, splashing through fast-rising floodwater until forced to turn back. As they sought another route, the Gang watched, up to their necks in water, hidden among reeds, their guns and ammunition wet and useless.

When the police moved on, the Gang picked up their horses, which were hidden in scrub, risked lighting a fire to dry themselves and their weapons, then struck west to try to cross the main channel by a punt at the Bungowannah wharf. It had sunk. Defeated, they swung their mob of horses and drove them back through the lagoons and channels, back south, towards Beechworth.

This was Wednesday, 30 October, the day on which the two-day-old reward for the Gang was increased to £2,000—£500 for each of the fugitives. Again, Ned and Dan were named and described. Joe and Steve were described and still designated 'Name Unknown', though Joe was now noted as 'supposed identical with Charley Brown'. Confusion reigned. Fitzpatrick thought that McIntyre's description of Joe matched George King, Ned's step-father. Bill Williamson, in Pentridge, gave a similar description of 'Billy King', who was, he said, 'like King who is married to Kelly's *sister*.' Yet, eventually, it was Steve Hart who was provisionally identified as 'William King of Greta' while Joe was still supposed to be 'Charles Brown of King River'.

On Saturday a bark stripper working in the bush near Sheepstation Creek saw the Gang at the Sherritt house, 'men and horses pretty well worn out'.

He rode straight into Beechworth to tell the police but was so shaken by his experience that he stopped for one or two drinks which became three or four. By the end of the night he was carried to the police lock-up 'in a speechless state of drunkenness'. He seems to have passed Sunday without saying anything to the police about the Gang, resumed drinking on the Monday and was, supposedly, still drinking on the Wednesday when he eventually told his story.

Meanwhile, the Kelly Gang had passed through Everton late on Saturday night, bought a meal there, then in the early hours of Sunday morning pushed on past Wangaratta, and crossed the swollen One Mile Creek by a narrow ledge under the railway bridge—betraying local knowledge that pointed to Steve Hart. Now it was almost a clear run to the Warby Ranges, offering cover and safe travel to home ground. Scanlon's horse (usually described, incorrectly, as 'Kennedy's pack horse') broke down on the last leg and was left behind. Two other police horses would be abandoned soon after. The Gang were 'completely done up...wet and tired out'. Driving six horses, they had travelled more than 200 miles, much of it through flooded country, in just over a week. They had evaded the police, if at least some of the police hadn't evaded them. They were back in their home ranges by Monday, 4 November. Three days later, and five days after the bark stripper had seen them at Sheepstation, the police mounted a raid on the Sherritt house. Aaron was about to enter the story.

CHAPTER 7

The Great Sebastopol Raid

November 1878

An Englishman, an Irishman and a Scotsman provide the archetypal trio for a myriad jokes and stories based on their contrasted perceptions of an event. Such was the human chemistry operating in 'The Great Sebastopol Raid', the much-lampooned set-piece which introduces Aaron Sherritt to history.

The Englishman was Captain Frederick Charles Standish, Chief Commissioner of Police, Chairman of the Victoria Racing Club, prominent Freemason, member of the Melbourne Club and 'foremost citizen of that city'. Now, an arrogant, abrasive man in his mid-fifties, he had been Chief Commissioner for twenty years and increasingly neglected those aspects of his work which did not appeal to him.

The Scot was Superintendent Charles Hope Nicolson, a grumpy disciplinarian (Aaron would call him a 'cranky Scotchman') who, against Standish's wishes, was named Assistant Chief Commissioner. Early in his police career, he had chased a bushranger who had just killed a fellow police cadet. Ignoring a hail of bullets, Nicolson galloped in pursuit of the man and eventually hauled him from the saddle without even drawing his own re-volver. He had been one of the captors of bushranger Harry Power and, though now 49 and best known for his sixteen years in charge of the detec-tive branch, as the officer elected to lead the Kelly pursuit he was about to demonstrate the same readiness to charge.

The Irishman was Superintendent John Sadleir who, as a flashy young of-ficer, had led gold escorts from the Woolshed. Now, an 'austere and dignified' 45, capable, humane but unimaginative, he was in charge of the North-Eastern District while subordinate to both Nicolson and Standish, an uncomfortable hierarchy whose shortcomings were about to be demonstrated.

Enterprising Constable Keating of Beechworth set the ball rolling on Wednesday, 6 November, when he at last heard the drunk bark stripper's story of seeing the Kellys at Sherritts. He gathered an armed posse of young

Beechworth townsmen—a group which caused Superintendent Sadleir some alarm when he rode back into town at 10.30 that night. However, Sadlier quickly heard Keating's story and proceeded to interview the grog-battered informant. The man believed that he had seen the Kellys two evenings before but, significantly, was confident that, even if they had left Sherritts, they would be nearby, 'somewhere in the rocks where it would take fifty men to get them out'.

On the basis of this report, Sadleir telegrammed Nicolson at his Benalla headquarters, 'Very positive information that Kellys are concealed in ranges near here. My informant is not quite sober, and has been talking rather openly, but I am convinced his information is genuine. But it may be a day or two late. I have but two constables here and the hiding place is most difficult to approach.' Sadleir asked for every available man, mounted and armed, and a black-tracker.

Nicolson quickly organised nine troopers and a tracker. By chance, the Chief Commissioner, Captain Standish, had arrived in Benalla that evening after officiating at the Melbourne Cup the previous day. He, too, accompanied the party, with two Melbourne reporters from the *Argus* and *Herald*— meaning that fourteen men and horses arrived in Beechworth by special train soon after three on Thursday morning.

Nicolson—already dubious about the operation—was further irritated when Sadleir and Standish were 'very much engaged talking' while he was trying to organise his horse. As a result, he professed to know nothing of any plans for the ensuing operation.

Eventually, the party set out for Sheepstation Creek at 4.30 a.m., the fourteen Benalla men now augmented by Sadleir, the sobering bark stripper ('with blackened face to help towards his incognito'), a senior constable who had arrived with Sadleir, and the two local constables, a total of nineteen horsemen. The civilian volunteers had been thanked and dismissed.

Two miles out of town Sadleir had arranged to meet some half dozen men from a Taylor's Gap search party led by Sergeant Steele. Unexpectedly, Steele's full party of thirteen was waiting at the roadside and a surprised Sadleir found himself now with a squadron of 32 horsemen as they swung across the main ridge of the tableland. Later, asked who was responsible 'for bringing this large party together' he replied, 'It was an accident.'

By now, Nicolson's resentment was at boiling point. To his jaundiced eye, there were 'upwards of fifty mounted men' in 'this great cavalcade'. He protested, 'This collection of men was improper, and calculated to defeat the object we had in view...we had to cross some very rough country, great ranges of granite, and the rumbling noise that the party made was simply just like thunder, and the people heard us a mile off.'

The Melbourne reporters gave a different impression. The Argus man wrote, 'The ground was anything but suitable for rapid progress, as in places it was quite rotten, the horses sinking at times up to their knees, while in other places patches of granite cropped up out of the soil and this being smooth and slippery from the recent rains, rendered it necessary for every man to keep a tight hand on his bridle...' The Herald reporter wrote in similar terms and spoke of 'the strictest silence being observed'.

As dawn began to break behind the party, the blackfaced informant led them to a scrubby ridge from which 'a clearing with a large slab hut was seen in the valley below'.

While Sadleir says that 'Nicolson took charge of the attack,' Nicolson claims that he did so only after Sadleir told him, 'Now Nicolson, this is the house of the Sherritts, you will do this and you will do that, and the outlaws are said to be here.'

As they both hurriedly selected two or three men, the irascible Scot barked at Sadleir, 'You look after the back and I will look after the front!' then wheeled his horse and spurred down the slippery slope, followed closely by his small group and Sadleir's. Turning sharply into a narrow, fenced race leading to the house, Nicolson reined in, leapt to the ground and burst through the door.

As he did, Constable Bracken tried to push past and the indignant Superintendent shoved him aside, causing his shotgun to go off.

The Sherritt family had been barely awakened by the pounding of hooves and the crash of their door, when the shotgun blast shattered the darkness. Four of the girls in the house were under twelve, the youngest only three, and Anne was eight months pregnant.

The shambles which followed was probably indescribable, but Nicolson manages to omit the Sherritts completely from his account. 'I went suddenly from room to room. I have been accustomed to that sort of duty. I rushed into the next room whipped off the [bed] clothes, and ran to the next room and did the same, and so all through, and I found the whole thing nothing.'

Sadleir found himself 'in a rambling sort of building without windows...The room in which I found myself was lined with bunks, the top row of bunks so high that one could not see whether they were occupied without climbing up. I passed around the bunks, with my hat placed on the point of my rifle level with the upper row, preferring that the bullets which were momentarily expected should find my hat when my head was not in it.'

Sadleir, too, omits the screaming women and girls, crying children, and indignant men of the house, though admitting, 'we...found a family, and they were all fast asleep when Mr Nicolson, who was first in, arrived, so they did not hear us.'

Bracken's shot had brought the rest of the party charging down to the house and the *Argus* reporter was there to hear John Sherritt protesting at this attack on his family and property. 'Of course the man Sherritt put on a virtuously indignant air, and asked whether he ought to be suspected of harbouring such persons after having been in the police at home.'

The police gave the two reporters a briefing on the Sherritts' connection with the Gang. John, they claimed, was 'well known to have long been intimately acquainted with the Kellys'. Further, after having identified one of the Gang's 'unknown men' as 'Bob Byrnes', the Herald man noted that John had 'a large family of children, the eldest being a girl of twenty-one years of age [Elizabeth was 22] who is stated to be the sweetheart of Bob Byrnes'. The Argus went further, saying that the 'eldest daughter was to have been married to one of the men now wanted by the police'.

After their assault on the Sherritt house, the police offered no apology. On the contrary, a reporter wrote, 'After warning Sherritt, the party withdrew.'

By now it was clear that the raid was, as Standish acidly put it, 'a day or two after the fair'. In spite of this, or perhaps because of it, the police were to try again, and yet again. The party remounted, rode to Aaron's selection, and burst into his hut. It was empty, the bed not slept in.

Then, as it grew lighter, the disguised bark stripper (believed by the reporters to be a second blacktracker) led the 32 horsemen down 'a precipitous and dangerous gorge about 800 ft' to the Woolshed Valley where 'a sharp turn to the left brought us in front of a slab hut in a nicely-cleared piece of land. This was the hut of Mrs Burns, who is known to be most friendly to the Kellys, and is further said to be connected with another of the gang.'

Margret, Denny and the three girls were milking when they heard the rumble of many hooves and saw the big band of horsemen galloping across Limeburner Flat, with the newly risen sun spearing from behind them across the shoulder of Native Dog Peak. Margret hustled the children down to the house and they watched from the windows as the police surrounded the Byrne paddock in a chaos of hissing, honking geese and barking dogs, horses fidgeting, steaming and blowing after the gallop.

When Margret eventually opened the door after a 'demand for admittance', the reporters noted that she was 'at first greatly scared' but soon 'became very bold and impudent. She could not, or more probably would not, give any information, and, in fact, denied all knowledge of the Kellys.' So the people of Melbourne met hard-working Margret Byrne. The Argus report would be reprinted by Beechworth's Advertiser on Saturday. Unlike the Herald's, it did not mention 'Bob Byrnes'. But the connection was made clear. To the people of Beechworth, Margret was now identified as the mother of a Gang member.

The three senior officers spent some time talking with her, trying to enlist her help in persuading Joe to desert his mates, obviously influenced by McIntyre's impression of his mildness and respectability.

Sadleir recalled, 'We pointed out to her that her son had got his neck into a halter, and that she could save him if she liked...and there was a good deal of persuasion of that sort used with her...I tried to work on her mother's feelings.' But Sadleir was dealing with something far more complex than a mother's love for a son in trouble.

Margret obviously knew of Joe's involvement with the Kellys and made no attempt to deny it, thus confirming police suspicion that he was a Gang member.

As Sadleir tried to appeal to Margret Byrne's motherly feelings—a loving Irish father talking with a loving Irish mother—he found little response in the pale blue eyes, in the strong face tautened by drawn-back hair. All she said was, 'He has made his bed, let him lie on it.' Icy words in the clear beauty of the morning.

A search of the house for 'property of the murdered men' had yielded nothing. The *Herald* reporter watched as 'Mrs Byrnes with her two little girls [Elly wasn't allowed outside after the police had arrived] and a son, continued the milking of their cows, which operation had been disturbed by the arrival of the police.' It was a nice observation of a life in which neither death, birth nor sudden notoriety could be allowed to disrupt the ongoing order of things.

Meanwhile, Captain Standish called for refreshments and lit a pipe while some men headed off to James Chappell's Reidford Hotel. Then, as the Great Sebastopol Raid settled into anticlimax and a scatter of miners and neighbours gathered to see what was happening, Aaron made his entrance, strolling up with an axe over his shoulder. He had probably stayed the night with the Byrnes (he sometimes slept there for weeks, even months, at a time) and was 'cutting wood a little way from the house' when the police arrived. (Elly Byrne who knew him better than she knew Joe, commented, 'Aaron would come and split up wood or anything.')

Sergeant Steele of Wangaratta and Constable Strahan noticed his arrival and had a word with him. Aaron merely nodded towards the blackfaced informant, 'I know that bloody dog.' According to Superintendent Sadleir, Strahan then approached him and pointed out Aaron. 'Here is a man that knows the Kellys well, and will be of use to you; he knows all that is going on.'

Aaron calmly watched Sadleir as the officer approached, measuring the level eyes, the square-trimmed grey beard.

Sadleir recalled his first impression of Aaron as 'a light-looking high-shouldered man', reporting, 'I spoke to him and asked him just to do what he could to assist us, and made certain promises which I forget. I was a stranger to him and he was not satisfied with my authority. I then called, I think, first Mr Nicolson and asked him to come and speak with him, and I think he was still uncertain about whether we had any authority. I then told him of Captain Standish, and I asked Captain Standish to speak with him. I think we were out of hearing of the police standing around us, but they could see all that we were doing.'

It was an extraordinary scene, the three officers with their grey and grey-ing beards, men of authority unused to having that authority questioned, standing there 'near the back of Mrs Byrne's house', trying to establish their bona fides with this tall young bushman whose eyes remained impudent and whose broad mouth seemed so close to amusement.

At that stage, so soon after the tragedy of Stringybark Creek and its first impact on him, Aaron's motivations were probably in their most clear-cut state. His admiration for Ned Kelly, his dislike of Dan, his lack of regard for Steve Hart—all were overshadowed by his concern for Joe, his mate.

Now three of the highest-ranking policemen in the colony were asking for his help—asking him to betray the Kelly Gang. Nothing could be easier. The Gang had already placed trust in him, a degree of trust matched only by that shown to their closest relatives. It was understood that he would con-tinue to help them. To do this, he must know their whereabouts, their movements. If he could help them, he could betray them.

The knowledge placed Aaron in a new and powerful position with the police, a position he had already defined by rejecting the authority of the officer in charge of the district and the officer in charge of the Kelly pursuit. Aaron could name his own price—that Joe should be spared the death sentence. Confronting the possibility of saving Joe, Aaron may have been pre-pared to sacrifice Dan, Steve, even Ned. Life imprisonment for Joe seemed preferable to his death, so, in this first unsought, unprepared-for interview, he saw a chance for Joe to live and took it. Yes, he told them, he would help betray the Kelly Gang. Perhaps, in that moment, he thought this the only way he could save Joe's life or perhaps he already glimpsed other opportunities.

The discussion was intense but brief and, as far as the three officers were concerned, successful. Sadleir reports, 'It was proposed that he should have an understanding that Captain Standish would recommend to the govern-ment that Joe Byrne's life should be saved, and that he should be tempted through Aaron Sherritt to lead the police on the other three.'

Yet Standish was to tell the Royal Commission, 'Mr Nicolson…told me he had been talking to Aaron Sherritt, and…if I held out to him [Aaron] the inducement that he would receive a considerable proportion of the reward, he would work loyally for us, and that I had better see him myself, that I could give him a personal guarantee, being the head of the department. I went up with Mr Nicolson and had a talk with Aaron Sherritt, and told him if he put us in the way of catching the outlaws shortly, that he would receive a substantial proportion of the Government reward.'

Sadleir gave a totally different picture of this seminal discussion with Aaron. He recalled no mention of reward nor of payment for Aaron, stress-ing, 'His bargain was if we would save Joe Byrne and guarantee his life, and Captain Standish said, "No doubt the government would act upon his recommendation in the matter." That was about the size of what was said.'

Pressed as to the terms of the agreement with Aaron, Sadleir reiterated, 'Only Byrne's life.'

It seems most likely that Standish had overstepped his authority in undertaking to save Joe's life. Always a political animal, he may have edited the deal with Aaron to a less contentious form.

The fact remains that, to the end, standing police orders were, if possible, to avoid killing Joe and to take him prisoner.

The refreshments arrived, and the police party had a bizarre picnic in the Byrne clearing, before splitting into groups to go their various ways.

However unconcerned he may have been with the nature of promises he had made to Aaron, Standish was greatly heartened by the discussion. The day before the Great Sebastopol Raid, it was reliably reported, 'The Chief Commissioner considers the early arrest of the outlaws hopeless.' Yet the day after the raid, Standish was saying 'that he has now information that leads him to a confident belief that the gang will either be shot down or be in the hands of the police within a very short period'.

Having worked this transformation on the lordly Standish, Aaron was left to face the dilemma of how he could meet his end of the bargain. He must have known that Joe would not betray his new mates and it is clear from Joe himself that Aaron never put this proposal to him. If Aaron was to betray the Gang, he would also be betraying Joe. Yet to save Joe's life he must convince the police that he was doing all he could to put the Gang in their hands. He would worry later about paying the piper. Another payment to be postponed.

CHAPTER 8

'The Tall Unknown Bushranger'

November–December 1878

Over the next week Aaron helplessly watched Joe become an outlaw. The very day of the Great Sebastopol Raid, the *Advertiser* published a notice calling on Ned, Dan and the two Unknown Men to surrender on or before the following Tuesday, 12 November—'the last legal proceeding necessary before the murderers can be declared outlaws'. This formality disposed of, Parliament passed an Act of Outlawry.

On Friday, 15 November, in a handwritten, handsomely sealed proclamation by the Governor—its text published in the *Government Gazette* and newspapers throughout the colony—Joe, still officially an Unknown Man, was declared an outlaw. He could be shot without challenge by policeman or civilian. Anyone helping him in any way could receive up to fifteen years' imprisonment. Similar proclamations were issued for Ned, Dan and the second Unknown Man. As Aaron probably read in the *Advertiser*, 'The Act... places Ned Kelly and his comrades altogether outside the pale of humanity, and makes them animals to be got rid of by any means, fair or foul.'

Now Ned had to find a way for himself and his three mates to live outside the law and depend as little as possible on their friends. He also felt compelled to counteract the anti-Kelly hysteria of the press. Despite McIntyre's accurate account of Lonigan's death to Sadleir, he had elsewhere claimed that the trooper was shot before he could even draw his revolver. Ned, he claimed, had shot Scanlon as he tried to unsling his rifle while running towards a tree. When Kennedy's body was found after several days, an ear was missing, supposedly cut off by Ned while the helpless sergeant was tied to a tree. Wild stories were told of Kelly's family background, the dubious Fitzpatrick version of the 'row' was further embellished, the tragic clash at Stringybark was seen as heralding a vendetta by a pack of blood-crazed killers. Police and public paranoia fed on its own by-products.

There had been talk before this of the Kellys robbing a bank—Oxley, Milawa and Howlong were rumoured targets. Now, a bank robbery offered both the means to survive and an opportunity to carry out an exercise in what the modern world calls public relations. Ned and Joe worked out a careful strategy which Joe put to paper for evaluation and improvement. First, a bank was chosen, far enough from their home territory to be unexpected, yet still in an area where friends and relatives could provide intelligence and support. Seymour, Violet Town and Euroa were likely targets. The National Bank at Euroa, 27 miles south-west of Benalla, was the eventual choice.

Next, a depot was needed, where the Gang could meet, consolidate for the strike at the bank, collect hostages, and bring the loot and bank staff after the robbery. To find a suitable site, they scanned the vast pastoral empire of Isaac Younghusband and Andrew Lyell MLA, who, since 1875, had scooped up ten stations in the district—an awesome half-million-acre conglomerate. Only three-and-a-half miles from Euroa was one of their out-stations called Faithfull's Creek, a twin-gable brick homestead and slab outbuildings in a corner formed by the willow-flanked creek and the main railway line on an embankment only 150 yards away. An overseer, three station hands, a cook-housekeeper and one or two other women lived here, with a few casual labourers cutting and stacking hay. Ned knew the property well and had friends working there. Other friends would arrive during the hold-up to be included among the prisoners, providing further security.

The adjacent railway line was both a plus and minus. It threatened the security of the operation yet placed the government and railway telegraph lines—one to either side of the tracks—within easy reach.

An old and loyal friend, hawker Ben Gould, who had a selection near Euroa, provided detailed local knowledge. Ned and Joe may have been tempted to use him in the execution of the plan, but Gould's known links with Ned would have made him too vulnerable to arrest and prosecution under the draconian Outlawry Act. (As it was, he was the first of the Gang's sympathisers to be arrested.) Gould may have suggested a fellow hawker, James Gloster of Seymour, to play a key role—bringing new town clothes for each member of the Gang, also providing a 'cover' vehicle for travel between the depot and the bank and to carry the bank staff.

Gloster's complicity was to be disguised by an elaborate charade, involving him being bailed up, trying to escape, having his van plundered, and subsequently being held prisoner.

A date for the robbery would be chosen during the full moon, for easy night riding, and sympathisers would give the police false leads to draw their attention elsewhere while the operation was under way.

It was a superb plan, worked out in extraordinary detail. With only a few finishing touches to be supplied immediately before the robbery, Ned and Joe turned their attention to a Victorian parliamentarian, Donald Cameron, who made the news on 14 November asking if the Premier, Mr Berry, would institute 'a searching inquiry' into the role of the police in 'the Kelly outbreak'. Ned was always too ready to trust a man—even a politician. He and Joe produced a long letter to Cameron, an extraordinary document which set out to state the facts of the Fitzpatrick incident and, instead, became a statement of the events leading up to Stringybark—Ned's trouble with Whitty, the raid on his horses, the police harassment of the Kelly girls, the shooting of the three police, and a series of injustices that had rankled through the years.

The letter is strongly rhetorical, with Ned's anger and bitterness and, eventually, his vainglory evident. Joe would have hurried to record it and probably helped to structure it, contributing the odd phrase. Joe's old teacher Cornelius O'Donoghue may have winced mildly at some of the spelling, grammar and punctuation, but how he would have enjoyed the colour, the passion, the imagery, the wild stream of consciousness.

The 3,500-word draft closed with a final attack on the police, in which Joe introduced a touch of whimsy with snatches of lilting verse:

I am really astonished to see members of Legislative Assembly led astray
by such articles as the police,
    for while an outlaw reigns their pocket swells
'Tis double pay and country girls.

by concluding as I have no more paper unless I rob for it, if I get justice
I Will cry a go.
    For I need no lead or powder
    To avenge my cause,
    and if words be louder
    I will oppose your laws.

With no offence (remember your railroads) and a sweet goodbye from
Edward Kelly
enforced outlaw*

*A Government copyist failed to recognise the verse and rendered it as part of the letter's prose. However, a reporter who saw the original, commented that it concluded with 'four lines of original poetry'. The description 'enforced outlaw' was also quoted by the reporter and subsequently used by Joe Byrne in a later letter. The copyist read the phrase as 'a forced outlaw'.

The draft would have been a hasty scrawl but there was no paper, or perhaps time, for a fine copy. This would have to come later.

Back in the Woolshed, Margret Byrne had more to worry about than her son's outlawry. In these increasingly hard times, she was slipping further into debt. Her account with Beechworth storekeeper Paddy Allen had reached a daunting £45—half a year's fair wages. Allen tells the story.

> The Byrnes used to be pretty hard up sometimes. They ran in a long score with me. Then things got worse and worse, and they had no tucker at all. So one day Mrs Byrne came along and said she was ashamed, but they had nothing, and would I just let her have a bag of flour. Well, I knew she had cattle running in the hills, and she said she'd sell some of them and pay me. Of course, a man had to keep sweet with people there, when they got in on him and all. He had to keep them going if he wanted to get his own back. So I packed the cart with a bag of flour and about twelve hundredweight of other food, and started off.
>
> Along the road, about dinner time, I met Mrs Byrne's two sons, Joe and Paddy. They said, 'Hello, where are you going with all that stuff?' I answered, 'I'm taking this to your mother.' 'What,' said Joe, 'My God, we owe you £45 now!' 'Well,' I said, 'Never mind, here's another £20 worth.'
>
> Joe, he seemed astonished. He thought for a while, and then he said, with a big oath to his brother, 'Look here, I'm going to pay this man if I have to rob a bank!'

Allen claimed that this happened only two days before a Kelly bank robbery. And on Sunday, 8 December, two days before the Euroa hold-up, Joe was seen at Sebastopol. Obviously, it was no spur-of-the moment decision to rob the bank and Joe's oath to his brother smacks of melodrama but this shouldn't make us doubt Paddy Allen's story. Joe was already starting to reshape his role of outlawed police killer to that of highwayman hero. Like Ned, he would seize every chance to portray qualities expected of such figures. Already, in the draft of the Cameron Letter, Joe had helped Ned compose speeches that would have won applause on the Victorian stage. Now, they were about to face their audience.

After being seen at Sebastopol on the Sunday, Joe rode straight to Euroa and reached the town that same day. It was a 65-mile ride—a stiff test for Music who was back in service after foaling.

Joe was seen with Ned's friend Ben Gould in the quiet Sunday streets of Euroa and visited De Boos's hotel only 40 yards from the National Bank. As one of the Unknown Men, he could still move about with comparative freedom and check the final details of the hold-up strategy. Steve Hart may also have been in Euroa that day, asking about Meade's gold mine near the town, which lodged its smelted gold at the National Bank.

The original plan may have been to rob the bank on Monday but the distractions of a sitting of the Licensing Court and the funeral of a local lad on the Tuesday afternoon would provide cover for the hold-up. So the bank robbery was set for four o'clock, Tuesday afternoon.

A little before one o'clock on Monday afternoon, the Gang converged on Faithfull's Creek homestead. There was nothing unusual about these four bushmen, except their horses, to be described as 'magnificent'. Joe was riding grey Music who was still, to an expert eye, in less than top condition. He wore his 'respectable' bush clothes—grey tweed coat, printed moleskin trousers, white felt hat with the brim 'slouched' over his eyes, a police Webley holstered at his waist.

The Gang dismounted at the gate of the home paddock and, smoking his pipe, Ned strolled over to the homestead. Quietly, he bailed up Mrs Fitzgerald, the housekeeper, and her husband, both of whom were probably sympathisers, then signalled Dan and Steve to bring in the horses while Joe stood guard at the gate. With a minimum of fuss, the Gang collected the other two station hands and a few casual harvest workers as they straggled in for lunch.

While the station groom, George Stephens, stabled the Gang's horses and fed them with crushed oats, the other men were imprisoned in a slab-walled store shed about 20 yards from the homestead. Fitzgerald, recently out of hospital, was allowed to stay in the homestead with his wife.

When the overseer, Macaulay, arrived back late that afternoon, he too was taken prisoner and the Gang ate dinner, two at a time.

At sunset, hawker James Gloster drove up in his white-hooded wagon emblazoned with his name and an advertisement for Singer Sewing Machines. He refused to bail up, tried to get a revolver from the wagon, and generally seemed to behave in an almost suicidal way, with Ned and Dan both losing their tempers and threatening to shoot him—before Macaulay persuaded him to surrender.

It was a splendid performance. No one seemed surprised that, after this reckless defiance of the Gang, Gloster was allowed to have a meal in the kitchen before he and his 18-year-old assistant joined the other prisoners in the store shed.

With twenty-odd men, plus stores and tools in the 25-foot by 15 foot building, there was little hope of comfortable sleep. Ned passed the night with the prisoners, talking freely of the Stringybark Creek gunfight and what had led up to it. Four of those men would be called as prosecution witnesses at Ned's eventual trial. Two were to give Ned's account of Lonigan's killing—which contradicted McIntyre's amended version—and Gloster stressed that Ned seemed to be trying to take sole blame for the killings 'as though he wished to screen the others'.

Joe maintained a low profile throughout the robbery and was described by one prisoner as 'the tall unknown bushranger' who 'scarcely said a word'.

For much of the time at Faithfull's Creek, Joe sat in the homestead at the overseer's desk, writing out a fair copy of Ned's letter to parliamentarian Cameron (and, probably, a second copy to be sent to the Chief Commissioner via Superintendent Sadleir). He used a bottle of red ink, brought for the purpose, and carefully transcribed the hurried scrawl of the original draft in twenty notepaper pages of his best copperplate, described by Mrs Fitzgerald as 'beautiful writing'.

He also spent 'a good deal of time' in the kitchen while she was cooking and was far more outgoing with her than with the male prisoners. She said that 'he chatted with her on general topics' and, in a surprising detail, 'played for her entertainment on a concertina'.

After lunch on Tuesday Joe sealed the Cameron Letter in a square envelope, addressed it and asked Mrs Fitzgerald for a stamp. 'She procured one, and stuck it on the envelope, but as she did so he held a piece of paper over the address. Byrne weighed the letter in his hand, and remarked that he did not think one stamp would carry it, and Mrs Fitzgerald gave him a second one. He then rolled it up in a piece of paper and placed it in his breast.'

Mrs Fitzgerald's contribution of the stamps would lead to the popular furphy that the letter was left with her for posting. Her denial of this would, in turn, see the letter dismissed as 'a myth'. But it lay by Joe's heart in blood-red ink, to be carried, by the grace of two tiny tuppeny portraits of Queen Victoria, to one of her law-makers.

Early on Tuesday afternoon, shortly before their planned departure to hold up the bank, Dan guarded the prisoners while Ned, Steve and Joe broke the telegraph lines on both sides of the nearby railway, smashing insulators, pulling down posts, cutting and tangling wires, to baffle normal repair methods.

Four unlucky railway gangers who came along on a trolley were made prisoners, and, almost at the same time, two Melbourne sportsmen, on a kangaroo hunt with two local farmers, came bowling up in a spring cart to cross the line. Joe appeared on foot in front of them and Ned rode up behind. Because both were holding revolvers and handcuffs, the hunters assumed that they were plainclothed police. One noted Joe as 'a tall, sandy young man whom his companion called "Jack"'.

In a piece of splendid comic relief, Ned ignored Scots and English accents and accused the party of being the Kelly Gang. He and Joe relieved them of a superb, large-bore rifle and a shotgun before letting an amused George Stephens formally introduce the Gang as 'Mr Edward Kelly and party'. The apoplectic hunters were taken to the store shed by Joe and joined the other prisoners.

The previous night the Gang members had taken their suits of clothes and hats from Gloster's stock. No one questioned how the hawker could completely outfit four men of such varying height and build—and hat and boot sizes—from the obviously limited range of 'clothes and fancy goods' in his wagon. In a further telling detail, the hats were fitted with the elastic chin-strap favoured by the members of the Gang.

Joe selected a grey tweed Paget coat, brown tweed trousers and vest, Rob Roy shirt, black tie, elastic-sided boots, and light felt hat. Ned and Dan

THE PRISON

Joe guards the prisoners in the store shed at Faithfull's Creek, one of several highly accurate sketches of the Euroa hold-up in the *Illustrated Australian News*.

favoured dark jackets and lighter pants; Steve, a dark silk mixture coat and tweed trousers. A wash and a splash of Gloster's perfume completed their toilet. Then the four lads made a small bonfire of their old, travel-stained bush clothing. Another rite. As the pile of cloth burnt to ashes, the fugitives, the Stringybark murderers, were no more. Four gentleman bushrangers, highwayman heroes, stood in their place.

Two prisoners were taken out of the shed—Gloster's young assistant and a mysterious young man called 'John Carson'. Then, about 2.30, Ned drove off to Euroa in the familiar hawker's cart, with Gloster's assistant. Dan drove the shooting party's spring cart, and Steve accompanied them on one of the station horses so his own mount would be fresh for the ride back through the ranges.

Joe, in his new tweeds, was left to guard the thirty-odd prisoners as the horses and vehicles drummed over the Faithfull's Creek bridge and receded down the track to the main road.

Armed with a double-barrelled shotgun, a brace of revolvers in his belt, and two rifles within reach, Joe patrolled to and fro in front of the padlocked store shed as the unnatural silence of the afternoon settled over the station and its shingle roofs shimmered in oppressive heat. While prisoners sweated and whispered in the stifling gloom of the store, Joe prowled restlessly backwards and forwards across the dusty yard. The liberated prisoner 'Carson', supposedly held by him as a hostage, waited nearby, a cattle dog drowsed in the narrow shade of its kennel.

After an hour and a half, the silence was disturbed by the huffing approach of a southbound luggage train, which slowed beside the broken telegraph lines. Joe watched tensely as a man jumped down to examine the tangled wires and fallen posts while the train gathered speed on its way.

Showing clearly that 'Carson' was a man he completely trusted, Joe left his gun with the two rifles. With careful casualness, hands in pockets, he strolled from around the corner of an outbuilding. The man dropped by the train was now approaching the homestead. Joe turned back, gathered the gun, bailed him up, and after searching him for firearms, took him to the store shed. He was a big man, over six foot, a line repairer called Watt. He recalled that Joe seemed 'so nervous that he could scarcely fix the key in the lock'. Joe had obviously been shaken by the train's unexpected slowdown, by the possibility of police being included in a party sent to investigate the broken telegraph line. Watt, however, was a pliant prisoner (concerned only for a gold watch he eventually hid in his boot) and was soon locked away with the others.

With this threat past, Joe may have relaxed. But behind the slab walls of the store shed, other threats were brewing. The 'ancient Scotchman' of the hunting party, Robert Macdougall, was a real firebrand. Noticing '14 or 15 axes' among the stores, he suggested that if groups of men simultaneously attacked all four walls, the lone bushranger couldn't stop them breaking out. However, he reported that his idea 'was condemned by the manager, and found no support indeed at all, as it was evident that at least one of us must be shot in the attempt, and each one appeared to think it likely that he would be the "one"'.

One prisoner was of sterner stuff—George Stephens, the station groom, an ex-policeman. Noticing that Joe occasionally stood in the shade of the shed with his back to a small window in the front wall, Stephens hunted among the stock of tools for a pitch fork to stab through the glass into Joe's back. Failing to find one (even the stable fork was being used in hay making), he picked up an axe and squared himself to chop through panes and glazing bars into the head and neck of the stylish, unsuspecting figure outside.

It wouldn't be easy. The window was small and at an awkward height. And he would have only one chance.

As Stephens was lining up the blow, the other prisoners saw what he was doing. Several grappled with him and took the axe away, threatening to hand him over to Joe. The planted sympathisers probably played a part, but most of the men in that shed had listened to Ned through the long night, weighing his words, reading the man, re-evaluating the Stringybark killings in terms of police treatment of his mother and family. They didn't hold with murder, but they didn't want a man's blood on their hands, even for £500. This was no fight of theirs. Let the police do their own dirty work.

Joe probably heard soon enough how close a thing it had been. Perhaps he considered himself simply lucky, or perhaps the audience was beginning to respond.

Detective Michael Ward, a ruthless and devious man, seemed 'a good-natured bloody fool' to Aaron, at the very time when Ward was setting him up as bait to draw the Kellys into the open. (*Keith McMenomy*)

Superintendent Hare displays his Tennysonian profile for this portrait, which nicely captures his impressive bearing and boundless self-confidence. He was also dogged, courageous, gullible, and never let facts spoil a story which could help his career or reputation.

Superintendent Nicolson, Hare's rival, was a shrewd tactician who distrusted Aaron and, like Hare, was prepared to sacrifice him for the sake of catching the Kellys. (*Victoria Police Historical Unit*)

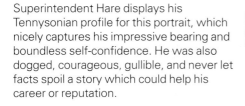

Dan Kelly was 15 or 16 when this photo was taken in Beechworth. His oversize clothes are probably hand-me-downs from his bigger brothers, Ned and Jim. While Joe easily stepped into the role of another big brother to Dan, the boy never seems to have accepted Aaron.
(*Victoria Police Historical Unit*)

Dan Kelly's mate, Steve Hart, slimmer and more youthful than in his outlaw days. Though Joe was only a few years older than Dan and Steve, he showed paternal concern for 'the boys'.

The Sherritt farm on
Sheepstation Creek,
photographed in 1960,
showing the last, and
smallest, of three Sherritt
homes erected on the site,
the last two using the same
white granite chimney. The
first house burnt down in
1873, the second in 1900.
This third homestead has
now vanished, almost
without a trace. The creek is
down to the left, below a
small garden and orchard.
Uphill to the right is the
ancient red box tree where
the family often tethered
their horses.

Sunrise on Reedy Creek, just
below the Byrne homesite,
very much as it looked in Joe
and Aaron's time. Today, the
gravel banks are choked with
scrub.

The site of the lower police camp, 'the Police Caves' (photographed in 1992), seen from beside the position where Aaron slept. Hare used the cave below the huge, overhanging rock.

A police party posed at Benalla as they prepared to set out for the Strathbogie Ranges on 20 June 1879. Standing, from left, O'Loughlin, Kirkham, Mills, Mayes, Superintendent Hare, Canny, Falkiner, Lawless; kneeling, Barry and tracker Moses. Most of these men took part in the 'cave parties', while Falkiner and Lawless were involved in the Whorouly races charade.

There was another hour and a half of boredom, heat and, for Joe, increasing tension and doubt. Then, at first no more than shimmering dots across the sun-bleached paddocks, a strange little cavalcade came jogging along the track to the station, raising pinkish dust.

The spectacled bank manager drove the huntsmen's spring cart, with Ned beside him and the family maid (who was an old school mate of Steve Hart) in the back. Dan drove the hawker's wagon, carrying a couple of the manager's older children and two bank clerks, while the manager's wife (dressed for the occasion in 'French muslin...with all its lace and ribbons...a shearer's hat all covered with tulle and flowers and a pair of long, white driving gloves') drove the family buggy carrying her mother, a nanny and the five younger children, including a five-month-old baby.

Under Ned's feet was a hessian bag containing £1,943 8s 6d in notes, sovereigns and silver, and a 31-ounce gold ingot, worth about £300—a total haul of some £2,260.

His tense wait over, Joe released the prisoners for the gala arrival, having signalled to Ned that all was well with 'a green flag' hung on the garden fence.

He soon heard what there was to tell of the robbery—gaining admittance to the closed bank on the pretext of cashing a cheque from Macaulay, scooping up the money and gold—and the unexpectedly large haul of prisoners— and jogging back past the funeral that had almost cleared the town.

As the sun set and the heat of the day began to pass, the Gang made leisurely preparations to leave, interrupted when yet another train stopped to examine the broken telegraph lines. They saw a man take some pieces of the cut wire and re-board the train which disappeared northwards.

Before leaving, the four lads, on their fresh horses, entertained the prisoners with an impromptu trick riding exhibition, Ned 'galloping about, lying or sitting upon his saddle in all kinds of apparently impossible positions'. With the sack of money and gold strapped on the front of his saddle, Ned gave a last short speech, telling the prisoners that no one must leave the station for three hours. Then, at about 8.30, the Gang rode out of the yard and spurred towards the full moon risen above the Strathbogies.

Galloping through the quickly cooling air and the sharpened summer smells of eucalypt and mown hay and cattle, Joe, in his new tweed outfit, revolvers in belt, gun or rifle slung across his back, new hat held firm on his head by its elastic chin strap, must have felt like a king. Those lads—Ned just turned 24, Joe just 22, Dan 17, and Steve barely 19—had carried off, as their first exploit, the most perfectly planned and executed bank robbery in Australian bushranging history. Without violence, leaving no enemies behind them.

The bulging hessian bag on Ned's saddle was only one measure of their success. An artilleryman, who was stationed in the town soon afterwards, reported, 'The people in the bank told me that with the exception of the robbers taking the money, they never offered the slightest insult to anyone. I also visited Younghusband's station where Joe Byrne was sentry over thirty persons while the others were in the bank, and was told everywhere that the outlaws were undoubtedly police-made criminals.'

Euroa had been, in every way, a strategic triumph for Ned and Joe. Yet their plans to divert police attention had yet to bear their most spectacular fruit, and provide an embarrassing exit for Nicolson as leader of the Kelly pursuit. The very day of the robbery he and Superintendent Sadleir were preparing to travel by train to Albury 'to warn all the police all the way up and down' that the Kellys were likely to try and cross the Murray into New South Wales. This theory was based on a letter to the Kellys' uncle Jack Quinn, recently 'fallen' into police hands. The day before the hold-up, another uncle, Pat Quinn, had visited Benalla in an attempt to draw Nicolson and a search party to the head of the King River. Nicolson believed 'his object was to lead the police off the track', yet he was prepared to head north to Albury on the strength of stale information from an equally dubious source.

As Nicolson and Sadleir were boarding their train, at eight in the evening of the Euroa robbery, an agitated police magistrate Wyatt appeared on the platform at Benalla 'carrying something in his hand like a bunch of flowers', actually a cluster of telegraph wires and insulators he had picked up beside the railway line at Faithfull's Creek. Wyatt hustled Nicolson into the ladies' waiting room, slammed the door on Sadleir and, in an 'almost incoherent' state, blurted out that the Kellys were at Euroa and had broken the telegraph line.

Nicolson would not be deterred. He and Sadleir boarded their north-bound train from Benalla while the Kelly Gang were still at Faithfull's Creek only 27 miles in the opposite direction.

The two officers arrived at Albury to learn officially of the hold-up at Euroa, now 95 miles to the south. They made a humiliating about-face and headed back to pick up another stale pursuit the following day. It was a final blow to Nicolson. Worn out by weeks of fruitless pursuit, blind in one eye from ingrowing eyelashes, he was replaced by Captain Standish's great favourite, Superintendent Frank Hare, a 'remarkably tall' 48-year-old with a reputation for galloping off after bushrangers in great style, but rarely catching them.

Hare had little understanding of the criminal mind and was wary, if not derisive, of Nicolson's detective-bred fondness for 'fizgigs'—criminal informants. Yet, as Superintendent Sadleir dourly observed, 'He did indeed use Aaron Sherritt, *if Sherritt did not use him*...[my italics]'

Hare's gullibility, to be exploited to the hilt by Aaron, was about to provide the basis for a long-running charade which, in its turn, would be exploited as the means to destroy the Gang—and Aaron.

CHAPTER 9

A Double Agent

December 1878 – January 1879

The colony was shaken to its roots by the Euroa robbery, and within three days, the £500 on Ned's head was doubled, bringing the total reward to £2,500. Rural banks panicked, 'sightings' of four horsemen riding three bays and a grey poured in from all quarters, police parties galloped on elaborate wild-goose chases, troops of Victoria's defence forces spread through the north-east to guard banks, and a casual remark from Ned about the vulnerability of the railway produced a spate of special patrols along the main line, with dire fears that there would be a sharp drop in the number of 'excursionists' travelling to Melbourne by train for Christmas.

Melbourne's daily papers—the *Age*, *Argus*, *Herald* and *Daily Telegraph*—ran the story for days, interviewing the Gang's prisoners, breathlessly recording each day's crop of 'sightings', trying, with waning confidence, to maintain an image of purposeful and confident police pursuit.

Out of it all emerged almost precisely the picture intended by Ned and Joe—a group of courteous young men, dangerous only when crossed, carrying out an audacious robbery with great professionalism and flair. The *Argus* and *Age* still used their standard heading 'The Mansfield Murderers' and trumpeted of 'this latest outrage' but reported, accurately enough, the glowing opinions of the Gang—especially of Ned, with high praise for his charm, good looks and horsemanship. Only Dan received a bad press, with unanimous reports of his ill-looks and of Ned supposedly having to curb his murderous ways.

Steve was at last officially identified (the maid in the bank manager's household had recognised him) and Joe's name was appearing fairly regularly—except in Beechworth's *Advertiser* which called him 'James Byrne', despite publishing details of the conviction over Feely's cow less than two years before.

For days there was rumour and counter-rumour about the mysterious letter supposedly left with Mrs Fitzgerald. A popular theory held that it contained Ned's plea for a pardon. Two or three days after the robbery, Sadleir's copy reached him, yet no mention was made of it to the press. It was clearly regarded as a dangerous document and the police probably imagined that their silence would consign it to oblivion. Then, on the afternoon of 17 December, a square envelope with two stamps, addressed in red ink, reached the office of Donald Cameron MLA, in the Treasury building. When Cameron eventually got around to opening it, he tore up the envelope. Then he started to read Joe's bold, red copperplate:

> Dear Sir
> Take no offence if I take the opportunity of writing a few lines to you wherein I wish to state a few remarks concerning the case of Trooper Fitzpatrick against Mrs Kelly W. Skillion and W. Williamson and to state the facts of the case to you.

Perhaps at this point Cameron checked the signature and then scrambled to retrieve the pieces of the envelope from his waste paper basket. He found a Glenrowan postmark of 14 December.

The Premier and Chief Secretary, Graham Berry, though much absorbed with his planned 'embassy' to London seeking reform of the Victorian constitution, read the letter shown him by a nervy Cameron and pronounced it 'a very clever and straightforward statement'.

The morning papers were given the story and allowed to examine the letter, while refused permission to publish it. The *Argus* damned it with faint praise as the work of 'a clever illiterate' and wrote of 'certain fiendish threats' made by Ned if his mother did not receive justice. The major content of the letter was dismissed in a sentence. 'He charges members of the police force with having wronged his relatives, and with being the cause of his crimes.'

That evening, the *Herald* published a balanced summary of its contents (which would be reproduced in Beechworth's *Advertiser*) noting 'a fair legible handwriting' and that the document 'exhibits both ability and manliness in its construction and tone'. While conceding 'some threats of a bloodthirsty nature' and reiteration of Ned's threat to the railways, the *Herald* recorded that there was 'no mention of a free pardon', that the letter concluded with 'four lines of original poetry', and that Ned signed himself, 'Edward Kelly enforced outlaw'.

Even before he had seen the more sympathetic *Herald* piece, Captain Standish was anxious that this exercise to gain 'public sympathy' should be nipped in the bud. He telegrammed Graham Berry that he had already seen the copy sent to Sadleir, which he dismissed as 'a tissue of falsehoods', and told the Premier, 'I think it inadvisable that publicity should be given to such a production and should recommend that Mr Cameron should be advised not to publish the letter.'

Berry was happy enough to comply and Cameron was relieved of the politically dangerous role of Kelly sympathiser. Both copies of Ned and Joe's letter were filed away from public gaze and it would never be revealed that Ned had offered to give up bushranging if he and his people received justice.

Failure to have the letter published—or at least read in parliament—was a bitter disappointment for Ned and Joe. They would try again but this time they would not place their trust in police or politicians.

The police had good reason to worry about 'public sympathy'. The press contained many reports of support for the Gang, coupled with stories of friends and relatives spending proceeds of the robbery. This could be comfortably dismissed as the Gang's predictable generosity to supporters and as payment for the services and silence of criminal accomplices. But already there were danger signs that couldn't be so easily dismissed.

Two days before Euroa Joe had been seen at Sebastopol, 'at Chappells'. James Chappell was a dairyman, publican, postmaster of the settlement and partner in the Scotchman's Claim, one of Sebastopol's most successful gold mines—a 48-year-old Cornishman, stocky, truculent with a grey 'billygoat' beard in the classic 'Cousin Jack' tradition. Apart from a dismissed charge of stealing washdirt during the gold rush years, his record was blameless. Yet this man was emerging as a Kelly sympathiser. Two other partners in the Scotchman's Claim, Richard Murphy and Archibald Batchelor, would also soon be recognised as sympathisers. The trio represented an uncomfortable problem for the police—part of the extraordinary phenomenon that would soon grip the north-east.

Margret Byrne was universally respected in the valley as an honest, courageous, hard-working member of the little community. It was well known that Joe hadn't been the most devoted of sons and his troubles with the police were common knowledge. Folk like Anton Wick and Jane Batchelor and Ah On had been intimately involved. But Joe hadn't been a *bad* young fellow. The news that he was a member of the Kelly Gang had set people back. Then came the stories of police outrages against Kelly womenfolk. The Gang's remarkable performance at Euroa confirmed the reassessment already taking place. If regard for Margret Byrne was a prime factor in the emergence of men like Chappell, Murphy and Batchelor as Kelly sympathisers, then their approval, in turn, encouraged her to accept Joe's role.

On 21 December Ned Kelly was seen at the Byrne house. The following day, Joe was seen there. Did Margret have any qualms at receiving proceeds of the Euroa hold-up? We'll never know. But at last, Joe was justifying her love, and repudiating all the disappointment and neglect she had suffered. He was giving her back her dignity, enabling her to go up to Paddy Allen's shop in Beechworth and pay him his £65. And if some folk wanted to point at her and whisper, let them. Her son was a member of the Kelly Gang and now she didn't care who knew it. As Paddy Allen put it, 'After that, the Byrnes always paid cash for what they got.'

Aaron's signature on his Application for Lease of March 1879, witnessed by James Ingram.
(*Victoria Public Record Office*)

Aaron, too, had been in dire straits before Euroa. Only days before Stringybark he had been warned by the Lands Department that 'arrears of rent must be paid at once or his land will be declared forfeit'. He was now more than two years overdue with his payments on the selection, the last had been made by his father while he was in prison. The day after Joe was declared an outlaw, the incomparable P. F. Murphy had written to the Department on Aaron's behalf (as usual, calling him 'Aarion Sherriott') explaining that arrears were unpaid because Aaron had 'met with some losses in cattle' and pleading for extension to 10 December, the day of the Euroa hold-up.

It wasn't until 11 January 1879 that Aaron took £10 14s to the Beechworth sub-treasury and, not surprisingly, payment was refused. That day Murphy sent off another heart-wringing letter, explaining that Aaron had not been able to pay until now, 'having to wait for his harvest to obtain Money to Supply his wants'. Forfeiture of the land 'would be the means of destroying not only Aarion Sherriott but his Father who had to support a helplefs family of Seven Children and his wife'. Murphy said that Aaron would readily pay a fine for his 'palpable neglect' but pleaded, 'Do not drive him to ruin in having his land forfeited on which he has spent money and labour and which he looked on as his living for life'.

The same day Aaron engaged Tuthill and Dickson, solicitors, of 'Beechworth and Melbourne' to write a coolly legal letter asking permission to pay his rent.

Aaron was again reprieved, his payment accepted on the condition that he apply for a lease of the land within fourteen days, otherwise his block would be put up for re-selection. This meant another three six-monthly payments to bring him up to date (he ended up paying £21 8s covering four payments) plus £2 for certificate and lease fees, and payments to Murphy and the solicitors—a daunting total of some £30—near £40 including his last payment. Yet he paid it promptly. Clearly, this was Euroa money—in recognition of his help on the flight to the Murray and, perhaps, for help at Euroa. He may have scouted for the Gang or even played one of the 'prisoners'. Might he have been the mysterious 'John Carson' so completely trusted by Joe? Certainly, a point near the Puzzle Ranges, only some twenty miles from Euroa and probably on the Gang's route to and from the hold-up, was later nominated by Joe as a meeting place familiar to them both.

At Euroa or not, Aaron was a uniquely valuable 'bush telegraph' for the Gang. The police were about to make him even more valuable.

In a gesture which smacks of frustration and impulsive overreaction, the police climaxed weeks of futile pursuit by swooping on a group of Kelly sympathisers. In an extraordinary Court of Star Chamber held by Standish, Hare and key district officers, a list of men was compiled and warrants sworn for their arrest on 2 January. Some had been named by Bill Williamson—in prison over the Fitzpatrick incident—who sang like a bird in his cage with a hopeful stream of information. Others were simply known to be friends and relatives. Initially, sixteen were brought in. Some were released, others arrested, until, out of 23 comings and goings, a core group of eleven remained in prison—including Wild Wright, Jack Lloyd and, eventually, Tom Lloyd. Hare would later make the startling admission that, although the group were remanded week by week, without trial, for three and a half months, the police had 'not a tittle of evidence against them'.

It was a bizarre move, initially applauded by the press, but enthusiasm eroded, week by week, until even the strongly pro-establishment *Advertiser* was vacillating between justification and condemnation.

One of many curious features of the exercise was the fact that no arrests were made in the Beechworth district, scene of the sympathiser trials and imprisonment. Aaron's 'arrangement' with Standish may have won him immunity but the failure to pick up other sympathisers in the district—home ground of Detective Ward, now a key figure in the pursuit of the Gang—may suggest that the police recognised a more complex situation here, and hesitated to open the Pandora's box of 'respectable' sympathisers concentrated about the Woolshed and centred on the Byrne family.

Whatever the reason, Aaron remained a free man and laughed at authority by wearing his chin strap under his nose—old badge of the Greta Mob and now the mark of the Kelly sympathiser—even swaggering into James Bray's Camp Street studio to be photographed in this rebellious guise.

With the ranks of their most trusted helpers depleted, Ned and Joe enlisted Aaron in their plans for a second bank robbery. He always claimed that he was asked to accompany the Gang on this exploit but declined. There is persuasive evidence that this wasn't true, suggesting that Aaron was keen to ride with the Gang but his offer wasn't taken up. Obviously, Aaron was still completely trusted, but Ned may have been reluctant to implicate him to this degree. (Tom Lloyd, who effectively became a fifth member of the Gang, had been far more intimately involved in the aftermath of the police killings and, according to some, had been present during the gunfight. He apparently rode with the Gang on their second hold-up.)

If, however, the Gang did ask Aaron to join them, why would he refuse? He was in a uniquely vulnerable position and had a lot to lose. He was one of the best-known friends of the Kellys and was liable to fifteen years' imprisonment under the Outlawry Act—a possibility uncomfortably highlighted by the arrest of the sympathisers. But there was more than his freedom at stake. He might lose his selection: the work, the money, the time invested in it, all wasted. Perhaps overriding these considerations was a reluctance to surrender his bargaining position to save Joe's life. By now, Aaron had rejected any idea of betraying the Gang (if he had ever truly considered the possibility). Yet only by convincing the police that he was still prepared to help them, could he maintain access to Chief Commissioner Standish's undertaking to use his influence on Joe's behalf. So Aaron makes his decision. His first approach to the police after his Great Raid recruitment will provide a vital link in the Gang's strategy for their next hold-up. He enters police service as a double agent.

Detective Ward was in Beechworth Hospital recuperating from an unusual accident. At two in the morning, two weeks before, he was supposedly on his way to see a telegraph operator, probably taking a short cut through a backyard, when he fell down a nine-foot pit, fracturing some ribs and injuring his leg.

Ward recorded that on Thursday, 30 January, Aaron Sherritt visited him in hospital with a story 'that he was speaking with two of the outlaws, and that they wanted him to go to New South Wales with them. He said if I came with him that we should be able to get them before they crossed the river.'

Ward didn't trust Aaron and, anyway, was in no condition for bush work. He suggested that he send 'two good men', Detectives Brown and Eason, in his place. Aaron wasn't interested. 'He said that he would go with no other person than myself.' Less than a year before, Aaron had made a similar 'exclusive' offer to Fitzpatrick in his attempt to lure him into Kelly hands—supposedly because he had a 'down' on Ward. Times had changed. At that stage, Fitzpatrick had represented the greatest threat to Ned, Dan and Joe. Now Ward was emerging as one of the few police who posed any significant threat to the Gang—a shrewd, manipulative, ruthless man with a keen nose on the Kelly trail, who also represented a rarity in the Force—a good bushman who knew the district. Perhaps most significantly, he had recently caught and prosecuted Ben Gould, first of the Kelly sympathisers to be gaoled.

Ward may have suspected a trap and, it would emerge, thought little of Aaron's story, but he saw a chance in it to gain some kudos. He telegrammed Standish in Benalla and, the following day, sent Aaron to see him.

Whatever Aaron had intended for Ward, this part of the plan had misfired. So, why not see Standish? Aaron hadn't yet made any attempt to explore his arrangement with the Chief Commissioner and, if the wind was blowing in that direction, he would go with it.

Next evening Aaron rode down to Benalla and ambled into the big police station on the edge of the town's business district to find that the Chief Commissioner was away overnight. Instead, Aaron was taken in to see the new leader of the Kelly pursuit, Superintendent Frank Hare. It was a fateful meeting.

In the gaslit austerity of Hare's office the two men summed each other up. Aaron made a vivid first impression on Hare, who recorded, 'He was a remarkable looking man, if he walked down Collins Street, everybody would have stared at him—his walk, his appearance, and everything else was remarkable.' Hare later called Aaron 'a splendid man, tall, strong, hardy, but a most outrageous scoundrel'.

Meanwhile, Aaron was making his own shrewd assessment of the policeman. Hare was South African born, son of a British army officer, and tended to dress like an English county squire on safari. At 48, his great, lanky frame was sagging to a paunch and his spade beard was blotched with grey, but he was still a handsome, imposing figure and, for all his towering ego, an engaging man, an amusing storyteller. Hare describes this first encounter in which each man played his own game: Aaron reluctant to relinquish his one-to-one contact with Standish; Hare, alert to the probable significance of the visit, but wary of seeming too interested.

'I explained to Aaron who I was, and asked him what he wanted Captain Standish for. He said, "I have some important information to give him, and I wish to speak to him privately." I told him Captain Standish would not be back that night. I led Aaron to believe I did not care to hear his news but kept him engaged in conversation.'

The conversation told Aaron a great deal about Hare—knowledge he quickly put to use.

For his part Hare had no doubt that 'somehow or other I made a most wonderful impression upon him. I had some drink with him, and saw that my influence over him was great.' This may have been true. More likely, 'guarded and cunning' Aaron saw that Hare was an easier mark than Standish and expertly played on his ego as a key to gullibility. Hare continued:

> Some time after—about an hour—Sherritt said 'I think I can trust you with my information;' and then he told me that on the previous afternoon, [Actually, two days before] about two o'clock, Joe Byrne and Dan Kelly came to his selection...He told me Joe Byrne jumped off his horse, and...came down and sat beside him; he said Dan Kelly was very suspicious, and would not get off his horse, and did not get near him, and he said they sat talking for a long time, and they asked him to join them, as they were going across the Murray, and intended going to Goulburn, in New South Wales, where the Kellys had a cousin. He said they urged him for a long time to go as a scout. Sherritt never told me at that time that they were going to stick up a bank. He told me he refused to go with them, and after some pressing, Joe Byrne said, 'Well, Aaron, you are perfectly right; why should you get yourself into trouble and mix yourself up with us.'

So this was Aaron's information: a Kelly strike at Goulburn, presumably to rob a bank.

Hare totally believed the story, never considering for a moment that this could be another Kelly strategy to decoy the police from an area where 'an outrage' was to be committed. It has been suggested that Aaron didn't know the information was spurious, that Joe gave him a false lead, suspecting that it would be relayed to the police. But the subsequent police action would have provided immediate proof of Aaron's 'betrayal' of the Gang. The fact that Aaron was trusted by the Kellys after this shows that he had deliberately misled their pursuers and, further, that the Gang were aware of his recruitment by the police.

At this stage, Aaron's role as a double agent was clearly defined and formed a valuable part of Kelly strategy. Yet the very value placed on his role meant that its true nature must be known only to the Gang and a few intimates. In this unique position of trust lay the seed of Aaron's destruction.

That seed could germinate only through Hare's credulity, which Aaron was carefully nourishing as he told Hare, 'You have a most difficult and dangerous job before you, but I will do all I can to assist you.' Hare's response established a naïve and almost obsessive degree of trust. 'I told him I would place myself unreservedly in his hands and do whatever he suggested.'

Soon after this, when Hare told Ward of his discussion, the detective gave him sound advice. 'He is only deceiving you, sir, please don't trust him; he would not sell his friend Joe Byrne for all the money in the world.' But Hare would not be swayed. 'I felt my opinion of the man was correct, and he meant to work for me honestly.' The die was cast. Hare arranged for them to meet again and Aaron prepared to leave.

Hare, though inexperienced with 'fizgigs', showed immediate enthusiasm for the undercover relationship he had established with Aaron. Subsequently, he gave Aaron the codename 'Moses' (brother of the Old

Testament Aaron) and, for reasons known only to him, 'Tommy'—sometimes calling Aaron with apparent affection, 'My boy Tommy'. Concerned that his first agent would be too easily recognised in the busier part of town along the main street, Hare urged Aaron to stay the night at a hotel in 'new' Benalla, down near the railway station, and gave him £2, a week's wages, 'for coming down to give this information'.

As soon as Aaron sauntered out, Hare hurried to share his news with Sadleir. A glance at the map showed 'a chain of hills running right across the Murray—right across to Goulburn in New South Wales'. Confident that this would be the Kellys' crossing place, Hare and Sadleir telegraphed an alert to 'all the border police on both sides of the river' and sent parties under Senior Constable Mullane and Sergeant Steele on a hundred-mile ride to the upper Murray, 'the other side of the Curryong', to guard the area. If anyone was reminded of Nicolson and Sadleir racing up to the Murray the day of the Euroa robbery, they kept their peace.

The following evening Joe Byrne and Dan Kelly were reported near Chiltern, riding north towards the Murray. In Hare's feverish state of enthusiasm, this *seemed* to confirm both Aaron's story of the meeting and the Gang's plan to cross into New South Wales. The fact that Joe and Dan had taken three days to travel 15 miles and were 100 miles downstream of the supposed crossing place did nothing to dent his belief. To Hare, the report 'in every respect corroborated Sherritt's statement'. Similar gullibility, demanding an extraordinary level of self-deception, would characterise Hare's future dealings with Aaron. To doubt Aaron's fidelity would have meant doubting his judgement, doubting himself, and that was unthinkable.

Exactly one week after Aaron visited Hare, the Gang crossed the Murray 160 miles downstream from the area being carefully watched by the police. They were heading, not for Goulburn, but for one of their horse stealing towns—a sleepy, dusty little place of 300 souls, about 40 miles across the border. Jerilderie.

CHAPTER 10

The Jerilderie Letter

February 1879

Jerilderie became a candidate for a Kelly robbery when Samuel Gill, editor of the *Jerilderie and Urana Gazette,* used the columns of his paper to inform the New South Wales government that the town had inadequate police protection. The government wasn't particularly interested, but the Kelly Gang was.

In return for this helpful piece of information, Ned and Joe decided to give Mr Gill a journalistic coup that had been missed by the Melbourne papers—a major letter from Ned Kelly.

Using the draft of the Cameron Letter as a basis, they produced a document that was far more ambitious in scope, scale and style. The opening lines set the tone.

> Dear Sir
>   I wish to acquaint you with some of the occurrences of the present past and future.

In part, the letter was Ned's criminal autobiography—telling the story of his brushes with the law since 1870, and alleging miscarriages of justice. Ned told the story of the dispute with Whitty that led to the big raid on his horses—claiming that only he and George King had been involved.

He gave a more detailed account of the Fitzpatrick incident, pleading the cause of his mother and the innocence of Skillion and Williamson, 'two quiet hard working innocent men who would not know the difference [between] a revolver and a saucepan handle'.

He told of the police raids on the Kelly homestead and gave another detailed account of Stringybark, again accepting all blame for the three killings and trying to lay the ghost of a tortured Kennedy. 'If Kennedy's ear was cut off it was not done by me and none of my mates was near him after he was shot I put his cloak over him and left him as well as I could and were they my own brothers I could not have been more sorry for them.'

The police came in for a vigorous lambasting as Ned spoke of 'the brutal and cowardly conduct of a parcel of big ugly fat necked wombat headed big bellied magpie legged narrow hipped splay-footed sons of Irish Bailiffs or english landlords which is better known as Officers of justice or Victorian Police who some calls honest gentlemen.'

This romping attack sparked a harder, more passionate tirade—underscored by the steady drumbeat of Irish rebellion which had already been heard as a recurring motif through the letter. Early, Ned and Joe had trumpeted, 'there never was such a thing as justice in the English laws but any amount of injustice to be had'.

Then the sonorous warning, 'It will pay Government to give those people, who are suffering innocence, justice and liberty. if not I will be compelled to show some colonial stratagem which will open the eyes of not only the Victorian police and inhabitants but also the whole British army And now doubt they will acknowledge their hounds were barking at the wrong stump. And that Fitzpatrick will be the cause of greater slaughter to the Union Jack than Saint Patrick was to the snakes and toads in Ireland.'

Now, Ned and Joe began to sound a harmony of those litanies of rebellion they had heard from infancy. The voice of 'Red' Kelly was there, and the Lloyds and the Quinns but, even more loudly and clearly, the voice of old Joe Byrne crying of the agony of Wicklow and Wexford in 1798 and the suffering of the transported rebels in New South Wales, and those brutally crushed Irish rebellions in the new land.

A Policeman is a disgrace to his country. not alone to the mother that suckled him, in the first place he is a rogue in his heart but too cowardly to follow it up without having the force to disguise it. Next he is a traitor to his country ancestors and religion as they were all catholics before the Saxons and Cranmore yoke held sway since then they were persecuted massacreed thrown into martyrdom and tortured beyond the ideas of the present generation. What would people say if they saw a strapping big lump of an Irishman shepherding sheep for fifteen bob a week or tailing turkeys in Tallarook ranges for a smile from Julia or even begging his tucker, they would say he ought to be ashamed of himself and tar-and-feather him. But he would be a king to a policeman who for a lazy loafing cowardly bilit left the ash corner deserted the shamrock, the emblem of true wit and beauty to serve under a flag and nation that has destroyed massacreed and murdered their forefathers by the greatest of torture as rolling them down hill in spiked barrels pulling their toe and finger nails and on the wheel. and every torture imaginable more was transported to Van Diemands Land to pine their young lives away in starvation and misery among tyrants worse than the promised hell itself All of true blood bone and beauty, that was not murdered on their own soil, or had fled to America or other countries to bloom again another day, Were doomed to Port Mcquarie Toweringabbie Norfolk island and Emu plains And in those places of tyrany and condemnation many a blooming Irishman rather than subdue to the Saxon yoke. Were flogged to death and bravely died in servile chains but true to the shamrock and a credit to Paddys land...

What would England do if America declared war and hoisted a green flag as its all Irishman that has got command of her armies forts and batteries even her very life guards and beef tasters are Irish would they not slew around and fight her with their own arms for the sake of the colour they dare not wear for years. and to reinstate it and rise old Erins isle once more, from the pressure and tyrannism of the English yoke, which has kept it in poverty and starvation and caused them to wear the enemys coat. What else can England expect...

After a final rant against the police, came a ringing coda.

I give fair warning to all those who has reason to fear me to sell out and give ten pounds out of every hundred towards the widow and orphan fund and do not attempt to reside in Victoria but as short a time as possible after reading this notice, neglect this and abide by the consequences, Which shall be worse than the rust in the wheat in Victoria or the druth of a dry season to the grasshoppers in New South Wales I do not wish to give the order full force without giving timely warning, but I am a widows son outlawed and my orders *must* be *obeyed.*

It was a huge project for Joe. In its final draft, the letter ran to 7,500 words, twice the length of the Cameron Letter. He wrote it on 56 pages of blue-lined notepaper with an 'AC & S Superfine' watermark—in red ink until it ran out, then the last twenty pages in black. In all, Joe devoted fourteen different sessions to the fine copy. In the longest, he produced eight pages, in the shortest only one, each session beginning with his best copperplate practised over those seven years in Cornelius O'Donoghue's little school by the creek, easing to a more mature and individual hand, and sometimes slipping into a tired scrawl before he rested.

For both Ned and Joe, it was a remarkable achievement—vivid, passionate, often funny, sometimes moving, occasionally trying too hard for its effects, yet often achieving them with considerable style and power.

When the 56 pages were at last finished, Ned honoured Joe's contribution in a unique way. He had signed the Cameron Letter, but left this Jerilderie Letter unsigned, as though reluctant to claim sole authorship. Then he folded it, and stowed the thick wad of paper in his pocket, this manifesto, this affirmation of a personal rebellion against injustice which was reaching inexorably beyond a family, a clan, to touch a widening pattern of lives, echoing the past, touching the present, challenging the future.

As soon as the draft was finished, the Gang rode north, on two bays, a black and a chestnut. The Murray was flowing its lazy, summer way and they easily avoided well-known crossings. The *Sydney Morning Herald* reported, 'The river is very low and is crossable at almost any point along a distance of a hundred miles or so.'

According to Joe, they crossed on the afternoon of Friday, 7 February, about halfway between Mulwala and Tocumwal.

'We first made sure the coast was clear, and that there were no bloody traps [police] about, and seeing none we crossed over.' Asked if the water was deep, he replied, 'Not very…it was only up to the saddle flaps in the deepest part.'

They struck north to the boundary of Barooga and Berrigan stations, in those days, 'a thick, scrubby forest', and made camp. Next day they rode through the forest at leisurely pace, past Wunnamurra station, out across a vast saltbush plain broken by belts of myall and box, and reached Pine Rise, five miles east of Jerilderie, at about four in the afternoon. They spelled their horses until near sundown, then rode on across the plain to Davidson's Woolpack Inn, two miles from Jerilderie on the main road, a substantial brick building shaded by pepper trees on the banks of Billabong Creek.

The Gang had some drinks and chatted with the barmaid. Ned said he'd been in the town four years before and asked if Mary the Larrikin was still around.

'Who do you call Mary the Larrikin?' said the barmaid. 'There's no such person.'

Just then one of the Davidson girls came into the bar and laughingly told Ned that there was indeed such a person. He had been talking to her, the one and only Mary Jordan. The laughter and drink flowed easily and Ned asked what the local people thought of the Kellys. He was told 'the Jerilderie people thought they were brave men but regretted they had shot the police'.

Casually, Ned established that there were still only two police in the town, Senior Constable Devine and Constable Richards. After unsuccessfully trying to sell Ned a watch, the irrepressible Mary entertained the lads with a song, 'The Kellys have made another escape, keep it dark.'

Joe was enjoying a rare chance to relax and, charmed by this brash and breezy female company (since his youth he had liked barmaids), tended to drink too much. Ned warned him to ease off and quietly told Mary not to serve Joe any more whiskey.

About ten o'clock the Gang took their leave, despite Mary's urgings for them to stay the night. Ned said 'they had a long journey before them' and tipped her two shillings, probably in gratitude for her help with his mate's uncharacteristic lapse.

After this lilting overture, the Gang rode to Jerilderie in brilliant moonlight and reined in at the courthouse on the edge of town, immediately opposite the police station, a simple slab homestead with a verandah. Joe, Dan and Steve dismounted, tethered their horses outside the court, then slipped across the main road, through the police paddock fence, and took

41

behind the tree my brother Daw advanced
and Kennedy ran I followed him he
stopped behind another tree and
fired again I shot him in the arm
pit and he dropped his revolver and
ran I fired again with the gun as
he slewed around to surrender I did
not know he had dropped his revolver
the bullet passed through the right
side of his chest & he could not live
or I would have let him go had they
been my own brothers I could not help
shooting them or else let them shoot me
which they would have done had their
bullets been directed as they intended
them. But as for handcuffing Kennedy
to a tree or cutting his ear off or bru
tally treating any of them is a false
hood, if Kennedys ear was cut off
it was not done by me and none

cuted massacred thrown into
martyrdom and tortured beyond
the ideas of the present generation
What would people say if they saw a
strapping big lump of an Irishman
rush holding sheep for fifteen bob a week
or tailing turkeys in Tallarook ranges
for a smile from Julia or even
begging his tucker, they would say
he ought to be ashamed of himself
and tar-and-feather him But
he would be a king to a policeman
who for a lazy loafing cowardly
billet left the ash corner deserted the
shamrock, the emblem of true
wit and beauty to serve under a
flag and nation that has destroyed
massacreed, and murdered their forefathers by the
greatest of torture as rolling them
down hill in spiked barrels

Two pages of the Jerilderie Letter showing examples of Joe's handwriting. At left part of
Ned Kelly's description of the Stringybark Creek gunfight; at right part of Ned's tirade against
Irishmen who had joined the police force.

up positions at either end of the station's front verandah. Ned rode back a little way then turned and spurred to a gallop, pulling up with a wild volley of yells about a drunken brawl at Davidson's and the certainty of 'murder before the morning'.

The two police pulled on trousers and hurried out, to find that Ned had opened the front gate and brought his horse up to the verandah.

'Are there not more than two of you?' Ned asked. 'The men are mad with drink.'

Assured that Jerilderie's only defenders of law and order stood before him, Ned drew a revolver.

'Throw up your hands. I'm Ned Kelly.'

Joe appeared on the verandah to their left, Dan and Steve to their right. Devine and Richards hopelessly raised their hands. The Kellys had captured Jerilderie.

Ned and Joe's plan was a brilliant development of the Euroa strategy. They had carefully analysed their first robbery, noted each weak point and carefully corrected it.

The Euroa depot, at Faithfull's Creek, had been too far from the actual hold-up. The Jerilderie police station was only half a mile from the Bank of New South Wales, their target. Joe had been left guarding prisoners for three hours, vulnerable to attack, while the rest of the Gang robbed the bank, with a policeman loose in the town. Here, the two police were secure and a secondary depot for prisoners would be set up in the Royal Mail Hotel nextdoor to the bank. Two of the Gang would guard hostages, two would slip nextdoor to carry out the hold-up.

At Euroa the Gang's 'cover' had been a hawker's cart and town clothes. Here, they would use police uniforms.

Senior Constable Devine's wife, who was pregnant with twins, was allowed to return to bed with her two children while the two police were locked in their ten-by-ten log cell with a drunk who had been arrested that afternoon. The Gang took it in turns to sleep.

Next morning, when it was discovered that Mrs Devine had to prepare the court house opposite for the Catholic mass at ten, Dan accompanied her in police uniform.

Luckily for the Gang, the officiating priest, Father Kieley, was making only his second visit to the town and did not investigate Mrs Devine's absence from his service. He saw unfamiliar troopers moving around the police paddock and assumed that these were men passing through town on their way to the Murray.

Probationary Constable Richards was a strapping young fellow who had been involved in a farcical gun battle at Tocumwal when New South Wales and Victorian police mistook each other for the Gang. He now suffered the humiliation of being forced to take police-uniformed members of the Gang around Jerilderie and, if necessary, introduce them as constables sent to protect the town from the Kellys.

The Sunday promenades gave Ned and Joe a chance to study final details of their hold-up strategy. They had been tempted to rob the bank that day. Even without knowing that the only two sets of keys were with the manager and accountant, both out of town, they decided to wait until the bank opened for business at ten on Monday morning.

There was something on Joe's mind apart from the problems of the bank robbery; that night he rode back to Davidson's Hotel to spend some time with Mary the Larrikin. Unfortunately, the two Davidson girls were also there. Joe consoled himself with several whiskeys and had to be helped on to his horse when he left at midnight to return to the police station.

Ned was tolerant of his mate's weaknesses for barmaids and grog. Later that day Constable Richards would ask him which of the Gang was his 'best and most reliable man'. Richards suggested Dan. Ned shook his head and pointed to Joe.

'No, that's the fellow. He's as cool and firm as steel.'

If Davidson's whiskey left him something less than cool and firm that Monday morning, Joe showed no sign of it, though, when he donned police uniform and took two horses to be re-shod, blacksmith Samuel Rea thought 'there was something strange in the manner of the man' and noted the brands.

Joe gave his uniform to Dan and, between ten and eleven, he and Ned walked down to the town with Constable Richards while Dan and Steve followed on horseback. Senior Constable Devine and the drunk remained in the lock-up; Mrs Devine and her children were free in the police station.

While Richards introduced Ned and Joe to the startled publican of the Royal Mail Hotel, next to the bank, Dan and Steve rode around the back, stabled their horses and started bailing up hotel employees and herding them inside. The parlour adjoining the front bar became a holding point for prisoners. Dan remained in the bar. Anyone who came in was invited to have a free drink, then sent in to join the growing throng, guarded by Steve.

With the depot established and hostages gathered, Joe strolled out into the hotel yard and crossed to the back door of the adjoining bank. Four years before, the Bank of New South Wales had rented a hall attached to the Royal Mail and partitioned it into two bedrooms, bathroom, sitting room and a banking chamber at the front.

The manager, Tarleton, had been away overnight and while a clerk called Mackie was out the front, keeping an eye open for his return, the accountant, Edwin Living, was working at his lofty desk behind the counter, sitting on a high, leather-seated stool.

Living, a tall, athletic man, heard footsteps and thought that the manager may have come in the back way. He turned and saw a well-dressed bushman standing with his hands in his pockets. Hotel patrons—sober and drunk—often entered the wrong door and made their way through the bank. Joe had obviously been told of this and played drunk while sizing up the situation. To Living, he 'appeared as if he had been drinking, and looked strangely about'.

'What do you mean by coming in here?' Living said as he left his stool and moved towards Joe. Suddenly the 'drunk' was transformed. Cool and firm as steel. With a revolver in his hand.

'I am Kelly.'

Joe could have said 'I am Joe Byrne.' The name may have hit home, but he knew that Kelly was the symbol, the icon he had helped create.

Hearing the voices, the clerk came in and was bailed up. Ned Kelly entered in his police uniform and he and Joe took £691 from the safe. Living tried to convince them that this was all the money in the bank but Ned pointed to the treasure drawer and ordered Living to open it. He needed a second key, held by Tarleton, the manager. After some French farce entrances and exits, the manager was found having a bath after his ride back to town. The treasure drawer yielded some £1,450.

School teacher, William Elliott, entered the bank and was made to hold a sack while the cash was dumped into it. A shrewd, observant young man, he had a brief conversation with Joe, quizzing him about the Gang's route across the Murray, until Joe snapped that he 'wanted to know too bloody much!' A few days later Elliott made a lengthy diary entry on the day's events and left us a detailed portrait of Joe.

> Joe Byrne was a man of 23 or 24 years. He was about 5ft. 10 ins. in height, loosely made, light complexion, inclined to be sandy, scant, sandy whiskers, light hair inclined to be reddish, blue, shifty-looking eyes, fair eyebrows, short upper lip, and light moustache. He seemed of a nervous, retiring disposition (which, however, his subsequent actions at the shooting of Aaron Sherritt belied), and was inclined to be talkative. His face showed no strong sense of character, but seemed to be that of a man who would rather follow than take the initiative. He had a hesitating, uncertain manner about him, such as is commonly seen in the countrified Australian youth who has spent the greater part of his life in the backblocks.

Another description of Joe from the local paper provides an interesting comparison. 'Byrne stands nearly six feet high, long features, fair complexion, and an effeminate cast of countenance, and of a nervous disposition; his manner is quiet, and he appears to a casual observer an inoffensive man.'

The robbery over, Joe left to ride down to the telegraph office. He missed a dramatic little incident which would impact strongly on the fate of the all-important letter he and Ned had written. Their manifesto.

Ned left a jockey called Tiffen in the yard of the bank to burn some ledgers and bank records, then went inside to change out of his police uniform, putting on a pair of superb riding breeches and boots belonging to the manager. While he was changing, three men arrived at the bank.

Gill, editor and printer of the *Gazette,* the man who was intended to print the Jerilderie Letter, had visited the police station for an interview with Devine about the four new police, probably believing that the government had heeded his warning. An alarmed Mrs Devine told him, 'I can't tell you anything. Run, for your life is in danger!'

Gill collected two local merchants, Harkin and Rankin, both justices of the peace, and they went to see the bank manager. They knocked, entered, found the bank empty. Ned called 'Just a minute...' but the strange voice triggered their growing alarm. The three turned and bolted. Harkin and Gill escaped but 22-stone Rankin fell in the doorway and was collared by Ned. After hauling his prisoner into the hotel and putting on a great show of threatening to kill him, Ned learnt that one of the escapees was Gill, the editor. He was furious. Eventually Constable Richards and Living, the bank accountant, took Ned to Gill's home where Mrs Gill convinced Ned that she didn't know where her husband was. Ned assured her that he meant the editor no harm.

'I want him to do some printing for me and I will pay him well for it.'

Ned produced the letter but Mrs Gill was reluctant to accept it and seemed unable or unwilling to suggest anything to help. Living, anxious to defuse the situation, offered to take the letter and give it to Gill on his return. Ned hesitated a moment, then handed the precious 56 pages to the accountant.

'This is a little bit of my life...mind you get it printed, or you will have to reckon with me next time we meet.'

Ned left Richards and Living at the hotel, then rode down to the telegraph office where Joe was checking through the day's telegrams, after getting the postmaster, Jefferson, to dismantle the morse key.

Ned and Joe 'cut the wires about in a fearful mess' and ordered the cutting down of a number of telegraph poles. Some locals started the job with a blunt axe until they borrowed a cross-cut saw and eventually felled eight posts.

Ned returned to the hotel, and Joe, carrying the sack of money, prepared to leave with Dan.

As they rode back to the police station to get one of the police mounts for use as a pack horse, they passed Rankin's store.

Rankin's 18-year-old son, William, had loaded a shotgun and took aim at Joe as he rode past. Finger on trigger, he hesitated and asked his mother if he should fire. She thought of her husband, a prisoner next door.

'Don't fire,' she said.

William lowered the gun and Joe rode on down the main street.

In the Royal Mail Ned delivered a speech to his prisoners. Then he and Steve returned to the police station as Joe and Dan were preparing to ride off, carrying the bag of loot on one of the police horses. They headed south, striking out past the court house and across the town common.

Ned and Steve released the drunk from the lock-up, placed Richards, the postmaster and his assistant inside, with Devine. There was a famous exchange with a congregational clergyman called Gribble, in which Ned made Steve return a watch he had taken, then Steve headed off, mumbling un-happily, after Joe and Dan.

Ned, apparently alone in the town, rode down to the Albion Hotel where a number of 'strangers' had gathered, some of whom had been 'prisoners' at the Royal Mail earlier in the day. They were, of course, sympathisers, who told Ned that the bank staff had defied his orders and ridden off for help. Ned had a quick drink with them, then, about four in the afternoon, mounted, acknowledged their cheers with a wave of his hat, and galloped out of town.

The Gang met near Wunnamurra station, made some inquiries after the bank men, then rode off in the direction of Berrigan station—and the Murray. As they left the open plains and entered the late afternoon shadows of the Riverina forest, the Gang again disappeared into a landscape of myth and misinformation, through which they would move like wraiths for sixteen months.

Another spectacular success lay behind them. Another £2,000 in the Kelly coffers, another romp, an even more outrageous thumb-to-the-nose to authority. The Melbourne *Herald* conceded the following day, 'The affair was managed with consummate judgement.'

But in one respect, Ned and Joe had failed. Living, to Gill's alarm, didn't give him the letter to be published. After a gruelling ride to Deniliquin, with the letter in his pocket, the accountant joined his manager in a train journey to the bank's Melbourne office. While there, he showed the letter to the police.

It was read by Hare, who found it 'a tissue of lies from beginning to end, a wandering narrative full of insinuations and complaints against the police'.

Hare closely read the account of the Stringybark Creek gunfight and marked several key passages. He wrote, 'It is obviously a string of falsehoods and it would be quite improper to have it published.'

Living carried the letter back to Jerilderie on Thursday. Schoolteacher Elliott read it and supplied a summary to Mr Gill, who telegrammed a copy to the Melbourne *Argus* and ran it in his edition of 22 February. Then, until a government copy was rediscovered and published by the Melbourne *Herald* in 1930, Ned and Joe's document vanished.

The published summary predictably failed to convey either the spirit or the detail of the original. Elliott, keen-eyed observer and well-organised chronicler though he proved to be, looked at the remarkable piece of prose with unseeing eyes. The very hostility of his reaction illuminated aspects of the letter which others missed. More than thirty years later, still derisive, dismissive, he remembered—far more accurately than some of the detail— the insistent, rebellious pulse that beat through the sometimes wayward prose. He wrote, 'Kelly was undoubtedly ambitious, and would seemingly have liked to have been at the head of a hundred followers or so to upset the existing Government or bring them to terms.'

Frustrated in attempts to have the Cameron and Jerilderie letters published, Ned and Joe used the Gang's long period of inactivity to conduct a carefully designed public relations campaign. A sympathiser produced a 16-page letter, clearly based on Joe's Cameron/Jerilderie draft but adding new and accurate material, which was quoted at length by the *Herald* and reprinted by Beechworth's *Advertiser.* Furthering the portrayal of the Gang as highwaymen heroes, the letter trumpeted, 'At present they are painted as black as print can paint them, but they harmed no man, woman, or child. Their actions are more like four sisters of charity than four outlaws.'

Using his talent for poetry and parody, Joe composed ballads which were soon being sung throughout the Kelly Country, and beyond. They included 'The Ballad of Kelly's Gang' (sometimes called 'The Kellys, Byrne, and Hart'), a spirited parody of the Irish rebel anthem 'The Wearing of the Green'. First drafted after Euroa, it was expanded to include Jerilderie, with a stirring coda,

High above the mountains so beautiful and grand,
Four young Australian heroes in bold defiance stand;
In bold defiance stand my boys, the heroes of today,
So let us stand together boys and shout again 'Hooray!'

G. Wilson Hall, editor of the Mansfield paper (and closet Kelly sympathiser) saw fit to include part of this ballad with some other Kelly songs in his pamphlet, *The Outlaws of the Wombat Ranges,* published in July 1879, pretending disapproval while describing them as 'hymns of triumph'.

Before the year was out, a pamphlet version of Joe's ballad had been published by a Mr T. W. Allen of Hobart who billed himself 'Sole Agent in Tasmania for Kelly's Songs', conveying an image of organisation and marketing not altogether inappropriate to the machine created by Joe and Ned.

While Joe's lyrics sank into folk culture, he also conducted and coordinated 'poison pen' campaigns against such prime targets as Detective Ward and Senior Constable Mullane—even distributing mock reward posters and caricatures for posting up in public places.

Effectively manipulated by Ned and Joe, the Kelly Country and Victoria-at-large sang the 'hymns of triumph', laughed at the bungling police pursuit and increasingly saw the four outlaws as huge shadow figures thrown across the antipodean landscape by the light of other heroes of other lands.

CHAPTER 11

'My Boy Tommy'

February–April 1879

Jerilderie was as rude a shock to Hare as Euroa had been to Nicolson. Hare arranged with Detective Ward for them to meet Aaron in Beechworth the following Saturday at 11 p.m.

That very day, though perhaps even Hare was unaware of it, decisions had been made to boost the Kelly reward to a staggering level. The Victorian reward was increased to £4,000—a figure now matched by £3,000 from the New South Wales government and £1,000 from 'certain banks' in that colony. The joint reward of £8,000, £2,000 for each member of the Gang, represented a present-day equivalent of more than A$2 million.

In hoodwinking Hare Aaron had helped the Gang earn this extraordinary measure of their success but, in providing an outrageously false trail, surely he had shown his hand? This Saturday night meeting with the police would, at best, see him discredited as a police spy and, at worst, exposed as an active agent of the Kellys.

It was a tricky moment for Aaron and he handled it masterfully. His first words to Hare were 'Didn't I tell you they would stick up a bank in New South Wales?'

Of course, he hadn't, but Hare often showed a loose grasp on facts. On his own account the best retort he could manage was 'Yes. But you told me they were going to Goulburn.' Perhaps Aaron shrugged: if Hare wanted to quibble about such details...

The Superintendent's next words set the tone for much that would follow. 'Well, what is to be done now?'

Aaron had grasped the initiative and clearly Hare was going to let him keep it. First, Aaron had another piece of information. Dan Kelly, he told Hare, had breakfasted with Mrs Byrne the previous Wednesday, two days after the robbery, worried that the other members of the Gang had failed to turn up at a rendezvous point.

Once more, Hare could find confirmation of the story. That very

Wednesday afternoon, he would claim, Dan Kelly had been seen riding towards the Buckland Gap, only four miles from Beechworth. (Actually, Dan was supposedly seen near *Taylors* Gap, some 15 miles from Beechworth, and Detective Ward considered the report 'doubtful'. Most significantly, news of the sighting had been published in the Melbourne *Argus* and the *Advertiser* two days before Aaron's meeting with the two police.)

Not only did Aaron have information: this time he had a plan for Hare.

'Now, you had better come tomorrow night. I have good reason to believe they will be at Mrs Byrne's—the other three men—you had better come and watch the place.' It was all patent nonsense. Had Ned, Joe and Steve been lost for six days? If Dan, with access to the Gang's superb 'bush telegraph' network, couldn't know their movements, how could Aaron? Perhaps Dan was now lost, and 'the other three' would turn up at Mrs Byrne's, looking for him!

Aaron arranged to meet Hare at eight o'clock the following night 'at a certain spot' in the ranges near Beechworth. Hare would bring a party of police from Eldorado. Aaron would then lead them to Byrnes' and show the police where the Gang hid their horses while eating supper.

Again, Ward tried to introduce a note of sanity, telling Hare, 'I have known Sherritt for years, and if he likes he can put you in a position to capture the Kellys, but I doubt him doing so.' Again, Hare would not be swayed.

Yet perhaps Ward managed to kindle a glimmer of doubt. Hare was to tell the Royal Commission, 'Of course, I had my doubts about Sherritt all the time; but still I thought he was true…but all my men were suspicious of him…the men all said, "You will come to grief with that man some day, he will "sell" you to the Kelly's." I said "I have the greatest confidence in him. I deserve to be "sold" if I did not know a man when I saw him, as I had the opportunity of seeing Sherritt…"'.

Reluctantly involved in Aaron's charade, Ward had injury added to insult the following day when he travelled with Hare to brief the Eldorado police. Hare entered splendidly into the clandestine spirit of the occasion, recording, 'As the detective was well known in the locality and I was not, I put him in the boot of the buggy under the seat, and he remained in that position nearly all the way.'

At eight o'clock that night Hare and Ward met Aaron in the ranges and they rode to meet the Eldorado police. After waiting an hour, Aaron became restive. 'We will be late, Mr Hare. We should have been nearly three miles from this by this time.'

Hare was 'very much put out' at the non-appearance of the police party but wasn't prepared to let this stop him catching three of the Kellys. In a splendidly dramatic moment, he turned to Ward and asked, 'Will you stick to me if we go by ourselves?'

Clearly confident that Aaron wouldn't take them within a bull's roar of the Gang, Ward rose to the occasion. 'Yes, Mr Hare, I will stick to you and do whatever you tell me to do.'

Like a character from some Imperial adventure, Hare then turned to Aaron and said in his unfortunately high-pitched voice, 'Alright; we are ready to go with you now.'

Aaron would have watched all this with near-disbelief—which Hare read as hesitation to accept that the two police would dare embark on such a hazardous expedition without strong armed support. So Hare drew himself up to his imposing height and said decisively, 'Come on.'

The expedition that followed is a luminous glimpse of Aaron in action. This is how it appeared to Hare:

We mounted our horses. I followed Aaron, the detective following me. The night was terribly dark, and Aaron took us at a good pace. The country was rugged and broken, but he rode ahead just as if he was in his own garden. He appeared to trust to his horse, and I trusted to him...Suddenly Aaron stopped, and in a whisper said to me, 'This is the bushrangers' country; no one ever comes in here but them.' We were then about ten miles from Beechworth on the ranges at the back of Woolshed, and so we rode along, winding round a drain one minute, and over logs and rocks the next, trusting entirely to our horses. Suddenly Aaron pulled up, and I went up beside him, the detective doing likewise. Aaron said, 'They are back from Jerilderie. Do you see that fire in the distance?...I have never before seen a fire in this place, and for some reason they have lighted one, and there they are.' We all three dismounted from our horses and sat down on the ground to decide what was to be done. Aaron said, 'What do you wish me to do? I will do whatever you like.'...I then told him...he had better take off his boots, leave his horse with me, and crawl along the ground as close to the fire as he could get...and find out whether the outlaws were there. He never hesitated for a moment, and did exactly what I told him to do, and the detective and myself were left alone...We stayed in the same spot for about ten minutes, deciding how we were to make the attack, when we heard footsteps coming towards us at a quick pace. The detective said, 'He has sold us; who is this coming towards us?' I said, 'Keep quiet.' We both, with revolvers in our hands, remained perfectly still until the footsteps came within a yard of us, and a voice we recognized as Aaron's said, 'Mr Hare, we have been deceived, that fire is on the opposite range and some miles away.'...

We mounted our horses and found what he had stated was perfectly correct. Aaron then said, 'We are awfully late, we must hurry on to Mrs Byrne's house,'... He commenced to go down a fearfully steep range. I said not a word but followed him, until he pulled up and said, 'I am afraid to go down here to-night, it is so very dark.' I said, 'Is there no other way you can get down?' He replied, 'Only by going a mile round.' He said, 'Be careful not to move from your saddle, for this is terrible steep range, and if you attempt to get off you will roll down some hundreds of feet.' He told me to get off the horse on the off side, he doing the same himself, and the detective also. We then led our horses round and got down another gap in the mountains. After riding about a mile Aaron told us that we had better dismount and tie our horses to a tree.

We did so, and we followed him down the ranges until we came to a house, which turned out to be Mrs Byrne's...Here...we met some watchdogs in the shape of a flock of geese, and they did give the alarm, and no mistake. However, after a short time, Aaron crawled up to the house, so as to ascertain if there was any one talking inside. Everything was quiet, there was a candle burning. He returned and said, 'They expect them to-night. You see, they have left the candle burning, and some supper ready on the table.' He then said, 'Let us go up to a clump of trees at the back of the house, where they generally tie up their horses.' I had previously been told by another agent of this clump of trees, where marks of horses having been tied up were to be seen. Aaron said to me, 'Go into that clump. They often tie up their horses there, and lay down beside them and have a sleep, after having their supper at Mrs Byrne's.' I walked into the clump, but found no horses there, and returned to Aaron. Aaron then said, 'We must now wait in this stock-yard, which leads up to the clump. If they come they will come through here.' It was then about two o'clock in the morning. We sat down and waited until daylight, and then, nothing happening, we started back to our horses, reaching Beechworth at eight o'clock.

Aaron suggested to me that I should bring a party of men and come and live in the mountains at the back of Mrs Byrne's house. He told me he could put me in a spot which was unknown to any one except the bushrangers, and the only danger of my being discovered was by them. He said I could stay in the mountains by day, and take up my position in the stock-yard behind Mrs Byrne's at night, and that if I had patience I was certain to get them...

The whole exercise should have stretched even Hare's credulity to breaking point. Why would the Kellys, acknowledged by the police as consummate bushmen, light a fire on top of a range, in mid-summer, especially when they were supposedly on their way to supper at the Byrne house?

Why would an expert bushman like Aaron crawl up to a house to see if the Gang was inside before checking the place where they 'generally' tethered their horses? Obviously, he knew what he would find in the house and that no horses would be found in the clump of trees.

The burning candle and the waiting supper were probably left by Kate Byrne for Aaron. The rest of the *Boy's Own Paper* touches ('This is the bushrangers' country; no one comes in here but them...I am afraid to go down here tonight, it is so very dark...if you attempt to get off you will roll down hundreds of feet') were tailored to Hare's self-dramatising taste—very successfully, as evidenced by his fulsome treatment of the episode in his autobiography and in a less detailed but equally savoured version given to the Royal Commission.

The clump of trees where horses had been tied (betrayed by chewed bark and manure) could have represented the only genuine link with the Gang. Aaron probably showed police this place because it was no longer in use. While these 'clues' justified watching only the front of the Byrne house, the normal approach was now via the back, using the high bank of the Chinese water race for cover. In fact, Joe repeatedly visited his mother while police, carefully supervised by Aaron, were in their positions by the stockyard, watching the front. Only once, for some unknown reason, would Joe revert to the old approach and almost step on Hare as he walked down to the house.

After the first night watch at Byrnes', Ward's suspicions must have been confirmed, though it was also clear that he would never convince Hare that Aaron was making a fool of him. Ward decided to play along with the charade and find opportunities to turn it to his advantage, eventually sacrificing Aaron in the process. Further, this bizarre foray had established the pattern of Aaron's involvement with the police and even the specific nature of police surveillance of the Byrne house—two other major factors contributing to his death in sixteen months' time. It had been a fateful night.

The next day Hare and Ward organised the first of the 'cave parties' to watch the Byrne house. Aaron showed them what was probably one of his boyhood haunts—a boulder-studded clearing in a corner of the range east of Native Dog Peak, directly above the Woolshed settlement and a mile-and-a-half from Byrnes. A small cave below a huge, shelving rock provided limited shelter at the top of the clearing, with various other places, beside and under boulders, where men could sleep.

Higher on the range, behind the shoulder of Native Dog Peak and about half a mile closer to the Byrne house, Aaron led Hare and Ward to the spectacular cave where he had guarded the Gang during the flight to the Murray. Hare thought it 'a wonderfully romantic spot, on the edge of a precipice, and only approachable on one side. Two men could keep off a dozen.'

Hare decided that he and six men would camp in the clearing, while four men under Senior Constable Mayes occupied the upper cave.

That evening, Monday, 17 February, Hare and Ward moved their men in. Some rode as close as possible and left their horses in Aaron's paddock. Others were driven by Ward in a buggy, probably down Maddern's Track which took them close to the lower camp.

They left blankets, rugs, billies and a few provisions, tucked away from sight and dew, then followed Aaron in a scrambling trek along the range and down to the clump of trees above the Byrne stockyard. While the police settled in the damp grass with their guns and rifles, each man behind a tree and some ten or fifteen yards apart, Aaron strolled down to visit Kate at the warm-windowed house.

Hare and his men waited, listening to the night sounds of the valley, humbled by the great pergola of the Milky Way arched from range to range, momentarily chilled by the shriek of a plover, tension easing to boredom as the hours passed. Then, at twelve or one o'clock, Aaron came ambling up the slope to settle on the ground by Hare and wait another four or five hours for the first lightening of the sky behind the blackness of the Peak. As the dawn chorus came to life, Aaron headed up to his hut on the tableland while Hare led his men in single file back to their comfortless camp.

That was the pattern for the next 25 days—sleeping by day among the rocks, heading down to the stockyard at dusk, watching all night, then trekking back to be in their possies by daylight. Already, in this last week of summer, the temperature dropped sharply with the sun. Soon, the nights were 'bitterly cold'. The police hung on.

'Night after night,' said Hare, 'Aaron used to go and see his young woman, and bring back hopes of success...He always used to take up his position beside me and relate all kind of encouraging reports he had obtained during the day as to the prospect of the Kellys turning up. Hardly a night that we took up our positions but we thought we should have some luck. As day broke in the morning we used to make back to our camp in the mountains in a very disappointed mood.'

Occasionally, as a special treat, Hare would let his men kindle small fires under their billies to thaw chilled hands and brew some warming, cheering tea. But most of the time they had only cold water to drink with their bread, tinned beef and sardines.

For the first few nights, provisions were brought in by pack horse. When this attracted the attention of a friend of the Byrnes, the food was carted to the Sherritt home by storekeeper Paddy Allen. From there, packed in sacks, it was carried to the camps by Aaron, his father or Jack or, occasionally, fetched by some of the men. Aaron used to bring water bags.

As the days and nights went by and it grew colder, spirit lamps were supplied to boil billies without tell-tale fires, and bottles of 'porter, ale and whiskey' were included among the provisions—all good business for Paddy Allen.

The onset of autumn made the eight-hour watches even more uncomfortable and the return to camp in the chill fore-dawn even more cheerless. Yet Hare noted that Aaron continued to pass these nights in his shirt sleeves, always the same 'peculiar dress...a white shirt, a pair of trousers and long boots, with his trousers tucked inside'.

Hare, who had spent many years among bushmen, commented:

I hardly think anyone out of Australia could possibly conceive the hardships that men of this stamp can endure. They have an extraordinary way of sleeping; they coil themselves up like dogs. I remember one night finding Aaron on my doorstep, about one o'clock in the morning. He came to my quarters, and not finding me, he lay down and fell asleep; his head appeared between his knees, and he said, when camping out he always slept in that position. He could go without sleep for a longer period than any other man I ever met, and he said that the Kellys could do the same.

The following year Aaron was to provide Hare with the most extraordinary display of his toughness when, on sub-zero mid-winter nights, he lay in the freezing grass from eight at night until four or five in the morning.

He was a man of most wonderful endurance. He would go night after night without sleep in the coldest nights in winter. He would be under a tree without a particle of blanket of any sort in his shirt sleeves whilst my men were all lying wrapt in furs in the middle of winter. This is an instance that occurred actually; I saw the man one night when the water was frozen on the creeks and I was frozen to death nearly. I came down and said 'Where is Aaron Sherritt?' and I saw a white thing lying under a tree, and there was Aaron without his coat. The men were covered up with all kinds of coats and furs, and waterproof coatings, and everything else, and this man was lying on the ground uncovered. I said, 'You are mad, Aaron, lying there;' and he said, 'I don't care about coats.'

This lay ahead, in the dark winter of 1880. For the present, in these 'bitterly cold' autumn nights of 1879, Aaron's ability to withstand cold was remarkable enough for Hare to ask him, 'Can the outlaws endure as you are doing?' Aaron's reply echoes down the years. 'Ned Kelly would beat me into fits…I can beat all the others; I am a better man than Joe Byrne, and I'm a better man than Dan Kelly, and I'm a better man than Steve Hart. I can lick those two youngsters into fits; I've always beaten Joe, but I look upon Ned Kelly as an extraordinary man; there is no man in the world like him, he is super-human…I look upon him as invulnerable, you can do nothing with him.'

Perhaps, as the steam of those words hung in the still, cold air, just for a moment Hare glimpsed something about Aaron and Ned that transcended mere hardiness and hinted at some supernormal quality bred into them to cope with existence in this harsh, strange land—some quirk of evolution that produced a first generation of European man with Aboriginal abilities to hunt and track and survive and endure, abilities they had honed to razor sharpness, which set them apart from men like himself from other lands, and even from most of the native-born who ignored or only partly realised their potential. If Hare glimpsed something of this in Aaron's words, it was too uncomfortable, too challenging, and he found easy reassurance in other words. 'He often told me that I had a kind of influence over him that no other man had ever had before, and he could not tell me a lie.'

With fervent belief in his mastery over this remarkable young man—a mastery affirmed by him to be more complete even than that exerted by Ned Kelly—Hare was armed for the incident that would have destroyed any other man's trust in Aaron.

About ten o'clock at night we were all in our positions, I at the opening of the stock-yard, lying under a post-and-rail fence with an old log fence at the bottom, as close to it as I could get, the men lying behind trees. There were six of us in all. I heard the footsteps of a man coming down the track from the hills. The footsteps came closer and closer, until I saw the figure of a man step on to the rails just above me. At the moment I thought it was most likely to be Joe Byrne coming down to see his mother, and I was just in the act of springing up as he jumped down, when I remembered that Aaron was down at the house, and if it was one of the outlaws he would be able to give us notice. So I decided to let him pass me. He walked right through the midst of my men. Not one of them moved, because I had not moved. He went straight to the house. About two hours afterwards Aaron came to us. I waited to see if he would say if there was anyone there or not. He did not. I asked him if there were any strangers at Mrs Byrne's. He said, 'Yes, a man named Scotty, who lives up on the hills, came there.' Some how or other I fancy the man was Joe Byrne. I have no real reason for thinking so, but I do, and we let him slip past us.

Everything suggests that Hare was right. The man had come on foot from the range by Byrne's Gully and there were no houses in that direction within normal walking distance. Only an exceptional horseman could have negotiated that country at night; suggesting that the unusually late visitor was such a horseman and, further, that he had some special reason to leave his horse far from the house.

According to local tradition, one of the troopers recognised Joe's distinctive walk and a contemporary noted that Hare's failure to act was 'much to the astonishment of the constables'.

It is hard to understand why Aaron's presence in the house stopped Hare challenging this man he believed to be Joe Byrne. Hare did not see the man leave the house and does not seem to have questioned Aaron as to whether he was still inside. So, by the time Hare led his men back to camp at four or five in the morning, Mrs Byrne's mysterious visitor had made an invisible departure from the house or was sleeping there.

Did Hare's inaction spring from cowardice (which, in all fairness, he did not normally display) or was it the result of his obsessive conviction that Aaron was true to him, a conviction of such personal importance that he was pathologically incapable of challenging its validity?

Joe's arrival must have given Aaron a nasty shock. Using some excuse— police in the area, horses, tracks—it was an easy matter to persuade him not to stay but slip away from the house using his normal route behind the high bank of the mining race, and circle back to pick up his horse. Certainly, Joe made no more unscheduled visits to his family. Mrs Byrne was always warned that he was coming and sent the children up and down the valley to make sure no strangers were about. Even little Elly, just turned eight, had a role on these occasions.

We had to clear the way—see the way was clear that evening, see who had come over the bridge and go down to the other houses to see who was there. Any of us would do that. They only had to say 'Watch the bridge and tell us who's coming over.' And we knew to a certain extent what we had to do and what it was for.

And if he was coming that night, we'd all be put to bed so we couldn't tell about it in the morning.

Sometimes Elly did lie awake, blue eyes wide in the darkness, listening to the murmur of voices, her young mind trying to cope with the paradox of this brother who was so fiercely loved and protected yet could not be seen or even spoken of.

It was ironic that, in this period when poor Hare believed that each new night would bring him success, the Gang were safest. This was despite the fact that, on 8 March, a contingent of six Queensland Aboriginal troopers arrived at Benalla, commanded by dashing, handsomely whiskered Sub-Inspector Stanhope O'Connor. Usually described as 'blacktrackers', these men were fully trained and armed as mounted police, combining an awesome ability to follow tracks with the potential to kill or capture criminals. Recruited from cannibal tribes of northern Queensland, they posed a formidable threat—and were rightly respected, if not feared, by the Gang. For an amalgam of reasons, including overt racism, they were never properly used, least of all while Hare's time was being wasted on the cave party. This became the sharp end of the Kelly pursuit. One night, even the urbane Captain Standish—who came to treat the Queenslanders with outrageous contempt—spent the night with Hare and his men among the trees at the end of the Byrne stockyard, demonstrating his view of the importance of the cave party, as well as his utter devotion to his friend.

One hot day a constable from the upper cave crept down to fetch water from Reedy Creek, almost half a mile from the foot of the range. He was seen by one of Margret's friends and she investigated. That night she told Aaron 'There is a party [of police] in the mountains here; go and look for them tomorrow.' Aaron shrugged. 'Alright.' But he added, 'I haven't seen anything of them.'

'No, but a man like a constable was seen walking with a bucket towards the creek, and I myself went to that creek, and I found where there was some soap. The fellow had washed his hands there, and he had been whittling a bit of stick.' Margret showed him the stick.

The next evening Aaron told Mrs Byrne, 'I've been in every direction, and can't find them at all.' There was little else he could say. Yet he must have known that Margret Byrne, used to following cattle in these stony ranges, could track almost like an Aboriginal and distinguish the tracks of police boots and government horseshoes. She was, in Hare's words, 'a very active old party'. That was Friday evening.

After the Saturday night watch Aaron didn't return to his hut on the tableland but went back to the camp with Hare and his men in the early hours of Sunday. Kate, who didn't seem to share her mother's suspicions of

Cornish dairyman James Chappell was described as 'a grumpy old devil' but proved a staunch friend of the Byrne family and baffled police as one of the 'respectable' sympathisers. (*Burke Museum, Beechworth*)

The Byrnes' next-door neighbours, Archibald and Jane Batchelor. Her evidence helped convict Joe and Aaron of the theft and butchering of a cow, while her husband later became a Kelly sympathiser and may have played a significant role in the events leading to Aaron's murder. He proudly displays a snuff horn, obviously a prized possession.

Looking out from the upper chamber of the Kelly Cave (in 1992), across a slope of native pine. Hare thought it 'a wonderfully romantic spot…two men could keep off a dozen'.

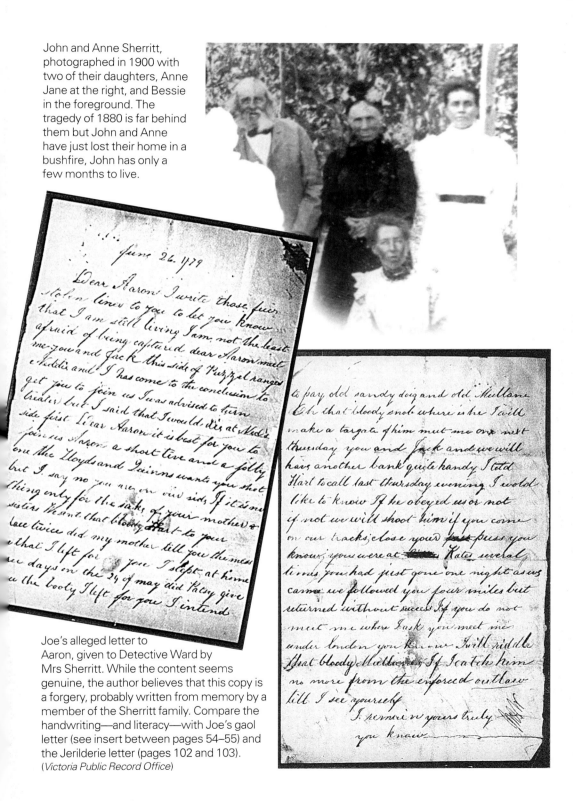

John and Anne Sherritt, photographed in 1900 with two of their daughters, Anne Jane at the right, and Bessie in the foreground. The tragedy of 1880 is far behind them but John and Anne have just lost their home in a bushfire, John has only a few months to live.

Joe's alleged letter to Aaron, given to Detective Ward by Mrs Sherritt. While the content seems genuine, the author believes that this copy is a forgery, probably written from memory by a member of the Sherritt family. Compare the handwriting—and literacy—with Joe's gaol letter (see insert between pages 54–55) and the Jerilderie letter (pages 102 and 103).
(*Victoria Public Record Office*)

A soaring view of the Woolshed Valley from the roof of the Kelly Cave (photographed in 1991). The Byrne homestead lay at the edge of the cleared land, to the extreme left.

The Chinese mining race (photographed in 1959) which crossed the Byrne clearing and provided safe cover for Joe's approach to his mother's home, just up the slope from this point. Native Dog Peak is in the background.

him, was home from Feely's for the day, and Aaron planned to spend some time with her.

This Sunday morning Margret Byrne put on her best white shawl and went to Mass as usual at Cornelius O'Donoghue's old schoolhouse almost opposite the lower police camp where Aaron was sleeping. Then, probably armed with information from Woolshed friends, if not from Cornelius O'Donoghue himself, she crossed the bridge, walked up to the range, and began to search its rocky, scrub-covered slopes. Standing on a rock, she saw something glinting in the sunlight on the opposite slope of a gully—a discarded sardine tin. She shed her shawl on to the rock and started to pick her way across the gully.

It was about nine o'clock and everyone was asleep in the police camp except the sentry posted among the rocks at the top of the clearing where Hare always slept. He called softly to Hare that 'the old woman' was in the camp. Hare cautiously raised his head in the small cave, screened in shadow, and saw Margret Byrne creeping up into the clearing. 'She stood for a moment, saw articles lying about the camp, then came a few steps further on, looked down in the direction of where one of the men was lying, then halted for a moment, and retreated...Directly she left, I jumped up and went to see who it was she had seen, and to my horror, I found it to be poor Aaron.'

Hare woke Aaron and told him what had happened. 'He turned deadly pale, and huge drops of perspiration broke out on his face. He could scarcely speak, and gasped, "Now I am a dead man."'

Aaron had been sleeping on his side, with his hat over his face. Despite the distinctive white shirt and long boots, Mrs Byrne may not have recognised him so Hare gave Aaron his greatcoat and white sun helmet, and urged him to head off immediately to establish an alibi with nearby friends. First, they watched Margret retrieve her shawl from the rock then, while the sentry kept an eye on her, Aaron slipped out of the camp.

That evening, Aaron told Hare that he was in 'a mortal funk'. Yet, when asked if he was going to call on 'his young woman', he said, 'Oh yes, I must go and see if the old woman recognised me this morning.' He had brought a penny whistle 'to break the ice' and headed down towards the Byrne house as Hare and his men moved off for their night's surveillance.

Jaunty in the dusk, despite his fears, Aaron started to play the whistle a hundred yards from the house as he approached the front gate. He played it all the way up to the door, but Kate did not appear. So he continued his cheery piping and walked inside to find a neighbour with Mrs Byrne. (It was probably Dick Murphy, a well-known Kelly sympathiser. Elly recalled, 'Dick was there every night. He'd come over at seven or eight and go home at half past nine or ten. He was always there—backwards and forwards. He'd walk in and he'd say "I'm coming in" and he'd sit down and he'd talk and he'd talk. From the time he came in. And then he'd go.')

Mrs Byrne said nothing to Aaron and he tried to read her mood; was this her now-normal coolness or a reaction to the morning's discovery? 'I watched her countenance, and I felt sure she had not recognised me,' he told Hare later that night.

After a time, Margret walked outside and Aaron followed her. She turned on him. 'A pretty fellow you are, going to search! I found the men in the mountains today.'

Relief surged through Aaron as she told him how she had discovered the camp, concluding, 'There must be a great number of men there, because of the way the ground is beaten about, but I only saw one man lying there.'

Aaron claimed that she wanted to find how many men were there and 'get Joe to shoot any number under fifteen or twenty.'

True or not, next morning Margret returned to the police camp. The sentry, Constable Barry, alerted Hare and they watched her circle up the slope behind the clearing, then creep forward on hands and knees. 'She used to go crawling along like a rabbit,' said Hare, 'and only her head over the rocks'.

Hare turned to Senior Constable Mills, his second-in-command, and told him, 'Go up and give the old woman a fright.' Mills, a lean, bearded country-man, crept up the slope to a boulder, let Margret crawl past, then 'gave a tremendous yell and jumped on her'. According to Hare, Mrs Byrne 'almost died of fright' and gasped out, 'What! What! I am only looking for cattle.' But she quickly recovered herself and told Mills, 'I'll get my son to shoot the whole bloody lot of you!'

After this, Hare reasonably decided there was no future in the camp. Unbelievably, Aaron urged him to stay. 'It is no use going away; she has no means of communicating with the outlaws. I am the only one who can do that, and when they come I will get the news.' If Aaron was speaking the truth even Hare must have wondered why he didn't make an appointment to meet the Gang instead of waiting night after night for three weeks to see if they turned up. To Hare's simple, 'I don't believe it', Aaron countered, 'Believe it or not, but don't go because she has discovered you.'

So Hare stayed for another five days—during which 'two old women' came up to have a look at the police camp. He then headed back to resume the pursuit of the Gang, yet left his men in the two camps for another twenty days. They had argued as strenuously as Aaron for the watch parties to continue, apparently having realised that, though boring and uncomfortable, the duty was completely free of danger and offered the compensation of plentiful free grog.

Once Hare had gone, Ward was able to provide added incentives: his friend of nineteen years standing, storekeeper Paddy Allen, did even better business, commenting, 'This cave…was full of bottles and tins and things. They were not allowed to light fires, and lived fat—and cut it thick. They had plenty of liquor, and they had fires when they wanted. It didn't really matter...The police thought she [Mrs Byrne] didn't know they were there. But I know that she did. I know that she knew it all the time. They were surprised that they didn't find out anything. But I wasn't. I wasn't interested in their hopes. I just served them with stores.'

With Hare gone, Aaron's attitude changed. He still watched with the men—to guard against any unscheduled arrival by Joe or other members of the Gang—but he lacked the credulous Hare as audience for his tales and Mrs Byrne was increasingly hostile to him.

Although Hare claims that she was 'constantly abusing him and telling him that she thought he had thrown his old friends overboard and was working for the police', she still held back from direct accusation, even though she stopped Kate from seeing Aaron. While Anne Sherritt said that, 'Mrs Byrne fully expected he would marry her daughter,' Margret would claim, 'he was not in a fair way to become my son-in-law'. This was her way. A dogged, uncompromising denial of something that had become so painful. By rejecting the fact that Kate and Aaron had ever considered marriage, no engagement had been broken by her. In holding back from a total acceptance that Aaron was helping the police, she could avoid the frightening repercussions of this fact. Eventually, it was Aaron who precipitated the final split between them.

Grazing near the Byrne house was a horse called Charlie, a gelding with an odd history. Three years before Aaron had given Kate a bay filly. In December 1871 Paddy had swapped the filly to a Chinese for £2 plus the bay gelding Charlie. With his engagement broken, Aaron did something roughly equivalent to taking back a ring: he took Charlie.

He told Hare, 'I couldn't help doing this. I didn't want the horse, but I felt I must do something to old Mrs Byrne. She has not behaved well to me lately, and her conduct towards me is so cool that I could not resist the temptation of stealing her horse.'

Aaron had often taken the horse and ridden it, so at first, with Paddy away, there was nothing unusual in Charlie's 'disappearance'. But with the bad blood brewing between Aaron and the Byrnes, it became the catalyst for a fatal rift.

A few days after Charlie disappeared, Margret went up to Sheepstation Creek and told the Sherritts that Aaron was 'after the bushrangers'. She claimed that he then came down to Sebastopol and confronted her. As on the night of her discovery of the cave party, she went outside to avoid the children (and probably Dick Murphy) and Aaron followed her. He demanded to know how she knew he was betraying the Gang, and when she refused to tell him, he made some wild threats.

There were no witnesses to this exchange, but Jack Sherritt and an old school friend, James Dawson, were at Aaron's selection when Mrs Byrne came up to the fence and called out to Aaron, 'What horses are those in the paddock?'

'I didn't know there were any horses in the paddock.'

'There are some there belonging to the police, and if I thought you knew it, I would burn your fences down!'

Margret finally hurled at Aaron, 'Go and take everything belonging to you out of my place. I want to have nothing to do with you!'

Later, in a welter of claim and counter-claim, Margret would admit only one widely reported fact in a court of law: 'We had a falling out about his giving the police assistance.'

By taking Charlie, Aaron guaranteed that his supposed betrayal of the Gang became common knowledge throughout the colony.

For the remaining weeks of the watch party Aaron would not be spending warm nights in the Byrne house. The relationship with Kate was over, though Aaron remained a brother-figure to the Byrne children and would still 'speak friendly' to them and bring presents from Beechworth. On his return from New South Wales, easy-going Paddy would be drawn into the hell-brew, inevitably taking his mother's part against Aaron.

Joe could do nothing to prevent it all, and would continue to believe in his mate. In the battle lines so strongly drawn in the Woolshed, all allegiance was with Margret Byrne and, to this key group of Kelly sympathisers, Aaron was increasingly regarded as an enemy. From here the cancer spread. The Kelly circle was, at core, Irish Catholic, but included several Protestants—among them, Wild Wright. While old suspicions and animosities were readily shelved in the interests of the Kelly cause, they remained deeply grained. To many prominent sympathisers, Aaron's background—not only an Irish Protestant, but also the son of an Irish policeman—provided early confirmation of his guilt. Aaron, once 'the scout or head-centre of the district', quickly became an outsider, distrusted by influential individuals and groups among the Kelly supporters and, increasingly, by many rank-and-file police.

Aaron seemed oblivious of it all. He continued to carry himself through the affair with a jaunty defiance and was about to mock his police 'allies' with another outrageous charade.

After leaving the cave party, Hare had continued sending men careering around the country, seemingly at random and, whenever possible, joining them. Then he was drawn back to Beechworth. A letter addressed to Aaron at Sheepstation Creek was passed to Ward by one of the Sherritts who had recognised Joe Byrne's writing. Hare tells us, 'I opened it and could not understand a word of it, as it was written in bush slang. I at once went for my boy Tommy...and met him on a large granite rock at the back of Beechworth', probably Sea Rock below One Tree Hill, with its sweeping views across the timbered gorge of Reedy Creek to the tableland and the Woolshed beyond.

Shown the letter, Aaron glanced sharply at the Superintendent. 'How did you get this into your possession?'

'Never mind, read it to me; and who is it from?'

It was clear that Hare knew who the writer was, so Aaron told him, 'Why, from Joe Byrne, of course.' It was equally clear that Hare couldn't understand the letter so Aaron sat down on the vast, curving tor and spun him a splendid tale.

Joe, he said, wanted him to come to the Whorouly races, due to be held within a week, and to meet him at the back of the course. He also claimed 'that Joe had the black mare which Aaron had ridden in a steeplechase previously, and that the mare was in good order and sure to win'. Joe wanted Aaron to ride it again.

Again, Hare looked to Aaron for a lead, asking him 'what he thought best to be done'.

Aaron had a wonderful idea: 'You must give me a good horse to ride at the races, and I will assist in every way possible.'

Hare and Sadleir arranged for the normal uniformed troopers to attend the meeting but also sent three hand-picked plainclothed men 'who were unknown in the district' Constables Lawless, Falkiner and Johnston. Hare thought the first two 'equal to any bush riders in the world' and also men of considerable courage. Johnston, too, he considered, 'a magnificent rider, but he required some restraint, being both wild and reckless, and inclined to lose his head'. (Hare was wrong about Falkiner being 'unknown'. He had ridden with one of Steele's search parties to Taylor's Gap and joined in the Great Sebastopol Raid.)

At the race meeting, Lawless set up a table and played the three-card trick, fleecing sharp-eyed racegoers with his sleight-of-hand; Falkiner put up an Aunt Sally booth, 'bawling out at the top of his voice'; while Johnston remained on horseback, playing a 'yokel' and prowling around the edges of the crowd.

Hare arrived, pretending 'to take great interest in the races', with some worries that the police on duty might arrest two of his men for gambling. They were quite safe. Lawless and Falkiner obviously knew a lot more about country race meetings than Hare did.

Aaron was cutting a spectacular figure, flashly dressed on a magnificent horse, and pointed out to Hare by several people as 'Kelly and Byrne's greatest friend'. They also asked why Hare didn't arrest Aaron 'for stealing the horse he was riding, as he could never afford to come honestly by such an animal'. Hare had bought the horse for the occasion a few days before. He 'pleaded ignorance about either man or horse'.

Falkiner, in between bellowing out the attractions of his Aunt Sally, had been studying Aaron. 'This was the man who was, I believed, to ride a horse for Byrne.' As Johnston came by on his horse, Falkiner remarked that, 'If this was the man, we could consider the information a hoax either on the part of Sherritt or Byrne...it was not at all likely that a man of twelve or thirteen stone was going to ride in a country hurdle race...'

In between cutting a 'flash' and generally enjoying himself, Aaron made sure for Hare's benefit to give the odd 'anxious' glance around the racecourse for the arrival of Joe and the black mare.

Paddy Byrne was back from seasonal work in New South Wales and, Hare noted, 'was a good deal with Aaron all that day'. Clearly, the disappearance of 'Charlie' was not yet troubling Paddy. Aaron later assured Hare that Joe was never mentioned.

The programme of races was slipping by and, as the time approached for the steeplechase, Lawless had the bright idea of abandoning the three-card table and riding his horse in the event as the best way of 'seeing everything all round the course'.

Just before the start of the steeplechase, Johnston saw three horsemen approaching. He, at least, was taking the whole thing seriously and, imagining them to be members of the Gang, clapped spurs to his thoroughbred and galloped towards the three newcomers. Falkiner caught Hare's eye. He shook his head. Quietly, they threaded their way out through the crowd as Johnston came riding back, 'terribly ashamed of himself'. Hare had been right about one thing—Johnston's impulsiveness.

Lawless won the steeplechase, but that was the only excitement for the rest of the day. Next night, after a second uneventful day's racing, they all attended a ball at a hotel near the racecourse, just in case the Gang 'put in an appearance' there.

After the ball, as they were making their way home, Hare asked Falkiner why he 'did not approve of the information he had received'. Johnston, an inveterate enthusiast in the Kelly pursuit, had obviously mentioned his colleague's misgivings. Falkiner repeated to Hare that no sane man would put a man of Aaron's size on a steeplechaser, adding that he 'could bowl Sherritt out in a week'. Hare drew himself up. 'You are very clever, Falkiner; how is it I have been sleeping with this man in the bush this last three weeks, and I cannot bowl him out?' Presumably, Falkiner had the good sense not to answer.

CHAPTER 12

The Strange Case of a Horse Called Charlie

April–July 1879

After the Whorouly diversion, Aaron returned to the nightly boredom of watching the Byrne house, now looking down at the glowing windows as an outsider, while increasingly aware of the cynicism of the rank-and-file police around him. They kept their thoughts to themselves, well aware of Hare's besotted belief in Aaron, and sensibly wary of a confrontation with this extraordinary man.

The end of the watch party, on or about 4 April, must have been as big a relief to Aaron as to everyone else. Now he could devote some time to his personal affairs—soured by the split with the Byrnes, his estrangement from Kate, and the uncomfortable revelation that a family member—probably Jack —had passed Joe's letter to Ward before he had seen it. Jack, always a competitor with Aaron, was now starting to play the same dangerous game. Aaron was making money from the police, so would he. Aaron was still in contact with the Gang, so was he. Jack was blundering on to the same narrow path that Aaron was carefully treading, and there was room only for one. Soon every adult in the Sherritt family except Willie would be actively helping the police, while apparently holding back from complete betrayal of the Gang.

Since the Gang's first contact with Aaron after the Stringybark killings, he does not appear to have confided in his family. Anne Sherritt was aware of the shots fired by the Kellys to attract Aaron's attention, but did not know that he had answered the signal. When Aaron started to play his curious double game, the family seem to have believed that he was genuinely acting as a police agent. According to an increasingly hostile Nicolson, they began to compete with Aaron for a share of the reward, while also receiving payment for their help or, more often, promises of help.

The family, to be codenamed 'Jones', first appears in police accounts on 10 March 1879, with a payment by Hare of £12 15s to 'The Sherritt family and others' for their 'promise to give information', with another £5 the following day. Only three days later 'The Sherritts and others' receive £10 for further promises of help, with another £5 on 24 March and £12 only two days later. On 1 April Jack (codenamed 'Jack Jones') receives £4 8s from Ward. Then over the next ten days, Standish makes three payments, totalling £25 to 'The Sherritts and Bruce [James Wallace]' with another payment of £5 from Hare on 15 April. In slightly more than a month the family had received a substantial share of £78 3s.

Yet Ward was to say, 'The Sherritt family were the easiest people I ever met about money,' a comment readily endorsed by Nicolson at a time when he had become a bitter antagonist to the family. Ward also reported that Jack Sherritt used to say, 'Ward you cannot afford it; I do not want money.'

It could be suspected that, despite their ongoing financial troubles, the Sherritts seemed disinterested in money because their eye was on the golden prize—a major share of the Kelly reward. Aaron showed a similar lack of avarice. Hare reports, 'I had not engaged him at any fixed salary, but whilst he was watching with me he used to ask me for a pound or two and I gave it to him. He often refused to take money from me, as he thought I was paying him out of my own pocket...and he only took sufficient to pay his expenses.' Hare recalled Aaron heading off for a couple of days, supposedly 'to look after some cattle'. When asked by Hare if he had enough money to tide him over, Aaron replied, 'I have a pound of the money you gave me last time.'

In the end, the Sherritt family's motivations are as elusive as Aaron's, particularly while Anne Sherritt retained Margret Byrne's complete trust and while Anne Jane and Julia continued their intimate friendship with the family.

On 6 April an anonymous correspondent who later called himself 'John Smith' wrote to 'Mr O'Hare, Commissioner of Police' with a tirade against Anne Jane and Julia, accused of carrying 'tucker' for the Gang, 'because they can ride and go over leaps like birds on the wing'. According to 'Mr Smith', the two Sherritt girls 'visits them often they would not tell on Kelly they are two of Kellys worst sympathisers they want locking up and the Kellys will soon be caught'.

Behind the indignation-cloaked admiration of these high-spirited girls was a core of disquieting news. 'Last Sunday', Anne Jane, Julia and Kate Byrne 'were all conversing very comfortable' at Sebastopol with Ned Kelly and Joe Byrne.

Ward did not see this letter until a year later when Nicolson referred it to him. As in 1879 Ward had a stake in the credibility of the cave party charade. Any suggestion that the two outlaws could visit the point of surveillance with complete freedom must be discredited. He set out to do this by claiming that on Sunday, 4 April 1880, Kate Byrne could not have been hobnobbing with Ned and the two Sherritt girls at Sebastopol because he had been talking with her in Beechworth, that she was driving her employer's buggy, and left to return to the Black Springs Hotel where she was 'at situation'.

Poor Ward didn't realise that the letter was a year old. 'Last Sunday' was 30 March 1879. His rebutting evidence was, on face value, weak, and, on examination, useless.

The letter had one last interesting piece of information. 'Kate Kelly visits the two Sherritt girls often'. Was Kate riding over to see Anne Jane and Julia, or seeing them on visits to Emma Crawford and, perhaps, Aaron? Certainly, it was this month, April 1879, that Aaron resumed wooing Kate with a view to marriage. Hare recorded that 'Aaron suggested to me that he would try Katie Kelly and see if she would engage herself to him.'

Aaron turned up at Eleven Mile Creek late in the month and, for the first time, met Kate's redoubtable older sister, Maggie Skillion. Aaron was riding the ex-Byrne gelding, Charlie and, reluctant to take the horse back to Beechworth, he asked Maggie if she'd like to buy it. Maggie wasn't interested but Aaron was so anxious to rid himself of this damaging piece of evidence, that he turned Charlie loose in the bush near the Kelly house and begged, borrowed or stole a horse to ride back home.

At some stage, Aaron had admitted to Maggie that he had taken Charlie from Mrs Byrne—hardly a strong selling point. Because of this, or perhaps from growing wariness of Aaron's police dealings, Maggie 'objected to his being about the place' and tried to discourage him from seeing Kate, but to no effect. Soon, Aaron's visits to Kate were known even to the Gang. Joe wrote to Aaron, 'You know you were at Kate's several times you had just gone one night as we came. We followed you four miles but returned without success.'

For a time, despite Maggie's disapproval, Aaron's courtship seemed successful. Hare records, 'Katie and he got on very well but she never mentioned her brother's name to him, nor he to her.' (Hardly likely but, clearly, Aaron didn't want to suggest that he was withholding any information from Hare, who continues.) 'They became great friends. One night, when Mrs Skillion went to see a friend, she left Katie and Aaron in the house together. Aaron induced Katie to come out for a walk with him, and when Mrs Skillion returned she found them both away. She was most indignant, and went to the nearest police station, Oxley, and laid some charges against Aaron. The police constable went to the Kellys' house, and when Aaron saw him coming up to the front door he bolted out the back way. The constable followed him and fired a couple of shots, but could not overtake him.'

Aaron was understandably rattled by the experience. Instead of heading for Benalla, only 10 miles away, he walked 18 miles to the home of James Wallace at Hurdle Creek and borrowed a horse. He then rode to Beechworth and told Ward what had happened, hoping to get help from Hare. No help was needed.

Maggie had laid a complaint of horse stealing against Aaron. Belatedly, the Oxley constable telegraphed Mullane at Beechworth to ask 'if a horse had been reported as stolen from Mrs Byrne at Sebastopol'. Mullane replied that 'there was no record in the police office of a horse having been stolen from Mrs Byrne'.

Once convinced by Hare and Ward that there was no charge against him, Aaron showed a surprising lack of ill will towards Maggie. He returned to Eleven Mile Creek on 1 May with another offer to sell Charlie. He stayed the night, Maggie thought it over, and eventually decided, yes, she would buy the horse. Next day Maggie, Aaron and Wild Wright rode out and found Charlie on the Fifteen Mile Creek. They took him to the Greta Hotel where a storeman duly drew up a receipt and witnessed Maggie's purchase of the gelding for £2.

Over the next week or so Margret Byrne became even more openly hostile towards Aaron and, apparently for the first time, threatened to prosecute him for the theft of Charlie. On the night of 13 May Aaron reappeared at Eleven Mile Creek, clearly shaken, anxious to give Maggie back her £2 and return Charlie to Mrs Byrne, 'who was going to give him five years'. By now thoroughly fed up with Aaron, Maggie refused.

On this visit, Aaron was accompanied by his friend, blacksmith Tom Straughair. As they were leaving, constables Arthur and Mountiford arrived, investigating this bewildering case. They found only Tom Straughair and Aaron's saddle. At the sight of the police, Aaron had galloped off, bareback.

Tom Straughair was also a close friend of Joe and Paddy. Perhaps as a result of what Tom learnt on this occasion, Paddy went to Greta and Constable Arthur showed him the recently purchased gelding and Maggie's receipt. Paddy identified the horse but held back from accusing Aaron of stealing it, well aware that Charlie was really a betrothal gift from Aaron to Kate, once removed. Paddy headed back to Sebastopol, apparently prepared to forget the whole thing, and Constable Arthur returned Charlie to Maggie.

But Margret Byrne was in a vengeful mood. On 31 May, two and a half months after missing the horse, she swore a complaint to Senior Constable Mullane and he issued a warrant. Aaron had vanished from Beechworth and the warrant was sent to Benalla.

On 11 June, Sadleir issued a Criminal Offence Report from his Benalla headquarters. He described Aaron as 'about 22 years, nearly 6 ft high, strong build. Brown hair and beard' and added, probably with some feeling, 'Well known to police of district.'

Aaron was now, officially, a fugitive from justice, prompting two approaches from the Kelly Gang to join them. On Thursday, 26 June 1879— one year to the day before Aaron's death—Joe wrote to his mate. This is the version of his letter that has come down to us.

Dear Aaron I write these few stolen lines to you to let you know that I am still living I am not the least afraid of being captured dear Aaron meet me you and Jack this side of Puzzel ranges Neddy and I has come to the conclusion to get you to join us I was advised to turn treater but I said that I would die at Ned's side first Dear Aaron it is best for you to join us Aaron a short live and a jolly one the Lloyds and Quinns wants you shot but I say no you are on our side If it is nothing only for the sake of your mother & sisters We sent that bloody Hart to your place twice did my mother tell you the message that I left for you I slept at home three days on the 24 of may did Patsy give you the booty I left for you I intend to pay old sandy doig and old Mullane Oh that bloody snob where is he I will make a targate of him meet me next thursday you and Jack and we will have another bank quite handy I told Hart to call last thursday evening I wold like to know if he obeyed us or not if not we will shoot him if you come on our tracks close your puss you know you were at Kates* several times you had just gone one night as we came we followed you four miles but returned without success If you do not meet me where I ask you meet me under london you know I will riddle that bloody Mullane if I catch him no more from the enforced outlaw till I see yourself

I remain yours truly
you know...

* A crossed-out word appears to be 'Citties'—an attempt to spell 'Kitty's'.

There is no signature and 'you know' is followed by a trailed-off scribble.

The letter is a total enigma. Joe's literacy seems to have deteriorated sharply since the Cameron and Jerilderie letters and even since the fly-leaf note smuggled out of Beechworth Gaol. While the handwriting displays some of Joe's characteristics (notably, an unusual capital 'D') it fails to show others (including the frequent up-sweeps at the ends of a word). The whole thing has the stamp of slow, slavish work. Groping for rationalisation, it could be claimed that Joe wrote the letter under abnormal conditions—perhaps while affected by opium or when his hands were very cold—and that the normally wide variation in his handwriting became further exaggerated.

It cannot explain why he would spell 'traitor' correctly in the Jerilderie Letter and come up with 'treater' six months later.

As a further unsettling detail, the letter is written on two sheets of the notepaper used at that time by Anne Sherritt—blue lined with an 'International' watermark. It is almost certainly a forgery. Yet it is, equally certainly, a letter handed to Detective Ward by Anne Sherritt on 1 July 1879. That day Ward arrived in Beechworth from Benalla to find a note waiting for him.

July 1st 1879
Sheepstation Creek

Mr Ward Dear Sir
I want to see you Immediately
I have some news of great
Importance

I remain yours
respectively
Mrs A. Sherritt
Sheepstation Creek

Mr Ward Please burn
my communication for
fear I might be found out

A S

Ward went to Sheepstation and was handed what purported to be the letter from Joe to Aaron. Anne told him that she had picked it up at the Reid's Creek post office 'and that Eldorado and Wangaratta postmarks were on it'. She did not produce the envelope. Interestingly, she did give Ward the gaol note written for Aaron by Joe three years before.

Ward seems to have some reservations about the letter—probably nourished by Anne's readiness to demonstrate its authenticity, and perhaps also by her anxiety to have her note to him destroyed.

He wrote to Hare (the report was received by Nicolson) 'You will be able to judge for yourself if the handwriting is alike, Mullane states that he could swear that the writing in the enclosed letter is Joe's writing.' Ward carefully avoids expressing an opinion.

What did Ward suspect? And where was Aaron? Had he seen the letter at this stage? If Anne Sherritt contacted Ward on Aaron's behalf—a reasonable line of action for a police agent who was also a fugitive from the law—why was she giving the detective a forgery?

The most likely explanation seems to be that Anne Sherritt was acting without Aaron's approval, though probably with his knowledge. Clearly, he had seen Joe's original letter, but refused to let it out of his hands. This then led Anne or another member of the family to write a copy *from memory* in a rather crude forgery of Joe's handwriting. Failure to produce the envelope suggests that Aaron kept it with the original letter, or that the envelope was held back by Anne because the forgery would have been exposed by such direct comparison.

This is all assumption, supposing that the *content* of the letter is genuine. Despite his reservations, Ward accepted that much and took 'we will have another bank quite handy' as a threat to the Beechworth banks. Further, he reported on 2 July, 'I will send Aaron to keep the appointment', also making it clear that he was in touch with this fugitive from the law. The following day, Thursday 3 July, Aaron claimed that he went to the meeting places but Joe did not turn up. Subsequent events were to suggest that Aaron lied and either avoided this meeting with his mate (which is unlikely) or didn't want to divulge his conversation with Joe.

There was much to talk about. Joe's 'I was advised to turn traitor' made it clear that Aaron had not canvassed this possibility with his mate. Did he now? And what was his reaction to the uncomfortable news that 'the Lloyds and Quinns wants you shot'? There were queries about messages sent via Margret Byrne and Steve Hart; and, more disturbingly, the question of 'booty' left with Paddy Byrne for Aaron.

Paddy Allen recalled, 'When they robbed the bank at Jerilderie Joe Byrne sent Aaron Sherritt £100 by another man. But Aaron says he never got it. Joe thought he did, though, and there was always trouble between them after that till Byrne went down and shot Sherritt. And when he shot him Byrne firmly believed that Sherritt had got the money. But I know he never did.'

Paddy Byrne didn't return from New South Wales until after Aaron had taken Charlie—well after the first signs of bad blood between Aaron and Margret Byrne. At this stage, it is easy to imagine Margret's hostile reaction to the news that Joe wanted Aaron to have £100. It is also easy to imagine mild Paddy being persuaded by his mother that they should keep the money, then taking the line of least resistance when he next saw Joe, claiming that he had given Aaron 'the booty'. Understandably, Joe would believe Paddy. Aaron's denial would form another splinter of doubt.

Twice in the body of his letter, Joe had written 'dear Aaron', trying hard to show that he wanted to keep their mateship alive. Yet this could be achieved only by Aaron agreeing to join the Gang. 'A short life and a jolly one.' In these words Joe showed that he had accepted the inevitability of his early death and was ready to 'die at Ned's side'. Why should Aaron condemn himself to an equally inevitable death when, in accepting the role of outlaw, he also sacrificed what still seemed the one chance of saving Joe's life? To throw in his lot with the Gang would mean death for them both. Did he try to make Joe understand that?

If Joe and Aaron met—and it's most probable that they did—they would have parted with an uncomfortable awareness of the chasm that was opening between them. A handclasp could still span the gap. But, as it widened, one must let go or they would drag each other to destruction.

It appears that Joe reported back to Ned and told him how he had failed to persuade Aaron to join them. One week later Ned and Joe returned to the Woolshed and the tableland. On the Thursday Joe and Paddy were seen on horseback near Sheepstation. Joe remained in the area overnight and was seen at his home the following day—recognised by Ah On, whose scarred face attested his reliability as a witness. Yet, on the Thursday afternoon, it was Ned who made the last attempt to demonstrate the Gang's belief in Aaron.

While Anne Sherritt was out, and two of her girls were looking after baby Hugh, Ned arrived at the Sherritt homestead. Anne describes what happened.

He said that he had a mob of cattle at the back of the hill, and that he wanted to get Aaron, as Aaron was a good bushman, to show him the way by the head of the King...He took the baby, a child of four or five months, in his arms and said that he was hungry. And there was some bread in the oven baking, and there was some dough in the dish, and he took some of the dough up, and he flattened it on the table and pulled out the fire with his foot and cooked two or three pieces...And then he made some tea, and said he was sending this tea up to his men that he had on the hill; and he had a flask of brandy in his pocket, and all the time he was inside he kept the baby in his arms, and he filled out a tumbler of brandy and put it on the cupboard, and told the children to give that to Aaron...and he would be back in a fortnight or three weeks...He said he believed there was a warrant out for Aaron, and the best thing he could do was to come along with them...

Ignoring Ned's 'cover' story of the cattle (for the benefit of the two girls who, obviously, didn't know him) this was a last, clear offer for Aaron to join the Gang. His failure to take up this invitation marked the beginning of final alienation from Ned and Joe—though both would be slow to believe the growing chorus of suspicion and open condemnation from 'the Lloyds and Quinns', from the other sympathisers and, probably, from Dan and Steve.

Out of the mess, Aaron could salvage some satisfaction. He knew that the watch parties had standard orders to try to take Joe prisoner. His agreement with Standish still stood—at least that far. Once Joe was captured, only Standish's political influence, for what it was worth, would save him from the gallows. As the realities of Aaron's life sank from under his feet, he clung to this fragment of hope, never to know that Standish had already betrayed him. The day before Jerilderie the Chief Commissioner had advised the Attorney General against a bargain to spare Joe's life.

While a brutal winter gripped the ranges, Aaron lived his fugitive life with occasional visits to his family and a handful of friends he trusted—a preciously small handful now that those with Byrne allegiances were against him. Among those still-trusted friends was his old school friend James Wallace.

After leaving Reid's Creek, Wallace had become a pupil teacher at the Eldorado Common School, to be appointed head teacher at Hurdle Creek in 1873. He married the following year and began to live beyond his means, a failing which contributed to his role in the coming tragedy.

The day after Ned had called at Sheepstation, Anne Sherritt sent word of his visit to Ward. The detective went to see her and found two other visitors— a draper calling about an unpaid bill and James Wallace. Anne Sherritt made them all a cup of tea while each man talked about everything but the real reason for his visit.

The next day when Anne Jane rode down to Sebastopol to see Paddy, Margret Byrne asked coolly how it was that the Sherritts 'were so friendly with Ward, the detective, to give him tea'. Anne Sherritt had no doubt that Wallace was her informant.

On another occasion, Wallace called at the Sherritt home at two in the morning and found Aaron sleeping in the hearth. Anne Sherritt heard 'that he told Mrs Byrne he could not make out what the Sherritts were doing, as he found Aaron in the ash corner'.

Wallace was playing a strange game.

He had approached Standish back in December 1878 with a proposal to become a police agent during his Christmas holidays. He supposedly operated in this capacity, as agent 'Bruce', for virtually all of 1879, writing lengthy letters later described by a Royal Commissioner as 'a perfect deluge of writing with not a particle of information in it'. Nicolson bluntly said that Wallace's Kelly intelligence was 'manufactured to raise money upon'.

It was certainly true, as Wallace admitted, that he was 'in financial difficulties' and that the £180 he supposedly made from the police in 'expenses' was very welcome. At the same time he was an active Kelly sympathiser. The Inspector General of the Education Department even suspected that he had helped in some alleged Kelly Gang hold-ups in December 1878. This notion was probably as groundless as the stories of the Kellys being involved, but the Inspector General's broader suspicions were confirmed by Ward and others. Wallace, like Aaron, was a double agent whose clearest loyalty was to the Gang. As such, he became another complicating factor in the already complex pattern of Aaron's dealings with the police and the Kellys.

Aware of Wallace's true allegiances, Ward combated his effectiveness as a Kelly agent by a simple expedient. He spoke freely in the district of Wallace being 'a detective' and made a point of telling Aaron that his old schoolmate was helping the police. Wallace had no doubt that 'if he [Aaron] knew that I was making enquiries about the outlaws he would put them on their guard, so as to prevent them from giving me any information'.

Interestingly, Wallace had played a similar game. One night, while drinking at Beechworth's Hibernian Hotel with Aaron and Ward, Wallace saw that Aaron had National Bank notes, which he admitted were 'portion of the notes taken from the Euroa bank'. Wallace drew Ward's attention to one of the notes, later claiming that this was to put the detective 'on his mettle'. Clearly, he was trying to discredit Aaron in Ward's eyes as a police agent. With the same intention, he repeatedly reported to Nicolson that Aaron had Sergeant Kennedy's watch. His influence on the Gang's view of Aaron can only be guessed at.

In the end Ward's strategy succeeded and the two double agents, whose basic loyalties were to the Gang, became mutually suspicious. Wallace was a last contact with the old life. When Aaron could no longer depend on

Wallace, there was only his family. And when they were gone, Ward. He could not have imagined such a future, even if moved to try. As ever, he lived day by day, now driven further into unreality by his lonely and furtive life.

Hare, running himself to a standstill with his wintry wild goose chases, watched Aaron's troubles from Benalla, and noted that his men, though 'delighted to hear that there was a warrant out for his arrest', couldn't find Aaron.

On Saturday, 21 June, the Eldorado police were alerted that Aaron had been home for the past week. Two troopers watched the Sherritt house all through a freezing night and, at daybreak, hurled themselves on the tall, young man who emerged. It was Jack. While the police dragged him off to be identified, Aaron slipped away.

Hare was 'greatly annoyed' with Aaron because this cat-and-mouse game 'crippled his usefulness immensely', eventually recording, 'When I was relieved from the district I left it to my successor to get him out of his difficulty.'

Captain Standish, bored with the Kellys, the winter and north-eastern society, had headed back to the fleshpots of Melbourne on 16 June. Hare followed on 3 July, his health and spirit broken by endless and aimless pursuit. Nicolson, who had left in a similar state seven months before, returned to Benalla to inherit a demoralised and depleted force—and the problem of Aaron as a fugitive from justice.

Nicolson's strategy was simple and pragmatic. Hare's wild pursuits had been expensive. Now, Nicolson had fewer men, less money. So he scaled down field operations, giving an impression of waning effectiveness and enthusiasm for the chase and so encouraging the Gang to become careless. At the same time, he built up a small, effective network of spies.

Nicolson the detective was back in power and Ward the detective was in power with him. No more being crammed in a buggy boot under the great bulk of Hare.

Probably through storekeeper Paddy Allen, Ward made contact with Aaron and urged him to face trial. Aaron came to realise there was no alternative; that as long as he remained in hiding, his land, his effectiveness as a Kelly agent, his ability to save Joe's life—all were jeopardized. But he wasn't prepared to surrender. Instead, Ward contrived an arrest by Constable Mullane—arranging for a 'coincidental' encounter in the bush. The arrest took place on Monday, 14 July, apparently without Mullane knowing of the set-up. Aaron was taken into Beechworth, charged, and locked up overnight, to appear in court the following morning before Police Magistrate Foster.

Inspector Brooke Smith prosecuted and applied for a seven-day remand to gather witnesses. Appearing for Aaron, Frederick Brown agreed to the remand and gained his client bail on two securities of £25.

The next day Aaron and Jack met Ward. The night of Aaron's arrest, Jack claimed that he had gone down to the Byrnes 'and stole up to the house and listened to Mrs Byrne and Paddy talking about the arrest of Aaron. Mrs Byrne said Joe would likely call home when he would hear of Aaron's arrest and that he [Paddy] should keep a good look out for which way he might come.'

Ward wanted to establish a three-man party in Aaron's hut and watch the Byrne house from Saturday night until after the trial on Tuesday. His idea was that Jack would accompany the watching police, something Aaron would not have wanted. Jack would too easily recognise the futility of watching the Byrne house only from the front.

Remarkably, Ward and Nicolson had plans for Aaron to be charged at his court appearance with 'aiding and abetting the outlaws on the 14th of June 1879 with arms and ammunition'—apparently as a device to restore his credibility as Kelly sympathiser. Constable Hayes of Myrtleford was to appear as witness. To make the whole thing doubly credible, Ward devised an extraordinary plan by which Aaron would default on his bail provisions—bringing about a repeat performance of the arranged arrest by Mullane.

Ward wrote to Nicolson on 17 July, 'I have made an arrangement with Aaron to have him arrested on Monday afternoon, he would be at the Woolshed Mullane to see him he will mount his horse and ride away Mullane of course will follow & then the chase will take place, this will be well circulated and the papers would take it up very warm...this is my suggestion and only requires your approval to be carried into execution.'

Alternatively, Ward suggested that the new charge could simply be brought against Aaron when he surrendered to his bail.

Ward finished his curious memo to Nicolson with an even more curious addendum. 'Since writing the above I have heard a rumour that I was about to be suppoenaed [sic] as a witness in the case. If so I would rather be out of the district as I cannot stand the test...'

None of Ward's plans came to fruition. There was no chase, no charge of aiding the outlaws, no subpoena for Ward.

In the intervening days Inspector Brooke Smith, who was prosecuting, telegrammed Nicolson, seeking approval for another remand, but received a curt reply, 'Sherritt's a police prosecution inconvenient to detain witnesses by remand therefore go on.'

On the back of the telegram, Brooke Smith noted to Mullane, 'I shall proceed on good grounds...' and finished, with characteristic paranoia, 'Have arrivals by train tonight watched!'

The case attracted enormous interest. On Tuesday a crowd of 200 thronged around the Beechworth Court, eager to catch a glimpse of Aaron, Mrs Byrne, Maggie Skillion and Kate Kelly who had come from Tarrawingee the previous night. The packed gallery was disappointed. Aaron's counsel, Frederick Brown, had been detained in Albury and, despite Brooke Smith's opposition, Mr Zincke, for Mrs Byrne, obtained a remand to the following Saturday, saying that Aaron would pay the expenses of witnesses 'remaining a few days'.

A correspondent of the Melbourne *Herald* noted, 'Sherritt is a young man about 25 years of age, tall and good-looking, of a very "horsy" appearance. He appears quite confident as to his defence.'

In Melbourne it was noted that a much-travelled Kate Kelly caught the Friday afternoon train back to Beechworth. Saturday morning's *Advertiser* reported, 'Much public interest is centred in the case, as it is expected that some disclosures with reference to the past movements of the outlaws will be made. Kate Kelly, sister to the principal outlaw, together with Mrs Skillion, nee Margaret Kelly, another sister, arrived in Beechworth last evening, the former from Melbourne, and the latter from Greta, where she resides.'

The day was dark and threatening. Proceedings began at eleven, again with Police Magistrate Foster on the bench.

Margret Byrne told the story of Charlie disappearing from her home and was at pains to deny an *Advertiser* report that she was Aaron's aunt. Paddy told how the horse had gone missing during his absence and that he had next seen it at Greta. Maggie told how she bought Charlie from Aaron, and the Greta Hotel storeman described the purchase. Mullane testified that he had arrested Aaron (oddly, dating the event as the day *after* Aaron's first court appearance). It seemed an open and shut case.

Aaron's Counsel, Frederick Brown, now called Ellen Byron (formerly Ellen Salisbury, an old sweetheart of Joe), who, three years before, had witnessed 'a transaction' in which Aaron gave Kate Byrne a filly and told her 'she was not to sell or chop it or he would have another in its place'. Willie Sherritt corroborated this evidence. Jack Sherritt then told the court that he had heard a heated exchange between Aaron and Mrs Byrne over police horses being kept in Aaron's paddock. Aaron had asked her if she was going to pay him for the filly he had given Kate, and Mrs Byrne said, 'Yes, I'll give you the horse Charlie, and take it away.' James Dawson, labourer, confirmed Jack's story.

The gallery was treated to some spirited cross-examination. In the course of a series of dogged denials, Margret Byrne said that she had not seen Charlie in Aaron's paddock, adding, with characteristically sharp tongue, 'I would not have been surprised to see anything in his paddock. I put a cow in it once, but it was home as soon as myself.'

There were probably a few chuckles at this shot. But the court was hushed as she said, 'We had a falling out about his giving the police assistance. I never said to his brother that if he left the colony I would withdraw the charge.' Sitting in the dock, Aaron may have met those pale blue eyes as she said coldly, 'I thought that Sherritt was giving assistance to the police in the pursuit of the bushrangers.'

The trial ended with anti-climactic abruptness. Brown concluded, 'That is the defence, your worship.' Magistrate Foster simply said 'The prisoner is discharged.'

A reporter from the Melbourne *Herald* hurriedly wrote his story and telegraphed it to Melbourne to catch that evening's paper. His piece concluded, 'Mrs Skillion claimed the horse and took it with her, leaving Mrs Byrne her civil remedy.'

Margret Byrne was left with much more—bitterness at having lost, a conviction that the police had conspired to save Aaron, perhaps a sense of violation at having her personal dealings paraded in front of the gallery. But at the same time there must have been some cold satisfaction. She had told the world that Aaron was helping the police. The people of Melbourne would read her remarks that evening, those people of Beechworth who hadn't heard or been told in the intervening days would read them in Tuesday's *Advertiser*. Aaron Sherritt had been denounced as a traitor by the mother of one of the Kelly Gang.

On Monday Inspector Brooke Smith packed up the prosecution brief and sent it down to Nicolson, with a memo summarising the case. He concluded, 'The witness James Dawson is an entirely disinterested witness and bears an excellent character. I am satisfied in my own mind that this witness was truthful.'

The police hadn't rigged the case to save their agent from gaol, but who would believe it?

CHAPTER 13

Tangled Web

August–December 1879

For the rest of the year, the behaviour of Joe and Aaron is totally erratic—if we believe our sources.

In a bewildering series of shifts, Joe writes two threatening letters to Aaron within a matter of days, then meets him less than a week later. Aaron does not report the encounter, yet supposedly reports a return visit by Ned Kelly to the Sherritt homestead the day after it happened. The day before Aaron tells the police of this appearance, Joe visits his mother. Aaron reports this another ten days later. Two months after this Joe appears at the Sherritt house, shakes hands with everyone, including Aaron, and invites Jack and Aaron to help rob a Beechworth bank. This incident is reported to the police by Jack, not Aaron. About a week later Joe and Aaron are seen together at Sebastopol, when Aaron is supposedly helping the police watch the Byrne house. Aaron does not report the meeting.

In all but two cases Ward is our source for this curious chain of events. Throughout, he demonstrated a highly politicised view of what should or should not be revealed to his superiors, and filtered material accordingly.

But two of the most contradictory incidents of the scenario—Aaron's failure to report a meeting with Joe less than a week after a written threat, and his unreported meeting while engaged with a police watch party—are directly from Aaron, confiding in Nicolson, and Jack, addressing the Royal Commission.

So, while Ward undoubtedly played a significant role in editing reports—to the point of serious distortion—he isn't totally to blame for the psychological slalom described above.

The Sherritt family certainly confused the issue with their curious game-playing, though this was abandoned when Mrs Sherritt and Jack became genuinely terrified. We are left with disquieting glimpses of Aaron and Joe in a strange state of mutual wariness and indecision.

While our view of Joe and Aaron in these months is fragmentary, distorted, two other figures emerge in comparative clarity—Jack Sherritt and

James Wallace. Both played significant roles in the deteriorating relationship between Joe and Aaron. And both were manipulated by Detective Mick Ward.

On the evening of Saturday, 16 August, Wallace met Ward on the road to Beechworth and promised to 'have an interview' with the detective later that night. Wallace failed to appear, but the following day turned up at Sheepstation Creek (significantly, described by Ward as 'Mrs Sherritt's'). Ward reported to Nicolson, 'He told Mrs Sherritt that his brother-in-law saw Ned Kelly on the Sunday night previous going in the direction of Greta he wore a brown over coat grey tweed trousers leggings & soft felt hat and rode Joe Byrns grey horse', a curiously detailed—and accurate—description for a supposedly third-hand account.

Ward continues, 'He would not tell Aaron anything, he accused Aaron of trying to sell and hang Joe Byrns, he said he would sell the other three but Joe Byrns he would not sell for eight thousand pounds.'

Aaron claimed that he rode four miles with Wallace on his way home. 'Aaron told Wallace that what he had done was to try and get a pardon for Joe Byrns, Wallace replied and said it is no use I have been to Mr Graves Member of Parlement he told me there is no reprief for Joe Byrns when he is caught he will be hanged,—strict watch will be kept on sabastapool Aaron is still in great hopes—'

The following Saturday Wallace drove his buggy to Beechworth on a shopping expedition, which was carefully documented by Ward. 'He bought a bag of bread and a case of brandy, half a dozen pocket-handkerchiefs, one bottle of scent, and a package of arsenical soap'. It was an extraordinary shopping list for a young married man with money troubles and Ward clearly regarded this unlikely collection as supplies for the Gang.

Wallace met Aaron by appointment and told him 'he came to see him to go to Melbourne with him, to try and get Graham Berry and the Marquis of Normanby to sign a reprieve for Joe Byrne by giving information to the police where the other three were to be caught. He said he would arrange everything if Tommy would go with the police, but he should get two thousand pounds of the reward, and cautioned Aaron if it could be arranged that he should take good care not to go as a target to the front.'

Ward's memo to Nicolson documents extraordinarily detailed proposals supposedly made by Wallace about 'laundering' the Kelly Gang's gold.

He said Byrne is treasurer and confidential for the gang; that their money is running short; they have only five hundred pounds and the gold. He wanted Aaron to go to Chiltern or Wodonga to sell the gold for him, and he would be well paid for it. Aaron refused, and said he was too well known to Sergeant Lynch, of Chiltern. He said he had 50 or 80 ozs.; that it would be melted down into 20-oz. pieces. He suggested to get a man with Aaron to go digging in the Stony Creek, near Beechworth, for a week or so, and then they could sell the gold.

Wallace said that Joe had called at his house two nights before, claiming 'that he wanted him to see Aaron and find out if he [Aaron] was after them yet; if so, tell him he would know the consequences'. Most remarkably, Ward reported, 'He wanted Aaron to shoot Ward, and it would be left on the Byrnes.'

In an intriguing tit-for-tat, Aaron now reported that Wallace had 'nineteen or twenty' National Bank notes and spent 'seven or eight pounds' during the night. The two drank together, spent the night at the Imperial Hotel and rode to Sheepstation early next morning. Wallace left for home about midday and, again, Aaron rode with him as far as the Golden Ball hotel.

On Saturday Ward had 'several' drinks with Wallace before he met Aaron and sounded out his views on the idea of saving Joe's life.

'It came down to this—the pardon of one to catch the other three.'

The week before Wallace had told Aaron that the proposition was hopeless, that Joe would hang, and he now reiterated to Ward, 'It can't be done.' Yet later that night he proposed this very plan to Aaron.

From all this, only one thing is certain. Aaron no longer trusted Wallace, and Wallace no longer trusted Aaron. Each would do what he could to warn the Gang against the other. Ward had divided, and conquered, but not completely.

The following Friday Aaron rode across to Wallace's place, supposedly to complete arrangements for the sale of the Kelly gold. When Ward had heard nothing by Monday, he went in search of Aaron, who eventually appeared on the Thursday, 'with very little news'.

During Aaron's absence, a letter from Joe Byrne reached the Beechworth police, containing threats to Aaron, Mullane and Ward, 'warning them of mischief before that day month', and, said Ward, 'offering a reward of eight thousand pounds for the apprehension and delivery in Wombat Ranges of Captain Standish, Senior Constable Mullane and myself'.

It transpired that the letter had been posted by Jack Sherritt, after being handed to him by Joe Byrne. Under threat of being shot if he revealed the truth, Jack told Ward that he had received it from an unidentified agent of the Gang.

Aaron told Ward that, from the description of this agent, he believed him to be 'Jack Fox, a particular friend of the Byrnes'. Ward's patience was running out. He reported to Nicolson, 'I am not at all satisfied with Tommy's tale. I am of the opinion that he has seen Joe Byrne himself, and most likely he is the identical person who gave the letter to Jack to post, and kept out of the way until yesterday himself.'

Immediately after this damning indictment of his chief agent, Ward goes on to tell Nicolson, 'He [Aaron] assures me that we will get them, and that before long.' Two days after this Aaron was paid by Ward to keep an appointment with Wallace at Chiltern on Friday evening 'to meet a person who knows where Joe can be seen'. The next day Aaron met Joe. He did not tell Ward, but mentioned the meeting in an interview with Nicolson ten days later.

As Aaron, understandably, slipped out of favour with Ward and Nicolson, Jack Sherritt was cultivated as a police agent. In a supreme irony, Aaron's decline in favour with Ned and Joe meant that Jack was courted by them as an agent and scout. He was quickly out of his depth.

Jack met Nicolson at the Wangaratta Agricultural Show on 12 September and was immediately engaged as a police agent. Jack quickly established regular contact with Joe, writing letters which Anne Jane gave to Paddy Byrne for delivery, then brought back Joe's replies. This correspondence produced a staggering '50 or 60' letters from Joe, all passed on to Ward.

After Jack had delivered the threatening letter, Joe sent Jack some carica-tures 'for posting up' around Beechworth, 'themselves represented on paper shooting police, and all that sort of thing'. Jack gave these to Ward and he put them up to help establish Jack's bona fides with the Gang.

On Friday, 19 September, Joe called home and left £2 in silver which Anne Jane brought up to Jack. So far so good. Paid by the Kellys and police, Jack's career as double agent was booming.

For a time it seemed that Aaron may have escaped the dangerous intrigue between the outlaws and their pursuers. His life took a new and apparently brighter turn. Five months after his aborted courtship of Kate Kelly, he found a new love.

Ellen Barry was fifteen, a tall, handsomely built Woolshed girl with red hair and a strongly Irish face. She was the oldest and prettiest of the Barry daughters and her nickname, Belle, honoured her looks.

After leaving Cornelius O'Donoghue's school (she had been in the Infants during Joe's last year in Fifth Class), Belle got a job as general maid with stationer James Ingram and his wife at their superbly sited home near Ingram's Rock where the road from Beechworth began its winding descent to the Woolshed.

Mrs Ingram was an exacting mistress—a redoubtable Scotswoman who had walked the 170 miles from Melbourne to Beechworth because she considered the public transport 'verminous'. She wore a plain frock in the morning and a silk one in the afternoon and, on special occasions, added a sash of Robertson tartan, affectionately damned by her as 'the oldest and ugliest'.

Belle worked in a black and white uniform, with a different cap and apron for mornings and afternoons, and slept in an austere little room off the kitchen. She had an afternoon and evening off each week.

After the easygoing Irish ways of the Woolshed, the ordered, scrubbed, and starched world of the Scots Baptist Ingrams demanded levels of discip-line and conformity quite beyond this high-spirited girl. Mrs Ingram found Belle 'untidy and incompetent' and reluctantly sacked her.

Soon after this setback, Belle met Aaron. Strange to say, their paths had never crossed, although in the small world of the Woolshed, she knew Joe, her mother had delivered Mrs Byrne's last two children, her father, miner Ned Barry, had been on the school council with Joe's Uncle John, and her brother went to school with Denny Byrne.

To Belle, Aaron was a glamorous figure, flashly dressed, well mounted, free-spending, boldly defying every level of Beechworth society as Kelly agent or police spy—and still flaunting both personae, wearing his chin strap under his nose Kelly fashion, as he paraded down Ford Street in a brown velvet dinner jacket given him by Superintendent Hare.

It was a springtime romance, which began as tiny, red spider orchids were unfolding on the hillsides, and was in full flower before the creamy, mid-summer blossoms of wedding bush.

Within two months of meeting Belle, Aaron proposed and was accepted.

Meanwhile, Jack was proving altogether too successful as a double agent. Anne Jane brought him a letter from Joe, 'short written, quick', asking Jack to meet him on Thursday, 5 November, at Thompson's farm on Sandy Creek near Peechelba.

Nicolson instructed him to keep the appointment and, with some misgivings, Jack rode over to Sandy Creek on the Thursday to find that Thompson was 'gone twelve months'. Sure that he had been watched on the way there, Jack had a long and nervy wait at the derelict farm among lengthening shadows, and camped the night. At 10 or 11 next morning, as he was riding back home along a scrubby track through the Warby Ranges, a man sprang from the bush and called him.

Jack swung around to see Joe on the track. 'He had no horse, but he had a pair of long boots, and his trousers were all over blood. He had long spurs.' Joe signalled Jack to follow and led him into the scrub until they were out of sight of the track.

In the course of a long and friendly conversation, Joe spoke glowingly of Hare as 'a bloody smart old cove', told Jack that search parties had nearly caught the Gang once, and that they were 'bloody well starved out'. Asked by Joe if he knew Nicolson, Jack said that he 'knew no-one'. Joe's mind 'appeared burdened about the murder of Sergeant Kennedy'.

Eventually, Joe came to the purpose of the meeting. He wanted Jack to scout the Yackandandah bank for the Gang, 'See how many police were stationed there, and see if I could detect any in private clothes, and loaf around and see where the police went in to have tea, and particulars about their movements.'

Joe told Jack 'that he was short of cash at present, but when he got the bank, he would give me a hundred or two'. Jack asked where the rest of the Gang were and was told 'not very far off'.

Jack arranged to meet Joe at Evans Gap on Sunday, 23 November, and thankfully rode on his way, with an even stronger sense that he was being watched.

Jack reported the meeting to Nicolson the following day and was appalled when the Scot did nothing beyond instructing him to keep this appointment with Joe and tell him it was too dangerous to stick up the Yackandandah bank. Jack had uncomfortable visions of riding with the Gang into a police trap or, if he tried to avoid joining them, being hunted by the Gang.

His fears seemed confirmed the following Thursday. Late in the afternoon he was working in Crawford's paddock, about a quarter of a mile from the Sherritt homestead, when one of the girls arrived with news that Dan Kelly had come looking for him and had searched through the house, revolver in hand. Dan had eventually left, saying he would be back at eight o'clock. If Jack had returned, a candle was to be left burning in a window.

Fearful that Dan had come to take him at gunpoint, Jack waited until dusk, caught his horse, and rode the four miles into Beechworth at a flat gallop. As he clattered down the hill of Ford Street, towards the police station, he claims that he saw by the clock in the post office tower that it was not yet seven o'clock.

He blurted out his news to Ward and Nicolson. He claims they wanted him to return to keep the appointment with Dan. He flatly refused. Jack was to swear on oath that this exchange took place at 7.30, giving time for a police party to reach Sheepstation before Dan's return.

At eight o'clock, while Jack was still supposedly arguing with Nicolson and Ward, the entire Kelly Gang appeared at Sheepstation, four miles away.

Eventually, seeing that Jack was worrying himself into a state of near collapse, Ward gave him half a sovereign and told him to ride down to Julian's shanty in the Woolshed, to 'play drunk and create a row and have it talked about' to explain his absence from Sheepstation.

Later, Nicolson claimed that he hadn't seen Jack until nine o'clock and that he didn't leave for Julian's until eleven. If this was true, Jack's half-sovereign's worth of drinking would have provided a very unconvincing alibi for his absence from home more than three hours earlier.

If, however, Jack did tell the truth (Nicolson's evidence on the starting time of their conversation was not corroborated by Ward or Mullane), it seems that Nicolson's 'softly, softly' approach had been taken rather too far. Certainly, Jack seems to have been completely disillusioned by the incident. His experience in negotiating the treacherous swamp of no-man's-land between outlaws and police was not yet over.

Ten days later on Sunday, 23 November, the Sherritt dogs started barking at about 6 p.m. They barked intermittently until 8 p.m. when Joe arrived.

Described as 'well dressed', he shook hands with all the family, including Aaron. He thanked Jack for his work in the past month and explained that Dan's visit ten days before had been to cancel the meeting at Evans Gap.

His main purpose for the visit was to ask Jack and Aaron to join the Gang in holding up one of the Beechworth banks. He and Ned couldn't agree on a plan. His own plan was to enter a bank at night, and stick up the manager 'in or out of bed'. If he did not have the necessary keys, one of the Gang and one of the Sherritt boys would go with Joe to find the employee in charge of the keys and get them, 'even if blood was shed'. One of the Sherritts and one of the Gang would remain with the banker until the safe was rifled, and Joe would then ride off with the haul.

Aaron and Jack agreed to take part in the hold-up.

In the course of a four-hour conversation, Joe told the family that the Gang's horses were bad, but Music was still the best. One of the girls raised the eternal possibility of him betraying the other members of the Gang to gain his pardon. He replied, 'People would say I was worse than Sullivan [a New Zealand murderer who had turned Queen's Evidence on his accomplices] and hunt me out of the colony'.

Joe said that the police were tired of watching his mother's home. Ironically, this visit would encourage renewal of the watch parties. To the Sherritts, 'he looked as if fretting' and appeared to have lost weight. They thought he was now less than ten stone.

Joe left at midnight, saying he would return the following Sunday.

Four days later the interview was reported to the police, according to Jack by 'my mother, or sister, or Aaron'. Ward identified Jack as the informant.

A subsequent interview with Nicolson saw Jack topple from favour as a police agent. In the face of Jack's obsessive fear that the Gang would kidnap him and force him to work as a scout, Nicolson had Jack—and Aaron—photographed, so the portraits could be circulated to police. Nicolson also advised Jack to sleep in the garden so he couldn't be surprised at night. All this did nothing to calm Jack's fears. Two years later he told Nicolson, 'You were under the impression, when you got my portrait taken, that I could lead all those outlaws to a bank, and first inform you and the bank, and then you would be waiting there with the police and catch them; and I would not do it, I told you, because I would be shot myself; I would not do it.'

Nicolson tried to deny that he had ever envisaged such a plan, but admitted, 'I saw he had not nerve to go, and was not fit to go with them,' later telling a Royal Commission, 'I can hardly convey to you what a coward this man Sherritt is.'

By contrast, Aaron showed no fear of joining the Kellys and seems to have gone along with Nicolson's plans. The 'cranky Scotchman' reported, 'I had no objection to their taking Aaron on a ride into New South Wales, I arranging that he would send back a telegram stating where he was going...'

For a time, Aaron was back in favour. The following Wednesday, 3 December, a cave party was re-established to watch the Byrne house. Aaron would accompany a four-man team which, because of the tedious and physically taxing nature of the work, was to be changed weekly. Even then, the morale and physical well-being of the party was to be a constant problem, at least one man coming down with severe rheumatism. Yet Aaron would continue, week in, week out, seven days a week, earning his seven shillings a day.

CHAPTER 14

'Strategic Movements and Well-laid Plans'

1879–80

Aaron's coming marriage to Belle had created its own problems. The match was bitterly opposed by the Sherritts, supposedly because Belle was Catholic. No such bitterness seemed to have arisen over the romance of Aaron with Kate Byrne, or Elizabeth with Joe, or Anne Jane with Paddy. Protestant–Catholic bigotry never clouded the close and long-standing relationships of the two families.

According to Jack, when Aaron said he was marrying Belle, he told him, 'What is the good? You will have to mix up with your wife's sisters or brothers, and very likely they will be going to the cave, and the house, and Byrne's sister and brothers go to school.'

Belle had her own views: 'His people said they were vexed about the religion, but I did not think it; I think it was because he left off working for them.'

She was clearly quoting Aaron, who had expressed similar views to Mrs Barry. 'Aaron…always said it was not the religion that was up with him. He used to say that they did not seem to him so very religious—he said they got very religious all at once…He used to say it was not that; it was just because he left them and got married.'

The fact remains that Aaron quarrelled over the marriage with his mother and father and 'was especially bad friends with his brother John'. Perhaps this rift in the family meant Ward's friendship became all the more to be valued. Ward set up an account with Joseph Wertheim, publican of the Hibernian Hotel, so that Aaron could have a meal when he came to Beechworth on police business. Payments of cash, occasional accommodation and purchases of tobacco, cigars and brandy were also provided via Wertheim. With regular payment for the cave party on top of all this, the strange limbo of the double agent's life had its compensations, and Aaron lived, day by day, in some unhappy illusion of luxury, hazed by Havana smoke and the heady vapours of Joseph Wertheim's best brandy.

Aaron began a strange seven months in which he played on the watch party stage by night, grabbed what little sleep he needed in the dawn hours, and tried to shape some semblance of a normal life during the day, clinging to the reality of his land, and his imminent marriage. His role was made harder by the increasing cynicism of the rank-and-file police who worked with him. But they remained unaware of the true depth of his allegiance to Joe.

Each night, as it grew dark, Aaron supposedly took up his position alone, watching the front of the Byrne homestead, before being joined by the four men of the watch party at 'eight or nine'. It was probably in this unmonitored early part of the evening, almost immediately after the establishment of the party on 3 December, that he appeared with Joe in E Fang's store in the main Chinese camp at Sebastopol.

Joe and Aaron 'got a bottle of gin and some tobacco, and something else, and went away'.

The next day, while Jack Sherritt was delivering a load of bark nearby, he called in at the store and was told by E Fang, 'Last night me see Ah Joe come along with Ah Jim to the store.'

Jack later surmised that Joe's companion must have been Ned Kelly: Aaron could not have been there, he suggested, because 'the police knew where he was with them this night'. Jack was apparently unaware that Aaron watched alone in the early evening. There could be no doubt about Joe being there, Jack said, 'because the Chinese knew him well, because he used to pelt them and hammer them with stones'. Yet the Chinese knew Aaron equally well and, in fact, he was the one who had thrown the stone or stick that seriously injured Ah On. It is inconceivable that E Fang mistook the identity of the man with Joe.

In this display of his true loyalties, Aaron spent his time with Joe then may have walked with him across the footbridge, past the scene of the clash with Ah On, along the creek bank, below the single Chinese hut and its garden, past the dam where they bathed together, until they were in sight of the house where Aaron was no longer welcome.

What did they speak of, and how did they part? With growing awareness of the real world slipping from beneath their feet? Of their friendship warping under the stresses of the role that each had chosen to play? Was there any sense of an ending in their handclasp before Joe slipped along the sheltering bank of the water race and Aaron walked up through the scrub towards the stockyard?

If Aaron called home on Christmas Day, it was probably the last time he saw his father. The next day he and Belle were to be married. All his money had been squandered on his free-spending courtship and his need to convince Belle that he had 'plenty of money'. Aaron faced his wedding day with something more than a groom's traditional nervousness.

Boxing Day dawned 'beautifully clear and fine' and, as Aaron rode into Beechworth, astir early for a day of carnival, the white streets were shimmering with latent heat. Already sweating in Sunday best jacket, collar and tie, he knocked up one of the last people he could turn to for help, storekeeper Paddy Allen, who recalled the near-panic of Aaron's opening words.

'Allen,' he said, 'What am I to do? I'm going to be married, and I haven't got a cent; and she thinks I've got plenty. Can you help me?' Well, I gave him about twenty pounds, and went to the Presbytery with him. I may say that I gave him stores beside the money. 'How much shall I give the priest?' he asked me. I told him that was a thing that had to be done properly. Well, I think he wanted to hand over fifteen pounds, but I think the fee paid was less than that.

Because Catholic Belle was marrying a Protestant, the marriage was celebrated 'behind the altar', in the austere parlour of Father Tierney's presbytery, beside St Joseph's Church. Official witnesses were Thomas Anderson and Eliza Woman, probably friends of Belle. Her parents and younger brothers and sisters were also undoubtedly there.

Conscious of the difference in their ages, Belle told the priest she was 17 (actually 15) while Aaron claimed he was 23 (he had turned 24 in August). Tierney had Edmond Barry's written consent for the marriage and it was no concern of his, merely a detail for the government certificate, which Aaron signed with agonising slowness, to run out of ink halfway through his surname. Immediately below, Belle scrawled her signature with bold self-assurance.

The wedding party walked out into the blazing sunshine of the day as a crowd of 2,000 lined nearby Ford Street to watch the Beechworth and Chiltern fire brigades compete in hose and reel contests.

Aaron, Belle and the Barrys may have laughed with the crowd as a Chiltern team drenched itself, and cheered Beechworth's win. If they then followed the crowd to a sports meeting at the racecourse, they saw Jack Sherritt's spirited performance in the Beechworth Handicap, decided over four foot races of 100, 440, 200 and 300 yards. Jack won the 440 and gained third place overall—worth a prize of £2 10s. In between handicap events, Jack took second place in the 150 yard hurdles and scored another pound.

Aaron and Belle probably spent their wedding night at the Hibernian Hotel as townsfolk romped their way through a ball in the nearby Oddfellows Hall, until the early hours of Saturday. They spent a two-day honeymoon at Aaron's little hut like a couple of children playing house, happily marooned with their windfall of stores from Paddy Allen. Then, on the Monday, Aaron left Belle at sunset and headed off to the Byrne homestead.

His three-day absence from the watch party sparked problems. Food supplies had been delayed (Jack had gone to Melbourne, running at another athletics meeting), and the men's wariness of Aaron was intensified by resentment. Constable Barry sent a note to Ward saying that he wanted to be relieved, and that the presence of the cave party was known. He said later, 'I did not consider it safe. The Sherritt family were rowing among themselves, and I wanted to get out of it.' He told Ward there was 'something crooked' about the whole thing.

Ward hastily soothed the situation, urging Barry, 'Mr Sadleir is here, so keep quiet' and, later, 'I would strongly advise all you boys to be kind to Moses for your own sake. Mr Nicolson is rather particular, and it would be unwise to quarrel on this duty.'

Barry took this as a clear statement from Ward that he wanted no talk of lax security, that the men were 'to keep quiet, and to hold our tongues and not to say anything about it'. This was Ward's first attempt to suppress the fact that the existence of the cave party was known. Later, he would actually falsify reports from constables who believed that the Byrne family knew they were there.

The watch parties had begun as charades staged by Aaron. They had become charades staged by Ward—some believed, with the purpose of putting money into the pocket of his friend, Paddy Allen, at the rate of £30 a month or, as Aaron suggested to a constable, merely, 'to show we were doing something'. A member of parliament would be told, 'Detective Ward expressed himself on several occasions to some of his friends in Beechworth, previous to the party going out, that he knew there was nothing in it, but he must do something to curry favour with Nicolson.' The parliamentarian's informant was also to say, 'Fancy a man in his proper senses engaging Aaron Sherritt to sell the outlaws. Why, he would rather cut his arm off.'

Earlier that year, in strikingly similar terms, Ward had warned Hare, 'He would not sell his friend Joe Byrne for all the money in the world.' Ward knew that this was as true in December as it had been in February. But he also knew that Joe's belief in Aaron was being steadily eroded by the hostility of his family and leading sympathisers. Aaron's continued participation in a surveillance that was becoming a matter of common knowledge in the Woolshed could only accelerate that erosion. Not quite fast enough for Mick Ward.

In the face of open hostility from the other members of the watch party, Aaron gave up all pretence of enthusiasm for the nightly watches. To Constable Barry, he was 'quite listless, and took no trouble in what he was doing. We had constantly to speak to him to keep him alive in what he was doing.'

Barry describes one curious incident. 'Through the night we heard some crackers being let off—at first they seemed like a stock-whip—and heard some voices, and we wanted Sherritt to listen for those voices, to see if he would know them. As soon as he heard them he cleared away in the bush from us—ran away in the scrub and planted, and after some search we found him asleep.'

Aaron's strange life placed an abnormal stress on his marriage and at one stage he and Belle separated 'for a few days'. This heightened the problems on the watch party and Ward enlisted Nicolson's help. After a talking-to, Aaron made an effort to 'settle down to his work shortly afterwards...and lived with his wife.' Perhaps at this stage of reconciliation, Aaron and Belle went to live with her family, in the heart of Woolshed village, on the banks of Reedy Creek just east of the Sunbury Bridge. Belle enjoyed being among family and friends, and her mother, plump, red-headed Ellen Barry, seems to have been genuinely fond of Aaron. But living with in-laws in a small house full of children was hardly an ideal existence for newly-weds. It also provided yet another pressure on the already dubious security of the watch party. Aaron was surrounded by Kelly sympathisers and it was virtually impossible to move to and fro without being seen.

Aaron had plans to find a place of his own—somewhere nearby, where Belle could still keep contact with her people. Before they left the Barry house, Mick Ward played his next card.

Aaron had bought Belle a sidesaddle from a Wangaratta saddler—an expensive gift which he managed to get on credit because one of his sisters had been a prized employee.

One day in January some travelling showmen arrived in the Woolshed to set up a 'hurdy-gurdy'—today's merry-go-round, or carousel—a huge, collapsible wooden wheel with wooden horses suspended from its spokes. Two men revolved it with a windlass while a third played the accordion.

In these lost days, when life's pleasures and excitements could be found in simple things, adults and children alike flocked to enjoy a ride. After dinner, before Aaron slipped across the creek to take up his position watching the Byrne house, he went down with Belle and the Barrys to join the fun. Paddy Byrne was there and Jack Sherritt. After a time, as the accordion played and the hurdy-gurdy whirled its laughing passengers in the smoky sweetness of the dusk, Jack was no longer to be seen.

When the Barrys arrived home, they found that a locked door had been broken open. Belle's new sidesaddle and a gold watch had disappeared. Somewhere in the house was found a discarded tie and a collar with Mick Ward's name in it. Ward had given some of his old collars and ties to Aaron. But also to Jack.

Acting on a report which came, surprisingly, not from Aaron but from the Sherritt family, Beechworth police searched the Byrne house for 'stolen jewellery'—presumably the missing gold watch. They found Belle's side-saddle. Mrs Byrne and Paddy were arrested by Ward.

Already suspicious, Aaron had no doubt who had taken the saddle. He mounted and headed for Sheepstation. Jack saw him coming, leapt on a horse, and spurred away, with Aaron galloping in pursuit along the dusty road to Beechworth.

Joe's brother Paddy (below right) was heavier than Joe but closely resembled him (the very heavily retouched photo of him at right was published in Superintendent Hare's book as a portrait of Joe). Blacksmith Tom Straughair (below left) was a friend of Joe and Aaron, suspected by the police as having made Joe's armour. Both young men wear unusual short overcoats favoured by horsemen.

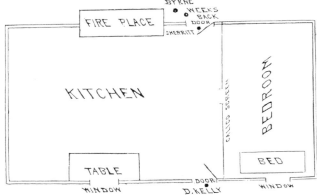

BYRNE
WEEKS
BACK
DOOR
SHERRITT

FIRE PLACE

KITCHEN

BEDROOM

CALICO SCREEN

BED

TABLE

WINDOW

DOOR
D. KELLY

WINDOW

Thomas Carrington of the *Sketcher* drew the back of Aaron's hut and an accurate ground plan (which reveals the one error in this drawing —placing the door too close to the corner, leaving no space for the bedroom).

Front Sherritts

An unknown artist sketched this front view of the hut where Aaron was killed. It is preserved among the papers of the 1881 Royal Commission.
(*Keith McMenomy*)

Bill Knowles, grandson of Anton Wick, shows where his grandfather was held up by Joe Byrne and Dan Kelly on the night of Aaron Sherritt's murder. The site of Aaron's hut is around the corner in the background. Photo taken in 1968.

German miner and market gardener, Anton Wick—here seen with his wife Margaret—was forced to decoy Aaron to his death. Margaret died in 1870, dating this Bray photo to at least ten years before Wick's involvement in the murder.

THE ILLUSTRATED
AUSTRALIAN
NEWS

No. 291.   MELBOURNE, SATURDAY, JULY 3, 1880.   PRICE { WITH TWO SUPPLEMENTS } 1s.

THE MURDER OF SHERRITT.
(FROM A SKETCH TAKEN IMMEDIATELY AFTER THE DEPARTURE OF THE KELLY GANG.)

Aaron's murder makes the front page of the *Illustrated Australian News*. Supposedly based on 'a Sketch Taken Immediately After the Departure of the Kelly Gang', the plate gets many details right, captures reasonable likenesses of Joe and Aaron (perhaps based on descriptions by neighbours), but is less successful with Anton Wick and errs badly in showing a curiously venerable Dan Kelly at the back door, rather than the front.

Though Aaron's horse had already covered three miles, he overtook Jack and managed to drag him from the saddle. In the course of a dusty, ugly fight, Aaron uprooted a sucker sapling from the roadside and swung a murderous blow at his brother's head. Jack dropped and lay still, deathly pale, and bleeding from a head wound.

Appalled at what he had done, Aaron caught his horse and galloped into town. He reined in at Paddy Allen's store and ran inside. Allen takes up the story.

> He looked so terrible that I called out to him, What's the matter with you?
>
> 'I'm after murdering Jack,' he said: and his face was white and drawn, and his voice trembled. 'I've come to see Mr Ward and give myself up,' he said.
>
> 'You fool, I told him, clear out of this—get over the border! Don't waste time!'
>
> But he wouldn't move. So I gave him a big tumbler full of whiskey and he drained it—just slid down. Then he had another. Then he started to tell me about it...And whilst he was at it who should come walking into the shop but the murdered man himself no less.
>
> Well, you can believe there was dismay. He looked dead enough to have been buried the day before yesterday. Pale he was, like a ghost, and the blood not yet dry on him. After a while the corpse looked hard at Aaron and said, 'You bloody wretch, you thought you'd murdered me!' Well, I thought, he came pretty bloody near doing it, anyway.
>
> Well, for a while it looked like there was going to be ructions. But they were both pretty sick of it—Aaron with the mortal fright that was put into him with his brother lying up there dead on the road; and Jack with the lick he got across the skull with the sapling. And there's a lot of real friendship in whiskey, anyway. I sent for a doctor, and he sewed up the hole in Jack's head almost like new. Then Ward came in and gave them advice that they never took, and never intended to. Then there was more whiskey—nothing like whiskey for a broken head, you know. And they went away as loving as two turtles.

Aaron and Jack's reconciliation lasted no longer than the effects of Paddy Allen's whiskey.

In the cold, sober light of the next day Ward was still charging Paddy Byrne and Margret with the theft of Belle's saddle, while Aaron, according to Sadleir, 'always laid the stealing of the saddle on Jack Sherritt'. This and some other odd facts of the case 'raised suspicion against the Sherritts' and Sadleir sent two of the Aboriginal police 'to search for any footprints or other marks that would help to clear the matter up'.

Sadleir reported, 'The trackers found large recent footprints both ways between Sherritts' and Mrs Byrne's houses and also the tracks of a horse, showing that some person walked part way at each end, then mounted the horse and rode the remainder of the way. The footprints were not those of any of the Byrne family, but would probably be such as Jack Sherritt or his father would leave.'

A strong, circumstantial case was assembled. The saddle had been found in the Byrne house in a position which indicated 'that it was placed there only a very short time before'. It was recalled that, when the Sherritts gave their information to Ward, they 'counselled a postponement of the search'. Meanwhile, Jack was clearly avoiding the police. He had also admitted to Hiram Crawford 'that the saddle, or a similar one' had been recently in his possession.

The case was to stay open for some ten months until the charges were withdrawn in December. Nicolson told the Royal Commission the following year. 'I knew that Sherritt…had stolen a saddle from his sister-in-law, and, as I have since learned, planted it in the Byrnes' farm.'

Meanwhile, Paddy and Margret Byrne had been arrested and charged—to be left with both the stigma of guilt and increasing bitterness towards Aaron. Joe had stuck to his mate through the saga of Charlie and the break-up with Kate. He had believed in him while 'the Lloyds and Quinns' wanted him shot as a traitor. This final blow against his family must be unforgivable.

It is hardly surprising that Ward's hand can be seen behind the affair of the saddle. He was to be briefly questioned about it by the Royal Commission. His answers are vague and evasive. It would remain for another policeman to mention 'the improper arrest of any of the friends of the late outlaws—for instance the arrest of the Byrne family for the saddle belonging to Aaron Sherritt. I think there is evidence forthcoming that will prove that is a put-up case.'

'If so, what policeman will be responsible?' asked the Commission.

'The family was arrested by Detective Ward.'

'You think that there will be evidence that that was the case?'

'If the Commission will examine the witnesses I will name them; and if they will allow me to repeat the statements made to me by Senior-Constable Mullane, so that he does not back out of it, it will be shown it was a put-up case.'

'By Ward?'

'Well, I would not like to say the name.'

The saddle case was a ploy in the strategy Ward had been developing ever since he had failed to convince Hare that Aaron would never betray Joe.

In supporting Ward's claim for a share in the Kelly reward, Nicolson was to testify that the detective 'rendered most valuable service in a very zealous and untiring manner *in working out the problem of the capture of the outlaws* particularly from July 1879 to June 1880 [my italics].' Nicolson considered that only men 'actually present at the destruction of the Gang has stronger grounds'. In fact, Ward was to receive a larger share of the reward than the trooper who ran forward under covering fire to set alight to the Glenrowan Inn.

A friend of Ward's, Enoch Downes, a truant officer with the Department of Education, also supported his claim, stating 'from personal knowledge' gained during his work in the district that 'it was...*the strategic movements and well-laid plans of that officer* that brought about the collapse of the gang at Glenrowan [my italics].'

Downes had been given an unusual insight into Ward's strategy—by Margret Byrne.

Denny Byrne had wagged school on 13 November—the day the Gang turned up at Sheepstation after Dan's earlier visit in search of Jack. During the first term of 1880 Enoch Downes rode down to the Byrne house to investigate Denny's absence and warned Margret against 'any future default', while reassuring her that there would be no prosecution for this truancy. Margret warmed considerably at this and invited Downes in for a cup of tea while Paddy turned his horse into the Byrne paddock to graze.

In an extraordinary two-hour conversation, Margret 'got a little lively' while talking about some bungling bank robbers who had tried to ape the Kellys. This gave Downes an opening to introduce the subject of the Gang.

> From that I spoke about her son, that she was quite right in saving him if she could; well, she hesitated about that, and she did not know whether she would or not; and there was something I was satisfied about that caused her to make up her mind that she would let her son go. She said he had made his bed and must lie on it—that was a reference to the horse-stealing case. [Downes meant the sidesaddle case.] She said it was a dodge of that—Ward; *he was using all sorts of dodges to bring Joe back again to have revenge on Sherritt,* but she said they would wait their own time, and I was satisfied from her words and actions that they intended to have Sherritt, and that Ward was not very safe [my italics].

At this point, Downes has recorded no more than Margret Byrne's astute theory of Ward's strategy. He provides a chilling confirmation of that theory —from Mick Ward himself—as he continues:

> I was not aware that there was any dodge at all, but Mrs Byrne was right in her surmises, but I told Ward on that evening that there would be no fear of them coming back yet awhile for Sherritt. She said the dodge would not take, it was a matter of time.

In these words, on 20 July 1881 in the Beechworth Court House, Enoch Downes told the Royal Commission that Detective Ward was setting out to incriminate Aaron Sherritt in the eyes of the Kelly Gang, that Ward knew the strategy was working, knew that 'they intended to have Sherritt's life', and that 'it was a matter of time'.

The Royal Commissioners, press and public seemed to find nothing remarkable in the revelation. Presumably, to them, the ends justified the means. In contriving the murder of Aaron Sherritt, Ward brought about the destruction of the Kelly Gang, therefore no guilt could be slated to him. To them, as to Ward, Aaron was expendable.

As Aaron had undoubtedly feared, Jack's time with a police watch party quickly exposed the obvious flaw. Jack was to say, 'I could go to the house and five or six men with me, and the men not see me—creeping along the deep rise there was in front of Mrs Byrne's house. The men used only to watch the front of the place.'

The watch party farce came close to exposure on Thursday, 19 February, when Jack paid a visit to Julian's shanty while Aaron and the party were watching the Byrne house, only a mile-and-a-half away.

> I got along with Patsy Byrne this night, and we got drinking together; he was drinking brandy and I was drinking 'soft stuff', so as to watch him. I stopped with him a considerable time, and he went home to his mother's place, and he came back again, and he told me, 'Joe has been home and got some clothes, and cleared out; is he not a bloody smart fellow?' It was close on morning then, so as soon as I got Patsy Byrne away, I took an axe with me, and gammoned [pretended] to go to my work...I met two of the cave party—Alexander and Armstrong—and I told them about Byrne being home last night, and they seemed like as if they were horror struck at Byrne being home and they watching.

Jack reported his news to Ward at eleven that morning. Two days later Ward wrote in a memo to Nicholson, 'I have made careful enquiries and the men tell me from the position of their watch on Mrs Byrnes house no person could arrive there at 11 o'clock or leave there at daybreak without their knowledge...they do not believe the tale...Moses distinctly states that he [Joe] could not come to his mother's house without being seen by the watch party.'

Ward shrugged off the incident with the theory that Paddy had spun a yarn to Jack 'to try and pump him', although he was almost certainly aware of the mining race and its role in Joe's 'invisible' visits to his home. Asked by the Royal Commission if he believed Jack's statement, Ward replied, enigmatically, 'I made enquiries.'

Significantly, two days after Jack made this potentially damaging report, he and Aaron came to blows—ostensibly over the marriage. Ward told Nicolson, 'Jack Jones and John Moses had a fight in the bush this morning. It originated on account of Aaron [crossed out] John Moses being married to a papist: they had several blows but I settled between the parties.'

The same afternoon Jack met Paddy in Beechworth and, on Ward's instructions, took six bottles of brandy down to the Woolshed, 'two is for Mrs Byrnes two for the French Man [Julian] and two for Jack'.

While Ward was playing his devious games, Aaron was left to continue in his self-destructive role.

In the early months of 1880 Joe was increasingly caught up in strange new forces that were swirling through the north-east. He had shared in and helped shape the transformation of police murderers into highwayman heroes. Now he was involved in an equally remarkable metamorphosis as the Kelly Outbreak was subjected to external pressure and internal ferment.

The police had provided the two most powerful forces that re-shaped the Outbreak. The first was the inept handling of the sympathiser prosecutions. The second was the use of the Land Act as a means to strike at the Gang's supporters. Not all Kelly sympathisers were selectors, but the selector class provided their most numerous, active and effective allies.

The previous May Standish had complained to the Acting Chief Secretary at the 'undue proportion of members of the criminal class' in the north-east, claiming, 'This evil is in some measure perpetuated by the facility afforded them of taking up selections for the ostensible purpose of cultivation but in many instances as a depot for stolen horses and cattle and as a base from which they can carry out their nefarious pursuits.' Already, Standish spoke of 'the remedial measures contemplated by the Hon'ble the Minister for Lands' as a means to 'modify that evil'.

Within a month, selections were being refused to known or suspected sympathisers of the Gang. Lists of applicants appearing at Land Board sittings were circulated to the police who marked men for refusal on the flimsiest grounds—one because he had come from Wallan ('Having come from there, he is likely to be a friend of the outlaws'), another because 'he had been a carrier on the Greta Road and is said to have been very friendly with the outlaws'.

Bill Tanner, a Kelly sympathiser who had been convicted with his brother-in-law, Tom Lloyd, over a brawl with police in Benalla, wrote to ask why his application had been refused. The Secretary for Lands replied bluntly, 'I have the honour to inform you that the land was refused on the recommendation of the police department.'

Use of the black list as a weapon against the sympathisers was a turning point. Farmers were being denied the right to take up land in the country they knew, among their friends and families. Ned Kelly saw himself as responsible for their plight and accepted the responsibility, just as he had when sympathisers were gaoled and Kelly money was paid for their defence.

Now the rhetoric of the Jerilderie Letter was transformed into action. The 'colonial stratagem' may have been a vainglorious boast, or a dream, twelve months before. As the summer of 1880 passed, it was becoming cold, hard reality—cold and hard as iron.

The plan put together by Ned and Joe first took shape in an increasingly elaborate bank robbery blueprint, as Nicolson's strategies helped convince Ned and Joe that hold-ups in the Euroa or Jerilderie models would be 'too dangerous'. From such beginnings came the fantastic idea of making armour for the Gang, a concept which appears to have been well advanced during

Joe's exploration with Jack and Aaron of the Beechworth and Yackandandah bank robbery plans.

About that time or earlier, 'not long after' August 1879, James Wallace visited Anne Sherritt at Sheepstation on a curious errand. Ward reported 'he came in a buggy he asked her in her daughter Mary Jane's presence whether she had any moulboards for sale giving as an excuse that his father was a dealer in old metals and he was purchasing for him at the same time he showed her one (moulboard) he had in a bag with him.'

Plough mouldboards—the twisting plate of quarter-inch steel which rolled back the sod after it had been cut by the ploughshare—was the material selected by Ned and Joe for their armour, an arresting symbol in itself.

Farmers had been denied land; the idle plough was to become a weapon.

The germ of the idea may have come from Ned's favourite book, *Lorna Doone,* where the outlaw Doones make a superb entrance as 'Heavy men and large of stature, reckless how they bore their guns or how they sate their horses, with leathern jerkins and long boots, *and iron plates on breast and head...*[my italics]'

Even though he opposed the idea and predicted to Ned 'that it would bring us to grief', Joe seems to have contributed the design of the body armour—based on the suit of ancient Chinese armour in Beechworth's Burke Museum—with its almost tubular cuirass, enclosing chest and back, separate pieces protecting the shoulder and upper arm, and short aprons slung back and front to shield the lower body.

The design for the helmet strongly resembled the 12th century 'heaume' of the Crusades with its cylindrical shape and single horizontal eye slit. A Melbourne scholar of the day had heard that the inspiration for the Kelly armour was 'a picture in an illustrated edition of one of Sir Walter Scott's novels'. A 'heaume' could have been found in an illustration for Scott's *The Talisman* or *Ivanhoe*—perhaps another contribution from Joe.

As the idea of the armour took shape and the materials were gathered to dictate its final form, the exploit it was intended for also took on a developing life of its own—first, with an enlarged 'Gang' to back up the four armoured shock troops in a bank robbery, and help prevent police intervention and pursuit. Then, as the plan began to emerge more and more clearly as an almost-military operation, it was all but inevitable that the strategy should take on the quality of rebellion which underscored the Jerilderie Letter.

An exploit of the scale now being contemplated could not hope to be executed without bloodshed. So, even if Ned and Joe had not begun already to interpret their outlawry in terms of insurgency against a corrupt arm of British rule (and the Jerilderie Letter suggests they had), the scale and nature of the coming fight demanded some such rationale or it would be seen simply as a criminal atrocity of monstrous scale.

At the most simplistic level, Ned and Joe had to offer their supporters in this wildly ambitious scheme something more than the proceeds of a bank robbery. They offered them some hope of relief from the black list, from the hated confederacy between squatter and trooper, from police retribution for loyalty to the Gang. They offered rebellion, and with it the lodestar of those who rebelled against the British Crown. The evergreen rebel dream. A republic.

Farmer rebels in South Africa nursed similar dreams of freedom from British rule and were about to launch their first, unsuccessful bid to make the dream reality. Twenty years on they would try again, and come magnificently close to success with formidable commandoes of men much like the Kellys and their mates—born and bred to the saddle and to the use of firearms, and brilliantly suited to guerilla warfare in a broad and hostile country which was at once their battlefield, their most formidable weapon, and their very reason for fighting.

When Ned and Joe discussed the mad dream of a republic with their closest supporters—the Lloyds, the Quinns, the Wrights, the McAuliffes, the Tanners— Joe was, as ever, 'scribe' and 'confidential' for their plans. 'Records of meetings' were kept in an exercise book and, eventually, Joe drafted a Declaration of the Republic of North Eastern Victoria in 'quaint, mock-legalistic language', a document undoubtedly stronger in rebel rhetoric and anti-British hyperbole than in any attempt to foreshadow even a rudimentary political structure.

As historian John McQuilton wrote, 'Kelly came from an Irish-Catholic background with its tradition of republican yearning, the concept of a republic becoming the symbol of an anti-British political system.'

In Les Carlyon's words, 'It was the *idea* that burned. The mood was rebellion.'

'The Seeds of Fire', carried by old Joe Byrne from troubled Ireland 46 years before, preserved and nurtured in fireside litanies, had at last found fertile soil in Ned and Joe's mad dream, now to be clad in steel.

Most of the mouldboards for the armour had been given by friends and sympathisers. Now, in late March, the total of 28 or 30 needed for the four suits was made up by thefts from 'two or three farms' in the Greta–Glenrowan district—apparently pointless crimes which were investigated by Aboriginal police. They found prints left by boots with the 'larrikin heel' favoured by Joe.

Then, by a creek 'on the far side of the Bald Hills', the Gang and Tom Lloyd set up a bush forge, built its fire to fierce heat with a huge bellows, and buried the first set of mouldboards in the coals. They stripped the bark from a freshly cut red box log with one end dipping into the water of a creek, and when the first of the boards were red hot, lifted them on to the sappy wood and hammered and chiselled them into shape in eruptions of steam and smoke. The living wood resisted fire and dulled the hammer blows, the waters of the creek helped absorb the sound.

The components of the first suit, made to fit Ned, were at last completed and the two halves of the breastplate riveted together. Then the finished piece was rested against a stump and a test shot fired from a Martini Henry rifle at only ten yards range. The massive bullet whined away, leaving a dent.

Now came the back plate, the apron, the shoulder guards, the helmet. And at last, held together with wire, straps and bolts, the complete suit was assembled on Ned.

After days of searing, bone-jarring work, he stood there with huge head and jutting shoulders, suddenly transformed into something more than a big man clad in fire-bloomed steel. Ned Kelly, without armour, was formidable. In armour, he became indomitable—a figure from the dreams of his allies, from the nightmares of his enemies. Myth, legend and reality were fused into a preposterous icon.

At other times and places, other groups made similar suits for Joe, Dan and Steve. Oxley blacksmith, William Culph, played a key role as did some of the Delaneys, a prominent sympathiser family.

Joe's suit was probably made by Beechworth blacksmith, Charles Knight, whose forge was in Camp Street, between the Railway Hotel and the bridge across Spring Creek. Tom Straughair probably helped.

Of all the suits, Joe's was the finest, breast and back plates clamped together by side plates in a perfect fit, the helmet with face piece shaped and beaten to meet the brow plate above the nose and divide the narrow eye slit into two dark orbits, evoking a Vendel helmet his Viking ancestors might have worn.

Completed, the four suits of armour were hidden away, ready.

On 20 May police spy Daniel Kennedy, usually called the Diseased Stock Agent (or DSA), reported, 'Missing portions of cultivators described as jackets are now being worked, and fit splendidly. Tested previous to using, and proof at ten yards'. The report would be ignored.

CHAPTER 15

At the Devil's Elbow

January–June 1880

The Englishness of Beechworth was most obvious in autumn as its streets and gardens glowed with reds and yellows. While the European trees and shrubs prepared for their winter death, the bush stirred with new life after the ordeal of summer. Gum trees ceased to shed bark and leaves, moss and rock fern and native grasses regenerated, orchids reappeared, creeks and springs began to flow again. In these greening days, Aaron found what he'd been looking for, a vacant house. It was at the Devil's Elbow, where Reedy Creek turned sharply south to begin the Sebastopol horseshoe, barely a mile from his in-laws and slightly farther from the Byrnes. Its present owner, 'a foreigner' called Henry Grose, hadn't been seen for some time.

The house stood at the side of the main road to Eldorado on a low, rocky hillock just past the slight dip of Maidenhair Gully—an unadorned cottage of thick, sawn hardwood planks, with a shingle roof, and a big slab chimney at the back. In front, a door and two windows were set square like nose and eyes, presenting a blank face to the road and the creek beyond and, across the valley, the crouching shape of Native Dog Peak, with its hindquarters sloping down to Byrnes Gap and the small, grey shape of the Byrne house.

Behind the hut, a shed and open-sided shelter stood among a straggling scrub of sucker saplings sprung from ground cleared by gold diggers, whose old shafts were still studded about. Through the scrub, the blunt dome of Sugarloaf rose, dark and mangy.

Pushing past 'great clumsy doors', the interior was snug enough, walls lined with a wattle-and-daub of saplings and mud partly covered with hessian and paper, a board partition cutting off a small bedroom.

It was all Aaron and Belle needed, once they had brought in an iron double bed, some chairs and a table—'an impromptu affair consisting of a zinc-lined packing case with boards laid upon it'. Aaron made a small garden for Belle in front of the hut—a few blue and white irises and lilies—behind a token length of sapling fence.

Each night Mrs Barry came to keep Belle company while Aaron was off with the watch party and his daytime life settled into a semblance of normality.

One intrusive reality could not be ignored. Aaron's selection was becoming an albatross around his neck. He had paid no rent since taking out the lease the previous year and the split from his family left the big paddock stranded in that lonely corner of the tableland—halfway between a hostile Sherritt household and an increasingly hostile Byrne household. Clearly, strong-willed Belle wanted nothing more to do with the 'squalid den', a pleasant enough hideaway for a brief holiday from reality but no place to live.

Aaron found a ready buyer in his old friend Emma Crawford, daughter of millionaire Hiram Crawford, and the sale of the lease was arranged. Money may have changed hands before his marriage. From habitual procrastination or some more deeply grounded paralysis of will, he hadn't made formal application for transfer of the lease until 3 February. He gave as his reason 'that I am desirous of leaving that portion of the district'.

Although final formalities of the transaction would not be completed at the time of his death, he had at last given up his land after the five-year battle to hold it. His cattle and horses must find other grass to graze as the old cherished dream, the 'nice farm' and the horse stud, slowly faded.

While Aaron saw virtually nothing of his family (his mother did not even know where his new house was), the Sherritts continued their close relationship with the Byrnes. Knowing this, the police of the watch party were understandably surprised when Bessie Sherritt, known to be Joe's former fiancee, visited the cave. Another day, Belle came to call. All this did little to encourage confidence in the secrecy of the operation.

Down in Melbourne, Captain Standish had other reasons to query the conduct of the party. The first month's account from Paddy Allen for £30 15s landed on his desk in January. The Chief Commissioner protested to Sadleir, 'I certainly cannot at this date ask the Chief Secretary to approve the purchase of jam, sardines, and such like items—including *150* bottles of liquor—as absolute requisites for a party of police on duty.'

Nicolson gave a spirited justification of this expenditure on 'a secret service party...of which there are five on at a time viz four constables and a spy.'

'The service,' he added, 'is one of unusual danger. The privations they have endured are quite exceptional particularly the want of good sound rest for a spell of eight days each.'

Stressing the long hours involved, the lack of exercise, and the scarcity of water ('they have no water for cooking or washing, only sufficient to make a little tea'), he considered that they 'could not perform their duty without the liquor supplied to them, especially *the porter*' and 'food and nourishment of an unusual character'.

Standish rose to the occasion with a well-turned memo to the Chief Secretary, conveying Nicolson's view and pointing out, 'The total charge does not exceed one shilling and fourpence per meal, allowing three meals per day to each man.'

In January bull-at-a-gate Senior Constable Johnston had seen Hare at the Police Depot in Richmond and, asked by him what was going on up in the Kelly Country, Johnston rattled off, 'There is a cave party up at Beechworth and it has been there for some time...they are watching Byrnes' house.'

Hare passed on the tidbit to Standish who was delighted to inform Nicolson that his 'secret' cave party was a matter of common gossip at the depot. Despite this, Ward continued to assure Nicolson that the party 'was a profound secret to anyone'.

Nicolson felt that a leak within the force posed no great threat but he needed Standish's continued approval of expenditure. After a spirited rearguard action for two months, Nicolson wrote to Mullane and Ward on 31 March, instructing that the party be 'carefully and secretly withdrawn, leaving no traces behind them, if possible...the secrecy of the duty at Sebastopol will still be preserved, especially as it may have to be renewed again'.

The constables were recalled to Beechworth (unbeknown to Nicolson, they had slept the last two days at Aaron's house) and Mullane asked them for reports on their duty. Three men, Barry, Falkiner and Alexander, wrote 'that they believed that Mrs Byrne was aware that they were watching her house'.

Falkiner was particularly enlightening. 'I beg to report to the Superintendent that the Sherritts have been continually backwards and forwards together at Byrnes, and as much as sleeping together, and from their intimacy together, it has been impossible to say this duty has been unknown to the outlaws' friends.'

Ward was appalled and returned the reports, advising the men, 'That was not what they wanted.' He told one of them, 'I beg of you and pray that you will not state in your report that the public knew of you being at the cave some time ago, because if Mr Nicolson hears that he will be awfully annoyed with me.'

Falkiner submitted a revised report which concluded. 'Though unsuccessful, this duty has been carried out with the greatest secrecy by the members of the force who were engaged on that duty.' Barry and Alexander expressed similar views.

The fourth man, Constable Armstrong, had first reported 'I simply carried out Mr Nicolson's instructions, and formed no opinion as to whether we were discovered or not.'

Ward asked him, 'Won't you report that we are not discovered?'

'No, I cannot,' Armstrong said firmly, and left Beechworth to return to his station at Wahgunyah.

So the watch party came to its ragged end. Appropriately, on April Fool's Day. Aaron walked away from it, probably glad that the whole wretched business was over. He didn't even pay a last visit to the cave to see if anything remained to betray the presence of police. That was left to his mother and father. Told the police had gone, Anne and John took a dray and drove up to the rim of the tableland by moonlight, then climbed down through the bush to the cave. It was an appalling sight. Tins, bottles, bags, even oilskin coats, were scattered around, eloquent testimony of the constables' eagerness to quit this wretched duty—and of their disregard for security.

The County Cavan runaways of 27 years before worked together, gathering up the debris, suddenly aware of the threat such carelessness posed to their firstborn son. They would demonstrate, each in their own way, that, behind the uncompromising façade they presented over the rift with Aaron, they still loved him deeply. For the moment that love could only be expressed in this effort to protect him, as the incriminating trash was packed up and carried to the dray. But a letter dropped by Constable Falkiner had already blown down the hill to lie among the rocks and scrub, waiting to be found.

As Aaron cut wood or pottered around his cottage at Devil's Elbow, he could see the Byrne house across the valley, arrowed by the deep notch of Byrnes Gully. Much was happening here.

Paddy, now eighteen, was playing an increasingly active role as a sympathiser. He had carefully cultivated his resemblance to Joe, growing a wispy first beard, dressing in similar jacket, waistcoat, flared riding pants and high heeled boots. Then he bought a grey mare at Tarrawingee, a handsome animal that cost him £20. Riding around the Woolshed, only his distinctive riding style—crouched over his horse's neck—prevented him being mistaken for Joe on Music; just as if Joe were to abandon his usually erect posture in the saddle and bend forward, he might easily be taken for Paddy. It would be claimed that Joe exploited this ruse to pay frequent visits to a girlfriend in Beechworth—a girl who would perhaps play a significant role in the coming apocalypse. Locals believed her suitor was Paddy.

Meanwhile, Paddy's mare was kept in the Byrne stable, under lock and key, fed on oats and hay, and exercised each afternoon by one of the family. Such training was 'an unusual thing in a small place of that sort'—especially training as a night horse, kept out of daylight for most of the time. Paddy had important work for her in the coming weeks.

All this made solid, hard-working, easy-going Paddy a more exciting and colourful figure in the eyes of Anne Jane Sherritt, who continued her regular visits to the Byrnes, supposedly on the instructions of Ward, who called her 'a secret, cunning, good girl'.

If Anne Jane was as loyal an agent as Ward believed, she played her role with extraordinary spirit, prompting, on 30 April, another indignant letter to Nicolson from 'John Smith'.

On going to Missis Byrnes I came in contact with Joseph Byrne and Edward Kelly two outlaws & murderers in Company with them a little girl named Anney Jane Sherritt I dare say she is about 16 years old was there to [too].

Those two looked at me very hard the little girl pointing the revolver and telling me she was going with Kelly to bushranging taking the revolver and firing it off as well as any of the outlaws.

Again, 'Smith' accused Anne Jane of supplying the Gang with food, declaring, 'if you see her in the bush you will see her going over logs and stumps and every thing that comes in her way. She goes in the greta fashion a band under her nose.'

He believed, 'she knows all about the outlaws if she only will devulge the secret'. But he couldn't hold out much hope of this. 'Pat Byrne the Brother of the outlaw is courting her and of cours she will not tell on them. They are going to be married first of January...They were in Wongaratta getting their pictures taken.'

'Smith' urged Nicolson to have Anne Jane and Paddy followed, while warning, 'It would be almost imposible to catch them when they get on their horses they go like a bird on the wing.'

Anne Jane and Paddy would ride together like a pair of birds for another two months.

From this period, autumn 1880, dates the final breakdown of Joe and Aaron's impossibly stressed friendship, the last fragile link broken by an unendurable pressure.

Thirty-one years later, brilliant journalist B. W. Cookson asked Jim Kelly why Aaron was killed. Jim was clearly reticent and Cookson asked, 'Was it merely because he was with the police?'

'No; they had known that for a long time. It was not that, no. I'll tell you what it was.'

'And he told me,' wrote Cookson. 'He said that after Mrs Byrne found Aaron Sherritt spying for the police she met him and spoke of what might happen if Joe should come across him. Sherritt then, he said, in the mother's presence, made use of a bloodcurdling threat of unmentionable atrocity, and swore to shoot Byrne on sight. Byrne was told of the threat. And Aaron perished.'

Another eighteen years passed before J. J. Kenneally supplied most of the missing detail, claiming that Aaron told Mrs Byrne, 'I'll shoot Joe Byrne and I'll......him before his body gets cold.' Kenneally left little doubt as to the missing word. Modern writers have supplied 'fuck' and one of them seems to link this with a shadowy suggestion of a homosexual relationship between Aaron and Joe.

The story is, on the face of it, highly unlikely. On no other occasion did Aaron display hostility towards Joe. It is true that Mrs Byrne attributed some wild threats to him at the time of the Charlie confrontation, but these were threats to property. If Aaron had been moved to make any such threat against Joe, he would not have hidden his feelings from his police associates. They reported no such enmity. On the contrary, a lack of ill-feeling towards Ned and Joe was one of the things that made many police doubt Aaron's loyalty.

Yet stories of threats made by Aaron had reached Joe. Mrs Barry reported that immediately after killing Aaron, Joe said, 'that he was told my daughter used to go about blowing about what her husband would do when he would catch him. But that was all false...'

At such a moment, it is unbelievable that Joe would quote a threat reported secondhand via Belle if Aaron had in fact made a foul threat directly to his mother. It is equally unbelievable that Belle would have repeated the 'blood-curdling threat of unmentionable atrocity'.

In the end, the real nature of the threat, if any, and even the identity of the person who carried the story, true or false, to Joe, is comparatively unimportant. What matters is that, in Joe's eyes, the months of doubt and half-belief were over. Worn down by the constantly reiterated warnings, by the longstanding hostility of 'the Lloyds and Quinns', it must have been almost a relief to him that it was Aaron who, apparently, had cast the die. With no sense of guilt or betrayal, Joe could go with the tide against his old mate.

Aaron would be shot. The police response to his killing could be seen as a threat to the rebellion strategy—or be made an integral part of it. So Aaron must live until all was ready. Weeks passed and Joe's resolution began to weaken.

In one of the many ironies of this story, it was at this critical period that Margret Byrne received a letter from Joe while Anne Jane was at her home. She gave Anne Jane a message for her trusted friend, Mrs Sherritt, 'not to let Moses know, nor to allow Joe or Dan to visit her house, lest Moses should betray them'.

The information was duly given to Detective Ward by Mrs Sherritt.

One member of the Sherritt family remained true to Aaron—Willie. While he was scrub cutting in the Woolshed for a couple of weeks he stayed with Aaron and Belle. Once a week Anne Jane would ride down with a supply of food.

On the night of 24 May, as she was on her way back to Sheepstation, she called at the Byrne house.

And who should come up but Joe Byrne leading a horse, and Dan Kelly. Each of them was leading one and riding another. Mrs Byrne then came out—there was a whistle—it is a very thick scrubby place, and after a little bit Ned Kelly and Hart came on foot, from the back of the place like, and those two came up the front of the house like, so, and got their provisions. There was some bread and I think it was boiled bacon, and then Patsy Byrne went up the Woolshed and he brought something down in a bottle and gave it to them, and Patsy...said,

'Which way did you come?' and Joe says, 'The way we always come. We came down the steepest part of Wall's Gully.'

The next day Jack Sherritt was doing some ploughing at the Sherritt farm and rode into Beechworth at night for a few drinks. Anne Sherritt woke up at dawn next morning and went to see if he was home.

I saw his bed had not been disturbed; and then I went out to listen if I could hear the horse-bells of the horses ploughing; and I went along my own paddock fence, and I could hear the bells still further on. It was the horses had got into the paddock of a man named Murphy that my husband had bought, and I went to bring the horses home; and it seemed to me that Byrne was waiting to see who would come over for the horses. But when I went over there was an old calf pen, and three or four old sheds. And I saw the man first, and then a man with a horse's bridle on his arm, and this was Joe Byrne. And as soon as he saw me he got up and came over and spoke friendly enough to me; and he said he had come to take my son Aaron's life, and also Detective Ward's. He said 'Those two had them starved to death.' And he said that Ward went about the hills like a black tracker; and that if he had them two out of the way, and also Senior-Constable Mullane, he said he could go where he liked. And I begged him not to take Aaron's life. I said, 'He has no harm; he would not hurt you.' And he said, 'You need not try to impress that on my mind, because I tell you now that there was Ward and him and Mr Hare very nearly twice catching us, and that tells you whether they will hurt me or not.' Then I strove with him—I don't know what I said—not to take poor Aaron's life. So when he had done I said to myself in the first place when he went away, 'I will run down and tell Aaron. I do not know where his hut is; I think I can find it out on the Woolshed.' Then in place of that I brought the horses home, and came to Beechworth, and on my way I met my son John, he was on horseback coming home; and I told him to go back and tell Ward what Byrne had said.

Anne Sherritt's fear for her son's life is uncomfortably real. It emerges as clearly today as it did to the police who first heard her story in 1880. Yet the power of her reaction to Joe's threat obscures two key facts. Joe knew that Aaron no longer lived at Sheepstation; by lying in wait there, he would clearly expect to see some other member of the family. Secondly, a man intent on murder does not advertise his intention with threats. If Joe's purpose was not to kill Aaron but to convey a clear warning to him and perhaps to frighten him away from Kelly country, the encounter with Anne Sherritt was to trigger a sequence of tragic events.

Whether or not Ward realised that Joe was still holding back from a final commitment to kill Aaron, the Murphys' hut meeting provided exciting proof that his strategy was working. As soon as the detective had telegraphed Nicolson, he rode down to the Devil's Elbow and asked Aaron to go at once to Murphy's hut and follow Joe's tracks.

Ward was never asked why he chose Aaron to track the man who had just threatened to kill him. Aaron agreed to see what he could find and arranged to meet Ward that night 'below the Lazzarino'—on the slopes of the gorge behind the hospital.

There, in cold and sheeting rain, Aaron told the detective that he followed hoofprints from Murphy's hut to Mrs Byrne's, then away from there until they were lost in a maze of muddy tracks on a roadway. Aaron argued forcibly, even passionately, that the rain made further pursuit futile, and that any attempt to mount a major operation would only jeopardise his safety. The latter argument would not impress Ward, but it helped persuade Nicolson and O'Connor.

In view of what was to follow, Aaron's excuse that he feared for his safety is unconvincing. Whether or not he had tracked Joe's horse to the Byrne house and beyond, he had managed to avoid being seen. He wouldn't be so lucky two days from now when he was again called on to follow a branch of this glacial trail with a party of police and Aboriginal troopers.

In late May of 1880 Nicolson, like Aaron, was living on borrowed time. The previous month he had been notified that he was to be replaced as head of the Kelly pursuit on 1 June. Now, far from relaxing his efforts, he hurled himself into his last days of leadership in a dogged bid to destroy the Gang.

He had been in Melbourne fighting for more time when word arrived that the Kellys had appeared at Mrs Byrne's—a report quickly followed by news of the Murphys' hut sighting. He hurried to Beechworth and on Saturday 29 May, heard from Anne Sherritt the vivid story of her encounter with Joe. Significantly, Joe's threat to kill Aaron was of no interest to Nicolson. All that mattered to him was the appearance of the Gang.

He ordered a party of four police to be placed in Aaron's hut to watch Mrs Byrne's, then raced down to Benalla and sent police spy 'Renwick'—a Carboar farmer named Lawrence Kirwin—to search the Sebastopol and tableland area.

Nicolson kept the telegraph line between Beechworth and Benalla open on Sunday and hovered near the Benalla Telegraph Office all day, while a party of troopers and Queensland Aboriginal police were held ready for immediate departure. At last, the telegraph rapped out an exciting message from Ward.

'Renwick' had seen a man he believed to be Joe Byrne lurking behind a rock at the head of Byrnes Gully near London Rock.

Nicolson telegraphed Ward to have 'Renwick' and Senior Constable Mullane at Everton station the next morning to meet the five o'clock train from Benalla. Aaron was to join the party later.

As he alighted from the train with O'Connor, the Aborigines and half a dozen troopers, Nicolson was appalled to see Aaron waiting on a nearby hill in full view of the station and the adjoining hotel and store. While a dozen horses were being unloaded, the superintendent sent 'Renwick' to tell Aaron 'to go away and watch where he could meet us'.

Aaron duly disappeared and joined the fourteen-man party when they were out of sight of Everton. He then guided them to his old selection, now 'Crawford's paddock', from where 'Renwick' could find his way to the spot in Byrnes Gully where he had supposedly seen Joe.

The event was a scaled-down replay of the Great Sebastopol Raid. The trail was certainly fresher, but the report was much more dubious. According to Nicolson's informant, Joe had a greyhound with him. As soon as he heard this detail the previous day, Ward claimed to have protested that the man was almost certainly Paddy Byrne. Yet Ward passed on the report without this comment and may have been less than specific in conveying Nicolson's instructions to Aaron.

While the party led their horses cautiously down from the tableland, to the head of the waterfall by London Rock, Aaron astonished Nicolson by riding carelessly down the cliff-like slope.

From the head of the waterfall, they could look straight down through Byrnes Gap to the Woolshed. While three mounted men patrolled each side of the gully, Aaron and the rest of the party followed 'Renwick' to the rock on the shadowed eastern slope where he had seen the man. The Aboriginal police found 'traces of a young man with a foot just such as described as Byrne's, with a small foot' (an effect created by the 'larrikin heel' of Joe's boots).

With O'Connor's men following the tracks, Nicolson, 'Renwick' and Aaron moved down the gully, below the cave under London Rock, beyond the tangled rock and fallen timber, past the granite throne and the wing fence that ran up to the once-secret horse yard, through the peaceful stretch of gully bed where groves of pine and gum sprang from a carpet of fallen leaves, past the derelict farm on the sunny western slope where Joe and Aaron had butchered Feely's cow, closer and closer to Byrnes', just beyond the low gully rim down to the right.

The trackers had already seen that the man's boot prints were on top of scattered cattle tracks and that they moved from one side of the gully to the other, collecting stray beasts. Now, the cattle were concentrated in a single mob heading for the Byrne house with the man following. As Aaron had already predicted, it was Paddy Byrne rounding up some of his mother's cows.

Suddenly, a figure appeared in front of them—a slim, middle-aged man with a spade beard. Impulsively, one of the Aboriginal troopers levelled his carbine. A brief exchange and the man went on his way. It was claimed that he recognised Aaron. Aaron certainly recognised him, and even his coolness was shaken. The man was Archibald Batchelor, the Byrnes' next door neighbour and a well-known sympathiser. Aaron is supposed to have told Constable Arthur that 'he was done now, it was all up with him now'.

Jack Sherritt and several police witnesses were to tell the Royal Commission that this incident doomed Aaron. 'Renwick' was to make it the major justification for his claim to a share of the Kelly reward. 'I am of the opinion that the out laws thought that Aaron Sherritt was the cause of the party going after them to Sebastopool and they afterwards went to his hut and shot him which was finally the cause of the outlaws being exterminated.'

Confronted by the Royal Commission with this statement, Nicolson merely commented, 'I cannot help 'Renwick' giving that opinion...Aaron was quite willing to come...it was quite of his own accord.'

Only two days before, Aaron 'Begged and prayed of Mr Nicolson not to go out...He also said, if we did not get the outlaws, they would know who had given the information, and would come and murder him and his connections.' Yet here he was, in broad daylight, with a fourteen-man police party, within a few hundred yards of the Byrne house. The difference was that two days before, it was a genuine sighting, not a charade. And in begging and praying, Aaron was not trying to protect himself, but his mother, the obvious source of information on Joe's visit to Sheepstation.

By riding with the 'Renwick' expedition, Aaron knew that he was engaged in a wild goose chase, which posed no threat to Joe. Therefore, he was quite fearless. Or, perhaps, his own safety was no longer an issue in this world he had helped create, in which puppet and puppeteer became indistinguishable.

After Nicolson's acceptance that the expedition was a fiasco, the party circled back via neighbouring Bullock Camp Gully, up beyond the waterfall, then climbed to the tableland and Aaron's old selection. There, on this remnant of Aaron's dream, surrounded by the fences that Joe and Ned had helped him build, the party split up. Some headed for Beechworth while Nicolson, O'Connor, 'Renwick' and the Aboriginal police made camp for the night.

The sun set on Nicolson's leadership of the Kelly pursuit. At daybreak next morning, Frank Hare would be, at least nominally, in charge. In these dying hours of the 'cranky Scotchman's' regime, Aaron and Nicolson made their peace. While the Aborigines huddled against the alien cold and the evil spirits of the night, perhaps Aaron yarned with Nicolson as he had yarned so often with Hare. Here, where he and Joe had joked and dreamt and plotted, at this fulcrum of his life between Sebastopol and Sheepstation.

Next morning, Aaron seems to have thrown caution aside and returned to Benalla with Nicolson. Was it just another piece of recklessness, or could it have been an affirmation that it just didn't matter any more?

Soon afterwards he told a policeman he had befriended, 'Nicolson is as cute as a fox; he would know your thinking. He would walk into the mouth of a cannon. I parted with him in Benalla, good friends, and he shook hands with me. This is the cap he gave us; I am wearing it; he gave his cap to me on leaving Benalla.'

Nicolson sent word back with Aaron for the four police camped in his hut to return to Beechworth. As he was leaving Benalla after the official handover to Hare on 2 June, he telegrammed confirming instructions to Mullane.

'Send Constable Armstrong back to his station. Withdraw the watch party and send them to duty. Any further orders from Superintendents Hare or Sadleir. Detective Ward already instructed that no further money or supplies to Tommy or his friends.—C. H. Nicolson A. C. P.'

Nicolson had been defying Standish's orders by continuing to pay Aaron out of his own pocket. Now it was up to Hare to make his own decisions in the matter.

Next day Ward was summoned to Benalla and strolled with the newly arrived Hare out along the Sydney Road. The detective's main concern seemed to be the expiry of the reward with the recent change of government. Hare assured him. 'It is not off. I can tell you privately that the reward is alright.'

Told by Ward of the order to suspend payment and supplies to the Sherritts, Hare asked, 'What have you done?'

'Oh, I have done nothing,' Ward replied. 'I stick to Tommy by all means.'

Walking thoughtfully along the muddy road, Hare decided that he had not *seen* any instruction to dispense with the Sherritts and that it would take him three or four days to read through all the papers left by Nicolson...

In a shrewd bid to encourage Hare's blind eye approach, Ward told him of Anne Sherritt's encounter with Joe and his threat to kill Aaron.

This was just the sort of news Hare wanted. He already had plans to send the Aboriginal police back to Queensland because 'it was said that as long as they were in the district the outlaws would not show out, *and I was anxious they should do something, as it would give us a better opportunity of falling across them* [my italics].'

He told Ward, 'You go back, keep the agents on.'

During this conversation, when Hare's and Ward's plans converged so neatly, it was decided to send a party of police back to Aaron's cottage. Hare claimed that this was at Aaron's suggestion but Ward admitted it was his idea.

'I will see it secure,' he told Hare.

That same afternoon Ward sent three men down to the hut at Devil's Elbow—three policemen who would live with Aaron and Belle on a main road, between two townships thick with Kelly sympathisers, with neighbours only a stone's throw away, in sight of the Byrne house, and with the Byrne children passing the front door twice each day, on their way to and from school. Preposterously, the party would be provided with a kind of uniform—old-fashioned blue diggers' smocks.

The men—constables Armstrong, Alexander and McCall—were to operate in the same way as the cave parties watching Mrs Byrne's house. With one major difference. They were not to post a sentry.

Armstrong commented to Aaron, 'It's a strange thing Ward gave us instructions to keep no sentry.'

Aaron smiled. 'Ward is a good-natured bloody fool; he has got no brains.'

CHAPTER 16

'Sherritt's Had His Last Supper'

June 1880

Winter of 1880 settled over the Woolshed and the tableland. In late summer a comet had poised in the sky, and now great windstorms lashed the trees as dozens of humble hearths heard talk of rebellion. Much of the talk was in the varied brogues of Ireland, echoing, to the sweet tang of gum smoke, the prologues to a hundred other rebellions that had been whispered of by bitter-smoking peat.

At the Cornish hearth of the thoroughly respectable Chappells a police agent was told 'that the Kellys were still in the country, that they were going to do something good, that Mrs Byrne's people were in great joy'. Mrs Byrne boasted openly 'that the gang was about to do something that would astonish not only the colony, but the whole world'.

Against these rumblings, Hare and Ward met Aaron in the bush near the fortress-like powder magazine just outside Beechworth, two days after their Benalla conference. They shook hands and Hare told Aaron he was sorry that he hadn't worked well with Nicolson. Aaron replied, 'He used to lose his temper with me sometimes, *and distrusted me in everything* [my italics].' An interesting comment, in view of his admission that Nicolson 'was as cute as a fox' and 'would know your thinking'.

Aaron assured Hare that everything would be different now, as ever, nourishing the big man's matching ego.

'I wish you to capture them, Mr Hare, and I am only sorry that you ever left the district...Beyond doubt you shall have them before long.'

According to Hare, Aaron was completely happy with the watch party living in his hut and assured him that their presence was a secret. 'I do not know any better place where they could be; nobody comes to my house, except my wife's mother...' (a sad comment, and almost true) 'and they are not likely to inform the outlaws of anything that I am doing.'

The party was now increased from three to four men, Constable Magor joining Armstrong, Alexander and McCall. There were now six people in the hut during the day. Each evening Mrs Barry came to stay with Belle, usually until Aaron and the four police returned from Byrnes' just before dawn. The constables settled down on the floor of the living room with their feet to the fire while Aaron joined Belle in the double bed nextdoor. Then, when Aaron and Belle got up, the police moved to the bedroom, two on the bed, two on the floor.

On one of Ward's visits (he always took some greyhounds with him 'as if for sport' when he went down to the Woolshed) the detective saw that security was too dubious, even for his taste. He bought 'three or four yards of calico' to make a curtain for the bedroom doorway and blinds for the glassless front windows.

Paddy Allen continued to deliver weekly cartloads of supplies to the hut by day and the party continued to produce empty bottles at the rate of some three dozen a week—an obvious threat to security.

A more immediate threat to the supposed secrecy of the party came one morning about eleven, when the police were awakened by a disturbance. The owner of the hut, Henry Grose, had turned up and wanted Aaron to clear out. Predictably, Aaron was refusing to budge. Grose marched off, announcing that he would get the police. Constable Armstrong was appalled.

'For God's sake,' he hissed at Aaron, 'Bring the man back here; he will turn us out and we shall be discovered.'

Eventually, Constable Alexander provided the money to buy the hut from the disgruntled owner.

On 16 June, Constables Magor and McCall were recalled to Beechworth to be replaced by Constable Duross from Mooroopna and Constable Dowling from Shepparton. Both were originally 'Melbourne men', both foot constables, formerly in the Garrison Artillery.

The two were given no briefing and, as they were about to leave for Devil's Elbow, the Spencer repeating rifles they had been trained to use were taken from them and they were given the shotguns of the men they were replacing, 'guns we had never seen before in our lives'. Asked if they could hit a haystack with them, poor Duross told the Royal Commission, 'I think we could.'

The two new boys were given one useful piece of advice about Aaron before they left. 'We were told by some of the constables in Beechworth to have our eye on him.'

So the two 'Melbourne men' joined Armstrong and Alexander. Harry Armstrong, a foot constable of nine years service, was in charge. While stationed in Melbourne, he had won a reputation for great courage but he had no experience of command. Aaron easily became the de facto leader of the group (he was the only person to give the new men any sort of briefing on their duties).

Duross and Dowling's suspicions of Aaron were quickly confirmed. Each night, at eight or nine, he led the party down across the creek to make their way along the bank and up through the bush to the old watching place in the clump of trees in front of the Byrne house. As usual while working with the police, he wore a white shirt which shone brightly through the bush on moonlit nights and was easily visible even by starlight. In case this did not warn of the party's approach, he had another trick up his sleeve—or, rather, in hand.

Alexander agreed with a Royal Commission proposition that Aaron 'knew the outlaws were about at the time' and was 'false'. He testified, 'Always, when going to Byrnes' he carried a towel in his hand, and I said to Dowling, "That must be a signal he has got," and we did not like to mention it to him; he was always swinging this about going forward in the bush.'

Aaron's excuse for taking the towel was that he sometimes carried the police across the creek and needed to dry his feet.

It was also obvious, even to 'Melbourne men', that the Gang could arrive at the Byrne house from the back without being seen from the police positions at the front.

Two nights after the arrival of the new men, Aaron and the four constables were on their way to Byrnes when 'a lot of Chinamen' began following them and calling out, apparently in fear that they were 'night fossickers' after the gold in the Chinese sluice boxes. Armstrong suggested that, if they pointed their guns, the Chinese would think they were the Kellys. Aaron agreed with the plan and the miners scattered.

Next day Aaron went to talk with the Chinese. Supposedly, they told him that they had seen the Kellys the previous night. Yet, after this interview with these staunch Kelly sympathisers, Aaron arranged with Armstrong that the party would not go out until ten o'clock that night—because of the moon, which was approaching full. (He told Duross another story—that, being a Saturday night, men would be going to and from Julian's shanty.)

This very night, Hare was on a visit to Beechworth and decided that he would call on the hut party. Aaron, Armstrong, and Dowling were cutting wood up the slope at the back, when Hare and Ward reached the hut between eight and nine. Finding two men inside and obviously concerned that this late departure might create a bad impression, Ward instructed Duross to tell Hare that the others were already at Byrnes, and sent Belle to warn the three wood-cutters. They hurried off to the watching place while Alexander led Hare and Dowling across the creek and through dense scrub in a roundabout search for the Byrne house, covering some two miles. Not surprisingly, by the time they arrived, Aaron and the other two police were already in position. Ward's odd deception had apparently worked, until Armstrong made a clean breast of the whole thing.

Much was made of this curious incident by the Royal Commission, but Ward's duplicity was overshadowed by the Commissioners' pre-judgement of the four constables—based on their appalling conduct exactly one week later.

There were two interesting sidelights. Aaron guided Hare back to his hut where Ward had remained and they had one of their usual conversations, with Aaron assuring Hare of success 'if we only stuck to it'. Hare was very concerned about Aaron lying out in the freezing bush all night in his shirt sleeves. After they had waded across the creek, Hare urged Aaron to come up to the hut and have a cup of tea to warm him, before going back to the watch party.

'He said to me, "No, Mr Hare, this is Saturday night, and I must go back at once to the men." I thought to myself, here is a man who has been working for the last eighteen months—is this put on or is it reality—so I sat on the bank of the creek to see whether he did return afterwards, and remained there, I suppose, about a quarter of an hour just to test him, and I could hear his steps further and further up in the direction of the ranges, and I felt confident that his whole heart and soul were in the work.'

It seems clear that Aaron's anxiety to get back to the watching police was related to his concern that the party shouldn't leave his hut until ten that night. Most likely, he had learnt from the Chinese that Joe was due home and wanted to minimise the risk of him being seen. Hare's arrival had thrown out the timing and Aaron wanted to be on hand in case the men tried to vary their watching position or Joe varied his approach to the house.

Earlier, while scrambling through the moonlit scrub, Hare asked Alexander 'if Sherritt was true to us'.

Alexander replied, 'Sometimes I think he is; again, judging by his conversation, I think different.'

Hare was having doubts about Aaron. Or, perhaps half-aware of the convergence of his strategy with Ward's, he was having qualms. Certainly, after the Saturday night visit, he discussed the shortcomings of the Devil's Elbow situation with Ward, who claims to have spent the next day combing the bush with Mullane in search of a better place to camp the four police. Nothing fitted his particular requirements as well as Aaron's hut.

The Royal Commission was to record, 'The first impression of your Commissioners when they visited the scene...was its unsuitability for such a purpose.' Ironically, the Royal Commissioners went on to define, very accurately, this final element of Ward's strategy. 'Whatever suspicions may have been engendered in the minds of the outlaws as regards Aaron Sherritt's treachery towards them previously, *the fact of his harbouring police in his hut was enough to seal his doom* [my italics].'

In the light of this judgement, it is surprising that the Commissioners blandly accepted Hare's astonishing admission: 'I thought they would run a great risk of being discovered, but I was going to leave them till they were discovered.'

Any shadows of guilt or doubt in Hare's mind were dispelled by a letter written to him by Jack Sherritt that Sunday, 20 June.

Joe, he said, was frequently home and slept in a haystack at Sebastopol. 'I cannot see how it is he is not caught before now. His brother Patrick does be out all night and sleeps all day. Mrs Byrne has their winter flannel and socks all ready to go to them, and she has provisions for six families stored by in her house.'

Jack urged 'for Patrick Byrne to be watched minutely day and night, *as this is a particular time*. As long as Aaron has the men down there, they will never do any good, as to my knowledge he lets too many of his mother-in-law's children to his house, and his mother-in law herself will go there night after night, and will stop sometimes until two o'clock in the morning, and this will be the means of discovering the police, as the Barry children and the Byrne children go to the same school and are on friendly terms. Dear sir, the reason I send you these few lines is this—anything I say up here, they will not listen to; therefore I would like to explain matters to yourself. *I am certain before long they are going to make another raid;* I have not yet heard what it is [my italics].'

Hare's great wish for the Kellys to 'do something' was about to be granted.

Next night, about 11.15, Aaron was mysteriously absent from the watch party when Paddy Byrne left home on his grey mare and, riding at a slow trot, headed up the slope past the police. Because it was bright moonlight they hesitated to follow and watched him riding along the foot of the range until he disappeared near Maddern's Gap.

Driven further from the house by the constant barking of the Byrne dogs, the police watched until 3.30 a.m. without seeing Paddy return.

When Armstrong reported the incident, Ward rode down to the Devil's Elbow the following afternoon. Aaron was away and didn't return until 5.30, with a tale of having left at noon to watch for Paddy's return. He also claimed to have searched for tracks without success.

Ward memoed Hare of the incident the following day, Wednesday. Hare replied on Thursday, foreshadowing local blacktrackers being stationed at Beechworth—'shortly'—an incredibly belated and inadequate response to the activity centred on the Byrne house.

Hare also stressed that Armstrong 'is not to leave the responsibility of the affair to "Tommy"; he is an irresponsible man...'

It was Thursday, 24 June. As part of Hare's plan to bring the Kellys into the open, O'Connor and his Aboriginal police left for Melbourne, the first leg of their journey back to Queensland. A policeman claimed that this night, 'a remark made by Aaron Sherritt to a mounted constable' spurred the final decision to kill Aaron—and trigger the rebellion.

The constable 'was sure that Sherritt knew where the gang was hiding, if he could only get him to open his mouth'. The trooper and Aaron made a 'pub crawl' through Beechworth, with the policeman buying, and reached the Vine Hotel at the very edge of town, the last licensed house before the descent to the Woolshed.

The Vine was a delightful place—established by Jacob Vandenberg, a former Drury Lane violinist who made his living as a miner and tent maker before becoming a publican. Vandenberg was a stout Dutchman, a generous host who had created an oasis of good food, drink and fragrant garden before his death in 1875. The hotel was now run by his family.

Working at the Vine was a girl known to history as Maggie. She was one of the girls in Joe's life—apparently the Beechworth lass whose regular nocturnal visitor was mistaken for Paddy. Described, inevitably, as 'a barmaid', she was actually a general servant who sometimes helped out in the bar.

As Aaron and the constable walked in, Maggie 'was leaning on her elbows on the counter talking to a miner, their heads close together'. To the constable, Aaron seemed 'stung by jealousy'. It is more likely that he was angered by her infidelity to Joe. Settling on a stool at the far end of the counter, Aaron nodded towards her.

'That girl often sees Joe Byrne.'

'Are you sure?'

'Well, I heard so.'

The two had their last drink and Aaron rode off to pick up the four police for the night's watch. The constable returned almost immediately to the hotel and asked Maggie about seeing Joe Byrne.

'The devil a man could tell you that but Sherritt.'

'No, he did not.'

'Oh yes, I know he must have, *and somebody else will soon know, too* [my italics].'

The story, told thirty years later, has a fine apocryphal ring to it. Within a week of the event, however, it would be reported that, on the Wednesday or Thursday night, Joe visited his Beechworth girl friend, 'the last time they met on earth'.

Some catalyst like the 'Maggie' incident may have triggered the rebellion. More likely the date was already set. The Kellys usually rode to action on a weekend during the full moon. The moon was passing full, the weekend one day off, the weather fine.

Ned was reluctant to believe Aaron's betrayal and he may have opposed his killing. But he was prepared for bloodshed—perhaps on a horrifying scale. If Joe was now committed to killing his mate, this death, like the others, must be seen in the context of warfare. If Aaron's death was inevitable, it must be part of the campaign plan.

On Friday, 25 June, the Diseased Stock Agent arrived at the Benalla police station to see Nicolson. Surprised to find Hare, he reiterated his information about the Gang making and testing their armour, reported that 'a fresh exploit was to be expected immediately', and advised that 'part of their plan was to effect something that would cause the ears of the Australian world to tingle'.

Sadleir records, 'Hare treated him with scorn, dismissed him from all further service, and turning to me, remarked: "If this is the sort of person Nicolson and you have been depending upon, it is no wonder you have not caught the Kellys."'

For the second time in four days Hare had ignored a warning.

Events moved quickly, lent significance by the hard light of investigation to come. At 2 a.m. that morning and again on the Saturday Paddy Byrne was seen riding away from the Byrne house on his mysterious errands. A horse was heard passing the Sherritt house on the tableland.

The previous Sunday, Paddy had halted his grey mare outside Aaron's hut and spent an hour 'watching what was going on'. Wednesday or Thursday, he was seen as he 'took stock of the back of the hut'.

Each morning on his way to school Denny Byrne checked the party's tracks leaving and returning to Aaron's cottage.

On Saturday morning, 26 June, Aaron saw Denny pass the back of the hut twice and peer inside. Aaron warned Armstrong, 'You are discovered...they can set fire to this hut, and shoot you one by one as you run out.'

'We'll have to chance that,' Armstrong replied. 'However, I'll go in tonight and tell Ward, and he can tell Mr Hare if he likes.'

This incident may have distracted Aaron from riding into Beechworth that day on a special errand.

Belle was pregnant. Perhaps this had led to a discussion of religion the previous night. Aaron always told Belle that he was 'nothing'. That night, something—perhaps no more than a wish to please Belle—prompted a decision. She recalled, 'He said he would turn Catholic...he said he would get the horses next day and come up to the Catholic chapel at Beechworth...'

Some weeks before, Mrs Barry 'had a dream of bad...that the Kellys came and stuck up the place'.

'That is how I believe it will be before long,' Aaron told her.

After this, Mrs Barry thought that Aaron looked 'downhearted' and she suggested 'Perhaps it does not agree with you to be out at nights.' Aaron dismissed her concern with a characteristic, 'It doesn't matter.'

The day passed and Aaron saw the southern range sink towards moonless darkness. For the last time he saw the crouching shape of the Peak and the notches of Madderns and Byrnes Gaps and the thread of smoke from Byrnes' and the feeble twinkle of lights there, before he went in to dinner.

He was dressed for the night's watch with his white cotton shirt over a flannel singlet, a scarf knotted at his throat, waistcoat hanging loose over dark trousers tucked into heavy boots. This night he was wearing clothes that had been given to him by Ward, eating a supper paid for by Ward, behind curtains supplied by Ward, in a house bought by one of the police in the next room. Perhaps it all seemed a huge joke, a long, rambling joke that twisted its way through comic situations and defied any attempt to predict its ending. He sat at the table, eating dinner by candlelight with his pregnant wife and his mother-in-law, a roaring log fire filling the stone fireplace with bright flame.

About six o'clock Anton Wick left his house opposite the Woolshed school, walked across the Sunbury Bridge, and up the main road towards Devil's Elbow. He planned to visit his friends, the Weiners, and enjoy a chat in German. The calico blinds of the Sherritt cottage were glowing with candle and fire light as he passed, but Weiner's, next door, was in darkness.

Wick turned around and headed back home. It was deep dusk, deeper as he descended the short rise and turned along a stretch of road gloomed with scrawny trees. He had travelled only about a hundred yards when two horsemen approached, one leading a packhorse. It struck him that both men's horses 'kept their heads up'. He said, 'Good evening.' Neither man replied, but the one with the packhorse turned and swung back beside him. It was Joe. The other horseman was Dan.

'What's your name?'

'Wick from the Woolshed.'

Joe took his horse closer to Anton and bent from the saddle. 'Do you know me?'

Wick peered into the blackness under the man's hat brim. 'No.'

'I'm Joe Byrne.'

'I don't believe you.'

Joe drew a revolver. 'Do you believe me now?' He nodded to his companion. 'That is Mr Kelly.' Then, gesturing to Wick, 'Put the handcuffs on.'

Dan dismounted and handcuffed the terrified German. Joe still looked down at him from horseback.

'Don't be frightened. You had a case against me about a horse. I forgive you for that. You have to go with me to Sherritt's place. If you do what I tell you, you need not be frightened.'

Wick thought, 'Aaron Sherritt's had his last supper.'

Joe led off along the road, with Dan following Wick. As they approached Aaron's hut, Joe turned up into the scrub on the short slope of Maidenhair Gully and dismounted. He turned Music loose and took a double-barrelled gun from the packhorse. Dan tossed his reins over a bush and walked out on to the road, then up the rise towards the front of the cottage. Joe took Wick around through the scrub to the back.

Joe saw the big slab chimney set in the windowless wall with the back door to the left of it, outlined by chinks of fireglow and candlelight. The gun was the Mansfield vicar's shotgun borrowed by the Stringybark Creek party, the gun that had killed Sergeant Kennedy, now loaded with massive lead slugs. Joe cocked both hammers back, the triggers set forward.

Aaron was finishing his meal with Belle and Mrs Barry, Constable Duross was warming himself at the fire, the other three police were lying down in the bedroom, when a knock sounded at the back door.

As Duross slipped into the bedroom and lowered the calico curtain, Belle crossed to the door and called, 'Who's there?'

'I've lost my way, Sherritt. Come and put me on the road.' They all recognised the heavily accented voice. Belle turned to Aaron. 'It's Anton Wicks. He's lost his way.'

Aaron laughed. The old German was less than a mile from his home! He left the table, followed by Mrs Barry, removed the prop stick holding the door shut, dragged it open, and leant out into the darkness.

'Do you see that sapling over there?' It was the start of an old bush joke.

A figure moved from behind the chimney.

Aaron went to step back.

'Who's that?'

Joe said something. And pulled the first trigger. A massive explosion. The huge slug took Aaron in the left side of his throat, just above the collar bone, and burst out through his right shoulder. He staggered for a moment, jugular, carotid arteries and windpipe severed.

Standing almost beside Aaron, Mrs Barry stared blankly at his face, in a moment of awful stillness. Belle was half behind her husband.

Then Joe stepped into the doorway and fired the second barrel. A second massive ball smashed into Aaron's ribs and out through his right hip, just missing Belle. Unable to make a sound, his wind gone, Aaron fell, and lived as long as there was blood for his heart to pump.

In the last few seconds of his conscious life, as the blood supply to his brain terminated, he may have been able to comprehend some of the forces that killed him. But not all.

Ward's ruthlessness, Hare's connivance, Nicolson's pragmatism, Jack's gullibility, Wallace's game-playing, Mrs Byrne's enmity, many peoples' Catholic Irish distrust of a protestant, his own naïve guile—all had played their role in the darkly Celtic brew that poisoned Joe against him. Many fingers had helped to squeeze the fine-set triggers of the clergyman's gun.

But, at the end, in the brief glimpse of Joe aiming the gun past Wick's right shoulder, how could Aaron begin to believe that this was happening? He knew that he had remained true to Joe. Beneath it all, Joe, too, must have known…

Shocked by the first shot, hardly aware of the second, Wick saw Joe look down at the bloody, dying remnant of his mate, and say, 'That is the man that I want.'

Belle had blundered through the calico curtain into the dark bedroom where the four police scrambled for their guns, stacked in a corner of the room with ammunition bags hanging beside them.

Mrs Barry dropped on her knees by Aaron's head as he died. She looked up at the tall figure by the open door, the boy of nine years before who had slept in the same bed while she waited to deliver Elly.

'Oh, Joe, Joe! What have you done, what did you shoot poor Aaron for?'

'The bastard will never put me away again.'

Later, he told her, 'I am satisfied now, I wanted that fellow.'

'I never heard Aaron say anything against you,' she countered.

'He would do me harm if he could; he did his best.'

Eventually, she would talk to him for some fifteen minutes 'about his mother'. In the course of this surreal exchange, she asked, 'Joe, how could you have the heart to shoot Aaron?'

'I have a heart, but it's as hard as stone,' he told her.

Aaron died at about half past six. For two-and-a-half hours a grotesque epilogue to the murder was acted out, underscored by the barking and, later, the howling of Aaron's dog, who knew, in the way of dogs, that its master was dead. The sequence of events becomes confused.

Joe ordered Mrs Barry to open the front door. Dan was there. As he walked into the room, Belle emerged from the bedroom to register a horrifying image.

'Dan Kelly...leaned his arm against the table, with his gun placed carelessly by his side, and looked around the room. When he saw my husband's body lying on the floor he smiled, as if glad at what had taken place. He said to me, "Good evening ma'am," and nodded. I looked at him, but never spoke...'

Joe had heard Duross go into the bedroom. Told it was a man who had arrived looking for work, Joe ordered him to come out. The police dithered over their guns, ready to follow Armstrong, they claimed, yet dissuading him from taking risks.

Holding a revolver at Belle's head, Joe ordered her to bring the man out. She went in and told the constables to come out or they would be shot. They refused. She came out again to find Joe 'foaming with rage and swearing and threatening what he would do'.

He had re-loaded his gun and fired a shot past Belle's head into the bedroom wall.

'The flash of the gun went so close to my ear that I and my mother thought I was shot, and I exclaimed that I was; but Byrne said, "It was only the flash of the gun in her ear."'

Again she went into the room to try to get the police out, again she came out, again she went in, until the constables held her there.

Ten minutes after the first shot Armstrong and Duross had been partly under the bed. Now, distraught Belle was forced under the bed—supposedly for her own safety, actually as a screen for the police. She was 'nearly suffocated, being huddled up into a corner'.

Joe and Dan fired a total of five shots into the bedroom, taunting the police to come and fight. They threatened to burn the house, made a half-hearted attempt to light some branches and a broken-up cask against a wall, let Mrs Barry go in to bring Belle out, but she too was kept in the bedroom by the police.

Joe and Dan considered sending Anton Wick in, but eventually gave up the idea and took the handcuffs off him. About nine o'clock, they disappeared. Wick stood there in the darkness. Aaron's dog was still howling. Wind blew through the open doors of the hut, stirring the calico curtain lit by the log fire and the guttering candle.

Aaron lay inside the back door as he had fallen, his face obliterated by blood, only his right eye and his teeth visible.

In the midst of the nightmare Belle 'took a weakness'. Her mother was trying to help her out from under the bed. Belle couldn't seem to hear what she was saying. The trauma—physical and mental—would prove fatal to the baby she was carrying and very nearly fatal to her.

Eventually, Anton Wick wandered off. The police heard voices outside the hut. One policeman would surmise they were members of the Byrne family. Armstrong knocked out the candle with a pillow and, about midnight, pushed the doors shut with his gun, doused the fire, and covered Aaron's body.

Approaching four o'clock, Aaron's dog at last went to sleep. The voices could still be heard. About a dozen voices, one man thought. Then, at last, as the dawn chorus cued the break of day, the voices were silent, and the cold, grey light proclaimed the ugliness and shame of the night. The four police would be branded as cowards, Armstrong disgraced as their leader. Their real leader lay dead.

At last the police ventured outside and began a new round of dithering. How would they get word to Beechworth? They stopped a passing Chinese and sent him with a letter, which he stuck in his boot. He came back with the excuse that he had work to do. They sent him to get Cornelius O'Donoghue. The schoolmaster agreed to alert the Beechworth police but returned after an hour and a half with the excuse that his wife was too frightened to let him go. He told the police that 'he heard the outlaws were in the ranges to shoot any person who would go in with word'.

Cornelius O'Donoghue, Joe's teacher, close friend of Margret Byrne, and known Kelly sympathiser, wasn't going to jeopardise Joe's safety by setting police on his trail.

Eventually, after another two abortive attempts with Chinese, miner Tom Duckett agreed to take word, and headed off to Beechworth with a letter. When hours passed without help arriving, Constable Armstrong made the belated decision that he should go.

As he was walking up the Woolshed, Paddy Byrne appeared from the bush and galloped towards him on his grey mare. Perhaps recognising Armstrong, Paddy veered off into the scrub. About three miles from Beechworth, Armstrong met a traveller and took his horse. He rode it to a standstill, saw Tom Duckett, still on his way, and eventually reached Beechworth police station at about 1 p.m.

'Shivering with cold and greatly excited', he had a constable fetch Ward, who interrupted his Sunday dinner to hear the news. Ward's plan was working. The Kelly Gang had emerged, after sixteen months, but already the trail was more than sixteen hours cold. The Beechworth telegraph office couldn't raise the Benalla station. Hare eventually received the news after 2.30, but would take no action until he contacted Standish in Melbourne, more than two hours later.

Alerted by the Beechworth telegraph officer of Aaron's death, magistrate and coroner Henry Foster hurried down to the Devil's Elbow with his clerk. He arrived at about 1.45 to find a crowd of more than a hundred clamouring around the hut.

Inside, the three police and the two women were in a wretched state, the hut so dark behind its drawn curtains that Foster failed to notice the corpse at his feet. When he asked for a light, Alexander said, 'Well, we do not care much about a light here, sir.'

Foster, who had discharged Aaron in the 'Charlie' case, finished the initial inquiries beside his body, then headed back to Beechworth. About a mile along the way, he met Mullane and four troopers on their way to the hut. They hadn't left Beechworth until 3 p.m. There was no chance of following Joe and Dan, because Hare had done nothing about stationing trackers at Beechworth, and the Queensland native police were in Melbourne, ready to return to Queensland.

It seemed that Ward's murderous strategy had sacrificed Aaron for nothing.

In an extraordinary irony, however, Aaron's death—planned to decoy Hare and the cream of his men to destruction—was about to destroy the Kelly Gang.

This gently sloping bench of park-like bush is tucked away high on the sheer, eastern slope of Byrnes Gully—a perfect hiding place for Joe and Aaron's stolen horses. The photograph was taken in October 2000, when three horses were brought onto the bench, almost certainly the first in 120 years. Only a few metres away (right) is a near-precipice which falls to the gully floor. The author talks with Roger Smitheram, one of the riders who carried out the exercise. (*Photos by Brendon Kelson*)

The rusted head of Joe and Aaron's shovel, just after it was found hidden under this boulder. The hiding place was on the slope of Byrnes Gully immediately below the point where a horseman could enter the secret yardsite. The shovel was needed to maintain a water supply for the horses held there. (*Brendon Kelson*)

The Glenrowan Inn, under police siege, after Ned's capture on the Monday morning. Joe lies dead in the bar room behind the centre window; Dan and Steve are still alive, somewhere within its walls.

Joe's grey mare Music, drawn by Thomas Carrington for the *Sketcher* after she had accompanied Ned Kelly in his last fight with the police at Glenrowan. Note the superb, lightweight saddle.

Joe Byrne's armour, photographed at the Antique and Historical Arms Collectors Guild exhibition in 1966. Although the best-made and best-preserved of the four sets of Kelly armour, the apron probably came from Dan Kelly's or Steve Hart's suit. Joe's breastplate has no provision for attachment of an apron, possibly explaining how he received a fatal bullet wound in the groin.
(*Neil Speed*)

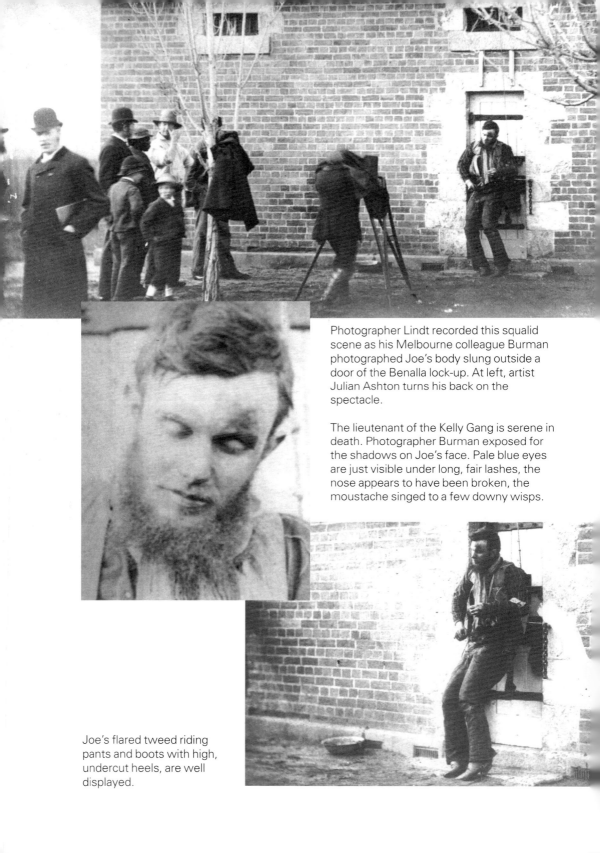

Photographer Lindt recorded this squalid scene as his Melbourne colleague Burman photographed Joe's body slung outside a door of the Benalla lock-up. At left, artist Julian Ashton turns his back on the spectacle.

The lieutenant of the Kelly Gang is serene in death. Photographer Burman exposed for the shadows on Joe's face. Pale blue eyes are just visible under long, fair lashes, the nose appears to have been broken, the moustache singed to a few downy wisps.

Joe's flared tweed riding pants and boots with high, undercut heels, are well displayed.

CHAPTER 17

Armageddon

June 1880

After Aaron's Saturday evening murder, Ned and Joe predicted that, while a small party of police might ride to Devil's Elbow from Beechworth, the main pursuing force would come from Benalla by train, perhaps twelve hours later. Because trains did not normally run on Sundays, troopers, horses and blacktrackers would travel to Beechworth by a police special.

Just past Glenrowan, in the heartland of the Kellys, the line dipped through the Glenrowan Gap and made a sweeping turn to the left around the lower slopes of the Warby Ranges. Here, on the curving embankment above a deep gully, the Gang would break the line. The police train would crash to destruction.

Two Chinese rockets would signal the gathering of a band of sympathisers armed with the Gang's best guns. The armoured Gang members, bearing the older, poorer weapons of their armoury, would then lead the tiny army in an attack on one of the Benalla banks, one of their pack horses carrying a drum of blasting powder and a coil of fuse to destroy the railway line beyond Benalla and isolate this key city of the north-east.

The mad, rebel dream of the Republic was scarcely a day from coming true. Then guerilla war would begin, with police, colonial militia and, eventually, perhaps even Imperial troops set against the farmer rebels in the battle ground of their choice—the ranges of the Kelly Country—while diverse groups with grudges against the British Crown or the colonial government rallied to the Kelly icon.

All this lay ahead as Joe and Dan rode through the night to meet Ned and Steve at Glenrowan. The only emotion Joe had shown was his anger with the police; no hint of hesitation or remorse—nor of recklessness. In moving around outside the house he had taken care to keep Mrs Barry or Wick between himself and the bedroom where the police were cocooned. He had called out a warning to Dan of windows in the front wall. He had remained in control of himself and the situation—supported, as he was, by an unknown number of sympathisers screening the operation. He was heard whistling signals to them and calling out that there were 'bloody dogs' inside. And he was in the Woolshed valley, crucible of passionate, Byrne-based support, where every person was so utterly loyal to the Kelly cause or so utterly cowed by the pervading pro-Kellyism that he and Dan could linger at the murder scene for two-and-a-half hours without the seven shots, screams, shouting and the awful death song of Aaron's dog bringing one person to help or investigate. Not a whisper of the killing escaped the valley.

On the ride to Glenrowan, he and Dan probably rode alone, the first three hours in moonless darkness. Their most likely route was up through Maddern's Gap and across the tableland by Sherritts'—along the track carefully checked by Paddy in the preceding two nights. Then, down by Everton, across the Pioneer Bridges, and over the Oxley Flats until the moon rose brilliantly behind them and speared their shadows ahead towards the Glenrowan Gap.

They rode hard, often girth-deep in water, bodies warm under flannel, wool and oilskin, legs chilled by wet tweed in the icy foredawn. For Joe, with an old crocheted scarf knotted around his throat, there was another coldness creeping through him as the chemicals of tension and crisis diluted in his blood, and the killing of Aaron slowly came into focus, clearer and uglier with every mile.

He had told Mrs Barry, 'I have a heart, but it's as hard as stone.'

In one pocket of his blue jacket was a Catholic prayer book and some cartridges. In the other, some bullets and a small brown paper package of poison. On the third finger of his right hand was Scanlon's topaz ring, on the little finger of his left, Lonigan's ring with its white seal.

Joe rode to his place of destiny with his hands proclaiming him a murderer, his pockets offering evidence of some search for absolution, yet asserting his readiness to kill again—bullets for his enemies, poison for himself.

While Joe and Dan were still riding across the Oxley Flats, Ned and Steve moved on Glenrowan. Wearing their body armour under oilskin coats, they rode into the little railway township between midnight and one.

In a broad saddle of open bushland below the steep, thickly timbered hill called Morgan's Lookout, the railway line levelled out after a steady climb and ran through railway gates to the station on the north side. Diagonally behind the station, almost level with the gates, was the Glenrowan Inn—a homely, white weatherboard building with a corrugated iron roof and a bark-and-slab kitchen immediately behind. Across the line was the Railway Tavern, an older, rougher pub run by Kelly sympathiser Paddy McDonnell. Here, the Gang's saddle horses were stabled. Ned and Steve woke seven labourers sleeping in a group of tents between Jones's Inn and the station, and brought the stationmaster from his house near the gates. Ordered to direct the workmen in breaking the line, the stationmaster said they needed platelayer James Reardon who lived half a mile out of town towards Benalla.

Steve guarded the labourers while Ned fetched Reardon—with his wife and eight children. Publican Ann Jones was roused from her sickbed (she suffered from neuralgia) and she and her 14-year-old daughter Jane joined the prisoners, while her four young sons were locked in the hotel.

Now, Joe and Dan arrived, later than planned and almost immediately Dan took charge of the prisoners. While Ned went back to get a crowbar from Reardon's and Steve took the railwaymen to start breaking the line, accompanied by Jane Jones, Joe downed a drink or two at McDonnell's. When he rejoined Dan at the gatehouse, he asked the stationmaster's wife for breakfast and she brought some bacon out to them.

Soon afterwards Mrs Jones came out and invited the two inside. Joe shook his head. 'No.'

He peered through the window of the house and saw the women and children at breakfast. 'No,' he repeated. 'There's females in there.' It was as though he was suddenly unfit to mix with these women and the brood of children.

Mrs Jones repeated the invitation. Again, Joe refused. 'No, thank you. We are right enough here.'

The rashers of hot bacon were not enough to fill that cold emptiness. He was conscious of a bottle of brandy Mrs Jones had brought down to the gatehouse and asked for 'her' bottle of brandy, adding, 'In fact, it did not matter whose it was as long as he got it.'

With a length of rails removed and dumped in the gully below the bend, Ned and Steve brought the railway gang back to the township and at Mrs Jones's invitation, they all trooped up to the Glenrowan Inn.

The morning dragged by as the Gang waited edgily for the train—unaware that knowledge of Aaron's murder was still locked in the Woolshed valley. About eleven, the Glenrowan schoolteacher, Thomas Curnow, joined the prisoners with members of his family. A tallish young man, lame in one leg, he sought a way of 'checkmating' the outlaws and systematically worked his way into Ned's confidence, first telling him of a revolver in the stationmaster's house.

Exhausted, at last relaxed by the liquor he'd put away, Joe had a sleep in the Glenrowan Inn towards midday. When he woke, 'he was quite straight' and, seeing Dan about to down a nobbler of neat brandy, was heard to say, 'Steady, old man'—prompting Dan to add water.

Anyone who came along was bailed up, until 62 men, women and children were held in the gatehouse and Mrs Jones's Inn, including five prominent sympathisers—Paddy and Denny McAuliffe and Michael, John and Paddy Delaney. Relaxed by Mrs Jones's liquor and the Gang's amiability, they all made the best of it.

Mrs Jones was charmed by Ned and thought Joe 'a very nice and handsome man, as nice as any she had ever seen'. The two did their best to keep up the spirits of the prisoners—and Dan and Steve—as the Sunday afternoon slipped away. Ned spoke of bailing up a nearby circus to entertain them and considered butchering a bullock for the evening meal.

Meanwhile, Standish in Melbourne and Hare in Benalla exchanged dithering telegrams. Swallowing his pride with some difficulty, Standish asked O'Connor and his Aboriginals to rejoin the hunt. O'Connor relished the moment, and agreed 'after a good deal of humming and hawing'. It was planned to send the Queensland contingent up by the first train on Monday, until the Chief Secretary stepped in and decided the issue. A special train would be provided that night.

Twenty-four hours after Aaron's death, his body still lay on the floor of the hut, and officialdom was still fumbling towards the first step in pursuing his murderers.

Surprisingly, Ned and Joe waited until late Sunday night to bring in the Glenrowan policeman, Constable Bracken. Until the previous day there had been four troopers at his station, going out for nightly surveillance of the Kelly homestead. They had been withdrawn on the verge of hospitalisation, and Bracken was in bed with flu.

Wearing armour, Ned and Joe took some locals, including schoolmaster Curnow, to bail up Bracken, the first policeman to face the awesome spectacle of a helmeted Ned Kelly. Warning Curnow 'not to dream too loud', Ned let the teacher and his family continue home before he and Joe took their police prisoner back to the hotel.

The Inn was 'a house of sport' as Mrs Jones put it. Dave Mortimer was playing the concertina, there was singing and dancing and card playing, a big bonfire blazed in the backyard. But it was past midnight, children were sleepy and tearful, and wives were reluctant to go home while their husbands stayed drinking.

Past two o'clock on the Monday morning, almost 32 hours after Aaron's death, it seemed that there would be no police special. Ned and Dan had decided to let the prisoners go when Mrs Jones called them all back to hear 'a lecture' from Ned.

Joe was on sentry duty outside in the still, icy darkness. The moon was behind him, by the shoulder of Morgan's Lookout, sketching the Gap and the ranges beyond with bleached, grey light and bold strokes of shadow, the group of tents shining coldly, trees out to the left caught by the flickering glow of the bonfire at the back.

When he was nine or ten, Joe had studied 'The Night Before Agincourt' from *Henry V*—Shakespeare's marvellous evocation of a moonlit landscape with two encamped armies preparing for battle. Many of the symbols may have struck chords—the moonlight, the fires, the tents, the horses, the armour—

Steed threatens steed, in high and boastful neighs
Piercing the night's dull ear; and from the tents
The armourers, accomplishing the knights,
With busy hammers closing rivets up,
Give dreadful note of preparation.
The country cocks do crow...

There was even a cock crowing. But then...it wasn't a cock: it was a train whistle.

Joe burst into the hotel. 'The train's coming!'

The Gang went into a back room to put on their armour, helped by a sympathiser. Four young men went into the room; four metal humanoids emerged, four Ned Kellys moving through the inn to the chime of steel on steel, as steam hissed from water-doused fires and kerosene lights were extinguished, room by room.

Constable Bracken had noted where the frontdoor key was kept—'on the end of the bar counter near the wall'. He slipped outside, locked the door behind him and ran down to the railway.

A pilot engine preceding the police train had been stopped by Curnow with a candle and red scarf. Alerted that the Kellys were at Glenrowan, Hare, backed by seven Benalla police and O'Connor with his Aboriginals, jumped from the train at the Glenrowan station and ran to the gatehouse. He had returned to the station and was getting the horses unloaded, when Bracken arrived to warn of the Gang in the hotel.

It was Hare's moment of glory. He led a wild charge of police (and two enthusiastic pressmen) towards the darkened hotel. Ned stood in armour, just in front of the building; Joe, Dan and Steve were on the deep-shadowed verandah.

Ned fired first, hitting Hare in the left wrist and starting a wild exchange of shots as the police dived for cover in a drain, behind fence posts and trees, to return the Kelly fire. As Ned took aim, a single bullet ripped through his bent left arm, inflicting four serious wounds. Another went through his right foot, another wounded his right hand at the base of the thumb.

Joe, too, was badly wounded. During those first wild volleys, a bullet tore into the calf muscle of his right leg.

Ned still managed to shout defiantly, 'Fire away, you bastards. You can't hurt us!' and the Gang retreated around the side of the hotel to the back-door, as Hare dropped out of the fight and his men formed a firing line in a scattered half-circle around the front.

One of them, Constable Phillips, heard an extraordinary exchange between Ned and Joe.

'Is that you, Joe?'

'Yes. Is that you, Ned? Come here.'

'Come here be damned. What are you doing there? Come with me and load my rifle, I'm cooked.'

'So am I. I think my leg is broke.'

'Leg be damned. You got the use of your arms. Come on. Load for me. I'll pink the buggers.'

'Don't be so excited; the boys'll hear us and it'll dishearten them.'

'I'm afraid it's a case with us this time.'

'Well, it's your fault; I always said this bloody armour would bring us to grief.'

'Don't you believe it. Old Hare is cooked and we'll soon finish the rest.'

Everything had gone wrong. Capping it all, Jack Lloyd, charged with firing the signal rockets when the train was wrecked, had set them off almost immediately after the start of the fight. Sympathisers would be riding to join the Gang; but instead of an almost unopposed attack on Benalla, they faced a pitched gun battle. They must be turned back.

While Ned headed off to the meeting place, Joe, Dan and Steve battled the police in a chaos of terrified civilians lying on the floor of the hotel. Young Jack Jones had been fatally wounded by one of the first bullets splintering through its walls, another would graze Jane Jones's head. Mrs Jones, demented with grief and anger, wandered around the battlefield and through her hotel, screaming abuse at police and Kellys alike. A railway worker risked death to carry young Jack to safety, a few others ran clear, another labourer was mortally wounded out in the kitchen. Reardon's son would be hit by a bullet near the heart while trying to escape.

Dave Mortimer, who had played the concertina for the dancing, lay on the bar room floor as 'the bullets continued to whistle through the building' and saw Joe living out his last couple of hours as an inspirational figure for 'the boys'. Mortimer recalled that he 'cursed and swore at the police. He seemed perfectly reckless of his life.'

In this nightmare, Dan showed genuine concern for the plight of the prisoners and kept a cool head. When Mrs Reardon was carrying a baby down the passage, about to make an escape bid, Joe's rifle tangled in her dress and Dan called, 'Take your rifle, or the woman will be shot.'

Outside, Ned had managed to reach the place not far from the broken railway line, where the sympathisers were to gather. He ordered them out of the fight and, helped by Tom Lloyd, prepared to come back to the hotel to rescue Joe, Dan and Steve.

Police reinforcements were arriving. Constable Bracken had ridden to Wangaratta to bring Sergeant Steele and four men on horseback. They moved into position shortly before 6 a.m. Immediately afterwards another trainload of police arrived from Benalla—Sadleir and thirteen men.

The distraction of these arrivals probably enabled Ned to move through the still-uncompleted cordon around the hotel, helped by a pre-dawn ground fog and slow-moving drifts of gunsmoke.

He reached the backdoor and limped down the dark passage. At that moment, Joe left his firing position at a front window and crossed to the corner of the bar by the passage doorway to pour himself a whiskey.

He probably saw Ned. Shortly before, daunted by the reinforcements, he had been heard calling the McAuliffe brothers to come and help. Suddenly, everything was different: Ned had returned. Joe raised the glass and called a defiant toast.

'Many more years in the bush for the Kelly Gang!'

A police volley smashed through the walls as Joe went to drink. A bullet ripped into his groin between breastplate and apron, severed the femoral artery and, probably, the femoral nerve.

Paralysed, in a moment that lasted for the rest of his life, he toppled and fell, his armoured weight shaking the floor.

James Reardon lay nearby. 'I heard him fall like a log, and he never groaned or anything, and I could hear like the blood gushing.'

Joe had fallen partly across one of the Delaneys and a farmer called Sandercook, and close to 9-year-old Kate Reardon. His blood splashed over her dress and pinny. The fatal volley had hit a clock in the next room and it started striking. Trying to ignore the horror of the moment, young Kate counted over a hundred strokes.

Ned stood in the passage, with the clock crazily chiming. Time had gone mad; Joe was dead. For the moment, Ned was on the verge of letting everything go, simply trying to survive. He said that 'when he saw his best friend dead, he had no more faith in them [Dan and Steve]'.

Yet he told Dan, 'We must make the best of it; my best friend is dead. I'll go out in the verandah and challenge them.'

'I went out and did so but the police wouldn't answer. I went back to the house. My brother and Steve Hart had gone outside or into one of the rooms. I thought they had cleared. I said "I'll challenge the lot myself" and walked out past seven or eight police. I could have shot them easily, and could have got away if I wished.'

Constable Gascoigne, who had swapped shots with Ned and recognised his voice earlier in the battle, now saw him walk up the backyard among the horses and saw one of them 'get out of the yard and get away into the bush'. The trooper reported this to the newly arrived Sadleir.

When Ned reached Tom Lloyd up in the bush and discovered that Dan and Steve hadn't left the pub, he fainted from loss of blood. Meanwhile the boys were calling for him. A prisoner heard one of them say, 'What'll we do?'

Ned regained consciousness and prepared again to rescue them. With Tom's help, he loaded three revolvers—two Colts and a Webley—and, at sunrise, began what has passed into legend as Ned Kelly's Last Stand.

Ned had been bleeding from major wounds for four hours, in sub-zero temperatures, wearing almost a hundredweight of armour, as he limped to attack the 36 police by now scattered in the bush around the hotel.

Looming from a dawn ground mist among the trees, his voice booming eerily in the helmet, he seemed a giant, unearthly figure. In a bizarre gun battle that lasted almost half an hour, he advanced doggedly towards the hotel, with police falling back around him. Bullets whined off his armour and, occasionally sent him staggering, yet, each time, he rallied and moved forward again, banging his revolver against the helmet to make it chime 'like a cracked bell'. His strength was waning; he could hardly raise the barrel at arm's length to take aim.

Dan and Steve emerged from the backdoor and caught the police in a crossfire. An escape corridor was opening. Ned rested and was seen trying to re-load one of the revolvers. Adding to the unearthly quality of this dawn battle, Music had appeared in the bush behind him, trotting backwards and forwards among the misted trees like a spirit horse. Now, she came forward, almost to where he was crouched, as though offering escape. Ned ignored her and resumed the advance.

Sergeant Steele had already tried to close in on Ned but was driven to ground in the crossfire. He saw his chance as Ned was turned aside to swap shots with a trooper and a plucky railway guard among the branches of a huge fallen tree. Steele ran forward. At that moment, Music moved between Ned and the advancing policeman. Ned started to turn, and Steele gave him a barrel of duckshot in the hip and thigh. Ned staggered, tried to brace his gun hand against the buckling leg as the second barrel blasted shot into it. He fell with an awful, echoing cry, 'I'm done!'

It was over. Stripped of his armour, he seemed on the verge of death, mangled by 28 separate shot wounds. Taken to the station, he showed no will to live, but was too tough to die.

At 9 a.m. Senior Constable Mullane reached the battleground with ten police from Beechworth—and Jack Sherritt.

Shattered by the news of Aaron's death, Jack had slept at the police barracks on the Sunday night. In the early hours of Monday, when news came of the Glenrowan battle, Jack galloped down to Devil's Elbow to bring back the police still guarding the death hut. He covered the 12 miles in a staggering 30 minutes. Then, armed with a police shotgun, he boarded a special train with the Beechworth contingent 'because he wanted to be avenged of his brother on Joe Byrne'.

Willie might have joined his brother but was needed at the inquest on Aaron which began that day.

At last, Aaron's body was taken from the hut and, because his death had occurred more than two miles from a police station, it was carried to the nearest hotel, as required by law. So, that Monday morning, a few hours after Joe's death, Aaron's body arrived at the Vine Hotel where 'Maggie' worked. It was placed in an outbuilding and Dr Dobbyn of the Beechworth Hospital performed a meticulous post-mortem, dissecting Aaron's chest and abdomen to trace the path of those two huge bullets. He observed dispassionately that the heart's ventricles and auricles were quite empty of blood and finished with the curiously pathetic note, 'The body was very healthy.'

That afternoon Magistrate Foster empanelled his jury. Its foreman was Aaron's confidant, storekeeper Paddy Allen, and it included James Ingram, who had chatted so often with Aaron and Joe in the back room of his shop, and publican Joseph Wertheim, who was still charging Aaron's brandy and cigars to Ward.

Willie and John Sherritt were the first witnesses. They had been taken to the outbuilding to view Aaron's body and now formally identified it. Mrs Barry had been subjected to the same cold ritual. She began to tell her story of the killing but the balance of her evidence was deferred because the four police in the hut had been sent to Glenrowan. Dobbyn described his post-mortem and the day's hearing concluded.

Foster released Aaron's body for burial. The police paid for his funeral and the Reverend Mr Mackie of the Presbyterian Church conducted a graveside service in the creeping cold of the highland dusk. If the bleak little ceremony brought together Belle and the Sherritts in their shared grief, there is no record of their presence. The grave was unmarked by cross or headstone but would be carefully tended. By the time Aaron was laid to rest in his police-bought coffin, it was all over at Glenrowan.

About an hour after Jack and the Beechworth police moved into position, the last of the prisoners were released by Dan and Steve. The siege became a tedious standoff. Sadleir sent for a field gun and considered the use of electric light.

At three in the afternoon, while Ned still lay in the station master's office at the railway station, the hotel was set alight by impetuous Constable Johnston. As flames swept through the building, a brave Catholic priest, Father Gibney, ran inside and found Joe's body.

> There was a door leading out of this room towards the [back] door. His body was lying there where he had fallen in a strangled [*sic*] kind of way. He seemed to have fallen on his back, like on his hip. He must have died soon, because he was just in the same position as he fell; he was still lying, and his body quite stiff.

Constable Armstrong, from Aaron's hut, and Constable Dwyer dragged Joe's armoured body outside as Gibney found Dan and Steve side by side in a back room—dead, their heads pillowed on sacking, armour at their sides, a dead dog beside them. The hotel became their pyre. After their charred bodies were recovered from the ashes of the inn, they were handed to the

Kelly girls and the men of the sympathiser army who had obeyed Ned's last order and kept out of the fight.

Joe's body remained in police hands. Stripped of armour, it was carried down to the railway station by two police, with press artist Carrington following to make a sketch. At the fence of the railway reserve, they rested the stiffened corpse on a post while the first trooper climbed between the wire. A Glenrowan lad watched as Joe's body see-sawed grotesquely for a moment. The two police laughed.

Eventually, after Carrington had made his sketch of Joe's sadly contorted frame, it was loaded on the same train that carried Ned to Benalla. That night Ned and his mate's corpse shared neighbouring cells in the Benalla lock-up.

Respected young English artist Julian Ashton, representing the *Illustrated Australian News,* had arrived late for the battle. He achieved a scoop of sorts by gaining admittance to the lock-up to make a study of Joe's body by candlelight. In what he described as 'the most miserable assignment I ever had', he made his drawing straight on to a wooden engraver's block.

Ashton posed an Aboriginal trooper with the corpse, which lay, stiff and awkward, on the board floor. Flared riding pants were soaked with blood, the knees flexed slightly, arms half-raised from the elbows. Brow and clenched hands had been scorched by flames. Blue eyes were half-open under long, fair eye lashes, bearded face thrust upward, mouth settled in a sad, half-smile.

Eager to be done, Ashton wrote his initials 'JRA' backwards, in a corner of the block—so hastily that he forgot to reverse the 'J'—and, gratefully, left.

Next morning, after Ned had been taken to the Benalla station on his way to Melbourne, photographers persuaded police to hang Joe's body on the lock-up door. Ashton's disgust is clear in one of their photos as he turns his back on corpse, photographers and lookers-on. Perhaps he still had his back to the squalid scene when a young woman burst from the crowd and hurled herself at Joe with an anguished cry.

'End the circus!'

Writer Max Brown surmised that it might have been 'Maggie'. Or any one of the many girls Joe had wooed or charmed. If Ashton had not been so thoroughly fed up with the whole business, he might have sketched the tableau. But the moment passed without record. The sobbing girl was led away, and the body was lifted back to lie in the merciful dimness of the cell while police formed up outside the open door and posed for the photographers in triumphant groups.

Police Magistrate Wyatt had set Joe's inquest for the following day, Wednesday. However, he had been dead for some 40 hours and, in Wyatt's absence, it was decided to hold a hurried 'inquiry' to enable burial as soon as possible.

That evening Captain Standish and squatter Robert McBean, both justices

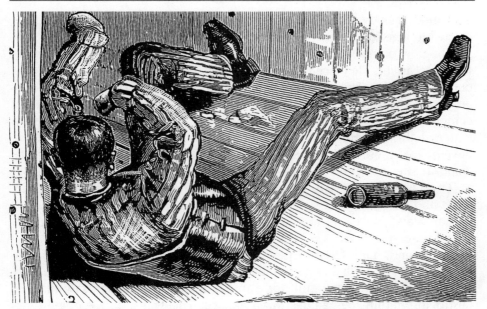

When police carried Joe's body down to the Glenrowan railway station, after its rescue from the burning hotel, *Sketcher* artist Thomas Carrington followed to make this study. The armour had been removed, and Carrington supplied some, unconvincingly. Joe's blue jacket has already been torn or burnt off; Carrington, or the engraver, has omitted his scarf and waistcoat.

of the peace, sat in the empty Benalla courthouse to hear four witnesses.

Constable McIntyre identified Joe as one of the party who had shot the police at Stringybark Creek, and as the man named in the Proclamation of Outlawry as Charles Brown. Railway contractor Alfonso Piazzi deposed that he had seen Joe at the hotel during the Glenrowan hold-up and, later, 'laying dead in the passage'. Constable Canny said that he had known Joe for eight or nine years, described the Glenrowan battle, and the removal of the bodies.

Sadleir offered the only semblance of medical evidence. He had seen the body removed from the inn. 'It was quite stiff, encased in sheet iron armour. It has a bullet wound on the inside of the right thigh, which caused death.'

McBean then gave his finding. 'After having heard the evidence given herewith, I find that the deceased Joseph Byrne, being an outlaw by proclamation in the *Government Gazette*, met his death from a gunshot wound in an encounter with certain members of the police force at Glenrowan on the 28th June, 1880.'

Tom Lloyd and other 'friends of the deceased' had been pleading for the chance to give Joe a Christian burial at Greta. The police fobbed them off until after the inquiry. If the application had been made by a member of the Byrne family, it might have been granted. Coming as it did from members of a group who had been holding a wild wake over Dan and Steve's remains, and who were planning to bury them the following day, the police clearly thought that another body would only inflame an already explosive situation. They elected to give Joe a secret burial.

The now-putrescent body was stripped and wrapped in canvas by undertaker McFarlane. He placed it in a roughly made coffin which was smuggled out the back of the police station to his cart. 'A well-armed constable' provided an escort through the dark streets to the farthest corner of the Benalla cemetery, where the coffin was buried in a waiting pauper's grave by lantern light, without prayers, tears or even a thought for those who might have offered these rites of interment. It was little more than an act of waste disposal after due process of law.

Their work completed, the constable and the undertaker 'saluted each other and went home'.

Aaron and Joe, closer than brothers, had been buried on successive days, 40 miles apart.

At the end, had Margret Byrne been too proud to claim the body of her outlaw son? What other stubborn, uncompromising position might have held her back? If she felt any guilt for Aaron's death, perhaps she saw that, in destroying Aaron, Joe had destroyed himself. This was a degree of guilt she could not accept, or confront.

On the tableland and in the valley below, the two families hugged their grief tight, and spoke of revenge; while rain drifted over the hills, and two anonymous mounds of freshly turned clay lost their rawness, settled, and sprang with grass.

CHAPTER 18

Afterwards

Ned Kelly was nursed back to health, tried and, as a matter of course, found guilty, sentenced to death, and hanged on 11 November 1880.

Belle lost her baby and nearly died. Under the care of two doctors, she recuperated in Beechworth, staying at the Hibernian and Empire hotels. Her accommodation, clothing, footwear and, later, groceries were paid for by the government, via Ward. Eventually, it was agreed to pay her a pension of £1 per week, retrospective to Aaron's death, which she continued to receive even after she married a Michael Murphy in 1884. They lived in the Woolshed and raised a family.

Hare, who recovered from his wound to enjoy brief adulation, was censured by the Royal Commission and retired as a police magistrate. He left a chilling valediction on Aaron.

> It was doubtless a most fortunate occurrence that Aaron was shot by the outlaws; it was impossible to reclaim him, and the government of the colony would not have assisted him in any way, and he would have gone back to his old course of life, and probably spent his days in gaol, *or he might have turned bushranger himself, when he would have been quite as dangerous a man as Ned Kelly* [my italics].

Aaron would have considered this a proud epitaph. Hare continued, 'The government gave his widow a comfortable allowance, and she was much better off without him.'

Detective Ward had early fears that there would be retribution for his use of Aaron as bait to bring the Kellys into the open. In November 1880 Belle told Armstrong, 'He [Ward] is afraid he will get into trouble for leaving the camp without a sentry, allowing the camp to be stuck up, and Aaron shot.'

However, by January 1881, Ward was prepared to claim in his application for a share of the Kelly reward, 'It was on my information that the authorities kept up the watch party at Sebastapool from December 1879 to June 1880 the day of Aaron Sherritt's death and I am of the opinion that the murder of Aaron was the catching [of] the Kelly gang.'

That year several details of his strategy and even its precise nature were revealed in evidence before the Royal Commission, though the Commissioners eventually censured him only for deception of his superiors. He was demoted one grade. He ended his career as a successful Melbourne private detective.

The Royal Commission recommended James Wallace's immediate dismissal. The Education Department readily complied.

The Sherritts were shattered by Aaron's death. On top of this, threats were made against the family. John Sherritt reported to the Beechworth police on 3 July that 'Tom Lloyd, Quinn, Pat Byrne, and Dick Hart were "out", and himself and his family were in fear of their lives, or of having their places burnt down.' Ward reported to Standish two days later, 'I believe they are in danger at the present time.' The same day, Sadleir urged 'early and liberal assistance' to enable the family to leave the district.

Jack was the focus of most resentment because he had taken arms with the police at the siege of Glenrowan. He left Beechworth within a week and he and Willie joined the police force in August. Their careers lasted only until October, peremptorily cut short by a hostile if not vengeful Nicolson. Considering a return to Beechworth suicidal, Jack went to South Australia briefly but, because 'it was too hot...and I got a fall from my horse', he returned to Victoria and settled near Gisborne. He lost touch with Willie who would drift back to Beechworth and eventually die a bachelor on his parents' old farm. Jack gave evidence to the Royal Commission at its Beechworth sittings in 1881 and, three times within a few minutes, told the Commissioners that he feared that Mrs Byrne herself might try to kill him.

The Sherritt family claimed compensation for the death of Aaron, to earn scathing condemnation from Nicolson, who reported that they had been 'very jealous of Aaron least he should earn a portion of the reward to their exclusion'.

Nicolson went further and said that 'the police had grounds for suspecting John Sherritt [Jack] of having given warning to the outlaws and their friends [of Aaron].' He told the Royal Commission that Jack was suspected of 'thwarting if not betraying' Aaron.

Ironically, Jack did receive a share of the reward—£42 15s 9d, the same amount granted to the other members of the Beechworth police contingent.

Jack's fears of Mrs Byrne were not unfounded.

On 24 July Anne Jane was at the Byrne house when Paddy and Denny threatened the lives of Ward and Mullane and were trying to find out who shot Joe 'that they would have revenge on him'. Anne Jane reported to Ward, 'Mrs Byrns said Paddy had not courage to shoot that bloody spy Ward' though she considered it a pity to kill Mullane because of his courage 'for coming down to Sebastopool so often in uniform.'

Ward urged Anne Jane to continue her visits in the hope that 'we might be able to prove something against Paddy and Denny before long' but soon realised that any attempt to prosecute members of the Byrne family would stir up enormous ill-feeling and place him in very real danger. When Constable Armstrong suggested that Paddy Byrne had been turning back the various messengers sent to Beechworth with news of Aaron's murder, Ward carefully debunked the theory—quoting Cornelius O'Donoghue to help clear Paddy, without indicating that the teacher was a Kelly sympathiser, a fact he later admitted to the Royal Commission.

Elly Byrne recalled O'Donoghue's daily visits to her mother at this time. 'I remember every day Mr O'Donoghue would let us out then shut up the school and run as fast as he could go, down across the creek and to our house. I can see him now, running as fast as his legs would carry him.'

Paddy Byrne—with Dick Hart and Jim Kelly—was regarded as one of the leaders of the 'new gang'—the continuation of the Kelly rebellion, which fermented uneasily for more than a year after the destruction of the Gang. With, at last, some judicious police work and, at last, more level-headed police participation in the administration of the Land Act, the threat was contained and resurgence aborted. In February 1881 Paddy Byrne took up a gold claim with four mates on Reedy Creek. Some time after this, Margret Byrne left the Woolshed. Elly recalled, 'I remember coming home and my mother had every-thing on a big lorry piled up sky high. And it was all ready to go to Albury.'

Margret had decided to leave the valley, in spite of the widespread sym-pathy and respect she commanded. In Elly's words, 'She thought she'd make a clean sweep and a fresh start.'

The Byrnes rented accommodation in Albury until Margret bought a substantial weatherboard house on a large block of land in Young Street. The family lived out their lives proudly, never advertising their kinship with Joe, but never denying it. In Elly's words, 'Whatever happened, well, it happened. It's been done, we can't undo it', echoing the view often expressed by her mother.

Margret Byrne died at her Albury home in May 1921, survived by five of her seven children. She was 87.

Elly was the last of the family, dying on 5 August 1964, at the Mercy Hospital, Albury. At 93, she was still bright-eyed and cheerful, with clear memories of her childhood in the Woolshed, and almost defiantly proud of her outlaw brother.

After Elly's death, her foster son continued to live in the old Byrne home. Eventually, it was sold and demolished to make way for part of the Georgian Motel. A section of the original property had already been given by Elly to the Catholic church for construction of a modest chapel, named, appropriately, St Joseph's, in which innumerable prayers have been offered for the soul of Joe.

Back in Beechworth, the Sherritts were left with their grief and the stigma of Aaron's supposed betrayal of the Gang. None of the Sherritt girls married until 1889.

At Christmas 1899 a bushfire swept up across the ranges from the Woolshed and the Sherritt homestead was destroyed. Old John never recovered from this final blow and died of influenza in June 1900 at the age of 73. He was buried in an unmarked grave beside Aaron. At the end, just as he had defiantly declared in court all those years before, he and his beloved eldest son were 'not separated'.

Anne Sherritt survived John by only eight years, and died at 70, in March 1908, to be buried with Aaron and her husband. She was survived by eleven of her twelve children. Her brother, Robert, had been killed in a riding accident five years before.

One of the last members of the Sherritt family living in Beechworth was a niece, daughter of baby Hugh who was nursed by Ned Kelly on that charmingly described visit to the Sherritt home in 1879. She had never heard Aaron's name mentioned until a school friend returned from a visit to Melbourne and told her, 'I saw your uncle in the wax-works.'

Revenge had remained an uneasy lietmotiv between the Byrne and Sherritt families for many years.

In 1906 Paddy and Denny Byrne, working as drovers, brought a big mob of sheep through the Woolshed on their way to Wangaratta. They camped the mob in a lane beside the home of one of the married Barry girls and visited their old Woolshed friends. Later Paddy rode up to Beechworth and enjoyed a few drinks in the Railway Hotel (today's Nicholas), at the corner of Camp and High streets.

Jack Sherritt was then working as a locomotive driver, earning the nickname 'Hellfire Jack'. That afternoon, he brought a train into Beechworth Station and went up to the Railway Hotel for a drink.

As he walked into the bar, the murmur of talk was hushed, and Beechworth witnessed one of those confrontations beloved by Western writers but rarely seen in real life. The tall engine driver faced the powerfully built drover.

Jack, who had gone to Glenrowan clutching a police gun, ready to kill Joe Byrne and avenge Aaron's death, faced Joe's brother, who had undoubtedly been an accessory to Aaron's murder.

The seconds stretched breathlessly. It was Jack who moved first. He crossed to Paddy, and extended his hand.

'It's been a long time, Paddy.'

Paddy shook his hand and the pair moved to the bar, apart from the other drinkers. They talked and drank together for hours, these two men whose Irish origins had been so different, one Protestant, one Catholic, one for the Rebel cause, one for the Crown. But two men with something in common that outweighed all else. Grief. And guilt. Each, in his own way, had helped to shape the tragedy which destroyed Joe and Aaron.

When they parted, out in Camp Street, late in the day, it was for the last time. They parted friends, warmed by whiskey and the memories of those long-lost days, when Joe and Aaron had walked this street, turning heads, brothers to be proud of.

Paddy untied his reins from their hitching ring and mounted. A cock of the head to Jack, and he reined his horse up across the hump of the hill, back towards the Woolshed. Jack watched for a moment, then turned and walked down towards the station. Some thought there were tears in his eyes. Others said he was smiling. Perhaps both were right.

Abbreviations

Age	Melbourne *Age*
Argus	Melbourne *Argus*
AONSW	Archives of New South Wales
cf.	compare with
Commission	*Minutes of Evidence Taken Before Royal Commission on the Police Force of Victoria, 1881*
Const.	Constable
Det.	Detective
Det. Insp.	Detective Inspector
DSA	Diseased Stock Agent
et al.	and others
et seq.	and those following
Herald	Melbourne *Herald*
ibid.	the same source
IRA	Irish Republican Army
MEHC	Ministry of Education Historical Collection
MLA	Member of the Legislative Assembly
n.d.	undated
op. cit.	previously cited
O & M	*Ovens and Murray Advertiser*
OUP	Oxford University Press
p., pp.	page, pages
PG	*Victoria Police Gazette*
Q.	Question in Royal Commission of 1881
q.	quoted
RC	Roman Catholic
RIC	Royal Irish Constabulary
Sgt	Sergeant
Sketcher	*Australasian Sketcher*
SMH	*Sydney Morning Herald*
Sr Const.	Senior Constable
Supt	Superintendent
v.	versus
VGG	*Victorian Government Gazette*
VPRO	Victorian Public Record Office
w.e.	week ending

CONVERSION TABLE

Length

1 inch = 25.4 mm
1 foot = 30.5 cm
1 yard = 0.914 m
1 link = 20.1 cm
1 chain = 20.1 m
1 mile = 1.61 km

Area

1 acre = 0.405 ha

Weight

1 ounce = 28 g
1 pound = 454 g
1 stone = 6.36 kg

Money

12 pence (d) = 1 shilling (s)
20 shillings = 1 pound (£)
1 guinea = £1 ls

Notes

1 THE BYRNES AND SHERRITTS, page 1

I am grateful to Dr Brian Byrne (no relation to Joe) for his research on the Viking origins of the Byrnes.

St Mullins described, Samuel Lewis, *A Topographical Dictionary of Ireland*, 1837, Vol. 2, pp. 412–13.

Details of Joe's family, Convict Indent, Vol. X636, p. 731 for the *James Laing*, 29.6.1834, Convict No. 34/1160, AONSW.

His date of birth is not documented. The convict indent shows that old Joe was 34 in June 1834. Although his death certificate, 9.9.1869, gives his age as 71, it seems likely that he was born in 1800.

His marriage to Catherine Brien (called Breen, O'Brien and Bryan in other Irish and Australian records) is recorded in the Marriage Register of St Mullins RC Parish but the date is uncertain, possibly 1823 or 1825. A daughter, Mary, was baptised in 1827 when Joe and Catherine were living in the village of Ballycrinigan, St Mullins Lower (Baptism Register St Mullins RC Parish, 23.4.1827, *General Alphabetical Index to the Townlands and Towns, Parishes and Baronies of Ireland*, Dublin, 1861). Their sons' baptisms are not recorded.

A useful sketch of Michael Dwyer, his Byrne links, and excellent detail on his Australian career are provided by George Cargeeg, *The Rebel of Glenmalure*, Carlisle WA, 1988.

The Whiteboys as 'ancestors' of the IRA, Robert Hughes, *The Fatal Shore*, London, 1987, p.194; the Whiteboy phenomenon discussed, A.G.L. Shaw, *Convicts and the Colonies*, Melbourne, 1977, pp.173–83.

Joe's trial and transportation, Convict Indent, *op.cit.* There is no record of Joe's trial in the National Archives nor in the surviving Wexford newspapers of 1833, the *Wexford Freeman* and *Wexford Conservative*. Ticket of Leave No. L3/2372, 11.10.1843 AONSW, endorsed. 'Ticket of Leave torn up Byrne having obtained Bond of Pardon No. 48/1949 Dated Nov 1848'.

For Joe working with Luke Hyland, see John, James, Patrick and Michael Byrne, List of Immigrants per ship 'Succefs' 18.12.1849, AONSW. Under 'Relations in the Colony' it is noted, 'Father Joseph Byrne per ship *James Laing* in [blank in original]. Tried in Wexford—Living with Mr Luke Hyland, Long Swamp, County Murray.'

For Hyland as sheep farmer, publican, son of convict transported for life, Memorials received from individuals relating to land, No. 492, 6.9.1824; Licence to Retail Wines etc. No. 37/221, 4.7. 1837; Census of the Year 1841, Return No. 25, p.75; Convict

Indent for *Rolla*, 12.5.1803 (Matthew Hyland sentenced to Life at Dublin, December 1801); all AONSW. The 1841 census shows no assigned convicts at Long Swamp, suggesting that Joe arrived after this date. See also Errol Lea-Scarlett, *Queanbeyan, District and People*, Queanbeyan, 1968, pp.25, 229.

In an intriguing coincidence, 'Pallerang' homestead on the site of Hyland's Long Swamp, where old Joe worked, was the home of film director Tony Richardson in 1969 while making his 'Ned Kelly'. Actor Mark McManus who played old Joe's grandson, was a frequent visitor.

Voyage of the Byrne brothers, List of Immigrants per ship 'Succefs' *op. cit.* This was the same *'Success'* which later became a convict hulk in Victoria and was eventually refurbished as 'a convict transport' to becoming a floating sideshow in Australia, England and America. One of its exhibits was a replica of Ned Kelly's armour. See *The Australian Encyclopaedia*, Sydney, 1977, Vol. 5, p.466; *The History of the Ancient Australian Convict Ship 'Success'*, Cleveland, 1929, pp.8–11.

Death of Joe's wife, see List of Immigrants, *op. cit.* Under 'Parents names, and if alive their residence' the Byrne brothers have supplied, 'Joseph and Catherine, father living in New South Wales'. Their sister, Mary, did not accompany them and had died before Joe's death in 1869.

Romance on the *'Success'*, interview, Mr Len Byrne of Goulburn, 1966; List of Immigrants, *op. cit.*

Margret White was the daughter of Dennis (or Denis) White, labourer, and his wife Margaret (or Margret) formerly Ryan. Age and marriage details from her Death Certificate (NSW 21.5.1921) reconciled with the date of her marriage and ages given at birth registrations of her children suggest a likely birth date of 1834 (with variant dates three years in either direction).

Wedding of Paddy and Margret, Marriage Register S.S. Peter and Paul's Church, Goulburn, Book 1, 20.7.1855. The witnesses were Paddy's brother James and Margaret Dunn of Goulburn. Father O'Brien, Administrator of the Cathedral of Saints Peter and Paul, who showed me the entry in 1966, pointed out that Patrick had signed his Christian name and that the priest, Father Kavanagh, had written 'Byrnes'. The Marriage Registration (No. 397, Vol. 101, Registrar General's Office, Sydney) shows Paddy as a marksman. The descriptions of Paddy and Margret are based on their portraits taken many years later.

Will of Joseph Byrne, NSW Probates, Supreme Court, No. 8295, Series 1.

The description of the Woolshed in 1856–7 is based on *The Ovens Directory* of 1857 published as an appendix to Roy Harvey's *Background to Beechworth*, Beechworth, 1978.

Young Joe's birth was not registered and we have yet to locate a record of his baptism. His birthplace is usually given as the Woolshed (Death Certificate, 28.6.1880) and the fact that this was baby John's birthplace in 1858 tends to confirm the location. His date of birth, usually given as 1857, is apparently confirmed by his death certificate and the age given by him during his imprisonment in 1876. At the birth registration of Joe's brothers and sisters by Margret Byrne, Joe's age is consistent with a birth date of January or February 1857. (Joe already 12 at the birth of Margaret on 7.2.1869 and 14 at the birth of Ellen on 12.2.1871). A date of February 1857 is confirmed by Joe's age as noted by a school inspector on 3.10.1864 (seven years and eight months) and on 19.4.1865 (eight years and two months). However, in our earliest school record of Joe's age (19.10.1863) it is given as seven years, suggesting a birth date of 1856, a date confirmed on 14.3.1864 when Joe's age is noted as seven years and four months, i.e. a birth date of November 1856. The precise date is confirmed in Joe's last school record (8.6.1869) when his age of twelve years and seven months again gives a birth date of November 1856 (G. Wilson Brown, Notebooks, VPRO and MEHC).

Comparing the registered birth dates of other children with their ages as given in these records, one can have no great confidence in the accuracy of the school data. However, it seems that the November 1856 birth date is fractionally more likely than the date of three months later, especially given John Byrne's birth in June 1858.

John Byrne, Birth Certificate, 7.6.1858; Death Certificate 1.7.1858. Catherine Byrne, Birth Certificate, 26.4.1860.

The original Byrne homesite was shown to me by Bill Knowles in 1960. Bill's mother, Annie Wick, had pointed it out to him. The clearing was then quite distinct. The irises and rose bush had survived. About a hundred yards up the slope, I found traces of what I took to be a dairy and outbuildings. However these were subsequently identified by Elly Byrne (interview, 14.6.1964) as marking the second Byrne homestead. Elly described the house and garden, the willow tree, the paling fence and remembered the original hut by the creek. The second homestead was apparently burned down not long after the Byrnes left the Woolshed, while the old creekside hut remained for many years.

The Register of Claims, formerly kept in the Beechworth Court House, records for Phillip Riley (or Reilly) on 23.12.1861, 'Creek claim 8 men abandoned ground under P Byrnes house'. On 28.3.1862 Riley registered 'bank claim south side Sebastopol Flat beside Patrick Byrnes hut'. Riley was a sponsor at young Paddy Byrne's baptism.

Joe's upper lip 'short', description by William Elliott, in Rev. H. C. Lundy, *History of Jerilderie*, Jerilderie, 1958, p.111; 'a double lip', Jacob Wilson quoting George Stephens in *Minutes of Evidence Taken Before Royal Commission on The Police Force of Victoria*, 1881, (hereafter *Commission*), Q.4680, p.203; Joe 'opposed to' having photo taken, *Telegram*, 11.5.1879, Kelly Papers. Ironically, Joe's moustache was singed to a few downy traces before his body was rescued from the burning Glenrowan Inn in 1880. Photos show full, well-shaped lips. There seems to have been some slightly unusual development of the *quadratus labii superioris*, the muscle which controls the upper lip. This imperfection would have been evident when Joe's mouth was in movement. Tom Lloyd said that Joe spoke with little movement of his lips, 'in a clipped sort of way' (interview, Tom Lloyd Jr, 4.1.1964).

The changing fortunes of Sebastopol and the Woolshed are charted in the Register of Claims, op. cit. The Chinese camp near the Byrnes was described by Bill Knowles (interview, 8.7.1961) and is marked in Mines Department map 340, *Woolshed, Parishes of Beechworth and Everton*, which can be dated to the late 1870s or very early 1880s by notations and the inclusion of the new Woolshed School No. 1900, opened in July 1877 *(Vision and Realisation* (L. J. Blake (ed.), Melbourne, 1973, Vol. 3, p.959).

Ah Shing's race, Register of Water Rights, 17.12.1867, (incorporated in Register of Claims, *op. cit.*), and Mines Department map 340 which shows its later extension. Byrne garden watered from it, interview, Elly Byrne, 14.6.1964; description of Chinese dress, interview, Bill Knowles, October 1961; Joe called 'Ah Joe', *Commission*, Q.14974, p.542; learns to speak Chinese, John Sadleir, *Recollections of a Victorian Police Officer*, Melbourne, 1913, p.201.

Mary Byrne, Birth Certificate, 10.5.1864.

Agnes Anne Nesbitt's mother was formerly Agnes Anne Richardson (cf. Victorian Death Certificates Agnes Anne Sherritt, 3.2.1908 and Robert Nesbitt, 14.10.1903). Anne's Death Certificate gives her age as 68—a birth date of 1840. However, the Birth Certificate of her daughter, Elizabeth, 8.7.1856, says that she was born at Cavan in 1838, making her 15 at her marriage, as stated on her Death Certificate. The name Nesbitt (or Nesbit), brought to Ireland by Plantation farmers, occurs in six of the eight baronies in Cavan (Index of Surnames, County Cavan, National Library). Anne's father may have been the Hugh Nesbitt who rented nine acres with a house and sheds from Lady Garvagh (R. Griffiths (ed.) *General Valuation of Rateable Property in Ireland,* Dublin, 1857).

John Sherritt was the son of John James Sherritt and Elizabeth McPhee (or McFee or McVie) (Victorian Death Certificate, 10.6.1900). The name, originally Sherruitt, is of French Huguenot origin, also found in England as Sherratt (Research of Bill Sherritt, St Mary's, Ontario, Canada). When John joined the Constabulary on 18 December 1849 (the day the Byrne brothers arrived in Sydney) he was 22, 5ft 8 ¼ins, a labourer, native of Leitrim. He was allocated to County Cavan on 1.4.1850 and promoted 1st sub-constable 1.6.1851 (No. 13700 Royal Irish Constabulary Register, National Archives). Family tradition had him stationed at Cootehill which possessed 'a chief constabulary police station' (Lewis, *op. cit.,* Vol. 1, p.398).

Marriage of John and Anne, Knockbride Church of England and Ireland Marriage Register, 7.6.1853. (The marriage is under 'Skerritt' in the Index of Marriages, General Register Office, Dublin.) Several unusual features of this registration, as noted in the text, could suggest that Anne was pregnant and subsequently lost the baby (or babies—a Sherritt family tradition says that Anne 'lost twins' at some unspecified time). This would explain the lapse of 26 months between Anne and John's marriage and the birth of Aaron.

John's punishments and resignation, RIC Register, *op. cit.* The enigmatic relationship between his resignation and a punishment the following day compounds the mystery of the marriage. If, as it appears, John deserted before his resignation became effective (a punishment recorded the day after the resignation on 10.4.1853 shows clearly that this date did not mark his departure from the force), then his RIC Register entry is curiously silent on this serious breach—but equally silent on the date his appointment terminated. John and Anne's migration, *Assisted Immigrants from U.K. 1839–1871,* p.452, VPRO; *Report of the Acting Immigration Agent upon Colonial Emigration and Immigration for the Year 1854,* printed 1855.

Description of Melbourne and suburbs, Antoine Fauchery, *Letters from a Miner in Australia,* translated from the French by A. R. Chisholm, Melbourne, 1969, pp.20, 24–5, 84.

Employment by Captain Harrison, wages, etc., *Disposal List, Assisted Immigrants, op. cit.;* obituaries of Harrison, *Williamstown Chronicle,* 24.7.1869, Melbourne *Age,* 23.7.1869; Harrison at the post-Eureka meeting, *Age,* 7.12.1854.

Aaron's birth was not registered and, again, we have yet to locate the record of his baptism. His Death Certificate, 26.6.1880 gives his age as 25 and his birthplace as Melbourne. On 30.5.1876 John Sherritt told the Beechworth Court that his son 'would be 21 years of age in August next'. *(Ovens and Murray Advertiser,* 1.6.1876.) This provides a birth date of August 1855 for Aaron. His prison record shows a birth date of 1856. This would have resulted from him giving his age as 20 on admission to Beechworth Gaol in May 1876, three months before he turned 21.

Attitude to gold-digging in 1855, Fauchery, *op. cit.,* p.93.

Reid's Creek's 15 murders in six months, Harvey, *op. cit.,* p.8; only ten businesses in 1857, *Ovens Directory, ibid.*

John as milkman, Baptism Register Christ Church, Beechworth, Elizabeth Sherritt, 12.10.1856.

Immigration of Robert Nesbitt, Unassisted Passenger List, *John Linn,* 3.10.1857, VPRO; John Sherritt. Birth Certificate, 28.3.1858. William George's birth was not registered and no record of his baptism has been found. Other Sherritt birth registrations show he was born in 1860.

Six girls in succession. Anne Jane (registered as Anne Eliza) 21.7.1872, Julia Frances 16.8.1864, Esther 8.2.1867, Mary 28.8.1869, Maria 5.5.1872, Martha 5.7.1875.

The long-winded vicar, Sadleir, *Recollections, op. cit.*, p.96.

Inspector's damning comments on Mrs Scott, G. W. Brown, Notebook, 21.10.1863, MEHC. Ironically, according to Sherritt family tradition, Anne was offered the job as teacher at Reid's Creek, but had to decline because of her babies.

Move to Sheepstation, John Sherritt's change of address in birth and baptism registrations, Julia Frances, 18.9.1864 and 8.4.1865; land rented from Dr Mackay, evidence of John Sherritt in Beechworth Court, 30.5.1876 *(O & M*, 1.6.1876*)*; Dr Mackay and the Tarrawingee run, *Letters from Victorian Pioneers, T.* F. Bride (ed.), South Yarra, 1983.

'The ancient red box' still stands. Buried in its bark is a length of chain used by the Sherritts to tether horses. The plum trees and lilac bushes are still alive. Anne's barefoot walks to Beechworth are a Sherritt family tradition.

Description of John Sherritt, Commission, Q.7557–60, p.288; 'looking for a big, bony bloody Irishman', interview, Bill Short, 9.7.1961; temporary truce with Christ Church and baptism of Maria, Martha and Hugh Nesbitt (born 13.12.1878), Christ Church Beechworth Baptism Register, 11.9.1879.

Willie's 'joke' is from family tradition, as are the descriptions of the children and the picnics with a billy of hard-boiled eggs.

The making of the sapling arch by Aaron and Will Robinson, interview, Clive Robinson (nephew of Will) 29.10.1962. Clive cut down the twin trees about 1930.

2 THE CARELESS YEARS, page 13

The establishment of the Woolshed Roman Catholic School (later, Woolshed Common School and School No. 689) is briefly described in *Visions and Realisations, Vol.* 3, L. J. Blake (ed.), Melbourne, 1973. Detail is drawn from the Correspondence Register Denominational Schools, Correspondence Register and Received Letters Register, Board of Education, and Building File, School No. 689, all VPRO.

The description of the school building is from interview, Bill Knowles and Clive Robinson, 29.10.1962.

The quotes from Elly Byrne are from interviews, 14.6.1964 and 15.6.1964. Elly described the Byrne children's route to school.

The picture of Cornelius O'Donoghue is built up from his Teachers Record, No. 682 (MEHC), Death Certificate, 3.8.1904, and the magnificent G. W. Brown Notebooks 1863–70, currently divided between the MEHC and the VPRO.

G. W. Brown, Notebook, 19.10.1863 offers the dry comment, 'The extraordinarily large no. present showed that I was expected.' He had earlier mentioned the district flooding. Details of G. W. Brown are from Teacher Record, No. 4024, MEHC.

Brown's subsequent visits to the Woolshed School are from his Notebooks, 14.3.1864, 3.10.1864, 19.4.1865, 30.10.1865, 15.5.1866, 26.9.1866 and 8.6.1869. With access to this material, it is difficult to explain Molony's statement that, 'Young Byrne...never failed to satisfy the examiners in every subject'. (John Molony, *I am Ned Kelly,* Ringwood, 1980, p.82). It is equally difficult to explain his contention that, 'there were Sherritts there'. There is no evidence that I am aware of that any of the Sherritt children except Aaron ever attended the Woolshed School. Even Aaron's attendance at the school currently defies documentation. He was not present during any visit by G. W. Brown. According to Superintendent Hare, Aaron said that Joe had been 'his schoolfellow' *(Commission,* Q.1270, p.63). But Hare is notoriously unreliable, as in his autobiography, where he claimed that Joe 'was educated at the Eldorado School, where he and Aaron Sherritt were most intimate friends' (Francis Augustus Hare, *The Last of the Bushrangers,* London, 1892, p.96).

James Wallace told the Royal Commission that he had been a schoolfellow of Aaron, *(Commission,* Q.14477, p.527) and his presence at the Woolshed School is documented in G. W. Brown's notebooks. But Wallace subsequently transferred to the Reid's Creek School which was attended by other Sherritt children. He could have met Aaron there. Elly Byrne commented, 'I don't think they went to the same school. We went to the Woolshed. Sherritt, I fancy, went to Reid's Creek.' (interview, 14.6.1964). Yet Annie Wick (who appears as an 'under 7' at the Woolshed School in G. W. Brown Notebook, 15.5.1866, and in First Class, 26.9.1866) spoke of attending school with Aaron and Joe at school No. 689 (her son, Bill Knowles, interview, 27.10.1970). It seems most likely that Aaron picked up most of his rudimentary education at Reid's Creek but occasionally (or briefly) attended the Woolshed Common School. It is easy to believe that his presence on comparatively few occasions managed to leave a vivid impression. The 'senior policeman' comments on Joe's education are from Hare, *op. cit.,* pp.177, 320.

Details of James Wallace and his family, L. J. Pryor, 'The Yea Teacher Linked with Ned's Gang', *Yarra Glen Chronicle,* 19.7.1989.

Wallace describes mesmerising Aaron, *Commission,* Q.14477, p.527, and speaks of him as 'guarded and cunning', Q.14472, p.526; Aaron as 'a better man than Joe...', Q.1282, p.65.

Joe's mention of a meeting 'under London', letter, 26.6.1879, Kelly Papers; Supt Nicolson describes Aaron's descent of Byrnes Gully, *Commission,* Q.13661–7, p.493; Joe riding down Wall's Gully and steep ranges, Q.13207, p.477; Q.12224, p.438.

Max Brown, *Australian Son,* Melbourne, 1948, p.62, for Beechworth memories of Joe and Aaron in 1946; Anne Sherritt's view of Aaron, *Commission,* Q.13180, p.476; Elly Byrne's memory of Joe as 'The Demon', interview, 14.6.1964; Annie Wick's description of Joe as 'wild', Bill Knowles, interview, October 1960; Joe attacks his sister, Melbourne *Herald,* 30.6.1880; Joe 'dangerous', Wm Williamson, Statement, 29.10.1878, *Commission,* Appendix 13, p.702; 'Bullet Eyes', Michael Woodyard, Statement to Supt Winch, 1.11.1878, Kelly Papers.

Paddy Byrne's Death Certificate, 7.11.1870, for duration of illness; G. W. Brown, Notebook, 13.5.1866 for corresponding lapse in Joe's schoolwork.

Birth Certificates, Dennis Byrne, 12.7.1866; Margaret Byrne, 7.2.1869; Baptism Register, St Joseph's Catholic Church, Beechworth, Dennis Byrne, 17.8.1866.

Death Certificate, Joseph Byrne, 9.9.1869.

Paddy Byrne's Death Certificate shows no priest at Paddy's funeral, identifies John Byrne as a witness to the burial, and the Death Register, Ovens and Murray Hospital, 1870, confirms that Paddy was 'buried by friends'.

Ellen Byrne, Birth Certificate, 7.2.1871, identifies Mrs Barry as midwife; Mrs Barry mentions sleeping in the same bed as Joe and Mrs Byrne *(Commission,* Q.12153, p.434); placement of double bed from Ellen Byrne (interview 14.6.1964); sponsors at Elly's baptism from Baptism Register, St Joseph's, Ellen Byrne, 17.2.1871. (There might be an error with the date of this entry. It seems very early—only ten days after Elly's birth—and the birth date is given incorrectly as 12.1.1871.)

Elly's memory of her mother's dairy business, interview, 14.6.1964; the number of her cattle, O & M, 1.6.1876; her use of the Woolshed Common, *Commission,* Q.12215, p.437; operation of the Common, interview, Bill Knowles, 24.10.1970.

Mrs Byrne's farm 'well conducted', from William Kyle, q. in Keith McMenomy, *Ned Kelly, the Authentic Illustrated Story,* South Yarra, 1984, p.61; goats from O & M, 1.6.1876; chooks and geese from Elly Byrne, interview, 14.6.1964; see also Hare, *op. cit.,* p.164.

Joe as cart boy, Clive Robinson, interview, October 1962; at Thologolong Station, John Peach, interview, September 1989; in Chinese store, Frank Clune, *The Kelly Hunters*, Sydney, 1958, p.116.

Paddy Allen's comment on the mystique of horse stealing, q. in B. W. Cookson, 'The Kelly Gang from Within—survivors of the tragedy interviewed' Sydney *Sun*, 4.9.1911; Annie Wick on 'borrowing' horses, from Bill Knowles, interview, 24.10.1970; tolerance of Joe's taking ways, from Max Brown, 'In Pursuit of the Kelly Gang', *Australian Monthly*, June 1949, p.7.

John's battle to establish and expand his dairy, Lands Department Files, VPRS 627, Unit 2, No. 31/95; Unit 140, No. 12123/31, VPRO, inc. Application for Licence, (Lot 2) 23.6.1865; Application to Purchase, 5.5.1872; completed, 23.8.1872; Application (Lot 6), 27.9.1867; Application to Purchase, 8.7.1872; purchase completed, 6.7.1891.

The Sherritt farm, outbuildings, and improvements described, Crown Lands Bailiff's Report, 27.6.1870 (File 31/95, VPRO). Fight at the wake, Sherritt family tradition; Kelty claims John 'got the worst of it', O & M, 1.3.1870. Dan Kelty & Anne, O & M, 18.2.1869 (thanks to Gary Dean & Kevin Passey).

The roadside clash with Kelty and the long-running prosecution, O & M, 15.2.1870, 1.3.1870, 4.8.1870, 18.10.1870, 4.2.1871; 'intent to do some grievous bodily harm', Criminal Record Book, Prothonotary, 1868–73, 15.6.1870, VPRO.

Sherritt farm burnt, Sherritt family tradition; note in Crown Lands Bailiff's Report, 29.1.1877 (File 12123/21, VPRO) that a certificate and letter of advice had been 'burnt along with Sherritt's house some time back'.

Joe's 'peculiar swagger', *PG*, 5.3.1879; Aaron's 'remarkable walk', *Commission*, Q. 1270, p.63. Ingram's memories of Joe, from Harvey, *op. cit.*, p.48; Warren's view of Aaron, in Max Brown, *op. cit.*, *Australian Monthly*, June 1949, p.7.

Images of the Chinese camp, Roy Harvey, interview, June 1959; details of Nam Sing, Baptism Register, Christ Church, Beechworth, 22.8.1871; reminiscences of Nam Sing's friendship with Joe, his home, garden, etc., Ernie Manton, interview, July 1960; Joe identified as an opium addict, Sadleir, Telegram, 27.12.1878, Kelly Papers.

'Half a Chinaman', Supt Sadleir, Australian *Life*, 1.2.1910. My thanks to Keith McMenomy for this reference.

The Chinese Procession in the Prince of Wales Birthday Carnival of 1873 is described at length in the O & M, November 1873, Harvey, *op. cit.*, pp.34–5, and Carole Woods, *Beechworth, a Titan's Field*, Melbourne, 1985, p.129. The *Australasian Sketcher* for 28.12.1874 provides details applicable to the previous year's procession. The O & M comment on Chinese civilisation, q. in Woods, *op. cit.*, p.129. The suit of Chinese armour is still on display in the Burke Museum.

Joe steals Wick's horse, summonsed by Wick, 'under Clause 73 of Criminal Law and Practice Statute', O & M, 23.9.1873.

Aaron's work on his selection is traced in the Lands Department file for the block, 47658/19.20 in VPRS 625, Unit 736 VPRO; his application, 11.12.1873; the original survey, 6.10.1873; the District Surveyor's Report, 11.12.1873 with endorsement by the Land Board, 6.2.1874; referral to the Mines Department, 2.3.1874, and approval of licence, 1.6.1874.

Aaron's 'ghosted' Statement of Improvements referred to later in the text records his initial six-months' payment on 1.4.1875 and his work to that date. The dimensions of the hut are from his Application for Lease, 26.3.1879. A bailiff's report of 29.3.79 identifies his fence rails as saplings and indicates that his 'chock and log' fences were built on 'post and spar'. Description of the hut, *Argus*, 8.11.1878.

When the author first located the selection in 1961, and inspected it with the permission of the then owner, Greg Forrest, there were still traces of Aaron's occupancy—the last vestiges of his hut, remains of 'post and spar' along which he had built a dogleg fence, some three-rail posts burnt in the 1900 fire, and a fallen three-rail corner post slotted for a slip panel.

Aaron drawn into the Sherritt-Kelty feud, prosecution of the Keltys, *O & M,* 30.7.1874, 1.8.1874, 3.9.1874, 5.9.1874.

Ned Kelly's fight with Wild Wright, the author's 'The Years Ned Kelly Went Straight', *Walkabout,* June 1962. Wild gets 'the hiding of my life', interview, 1962, with entertainment figure Charlie Fredricksen, 'The Man Outside Hoyts', who 'spruiked' for a boxing sideshow in which Wild appeared.

Aaron's clash with John Kelty, *O & M,* 2.1.1875. 1 am grateful to Graham Jones who alerted me to this case in the excellent *Court List* appendix to his *Ned Kelly—the Larrikin Years,* Wangaratta, 1990.

Bill Knowles told me of Joe and Aaron's secret yardsite, 'a corner in Byrnes Gully fenced for their horses', mentioned to him by Bill (Willie) Sherritt, (interview, September 1960). He had also identified traces of a wire fence running from the tableland almost to the gully bed as, traditionally, 'Sherritt's', believing it to be a boundary fence. But none of Aaron's boundaries entered Byrnes Gully.

In 1962 I discovered the extraordinary, near-level bench, a little to the south of this fence. After many years of unsuccessful searching for an alternative site, I am confident that this bench provided the hiding place for stolen horses mentioned by Bill Sherritt and described in a letter from Aaron to Jack Sherritt in 1876 (see chapter 3). Although the passage directing Jack to the site is missing, a fragment includes the words 'right-hand'. The normal line of approach for Jack would be from the south, with the bench on the 'right-hand', eastern slope. In October, 2000, when three expert local riders—Lorraine Lucas, Jan Robinson and Roger Smitheram—brought horses into the bench, a chance discovery confirmed the identification of the site. Jan Powles, member of a support party, found a rusted, goose-neck shovel head (its handle long since rotted away) hidden under a boulder immediately below the point where horses could enter the bench from Byrnes Gully. Clearly, the shovel had been used by Joe and Aaron to maintain a water supply, as described in the text.

Aaron and Jack's 'unlawfully taking and using' case, Cause List Book, Beechworth Petty Sessions, and *O & M,* 27.11.1875. For the first appearance of the advertised reward, see *O & M,* 13.11.1875.

Phelan 'illegal impounding' case, Aaron's involvement and Joe's alleged theft of Phelan's saddle, Cause List Book and *O & M,* 30.11.1875, 7.12.1875, 9.12.1875, 11.12.1875 and 18.12.1875.

'Dick Turpin's Ride' advertised, *O & M,* 18.12.1875, and described, Thomas Hardy, *Far from the Madding Crowd,* Pan, 1969, pp.340–1. (Thanks to Helen McGladdery for this reference.)

3 DAY OF RECKONING, page 34

The major source of this chapter is the virtual transcript of Joe and Aaron's trial in *O & M,* 1.6.1876; details of charges, bail, etc., Beechworth Petty Sessions Cause List Book.

Aaron's boxing skill, beats Const. Jim Dixon, Cookson *op. cit.,* Sydney *Sun,* 4.9.1911.

Michael Byrne died in Beechworth on 26.4.1876, Death Certificate.

The quote from Mrs Byrne about Joe's absence, *O & M,* 1.6.1876; Elly Byrne's memories of Joe, interviews, 14.6.1964 and 4.8.1964.

Kennedy's farm was on two acres of 'bought land' (*O & M,* 1.6.1876) which appears on

Lands Department maps, Central Plans Office. The remains of his fireplace mark the site, just uphill from traces of a hut built in the 1940s and burnt down in 1964. This is often identified as the Byrne homesite (as in Brown, *op. cit.*, p.62 and Clune, *op. cit.*, p.115) and seems to fit the Royal Commission siting 'at the mouth of Byrnes Gully' *(Commission,* Q.801, p.35, Q.13661, p.493). But the Kennedy site is at the mouth of Byrnes *Gap.* The gully proper continues below it to Reedy Creek.

Sandy Doig's reputation was known even to young Elly Byrne, who commented, 'I think he must have been a tell-tale' (interview, 4.8.1964), and was familiar to Bill Knowles some thirty years later.

Details of Ward's appearance and police career, Record Sheet. His reputation for interfering with schoolgirls, *Commission,* Q.14674–6, p.533, Q.14797–108, p.537. In a remarkable confrontation, school teacher James Wallace accused Ward of 'tampering' with girls at the Beechworth State School and said, 'I know no-one in the North-Eastern District who bore a more unenviable character for immorality than yourself'.

Ward's version of the case is quoted in Cookson, *op. cit.*, Sydney *Sun,* 5.9.1911. Ward claims that he found Joe and Aaron skinning 'a beast' and that he 'noted the brands'. He claims that the case collapsed on the refusal of James Foley (*sic*) to identify the animal and that he subsequently gained a six months conviction of Joe and Aaron on possession of mutton for which 'they could not prove ownership'. The story is nonsense from start to finish.

Ward's seduction of Kate Byrne is mentioned by James Wallace in his Royal Commission evidence, quoting Jack Barry of Hedi, *(Commission,* Q.14669, p.532). Local tradition adopted, or more likely, confirmed the allegation.

Margret Byrne's extraordinary version of the case, interview, Elly Byrne, 4.8.1964, the day before her death.

The prison descriptions of Joe and Aaron are from *Victoria Police Gazette* (hereafter *PG*) 'Prisoners Discharged' w.e. 20.11.1876 (in which Joe is incorrectly entered as 'James' Byrne). These descriptions are fuller than those in the *Prison Register* file.

4 THESE TWO STRAPPING LADS, page 42

Constable Mullane's much-endorsed report on Aaron's inability to satisfy Land Act requirement while in prison is from the selection's file, VPRS 625, Unit 736, VPRO, as is Murphy's pleading letter and the Department's cover sheet with its palimpsest of referral and comment. John Sherritt's attempt to pay Aaron's arrears seems to have been quite independent of the police action and is consistent with the loyalty and concern he always showed for his son. There is no receipt for the money, merely a query from Wimble on 2 September asking if the rent has been paid and a note on 6 September confirming payment.

Aaron and Joe's prison letter is now in Kelly Papers and was transcribed by me in 1960 from police file 0.6650. It is reproduced in McMenomy, *op. cit.*, p.139. The fate of the letter and the recovery of the foals are described in an accompanying memo from Mullane.

Detective Ward's theory that Joe and Aaron met Ned and Jim Kelly in Beechworth Gaol, Cookson, *op. cit.*, Sydney *Sun,* 5.9.1911.

Jim Kelly's imprisonment details, *PG* 'Prisoners Discharged', w.e. 28.8.1876; Wild Wright's, *PG* 'Prisoners Discharged' w.e. 21.5.1877; Steve Hart's, *PG,* 'Prisoners Discharged', w.e. 17.6.1878; Dan Kelly's trial, *O & M,* 14.10.1876.

Elly Byrne's story of Joe's release, interview, 4.8.1964. Incorrect interpretation of Elly's version led to my belief that Joe had met the Kellys via Jim, a view I published in

Ned Kelly, Man and Myth, Melbourne, 1968, p.65 and which was apparently adopted by Molony, *op. cit.,* p.84.

The friendship between Kate Kelly and Emma Crawford, interviews with Emma's daughter, Mrs J. Agar, in 1964.

Description of Kate Kelly, Det. Ward, Report, 21.12.80, Kelly Papers.

The quotes from Aaron about Ned Kelly, Hare, *op. cit.,* p.158 and *Commission,* Q.1282, p.65.

Ned's question about Aaron being tortured, *Commission,* Q.12214, p.437; his description of Joe as his 'best friend', Q.9486, p.343; as his 'best man', etc. Melbourne *Herald,* 19.2.1879.

Ned Kelly's career as a timber worker and the role of the Martins, the author's 'The Years Ned Kelly Went Straight', *Walkabout,* June 1962, p.17. The Martin brothers at 'Mother Byrnes', Telegram, 12.12.1878, Kelly Papers.

Harry Power's work as a digger in the Wombat Ranges area, *Mansfield Independent,* 12.6.1869.

Aaron's ill-treatment of a horse, Cause List Book, Beechworth Petty Sessions and *O & M,* 13.1.1877.

Details of the Ah On case, Cause List Book, Beechworth Petty Sessions; Criminal Record Book, Beechworth General Sessions; *O & M,* 8.2.1877, 15.2.1877, 1.3.1877 and 3.3.1877. The case has been handled in curiously cavalier fashion through the years. Brown, *op. cit.,* in the earliest account of the incident (p.62), does not mention the result of the trial. Unaccountably, Clune, *op. cit.,* has Joe and Aaron found guilty and sentenced to six months (p.122) supposedly enabling them to meet Steve Hart in Beechworth Gaol. Molony, *op. cit.,* also has Joe and Aaron found guilty (p.85) but does not mention a sentence. Correctly, Woods, *op. cit.,* p.152 and John McQuilton, *The Kelly Outbreak,* Melbourne, 1979, p.101, both have the boys acquitted.

The facts of the case are cloudy. The hostility of the *O & M* reports and editorial was based, commendably, on disapproval of what seemed to be a pair of larrikins baiting inoffensive 'Chinamen'. Yet, as we've seen, our two larrikins weren't, typically, hostile to Chinese. In this light, a comment made by Ah On in his evidence is particularly illuminating. He said that he had lived at Sebastopol about ten years and had known Joe all of that time. 'Had no dispute with Byrne before this, but Byrne had several times thrown stones at the house' (*O & M,* 3.3.1877).

Ah Seong, one of Ah On's two hut mates, lived the rest of his life at Sebastopol, to become the last of the Woolshed's Chinese. Bill Knowles, who knew Ah Seong well, recalled that he was treated as an outsider by other Chinese who called him 'a black Chinaman'. On one occasion, a group of Chinese attacked him and Ah Seong beat them off with a bamboo. As noted, Ah On, Ah Seong and Ah Sin shared a hut some distance east of the Chinese camp by the back Eldorado Road. It seems likely that all three were 'black Chinamen' and that Joe's hostility to them derived from the attitude of his other Chinese friends. Poignantly, Bill Knowles remembered Ah Seong as a kindly man, fond of children, who would 'knock up a bridge of slabs' for youngsters wanting to cross the creek (interviews, June 1962, July 1970).

The second Dan Kelly saddle case, Cause List Book Beechworth Petty Sessions and *O & M,* 1.3.1877. Curiously, Molony, (*op. cit.,* p.85), mentions Dan's case coinciding with Joe and Aaron's appearance over the assault on Ah On, but ignores Ned's presence at the trial and the significance of the occasion as the first documented encounter of Ned and Dan with Joe and Aaron.

The story of Mrs Byrne and Anton Wick 'exchanging portraits', from Bill Knowles (interview, October, 1962) who still had the photo of Joe given to his grandfather by Mrs Byrne. See insert between pages 22 and 23.

5 THE COMING OF THE TROUBLE, page 53

Ned's dry description of the horse stealing trade, from his Jerilderie Letter, a 7,500-word
  statement discussed in Chapter 10; Ward's from Cookson, *op. cit.*, Sydney *Sun*,
  5.9.1911, Aaron's from Hare, *op. cit.*, pp.170–1.
Ned and Joe as 'good-looking and well dressed', Hare, *op. cit.*, p. 135.
The Sherritt troubles in 1877, from Cause List Book, Beechworth Petty Sessions, 5.7.1877,
  30.7.1877, 7.8.1877 and 20.4.1877.
Jim's resisting arrest and conviction for horse stealing, *Wagga Wagga Advertiser*,
  30.6.1877.
Ned Kelly describes the Whitty horse stealing coup and its aftermath in his Jerilderie
  Letter. Details of the crimes, the value of the horses, and pursuit and arrest of the
  suspects, *PG*, 26.9.1877, 21.11.1877, 28.11.1877, 5.12.1877 and 12.12.1877. See *PG*,
  Prisoners Discharged, w.e. 17.12.1877 for Wild Wright imprisoned at Jamieson. For
  Dan Kelly and Jack Lloyd's implication, *PG*, 10.4.1878.
Identification of 'Billy King' as Joe, Wm. Williamson, Statement, 29.10.1878, (*Commission*,
  Appendix 13, p.702). In describing 'Billy King—but that is not his proper name',
  Williamson gives a clearly recognisable description of Joe, apart from specifying
  'stout' build, which could mean 'strong', or perhaps 'broad shouldered'. An unlikely
  detail of 'King' having 'thick legs' is borne out by two full-length death photos of Joe
  and the Bray portrait which suggest powerful thighs.
For Ned Kelly's Benalla brawl, Cause List Book, Benalla Petty Sessions, 18.9.1877 and
  Jerilderie Letter.
Ned's disposal of his horses, Jerilderie Letter; Joe visiting his uncle, John Byrne, *PG*,
  3.7.1878; John Byrne's Death Certificate, 15.6.1878, states that he had been suffering
  from an aneurism of the aorta for two years.
Elly's comment on Ned and Joe's friendship, interview, 4.8.1964.
Ned and Joe's mares were to be frequently described, their names preserved in family
  traditions. Max Brown records the name of 'Mirth' but assigns it to Joe's grey mare
  which he assumes, incorrectly, to be the Kelly mare bought by actor George Coppin
  (Brown, *op. cit.*, p.270). Elly Byrne remembered Joe's grey as 'Music', interview,
  15.6.1964.
Ned's description of the police raids on the Kelly homestead, Jerilderie Letter.
The Fitzpatrick incident is documented in a lengthy deposition from Fitzpatrick and other
  shorter statements from him in Prosecution Brief Queen v. Ellen Kelly *et al.*, in Kelly
  Papers, in Fitzpatrick's evidence before the Royal Commission of 1881–2,
  (*Commission*, Q.12809–87, pp.463–5), and in a virtual transcript of the trial of Mrs
  Kelly, Williamson and Skillion, in *O & M*, 10.10.1878. Ned Kelly gives his version in
  the Cameron Letter (a 3,500-word statement discussed in Chapter 8) and the
  Jerilderie Letter.
For Mrs Kelly's baby being two days old on the day of the Incident, Letter, Ned Kelly to
  the Governor of Victoria, 3.11.1880, Capital Case File, VPRO, 'They handcuffed her
  and took her away to the lockup & only the third day after her confinement'. Mrs
  Kelly was arrested the day after Fitzpatrick's alleged wounding.
Evidence of Fitzpatrick having mistaken Joe Byrne for Bill Skillion is found in two of
  Williamson's statements dictated in prison, and in a 1928 letter.
On 29.10.1878 Williamson dictated a statement to Inspector Green in Pentridge in which
  he described 'Billy King—but that is not his proper name', who 'was in Kelly's house
  when Constable Fitzpatrick was fired at'. As previously discussed, the description of
  'Billy King' fits Joe Byrne.
On 6.8.1881 Williamson dictated a letter to the Inspector General of Penal Establishments,

asking for 'mitigation of sentence'. He gave a detailed version of the Fitzpatrick incident and described how he held 'King' back from joining the scuffle.

He went on to make the intriguing comment, 'I understand that recently the police have discovered that Byrne was at the Kelly hut at the time Fitzpatrick was shot in the wrist'.

On 25.2.1928, Williamson wrote to J. J. Kenneally, belatedly admitting that he blamed himself for the arrest of Skillion, who was mistaken for 'Burns' when he [Williamson] 'pulled Burns back in the dark', as he was about to enter the house 'after the brawl'. (J. J. Kenneally, *The Complete Inner History of the Kelly Gang and their Pursuers*, 8th edn., Moe, 1969, p.38).

In the light of the previous statement, there can be no serious doubt that by 'Burns' Williamson meant Joe Byrne. This spelling was frequently used in the Kelly Country. Even the Beechworth priest recorded Joe's brother as 'Patrick Burns' in the record of his baptism (Baptism Register, St Joseph's, Beechworth, 20.4.1862).

The only feasible explanation for Williamson's reluctance to name Joe in 1878 is that he was frightened of him, regarding Joe as 'dangerous'.

By the time Williamson dictated the 1881 letter, Joe Byrne was dead, but Williamson was clearly reluctant to admit to the police that he had previously misled them. Hence, he continued with the 'King' charade, though effectively admitting that Joe had been involved.

Williamson was a poor type and one is reluctant to accept any of his statements as reliable evidence. However, on this one point, he appears to have told the truth, eventually.

Joe's presence at the Kelly homestead demands careful consideration of evidence that Ned, too, was there.

In his 1881 statement, Williamson claimed that Ned was present and shot *at* Fitzpatrick. But, in the context of Williamson seeking a remission, the claim must be treated with caution.

At the trial, the Kellys' cousin Joe Ryan said, 'I bought a horse from Ned Kelly on the 15th [day of the Fitzpatrick incident] and gave seventeen pounds for it'. The receipt was produced in court (*O & M*, 10.10.1878).

Molony dismisses this evidence (Molony, *op. cit.*, Note 10, p.274), failing to recognise that its presentation demonstrated clearly that, in contriving or allowing presentation of this evidence, Ned had no thought of trying to prove he was hundreds of miles away—an alibi that was clearly developed later. Ned's ambiguous statement that, when he heard of 'this transaction', he was 'over 400 miles from Greta', is from the Jerilderie Letter of February 1879. During his outlawry, Ned made several unambiguous claims that he was varying distances from Greta on 15 April—clearly aimed at discrediting Fitzpatrick and gaining a remission for his mother, rather than trying to prove his innocence, by then a pointless exercise.

On 26 October that year, he made the quoted, off-guard admission to Constable McIntyre that he had been present (McIntyre Deposition, Prosecution Brief, Queen v. Edward Kelly, Kelly Papers), and, eventually, on 29.6.1880, supposedly admitted to Senior Constable John Kelly that he had shot *at* Fitzpatrick (Kelly Deposition, Prosecution Brief, Kelly Papers).

As indicated, the weight of evidence suggests that both Ned and Joe were at 'the row'— the clear evidence of Joe's presence in itself suggesting that Ned was there, with his mate.

Dr John Nicholson's guarded views about Fitzpatrick's wound, Deposition, Prosecution Brief, Queen v. Ellen Kelly *et al.*, Kelly Papers. His evidence reported, *O & M*, 10.10.1878. The same issue contains the 'extraordinary' editorial comment on Fitzpatrick's evidence about his wound.

For a major re-evaluation of the above evidence, see the author's *Ned Kelly: A Short Life*, Melbourne, 1995, Chapter 7, 'The Fitzpatrick Mystery'. Here, the conclusion is reached that Ned Kelly did fire the shot that wounded Fitzpatrick—under circumstances amounting to accidental wounding

6 A RESPECTABLE-LOOKING MURDERER, page 61

Aaron and Jack's money troubles, Cause List Book, Beechworth Petty Sessions, 3.1.1878, 18.4.1878.

Ned Kelly 'and a man supposed to be his brother Dan' were reported to have crossed the Murray River at Barmah and passed near Deniliquin, apparently heading for the Darling (*O & M*, 14.5.1878). Only six weeks later, when Joe was suspected of having stolen a horse in the King Valley the previous October, it was reported that he was 'believed to be residing with his uncle, John Byrne, at Wagga Wagga, N.S.W.' (*PG*, 3.7.1878). It seems likely that Joe was the man travelling with Ned, and may have been at Wagga when his Uncle John died on 15 June (Death Certificate).

The Bullock Creek gold workings and the pot whiskey project are described in Letter, Edward Kelly to the Governor of Victoria, 3.11.1880, Capital Case File, VPRO; Ned Kelly speaks of the gold claim making 'good wages', Jerilderie Letter.

Aaron's dealings with Fitzpatrick, (*Commission*, Q.12925–9, p.467).

Johnny Byrne's relationship to Joe Byrne, skill as a blacksmith, etc., from his son-in-law, Jack Walsh of Tolmie, interview, January 1960.

Trial of Mrs Kelly, Skillion and Williamson, Criminal Record Book, Beechworth General Sessions, 9.10.1878; *O & M*, 10.10.1878; sentences, Criminal Record Book, 12.10.1878; *O & M*, 15.10.1878.

Ned's attempts to finance a new trial for his mother, Letter to Governor of Victoria, 10.11.1880, Capital Case File, VPRO.

Ned's old carbine described, McIntyre and Living Depositions, Prosecution Brief, Kelly Papers.

The Kelly armoury after the Euroa robbery (see Chapter 8) consisted of 'two double barrelled guns two single barrelled guns a Spencer rifle fully loaded eight revolvers' (telegram, Sgt L. Burland, 12.12.1878, Kelly Papers). A comparison of this armoury with the weapons taken during the hold-up and from the Stringybark Creek party suggests strongly that Joe and Steve were unarmed at Stringybark Creek while Ned may have carried a revolver, as claimed by McIntyre.

Bullock Creek hut and improvements described, Argus, 18.11.1880; Telegram, Sr Const. James to Pewtress, 24.11.1878, Kelly Papers; for tank-iron on door, Sadleir, *op. cit.*, p.193.

For police readiness to shoot Ned Kelly, McIntyre Deposition, Prosecution Brief, Kelly Papers; Argus, 10.11.80; Letter, E. Kelly to Governor of Victoria, 3.11.1880, Capital Case File, VPRO; Letter, James to Sadleir, 24.6.1898, Sadleir Papers, Latrobe Library, q. in McQuilton, *op. cit.*, p.99.

Straps for carrying bodies, Kinnear Papers, transcribed by the author, 1952. 'Two long straps 10 feet by 3 inches wide to strap bodies on the pack horse. These were made by Boles the Mansfield saddler & are now in 1934 in the possession of J. Egan farmers of Mansfield.'

'First blood, Lonigan', McIntyre typescript, MS.6342, Latrobe Library.

The movements of the police party, McIntyre Depositions, Prosecution Brief, Kelly Papers.

For visit to Johnny Byrne's on 25.10.1878, see Jerilderie Letter in which Ned describes how he found the tracks of police horses 'between Table Top and the bogs'. In January 1960, standing outside Johnny Byrne's hut, I asked his son-in-law, Jack Walsh, to point out the place Ned had described. Jack laughed. 'Right here!' There can be little doubt that Ned and, probably Joe, were paying a visit to the Byrne hut when they stumbled on the tracks.

It is intriguing that Ned believed he had found a different set of police tracks on the range between Emu Swamp and Bullock Creek (Cameron Letter), 'making for the shingle hut', (Jerilderie Letter). There was, of course, only one set of police tracks involved, but Ned had clearly been alerted to the departure or imminent departure, of both police parties and was therefore prepared to find a second set of tracks. According to the Mansfield newspaper editor, G. Wilson Hall, Ned received this information on 21 October (*Outlaws of the Wombat Ranges*, Mansfield, 1879, p.23. Hereafter, *Mansfield Pamphlet*). Ned had certainly been told of the Greta party's departure and its make-up, and was thus prepared to see Strahan, one of its members, at Stringybark Creek. In the Cameron Letter, Ned incorrectly assigns the finding of the tracks to 26 October, but in the Jerilderie Letter, he corrects the date to 25 October.

Aaron stressed to Supt Hare the element of chance in Joe and Steve being at Bullock Creek on 26 October (Hare, *op. cit.*, p.107). Clearly, he was conscious of how easily he might have been involved in the killings.

Ned's account of the council of war, Cameron Letter.

McIntyre's account of the shooting of Lonigan is that given by him to Supt Sadleir on 29 October and quoted by Sadleir in his *Recollections*, pp.187–8. (Sadleir dates it to 'the second day following the Police murders', but the Mansfield Occurrence Book shows that he did not arrive at Mansfield until 29 October.) The account is remarkable in tallying almost precisely with Ned Kelly's version—that Lonigan was behind cover and preparing to fire at Ned when he was shot. In all other versions, including those given at Ned Kelly's trial, McIntyre claimed that Lonigan was shot *before* he could draw his revolver and as he was moving *towards* cover, carefully removing the critical element of self-defence implicit in the Kelly version and in the version given to Sadleir.

Dan's near-hysteria, McIntyre typescript, MS.6342, Latrobe Library.

McIntyre's first description of Joe and the amended description, *PG*, 6.11.1878. 'Not the villainous expression of the others', *Sketcher*, 23.11.1878.

The exchanges with Ned and Joe, McIntyre Deposition, Prosecution Brief, Kelly Papers.

The gunfight involving Kennedy and Scanlon, Jerilderie Letter, Cameron Letter, and McIntyre Deposition.

Ned's denials that Scanlon was on his knees when shot, Statements, Sr Const. Kelly, 15.7.1880 and Sr Const. Johnston, 7.7.1880, both Kelly Papers. To understand this crucial discrepancy between Ned's account of Scanlon's death and that given by McIntyre, it is essential to establish the positions of the police and the four Kellys during the gunfight. This can be achieved by a careful comparison of McIntyre's various depositions in 1878 and 1880, Ned Kelly's accounts in his two letters, a sketch plan of the action by McIntyre (Prosecution Brief, VPRO), two views of the clearing by the Melbourne photographer Burman (with important annotations to an engraving based on one of these photos in the *Australian Sketcher*, 23.11.1878), and the account by G. Wilson Hall in the *Mansfield Pamphlet*. The resulting orientation of the action shows that Joe Byrne and Dan Kelly were closest to Scanlon—perhaps only 12 or 14 yards to his right—as he knelt, already wounded by Ned, trying to unsling his rifle. Either Joe or Dan could have fired the fatal shot. Oral tradition pointed to Joe, a tradition, intriguingly, recorded by 'Lucky Doolan' in his 1940s comic *The Kelly Gang Rides*, a vivid and naïve creation showing no evidence of research and clearly based on family and/or district lore. The relevant frame of the Stringybark Creek gunfight is captioned 'Ned & Joe both shoot Scanlan'.

The death of Kennedy, Cameron Letter and]erilderie Letter. 'Kennedy kept firing...' (Jerilderie); 'My brother advanced...' (Cameron); 'I shot him in the armpit...' (Jerilderie).

The aftermath of Kennedy's shooting, G. Wilson Hall, *Mansfield Pamphlet*, pp.32–5. Wilson Hall discusses his informant in *Commission*, Q.15555–6, p.566, and attempts to preserve his anonymity, but the Commission immediately identifies the source as Henry Perkins, a district selector later arrested as a Kelly sympathiser, and believed by some to have lured Kennedy and party into a trap at Stringybark, a theory accepted by Hare, *op. cit.*, p.98, and rejected by Sadleir, *op. cit.*, pp.184–5. Ned's dialogue with the dying Kennedy is discussed in Statements, Sr Const. Kelly, 15.7.1880, and Sr Const. Johnston, 7.7.1880, both Kelly Papers. Ned told Kelly, 'Kennedy never said a word but God forgive you', but in front of Johnston told a Mr Gale of the *Daily Telegraph* that the dying sergeant sent his love to his wife.

Scanlon's ring, worn by Joe at Glenrowan, described, *PG*, 4.12.1878; the stone identified as a topaz, *Weekly Times*, 3.7.1880; the second ring described, *Weekly Times*, 3.7.1880; identified as Lonigan's ring, returned to his widow, Memo, W. B. Montfort to Det. Insp. Secretan, 31.5.1881; Detective Ward to Det. Insp. Secretan, 1.6.1881; both Kelly Papers.

In their extraordinary dash to the Murray and back, the Kelly gang are as elusive today as they were in 1878; Kelly writers have produced wildly varied versions. Sadleir provides a useful sketch of their movements in his Royal Commission evidence (Q.1858–9, p.111) and in his *Recollections*, pp.193–6.

The Gang's detour via Taylor's Gap is from Telegram, 4.11.1878, Kelly Papers. This previously neglected report fills in a puzzling time gap between the Pioneer Hotel and Everton, and also explains the search parties subsequently recalled from Taylor's Gap for a raid on Sherritts (see later in the text).

The Gang's movements through Oxley and Everton are covered by Ward, *Commission*, Q.314866, pp.164–5, and *Age* 8.11.1878. (Ironically, the *Age* piece was ridiculed at the time, but is remarkably accurate and clearly based on information from Ward.)

Mrs Sherritt describes the eight shots to signal Aaron and places them on a Monday 'at the beginning of the outlaws', (*Commission*, Q.13157, p.475; Ward fixes the date as 28 or 29 October (Q.3162–4, p.165). Hare confirms that Aaron supplied the Gang with food and guarded them (Hare, *op.cit.*, pp.140–1) and describes the location, which can be identified as 'The Kelly Cave', Hare, *op. cit.*, p.168. Telegram, Det. Sgt D. S. Kennedy, 1.11.1878, q. in *O & M*, 5.11.1878, describes and dates the encounter with Margery; see also *O & M*, 7.11.1878; Sadleir, *op. cit.*, p.194, gives an excellent account of the Gang's close call in the floodwaters.

At this point Sadleir's account loses its reliability. The credibility of the Sebastopol Raid, described in Chapter 7, and his own credibility, both hinged on the date the Kellys were sighted at the Sherritt farm *vis à vis* the police raid of 7 November which resulted from that sighting. In his Royal Commission evidence, Sadleir has the Gang reach Sherritts' on 3 November and pass through Wangaratta 'on the morning of the 4th or 5th', (*Commission*, Q.1858, p.111). However, in his *Recollections*, pp.195–6, he has them stay at Sherritts' 'until the night of the 4th, passing through Wangaratta before daybreak [of the 5th]'. This dating gives a delay of only two days before the police raid on Sherritts'. However, the Gang was actually sighted at Wangaratta at dawn on Sunday, 3 November, according to the local stationmaster (*Commission*, Q.13960–1, pp.508–9) or on 1 November, according to Sergeant Steele (Q.8856, pp.320–1). Because no trains ran on Sunday, a stationmaster assigning an event to that day had a clear anchor point for his memory. The 3 November dating is confirmed by a Telegram Brooke Smith to Sadlier, 4.11.1878 *(Commission,* Q.17309–10, pp.652–3), placing the Gang briefly at Sherritts' on the afternoon or evening of 2 November, *five days before the police raid.*

7 THE GREAT SEBASTOPOL RAID, page 72

There is a useful contemporary biography of Standish in David Blair's *Cyclopaedia of Australasia,* Melbourne, 1881, nicely filled out and balanced by Sadleir's sketch in his *Recollections,* pp.266–8. Standish as 'Melbourne's foremost citizen', Ernest Scott, *Historical Memoir of the Melbourne Club,* Melbourne, 1936.

Aaron's view of Nicolson, *Commission,* Q.1480, p.82; Nicolson's exploit with the bushranger, Sadleir in *The Victorian Historical Society Magazine,* September 1911.

Sadleir's background is from his *Recollections,* with the comment about his 'austerity and dignity' from Mrs Val Murray, whose parents were neighbours of Sadleir (interview, 1974).

'The Great Sebastopol Raid' is a quote from Constable Meehan, *(Commission,* Q.17654, p.668). The main sources for the operation are the evidence of Standish, Nicolson and Sadleir in *Commission* and eyewitness press accounts in the *Herald,* 7.11.1878 and the *Argus* 8.11.1878. (The *O & M* account of 9.11.1878 is a reprint of the *Argus* story.) Sadleir gives some additional detail in his *Recollections* and in the *Victorian Historical Society Magazine, op. cit.* A major problem with the Commission material is the degree of bias and distortion caused by the politicking of the three officers, coupled with probably unintentional errors.

The text of Sadleir's telegram, *Commission,* Q.1768, p.107. The make-up of the party, Sadleir's evidence, Q.1768, p.107, which tallied with press estimates (give or take one or two, due to some ambiguities). Nicolson's claim of 'upwards of 50' is a clear distortion which sets the tone for his evidence.

Nicolson's often quoted claim that 'the people heard us a mile off', is usually taken as referring to the police party's approach to Sheepstation Creek. Yet, as noted, the Sherritts were asleep and Nicolson did not speak to any other member of the public before reaching the Byrne house at Sebastopol. By that stage, as noted later in the text, the party had made a fast ride over about a mile of open country, and the *Herald* account makes it clear that the Byrne family had been warned of their approach by the drumming of hooves. Clearly, Nicolson's remarks about being heard a mile away, referred to this later, less critical phase. The contrasting press pictures of the ride to the Sherritts, stressing the silence of the operation, are from the *Argus* and the *Herald.*

In *Recollections,* p.196, Sadleir has Nicolson take charge of the attack on the Sherritt house, while Nicolson *(Commission,* Q.402, p.17), produces a curious picture of each officer seeming to give orders to the other.

Nicolson's account of searching the Sherritt home, *Commission,* Q.403, p.17; Sadleir's account, *Recollections,* p.197. Sadleir's comments on the Sherritt family being in the house and asleep, *Commission,* Q.1773, p.108.

Sadleir, Q.1771, p.108, suggests that there may have been some confusion about Aaron's hut. However, the only dwelling it might have been confused with was the Murphy house and the previously quoted *Argus* description makes it clear that this 'squalid den' with its single bed was no family home.

The 'left hand turn' and other press references to the openness of the country en route to the Byrne home, suggests that the party rode down into the Woolshed via Maddern's

Gap, which gave them almost a mile ride to the house across Limeburner Flat. A descent via Byrnes Gully would have been extremely difficult and would have demanded a *right* turn to the Byrne house.

The *Herald* specifies that the Byrnes were milking when the police approached. Both the *Herald* and the *Argus* confirm—perhaps too closely to be regarded as completely independent—Mrs Byrne's initial fear giving way to impudence.

Sadleir's account of the discussion with Mrs Byrne, *Commission,* Q.1843–5, p.110. Steele's description of Aaron with the axe over his shoulder, the 'bloody dog' reference, and his version of the subsequent discussion with the officers, Q.8872–8, pp.321–2.

Elly Byrne's memories of Aaron at the Byrne home, interview, 14.6.1964. She remembered the morning of the raid, and described it, but did not recall Aaron being present on that specific occasion, though, as I point out in the text, he was far more familiar to her than Joe—a frequent visitor who 'often stayed there for weeks and months together' (*O & M,* 29.7.1879).

Sadleir describes the crucial interview with Aaron in *Commission,* Q.1786–1813, pp.108–9 and Q.1834–51, pp.110–11; Nicolson, Q,405 and 405a, p.17; and Standish, Q.15775–7, pp.573–4 and Q.15873–9, p.577.

There is an area of doubt as to whether Nicolson or Sadleir first spoke to Aaron. However, there can be no serious doubt that Sadleir, in stressing and re-stressing the fact that Aaron was interested only in saving Joe Byrne's life, was speaking the truth. He had nothing to gain by making such a claim. Standish's insistence that Aaron was interested solely in the reward must be seen as a deliberate or accidental distortion, which I seek to explain in the text.

For standing orders that Joe to be taken prisoner, if possible, Q. 5251, p.217; Q.7972, p.298; Q.12212, p.437; Q.13082, p.472; Q.13113, p.474. The last three references show that the orders still applied at the time of Aaron's death.

8 THE TALL UNKNOWN BUSHRANGER, page 79

The notice of surrender, *O & M,,* 7.11.1878; the Proclamation of Outlawry, *O & M,,* 16.11.1878.

O & M, reported on 16.11.1878 that because of hold-up rumours, the gold and silver from the Bank of Victoria, Oxley, and the Bank of New South Wales, Milawa, had been sent to Wangaratta.

For Joe as the Gang's scribe and for the written analysis of their strategies, Hare, *op. cit.,* pp.320–1.

It is usually assumed that the house bailed up by the Kellys was the homestead of Faithfull's Creek Station. However, this property's western boundary was a half-mile to the east, along the main road. The homestead on Faithfull's Creek was on the Euroa run and described by Andrew Lyell as 'an out-station', *Herald,* 12.12.1878. Ned's familiarity with the property, and the connivance of employees, *Herald,* 12.12.1878. For presence of sympathiser Andrew Morton, see Report, Const. Thomas Blade, 6.7.1880, Kelly Papers.

Ben Gould's role discussed by the manager of the Euroa bank, Letter, 13.12.1878, Kelly Papers. See *Argus,* 16.12.1878.

Gloster's role as a Kelly agent is revealed by his extraordinary ability to outfit completely (and stylishly) the four members of the Gang, from boots to elastic-chin-strapped hats (see later in the text), and in a Report from Sr Const. James Gill of Avenel, 13.10.1879, Kelly Papers. Gill states that Gloster was in debt before the Euroa robbery, had 'plenty of money' after it, showed no concern at camping in the bush well away from townships, and had been supplying the Kelly Gang with 'goods' the previous week. In a note of 14.10.1879 on Gill's report, Standish simply refuses to believe Gloster's involvement, thus laying the way for Gloster and his 18-year-old assistant, Beecroft, to be called as witnesses at Ned's trial and give accurate descriptions of Lonigan's death. Both stressed that Ned's version of the police killings was clearly intended to protect his mates. Beecroft's participation in the bank robbery, his obvious enjoyment of the event, his unsupervised freedom, and the fact that he was given Scanlon's watch, all suggest that he was, like Gloster, a member of the Kelly team. (See *O & M*, 14.12.1878.)

The government copy of the Cameron Letter is in Kelly Papers. The original has yet to be discovered and the version sent to Supt Sadleir has also disappeared. However, an interesting detail in the extant copy of the letter tends to confirm Joe as having written the original. On the fourth page, the copyist originally wrote 'last' but later corrected it to 'rest'. Joe sometimes wrote his 'r' with an unusually high loop which made it easily mistaken as an 'l'.

Paddy Allen's story of the Byrne debt and the encounter with Paddy and Joe is from Cookson, *op. cit.*, Sydney *Sun*, 4.9.1911. Paddy places the meeting two days before the Jerilderie hold-up. However, Mrs Byrne would not have been in debt at this stage. As noted, two days before the Euroa hold-up, Joe was seen, 'At Chappells, Woolshed Creek', (*Commission*, Appendix 5, p.690).

'Music' having recently foaled, Telegram, Sgt L. Burland, 12.12.1878, Kelly Papers.

It is usually claimed that Steve Hart reconnoitred Euroa on the Sunday. However, the Euroa publican, De Boos saw Joe's body at Benalla eighteen months later and identified him as the man who had visited his hotel two days before the robbery. (Evidence of Hon. J. H. Graves, MLA, *Commission*, Q.15545, p.566); Steve Hart (or Joe?) enquiring about smelted gold at bank, *Argus*, 14.12.1878.

Rave reviews of Gang's horses, *Herald*, 12.12.1878; *O & M*,, 14.12.1878.

Joe's clothing described, undated Statement, Stephens to Ward, Prosecution Brief, Kelly Papers.

The events of the hold-up are described at length in reports run by Melbourne and provincial papers and in a series of depositions and statements belatedly collected by local police and detectives for evidence at Ned's trial.

For Ned trying to take sole blame for police killings, Gloster Deposition.

Joe as 'tall, unknown bushranger', *Argus*, 12.12.1878; Mrs Fitzgerald chats with Joe, stamps for letter, etc., *Argus*, 14.12.1878; letter dismissed as 'a myth', *Herald*, 13.12.1878; the remarkable complexity of the telegraph line breaking and tangling exercise, *Age*, 13.12.1878; Joe as 'tall, sandy young man', *Argus*, 12.12.1878; the Gang's new clothing described by Detective Ward, Supplementary Report, 17.12.1878, Kelly Papers.

For the role of 'John Carson', Memo, Const. Henry McGuirk, 8.7.1880, Kelly Papers. McGuirk notes, 'Address unknown this man assisted Byrne to guard the prisoners'. For Carson as 'hostage', *Age*, 13.12.1878.

Joe's capture of Watt, Stephen's attempt to attack Joe, Sadleir *Recollections*, p.203; Macdougall's plan for escape, *Argus*, 12.12.1878.

Mrs Scott's outfit and Joe's 'green flag', Mrs Scott, The Kelly Gang at Euroa, typescript, Mitchell Library; proceeds of the robbery, *PG*, 18.12.1878; Ned's trick riding, *Herald*, 18.12.1878.

The prisoners' view of the Gang as 'police-made criminals', Cornelius Crowe, *One Big Crime*, Melbourne, 1920, p.15.

Nicolson and Sadleir's ill-timed expedition, *Commission*, Q.473–524, pp.20–2; Q.1996–2001, p.117; Q.2152–3, pp.124–5. See also Sadleir, *Recollections*, pp.203–6, in which he makes the astonishing admission, 'There was no pressing reason why Nicolson and I should both proceed to Albury'.

Nicolson's semi-blindness is usually ascribed to 'blight' (conjunctivitis). For 'ingrowing eyelashes', interview with Nicolson, *Argus*, 17.12.1878.

Sadleir on Hare, 'remarkably tall', *Recollections*, p.126; his futile galloping, *ibid*, pp.71–2; Hare used by Aaron, *ibid*, p.207.

9 A DOUBLE AGENT, page 89

Fear of the Kellys discouraging railway 'excursionists', *Herald*, 17.12.1878. The *Advertiser's* identification of 'James' Byrne, *O & M*, 12.12.1878.

Sadleir's copy of the Cameron Letter reaches him, *Herald*, 23.12.1878; Telegram, Standish to Berry, 18.12.1878, Kelly Papers; Berry's comments on letter, *Herald*, 18.12.1878; 'clever illiterate', etc., *Argus*, 18.12.1878; 'ability and manliness', etc., *Herald*, 18.12.1878.

Joe's appearance at Chappells, *Commission*, Appendix 5, p.690; description of Chappell, Bill Knowles, interview, 24.10.1970; charge of stealing washdirt, Minutes of Proceedings General Sessions Beechworth, 18.12.1856; partners in Scotchman's Claim, Register of Mining Claims, 1876 and 1877.

Ned and Joe at the Byrne home, *Commission*, Appendix 5, p.690.

Mrs Byrne settles her debt, Patrick Allen q. in Cookson, *op. cit.*, Sydney *Sun*, 4.9.1911.

Aaron's continuing battle for his land, the selection's file, 47658/19.20, VPRS 625, Unit 26, VPRO; Memo, 30.10.1878; Murphy letter, 16.11.1878; second Murphy letter, 11.1.1879; Tuthill and Dickson letter, 11.1.1879; Bailiff's report, 29.3.1879; Application for Lease, 26.3.1879. (This time, Aaron's signature is witnessed by James Ingram, who knew him well but, again, the body of the Application has been filled out by a representative of Tuthill and Dickson—tending to confirm that Aaron was, effectively, illiterate.) Payment details are from Notification of Approval, 28.5.1879.

'Puzzle Ranges' as meeting place, Letter, Joe to Aaron, 26.6.1879, Kelly Papers.

The 'Court of Star Chamber' to select sympathisers for arrest, described by Hare, *Commission*, Q.1266, p.63; among sympathisers named by Williamson and subsequently arrested were Richard Strickland, Robert Millar and Jack McMonigle, as well as Jack Quinn and Tom Lloyd, already well known to the police. Statement, Williamson to Inspector Winch, 6.12.1878, Kelly Papers.

McQuilton, *op. cit.*, p.114, publishes an excellent table which encapsulates the three-month history of the sympathiser debacle, showing date of arrest, reason, number of remands and release date for each of the 23 men. Hare's admission that there was 'not a tittle of evidence', Hare, *op. cit.*, p.193.

Aaron photographed as a Kelly sympathiser, see insert between pages 22 and 23.

Ward's accident reported, *Herald*, 24.1.1878; his interview with Aaron in hospital, *Commission*, Q.13847, p.500.

Aaron's first meeting with Hare, Q.1270–3, p.63; Hare, *op. cit.*, pp.140–1.

Hare's self-deception led to significant distortions of fact, even in Royal Commission evidence. As noted, Aaron's meeting (or alleged meeting) with Joe and Dan, which Hare assigns to 30 January (Q.1270, p.63), was said by Aaron to have occurred on 29 January (Appendix 5, p.691). Hare claims that Joe and Dan were seen heading for the Murray 'the evening of the day that he [Aaron] saw them' (Q.1276, p.64). Actually, they were seen on 1 February (Appendix 5, p.691), *three days later*. This meant that they had supposedly taken three days to travel 15 miles.

Hare's statement that this report 'in every respect' bore out Aaron's story, Q.1276, p.64.

10 THE JERILDERIE LETTER, page 98

For Gill publicising inadequate defence of Jerilderie, see William Elliott, schoolteacher and later editor of the *Gazette* (by then the *Jerilderie Herald)* in his superb 'The Kelly Raid on Jerilderie' by 'One Who was There', an appendix which makes up more than half of the Rev. H. C. Lundy's *History of Jerilderie*, Jerilderie, 1958. Elliott/Lundy provided the major source for my account of the hold-up.

The description of the Jerilderie Letter, details of its writing, etc., were from a study of the privately owned original. Up to this time, it had been known only from a copy made while it was, briefly, in police hands. (The original was presented to the State Library of Victoria in October, 2000, and is available on the library website, http://www.slv.vic.gov.au).

For Ned and Joe working on the Letter immediately before leaving on the raid, see Ned's comment, 'He regretted he had not time to finish it', *Argus*, 11.2.1879.

Joe's account of crossing the shallow Murray and the route to Jerilderie, Lundy, *op. cit.*, p.67; river 'very low', etc., *Sydney Morning Herald*, q. in *Herald*, 14.2.1879. The elaborate and widely copied account of the crossing via a stolen boat, in Kenneally, *op. cit.*, pp.113–15, is inexplicable—especially in having Tom Lloyd's horse swept downstream during his first attempt to cross.

The Gang at Davidson's hotel, Lundy, *op. cit.*, pp.67–8; *Herald*, 14.2.1879; *Jerilderie Gazette q.* in *Herald*, 18.2.1879.

Joe's return to Davidson's Hotel, *Jerilderie Gazette* q. in *Herald*, 18.2.1879. In this account Ned is the later visitor. Other sources make it clear that Joe was the culprit, cf. McQuilton, *op. cit.*, p.118.

Ned's description of Joe, *Herald*, 19.2.1879; Samuel Rea's reaction to Joe, Tarleton q. in *Herald*, 12.2.1879.

Elliott's diary entry about Joe, Lundy, *op. cit.*, p.111; *Gazette* description q. in *Herald*, 18.2.1879. It should be noted that Gill, the Jerilderie editor, did not meet Joe and that Elliott may have influenced the pen portrait published by the *Gazette.*

The encounter with Mrs Gill over the letter, Lundy, *op. cit.*, p.86; *Herald*, 12.2.1879. Wires in 'a fearful mess', *Argus*, 11.2.1879. Joe nearly shot by William Rankin, Lundy, *op. cit.*, p.88.

For the presence of sympathisers, *Jerilderie Gazette* q. in *Herald*, 18.2.1879. 'We never remember seeing so many strangers about'.

'Consummate judgement' in hold-up, *Herald*, 11.2.1879.

Hare's examination of Jerilderie Letter, comments, Hare, *op. cit.*, pp.154–6. It is interesting that Hare's alleged verbatim quotes from it are actually loose paraphrases.

Elliott's review of the Letter, Lundy, *op. cit.*, pp.105–6.

The 'sympathiser letter', *Herald*, 4.7.1879; *O & M*, 12.7.1879.

The Kelly songs are widely published. A notable early collection is John Meredith's *Six Songs from the Kelly Country*, Sydney, 1955. A more exhaustive and well sourced collection is presented by Meredith and Bill Scott in their eclectic *Ned Kelly After a Century of Acrimony*, Dee Why West, 1980. Graham Seal's important *Ned Kelly in Popular Tradition*, Melbourne, 1980, gives an excellent selection with incisive commentaries, and J. S. Manifold's *The Penguin Australian Song Book*, Ringwood, 1980, offers an amiable cross-section.

The well-known Melbourne saddler Kinnear, a Melbourne sympathiser and agent of the Gang, had a manuscript of 'The Ballad of Kelly's Gang' in Joe's handwriting. It has since disappeared. Other Kelly songs are attributed to Joe but provenance is, of course, impossible.

The 1879 Hobart broadside is in the Mitchell Library, reproduced Seal, *op. cit.*, p.21.

11 'MY BOY TOMMY', page 110

Reward to £8000, Supplement to VGG, 14.2.1819.

Aaron's first words to Hare after Jerilderie, Hare, *op. cit.*, p.159; Hare's account of the interview, *Commission*, Q.1276, p.64.

Taylor's Gap sighting, *Commission*, Appendix 5, p.691; Ward's views, Q.13849, p.501; press reports, *Argus*, 13.2.1879; *O & M*, 13.2.1879.

Ward's reiterated warning about Aaron, Hare, *op. cit.*, p.160; Hare: 'I deserve to be sold', *Commission*, Q.1276, p.64; Ward in the buggy boot, Hare, *op. cit.*, p.160; Hare 'very much put out', *Commission*, Q.1278, p.64.

Aaron leads Hare and Ward to Byrnes', Hare, *op. cit.*, pp.160–5; 'equally savoured version given to the Royal Commission', *Commission*, Q.1278–9, pp.64–5.

Establishment of cave parties, Q.1279–80, p.65; Q.7781–92, p.293; Hare, *op. cit.*, pp.165–8.

The site of the main police camp is known locally as 'The Police Caves', although there is, strictly, only one 'cave'. Several locals, including Bill Knowles, Jack McIntosh and historian Roy Harvey, independently identified the site in the early 1960s. In 1966 I examined the 'caves' with Albert Tucker. We found a few shards of bottle glass and recovered several beef and sardine tins from leaf mould around the base of a large sheltering boulder described by Hare as Aaron's sleeping place. At Albert's suggestion, we scoured the slope below the camp site and found dozens of bottle bases, necks and shards. With my son Darren, I recovered a further collection of bottle fragments in 1991.

Local tradition also pinpointed 'The Kelly Cave' below the crest of Native Dog Peak where the Gang sheltered after Stringybark. Hare identifies this as the camping place for his second party (Hare, *op. cit.*, p.168). A total lack of debris suggests that Senior Constable Mayes and his four men were a far more responsible and disciplined group than those in the lower camp, who probably relaxed their standards after Hare's departure—by then knowing that the location of the site was almost common knowledge in the Woolshed.

Aaron brings 'hopes of success', Hare, *op. cit.*, pp.161–8; Aaron's 'peculiar dress', *ibid.*, p. 187.

Hare's description of Aaron's ability to withstand cold and Aaron's estimate of Ned as 'superhuman', *Commission*, Q.1280–2, p.65. This incident is usually attributed to the autumn of 1879, despite 'water…frozen on the creeks'. It was clearly in the winter of 1880. See Q.1487, p.83.

Hare's alleged power over Aaron, Hare, *op. cit.*, p.181.

Hare lets Joe pass to the Byrne home, *ibid.*, pp.191–2; local tradition that Joe's walk recognised, Bill Knowles, interview, 24.10.1970; 'astonishment of the constables', C. H. Chomley, *The True Story of the Kelly Gang of Bushrangers*, Melbourne, n.d., but 1940s, p.104.

Preparing for Joe's visits, Elly Byrne, interview, 15.6.1964.

Arrival of the Aboriginal police, *Commission*, Q.1285, p.66.

Standish with a watch party, Q.47, p.3.

Claim that police horses seen in Aaron's paddock on second day of cave party, Q.7795, p.293; Margret finds the whittled stick, Hare, *op. cit.*, p.169, *Commission*, Q.1284, p.66; Margret, 'a most active old party', Hare, *op. cit.*, p.168.

Margret Byrne's discovery of Aaron in the police camp is described by Hare in *Commission*, Q.1284, p.66 and Hare, *op. cit.*, pp.186–7. Both sources describe that evening's conversation between Aaron and Mrs Byrne. In Hare's autobiography, he claims that Mrs Byrne immediately accused Aaron of having 'put the police into that camp', *(ibid.,* p.190). I have followed the less melodramatic version presented to the

Royal Commission eleven years earlier.

Margret Byrne's second visit to the police camp is, again, described in both sources. In his autobiography Hare claims that it occurred the same day as the first visit. However, his Royal Commission evidence, which is, surprisingly, far more detailed than the written version, assigns it to the following day.

The exchange between Aaron and Hare, *Commission*, Q.1285, p.66.

The 'two old women' discover the camp, Hare, *op. cit.*, p.191.

Paddy Allen's views on the cave party, q. in Cookson, *op. cit.*, Sydney *Sun*, 4.9.1911.

Margret Byrne 'constantly abusing' Aaron, Hare, *op. cit.*, p.182.

Mrs Byrne expects Aaron to marry Kate, *Commission*, Q.13174, p.475; Margret denies engagement, *O & M*, 29.7.1879.

Sources for the story of 'Charlie' are cited in chapter 12; Aaron's comment on taking the horse, Hare, *op. cit.*, p.176.

The exchange between Aaron and Margret Byrne, *O & M*, 29.7.1879.

Aaron remains 'brother' to Byrne children, *Commission*, Q.15155–6, p.549.

James Dawson as school friend of Jack, G. W. Brown, Notebook, 15.5.1866.

Hare's random 'search parties', Hare, p.205.

The story of the Whorouly Races adventure is from Hare, *op. cit.*, pp.177–81, and *Commission*, Q.5312–28, pp.219–20, in which Constable Falkiner gives his version. Hare provides some useful and conflicting details in Q.1362–5, p.74. Here, there is no Aunt Sally, Johnston is a bookmaker and Falkiner plays the 'yokel' race patron. Because the behaviour of the third man is so consistent with Johnston's character, I have followed the version from Hare's autobiography. The assessment of the three troopers, Hare, *op. cit.*, p.210. The final exchange between Hare and Falkiner, *Commission*, Q.5312, p.219.

12 THE STRANGE CASE OF A HORSE CALLED CHARLIE, page 125

The 'John Smith' letter of 6.4.1879 is in Kelly Papers with a Memo from Nicolson to Mullane of 7.5.1880, prompted by the second 'Smith' letter of 30.4.1880. This letter had been dated, in error, '1879' but the postmarks on the envelope clearly place it in April 1880. In a further confusing detail, a Memo, Ward to Nicolson, 14.4.1880 (16 days before the second letter was posted), comments on the previous year's letter and, as indicated in the text, treats it as though written in the current year. Adding to the general confusion, the second letter is catalogued as being from 'A. Sharpe', a misreading of 'As I hope'.

The story of Charlie the gelding is basically drawn from Prosecution Brief, Queen v. Sherritt, which includes the depositions of Margret Byrne, Paddy Byrne, Margaret Skillion and William Jefferson (Greta Hotel storeman). Bemusingly, a deposition from Sr Const. Mullane consists of 'I arrested'. This brief, with attached Warrant, Criminal Offence Report, and Correspondence between Brooke Smith and Nicolson, before and after the trial, comprises a dossier sent to Nicolson in Benalla and preserved in Kelly Papers.

Additional material, including evidence from Ellen Byron, James Dawson and Mullane, *O & M*, 17.7.1879, 24.7.1879 and 27.7.1879, and Melbourne *Herald*, 26.7.1879.

Hare's account of Aaron's foiled wooing of Kate Kelly is from Hare, *op. cit.*, p.201. His page heading, 'Off with the old love', makes it clear that Aaron was renewing, not initiating, the relationship.

Hare does not link the curious incident of Aaron's attempted arrest with the 'Charlie' case, but this emerges from the evidence of Mullane, *Herald*, 26.7.1879, and *O & M*,

29.7.1879, from Maggie Skillion's evidence in *Herald*, 26.7.1879, and from a rather perfunctory marginal note to Maggie's deposition in Prosecution Brief. On the basis of pure credibility, one hesitates to place the attempted arrest, complete with firing of shots, between Aaron's first and second attempts to sell Charlie to Maggie Skillion. However, Mullane is quite specific that the communication between Oxley and Beechworth was in April, before the transaction was completed *(Herald,* 26.7.1879; *O & M,* 29.7.1879). This communication, which exonerated Aaron, could not pre-date the attempted arrest.

The curious incident on the night of 13 May is described in a series of endorsements to a Memo from Sadleir of 19.9.1879 seeking information about Aaron's saddle, which was still missing. Arthur's note of 23.9.1879 provides some useful detail (including that he and Mountiford were not trying to arrest Aaron but were there 'to ascertain if Mrs Skillion's statement was true, regarding a horse'). Further detail, including the involvement of 'Tom Sawyer' (Straughair was pronounced 'Stroy-yer') is supplied by Mountiford's Report, 15.10.1879, in reply to Sadleir's Memo. All are in Kelly Papers.

Anne Sherritt's letter to Ward, 1.7.1879, Ward's Memo to Hare, 2.7.1879 and Joe's alleged letter to Aaron, 2.6.1879 were originally together in Police File 0.6650. They are now scattered in Kelly Papers. The alleged Joe/Aaron letter was first quoted by the author in *Ned Kelly, Man and Myth, op. cit.,* pp.90–1. McMenomy, *op. cit.,* reproduces the letter (p.138).

Paddy Allen's account of the £100 failing to reach Aaron, q. in Cookson, *op. cit.,* Sydney *Sun,* 4.9.1911.

The movements of the Gang on 10.7.1879 and 11.7.1879, *Commission*, Appendix 5, p.691, and Memo, Ward to Nicolson, 17.7.1879, Kelly Papers.

Anne Sherritt's extraordinary description of Ned Kelly's visit to her home is from Commission, Q.13166–8, p.475. I have assigned the visit to 10 July (*Commission*, Appendix 5, p.691) because, although Ward told the Commission that this was the date of an alleged encounter between Joe and some of the Sherritt children on the way home from school, he was speaking without any notes except a printed list of sightings (the basis of Appendix 5), and his evidence suggests some confusion between the two incidents ('they took some bread from them').

Appendix 5 also contains detail which seems drawn from both incidents—more than one outlaw involved, while identifying the location as 'At Mrs Jones near Beechworth' rather than en route to Reid's Creek.

Mrs Sherritt says that during the school homecoming encounter (actually, she has them going *to* school) Joe warned Aaron to sleep outside because 'Ned Kelly was coming in to shoot him'. (*Commission*, Q.13179, p.476). Yet if this occurred on 10 July, it would be only one week after the meeting between Joe and Aaron following on Ned and Joe's invitation for Aaron to join the Gang. Ned's friendly visit could hardly intervene and, clearly, did not predate Joe's written offer. Yet it is equally illogical that if it occurred *after* 10 July, Ned's amiable invitation to Aaron could occur within four days of the threat conveyed by Joe (Anne Sherritt was quite specific that Ned called while Aaron was a fugitive and he was arrested on 14 July).

On all these grounds, I reject the date of 10 July for the alleged homecoming encounter and assign to it Ned Kelly's baby-nursing visit.

We are left with the aberration of the alleged interception of the Sherritt children, which plunges further into confusion with Anne Sherritt's suggestion that the man involved may not have been Joe Byrne at all, but James Wallace (*Commission*, Q.13179, p.476)! Unless we locate the detailed report on which the 10 July entry in Appendix 5 was based, the confusion remains.

Hugh Sherritt had been born on 13.12.1878. Anne says that the two girls were 'fifteen', suggesting that one of them was 15-year-old Julia, who knew Ned well. Yet Ned's 'cover' story about a mob of cattle makes it clear that neither girl knew him. This and Mrs Sherritt's reference to 'little girls' would favour two of the younger Sherritt daughters, possibly 12-year-old Esther (who was 14 when Anne gave her evidence) and 9-year-old Mary. Two younger girls, Maria (7) and Martha (3) were probably away with Anne.

Standish advises against a deal to save Joe's life, Letter, Standish to O'Loghlen, 9.1.1879, Kelly Papers, VPRO.

Anne Sherritt's account of her afternoon tea party and her suspicions of Wallace, *Commission*, Q.13176, p.476.

The scathing assessment of Wallace's information by the Royal Commission and Nicolson, Q.14769 and 14772, p.535.

Wallace's admission of financial troubles, Q.14663, p.532; Ward's betrayal of Wallace as a police agent, Q.14639–57, pp.531–2; Wallace's belief that Aaron would warn the Kellys about him, Q.14639, p.531; Wallace's behaviour over Aaron's Euroa money, Q.14629–33, p.531.

Hare, *op. cit.*, p.176, has the superintendent's comments on Aaron's evasion of arrest and on pp.176–7, he describes his 'capture'. The date of the arrest is noted on the back of the Warrant in Prosecution Brief, Kelly Papers.

Aaron's first court appearance, remand, and bail, *O & M*, 17.7.1879; the second appearance and remand, *Herald*, 22.7.1879, and *O & M*, 24.7.1879.

Memo Ward to Nicolson 17.7.1879 in Kelly Papers describes Jack eavesdropping at the Byrnes, discusses arrangements for the proposed prosecution of Aaron as a Kelly sympathiser, and contains Ward's proposal for Aaron's second staged arrest.

Telegram Nicolson to Brooke Smith, 21.7.1879 in Prosecution Brief, Kelly Papers, refuses request for further remand of Aaron, with Brooke Smith's note to Mullane.

Aaron's trial described, *Herald*, 26.7.1879, and *O & M*, 29.7.1879. It is interesting that the *Herald* account, while using supposedly verbatim quotes, has clearly paraphrased. In marked contrast, the *O & M* story captures the flavour of witnesses' speech.

Memo Brooke Smith to Nicolson 28.7.1879, accompanying Prosecution Brief, Kelly Papers, provides clear proof that Aaron's discharge had not been contrived by the police. Yet many writers have made this assumption. Hare is probably to blame, with his highly inaccurate claim that 'the evidence was not sufficient for the magistrates to commit him for trial, as the horse was not forthcoming, and Aaron was acquitted'. (Hare, *op. cit.*, p.177.) This led the usually reliable Chomley to the dangerously embroidered paraphrase, '*It was contrived* [my emphasis] that not enough evidence should be brought forward to commit him for trial' (Chomley, *op. cit.*, p.110). Brown, *op. cit.*, p.151, and Clune, *op. cit.*, p.241, make similar claims.

13 TANGLED WEB, page 138

The 'totally erratic' behaviour of Joe and Aaron is summarised in *Commission*, Appendix 5, pp.691–4, except the last-mentioned meeting with Joe when Aaron was supposedly watching the Byrne home with a police party. This is discussed in Chapter 14.

The 16 August meeting between Ward and Wallace, Aaron trying to get pardon for Joe, Memo Ward to Nicolson, 19.7.1879, Kelly Papers.

Wallace's shopping expedition, plot to betray Gang and save Joe, laundering Kelly gold, etc., Memo, Watd to Nicolson, 26.8.1879, q. in *Commission*, Q.14773, p.535.

Aaron's long and unproductive stay with Wallace, Memo, Ward to Nicolson, 1.9.1879,

Kelly Papers; threatening letter from Joe, *Commission*, Appendix 5, p.692; offer of reward for Standish *et al.*, Q.13583, p.501; 'reward' letter posted by Jack, Q.15671, *et seq.*, pp.570-1; Ward's suspicions of Aaron fail to discourage the charade, Q.14791, p.536; the Chiltern meeting with Joe, not mentioned until ten days later, Appendix 5, p.692.

Jack engaged as police agent, *Commission*, Q.14896-8, p.540; Jack's regular contact with Joe, Q.14893-5, p.540; '50 or 60' letters from Joe, Q.15384 *et seq.*, p.557; Jack receives caricatures of police, etc., Q.15105, p.547.

Description of Ellen Barry, Bill Knowles, interview, 24.10.1970, and Sherritt family tradition, which also provided the nickname 'Belle'.

For Belle's job with the Ingrams and details of the Ingram household, interview, 1962, with Miss Ingram and Mrs E. Ellis Bird, both granddaughters of James Ingram.

Belle met Aaron 'two months before we were married', *Commission*, Q.13291, p.479.

Belle knew Joe, *Commission*, Q.13283, p.479; Q.13788, p.498; mother delivered last two Byrne children, Birth Certificates, Margaret Byrne, 7.2.1869, and Ellen Byrne, 12.2.1871; father on school council with John Byrne, Building File, School 689, VPRO; brother goes to school with Denny Byrne, *Commission*, Q.12196, p.436.

Aaron wearing Hare's dinner jacket, Brown, *op. cit.*, p.153. The source is unattributed but was clearly Richard Warren who described Aaron's flash appearance to Brown.

Joe's letter to Jack, and the wait at Thompson's, *Commission*, Q.14904 *et seq.*, p.540; encounter with Joe, Q.14904, p.541; Q.15613, p.569; Q.15104, p.547; Appendix 5, p.693; scouting bank for Gang, Q.14908, p.541; short of cash, Q.15104, p.547; meeting at Evans Gap, Q.15245, p.553; Jack's sense of being watched, Appendix 5, p.693.

Jack to tell Joe it was too dangerous to stick up Yackandandah bank, Q.14945, p.542.

Jack's account of Dan Kelly's call at the Sherritt homestead, his ride to warn the police, and their inactivity, is from his Royal Commission evidence, Q.14912-51, pp.541-2, and his affidavit, Q.15216, p.551. Nicolson's version, Q.16894, pp.629-30.

For the whole Gang at Sherritts at 8 p.m., *Commission*, Q.14921, and 14933, p.541.

Joe asks Aaron and Jack to help in hold-up of Beechworth bank, etc., *Commission*, Appendix 5, pp.693-4; Jack claims that mother, sister or Aaron told the police of the visit, Q.15149, p.549; Ward names Jack as informant, Q.15624-6, p.569.

Jack claims that Nicolson wished he and Aaron to take part in bank robbery, Q.15464-5, p.559; Nicolson's oblique admission, Q.15474, p.559; Jack 'a coward', Q.16896, p.630; Nicolson happy to let Aaron be taken to New South Wales by Gang, Q.16895, p.630.

Second cave party set up 3 December, Q.13541, p.489. Surprisingly, Nicolson dates it to 2 December, Q.16911, p.638. The 3 December date confirmed, Appendix 5, p.694.

Constable Barry contracts rheumatism during cave party, Q.7948, p.297.

The second cave party (Nicolson's) was in a new location which has not yet been identified. Nicolson is vague, if not misleading, as to its whereabouts. However, Jack Sherritt places it 'on top of the hill', (Q.15122, p.548); Mullane, a good bushman, says it was 'about a mile or a mile and a half', from Byrnes (Q.13544, p.489); Falkiner says that Mrs Barry, whose home was just east of the Sunbury Bridge, lived 'facing the cave' (Q.5574, p.226). All this suggests that the cave was on the north-east face of Native Dog Peak and almost on the rim of the tableland, consistent with Anne and John Sherritt being able to drive a dray close to it (Q.1320, p.477).

14 'STRATEGIC MOVEMENTS AND WELL-LAID PLANS', page 146

Jack's disapproval of Aaron marrying Belle, *Commission*, Q.15024, p.544; Belle's view of the Sherritt attitude, Q.13286, p.479; Mrs Barry's view, Q.13441–2, p.485.

Aaron's quarrel with mother, Q.13287, p.479; with father, and 'specially bad friends' with Jack, Q.13440, p.485.

Aaron's account at the Hibernian Hotel, attachments Memo, Monfort to Acting Chief Commissioner, 24.6.1881, Kelly Papers.

Aaron watches the Byrne house alone until 'eight or nine', *Commission*, Q.13855, p.502.

Jack describes Joe and Aaron's visit to E Fang's store, Q.14973, p.542. Nicolson wrings out of Jack the approximate date of Joe and Aaron's visit—about a week after Joe calls at Sheepstation on 23 November, Q.15320–8, p.555; Q.15288–90, p.554. This would place the visit about 1 December. Yet Jack stresses that 'the police knew where he was with them this night', (Q.14973, p.542), making it clear that the incident occurred after 3 December, when the watch on the Byrne house was re-established.

Paddy Allen's account of Aaron and Belle's marriage, q. in Cookson, *op. cit.*, Sydney *Sun*, 4.9.1911; details from Marriage Certificate, Aaron Sherritt and Ellen Barry, 26.12.1879. Belle's mother may have encouraged her to add two years to her age. Mrs Barry, too, had married at 15 and claimed to be 17. Earlier birth certificates for her children falsify her age, while later she is happy to lose the two years. Cf. Birth Certificates, Ellen Barry, 2.2.1864, and Bridget Barry, 20.8.1875.

Details of Beechworth's Boxing Day celebrations, *O & M*, 27.12.1879; two-day honeymoon, *Commission*, Q.14164, p.516.

Jack at Melbourne athletics meeting, Q.15353–4, p.556.

Barry's note to Ward, asking to be relieved, Q.7515, p.287; 'something crooked' about it. Q.7964, p.298; told by Ward to 'keep quiet', Q.7968, p.298.

Paddy Allen making £30 a month from cave party, Q.12108, p.431; Aaron: 'to show we were doing something', Q.12113, p.432; Ward out to 'curry favour' with Nicolson', Q.14829, p.538; Ward's view that Aaron would not sell Joe, Hare, *op. cit.*, p.158.

Barry describes Aaron as 'listless', crackers incident, *Commission*, Q.7312, p.282; Aaron and Belle separate, are reconciled, Q.14170, *et seq.*, p.516; Aaron and Belle live with Mrs Barry, Q.800, p.35; cf. Q.5575, p.227.

Aaron gets saddle on credit, sister prized employee, Q.14044, and Q.14059–60, p.511.

The 'hurdy gurdy', described by Bill Knowles, interview, June 1960.

The extraordinary story of Belle's stolen saddle emerges from Memo, Sadleir to Acting Chief Commissioner, 16.12.1880, Kelly Papers, in which Sadleir describes the police investigation and his growing suspicion of Jack Sherritt, leading to withdrawal of charges against the Byrnes. Ward discusses the case, *Commission*, Q.15635–70, p.570, and Q.15694–707, p.571, carefully skirting around his involvement while forced to make some damaging admissions concerning the collar and tie found in the Barry house after the theft. When Ward is asked, 'Your collar and tie might have been found there?' he admits, 'Yes, they might.' (Q.15704, p.571.) Constable Armstrong's claim that Ward contrived the case, Q.12184–7, p.435. Nicolson's statement that Jack stole the saddle and planted it, Q.16896, p.631. When Nicolson questions Jack about the saddle, Jack both protests his innocence and admits guilt in a single remarkable speech: 'I say, gentlemen, Mr Nicolson must think I am very ignorant and low, if you want to make out that I took the saddle. If I *give any evidence I will only be criminating myself*' [my emphasis] (Q.15414, p.557). Mrs Barry briefly mentions the incident, Aaron's belief in Jack's guilt, Jack's claim that 'young Byrne' had taken the saddle, and comments, 'But young Byrne did not know where the saddle was at my place', Q.13447, pp.485–6.

Paddy Allen's account of the fight between Aaron and Jack and its aftermath, q. in Cookson, *op. cit.*, Sydney *Sun*, 4.9.1911.

Nicolson's comments on Ward 'working out the problem of the capture of the outlaws', etc., endorsement to Ward's claim to Kelly Reward Board, 20.8.1880, Kelly Papers; Downes's opinion of Ward's 'strategic movements and well-laid plans', Letter, Downes to Sadleir, 14.9.1880, Kelly Papers.

Downes's conversation with Margret Byrne, her view of Ward's using Aaron as bait, etc., *Commission*, Q.13490, p.487. Downes's comment 'there was a horse stealing case *at the time*', shows that he had confused the 'Charlie' case and the case of Belle's saddle. It is interesting that, in a letter to a friend, written immediately after Aaron's death, Downes claims that, after his talk with Mrs Byrne, he took the information to Ward 'in order to save him [Aaron] from an untimely death', Letter, Enoch Downes to John Blight, 6.6.1880 (completed 3.7.1880), MS 10612, Latrobe Library. (I am grateful to Kevin Coleman for drawing my attention to the Downes letter.)

The Kellys constantly at Sebastopol during police surveillance, *Commission*, Q.15846, p.559.

Jack exposes the farce of watching only the front of the Byrne house while the mining race, 'the deep rise there was in front of Mrs Byrne's house', provided cover for arrivals and departures, *Commission*, Q.15032, p.544; Paddy Byrne reveals that Joe has visited home while police were watching, Q.15028, p.544; Ward debunks the story, Memo, Ward to Nicolson, 21.2.1880, Kelly Papers; Ward's enigmatic, 'I made enquiries', Q.15648, p.570; Aaron and Jack come to blows, six bottles of brandy, Memo, Ward to Nicolson, 21.2.1880, Kelly Papers.

Standish's concern at 'undue proportion of criminal classes', in north-east, selections as depots for stolen horses, etc., Memo, Standish to Acting Chief Secretary, 4.5.1879, Kelly Papers; police comments on applicants for land, Memo, Whelan to Nicolson, 8.10.1879, Kelly Papers; Bill Tanner's reply from Secretary for Lands, *Commission*, Q.3553, p.177.

James Wallace collecting mouldboards, *Memo*, Ward and Considine to Secretan, 22.12.1881, Kelly Papers; description of outlaws with 'iron plates on breast and head', *Lorna Doone* by R. D. Blackmore, OUP, Melbourne, 1949, p.10; Joe's opposition to the idea of armour, *Commission*, Q.17786, p.674; inspiration from an 'illustrated edition' of a Scott novel, E. E. Morris, Professor of English, Melbourne University, in *Cassell's Picturesque Australia* of 1889; Child and Henry facsimile, *Australia's First Century*, 1980, p.857, cf. *Herald*, 2.7.1880.

My thesis of the Kelly rebellion and the shadowy Republic of North-East Victoria was first presented at the Wangaratta Seminar of 1967 and published the following year in *Ned Kelly Man and Myth, op. cit.* The initial academic reaction was dismissive or derisive. However, in 1979, McQuilton's superb *The Kelly Outbreak, op. cit.*, developed the thesis and linked it with a masterful analysis of the Kelly phenomenon in terms of E. J. Hobsbawm's theories of primitive rebellion. The following year, Molony, in *I am Ned Kelly, op. cit.*, without reference to my work or McQuilton's, accepted rebellion and Republic as fact, on the basis of oral material from Tom Lloyd, jr.

I first encountered the idea of the Republic in Max Brown's landmark *Australian Son* of 1948 in which he quoted a legend that the Declaration of the Republic had been found in Ned's pocket at his capture. The notion remained dormant until an interview with Tom Lloyd jr on 4.1.1964 in which he first confided to me his father's story of the Glenrowan campaign—the firing of the rockets, the gathering and dismissal of the sympathisers, and Ned's attempts to rescue the other members of the Gang. As I advanced the work of cross-checking Tom's version of events with documented incidents and statements, Tom volunteered some material about the Republic at an interview on 10.5.64, in the presence of Keith McMenomy and my son Darren. Later that year Joe Griffiths and Les Tanner confirmed some details, challenged others. Subsequently, Tom told me of the preservation of a copy of the Declaration and of the 'exercise books containing records of meetings'.

Some years later, in 1969, senior Melbourne journalist Leonard Radic told me that in the winter of 1962–3 he had come across a printed copy of the Declaration in the Public Records Office in London. While unable to remember detail of its contents, he clearly recalled its 'quaint, mock-legalistic language'.

The PRO denied the existence of the Declaration and, perhaps predictably, in the light of this denial, an intensive search in 1969 and 1970 (with the valued help of Barry Jones and Tony Richardson) failed to locate it. However, Radic was a trained and highly reputable reporter with no conceivable motive for imagining or inventing such a document. His encounter with the Declaration and its subsequent disappearance create a titillating mystery. See Jones, *Ned Kelly: A Short Life*, Port Melbourne, 1995, Note, p. 377.

The making of Ned's prototype suit of armour is described by Kenneally, op. cit., pp.113–16. Based on Tom Lloyd's account, the Kenneally version is broadly accurate, but contains some anomalies—all the mouldboards stolen, much of the work done at the smithy near the Kelly homestead, all four suits made by the same men at the same time, and a helmet made only for Ned's suit. The last-mentioned furphy is slow to die, in spite of clear documentation of the other helmets. See the author's 'The Kelly Armour, fact and fantasy' in *The Last Outlaw*, Melbourne, 1980, pp.68–70 (including the identification and siting of the components of Ned Kelly's armour, which were 'discovered' 20 years later).

Some details in my account are drawn from interviews with Tom Lloyd jr (January 1964), Jack Plant (February 1964), and Bill Knowles (October 1970).

The 'DSA' description of the making and testing of the armour, *Commission*, Q.755, p.33.

15 AT THE DEVIL'S ELBOW, page 159

Descriptions of the hut at Devil's Elbow, *Commission*, Q.1481–3, p.82; Q.3639–48, p.180; Q.3703, p.181; Q.10442–53, p.376; Q.13082, p.472; Q.12192, 12196, p.436, etc. 'Great clumsy doors', Q.10448, p.376; 'impromptu' table, Argus, 2.7.1880.

The back of the hut and a ground plan were drawn by Thomas Carrington (*Sketcher*, 17.7.1880). An anonymous artist sketched the front of the hut and a plan for the Royal Commission. The plan only was included in *Charges Against Members of the Police Force*, 24.12.1881, a supplementary Return published with the Minutes and Report of the Commission.

Aaron's application for transfer of the lease to Emma Crawford, the selection's file VPRS 625, Unit 736, VPRO. Mrs Barry says that he sold the selection before his marriage (*Commission*, Q.13456, p.486). The formalities were completed on 5.7.1880 with a transfer fee supposedly received from Aaron *ten days after his death* (receipt in selection's file, *op. cit.*).

Bessie Sherritt visits the cave party, Q.7958–61, p.297; Belle drops in, Q.5590, p.227; Q.7330, p.282; Q.7561, p.288.

Standish protests at cave party luxuries, Memo, Standish to Nicolson, 15.11.1880; Nicolson replies, 2.2.1880 and 11.2.80; Standish defends the expenditure, 13.2.1880; all in Kelly Papers.

Johnston tells Hare of the cave party, *Commission*, Q.862–3, p.37, and Q.16421, p.602; Ward's assurance of secrecy, Q.17225, p.649; orders for winding up the party, Q.17225, p.649.

The three damning reports on the party, Commission, Q.13558, p.490; Falkiner on the

Byrne/Sherritt 'intimacy', etc., Q.13572, p.490; Ward's plea for re-written reports, Q.1618, p.199; Falkiner's about-face, Q.5334, p.220; Armstrong refuses to falsify report, Q.12107–8, p.431; Anne Sherritt describes cleaning up the cave, Q.13206, p.477.

Paddy's cultivation of his resemblance to Joe, (Q.1110, p.52) is attested in the portrait of him published by Hare as a photo of Joe (see insert between pages 174 and 175). Paddy's thicker build, heavy jaw and powerful hands identify him.

Paddy's purchase of the grey mare, Q.12217, p.437; Paddy rides in 'stooping position', Q.12137, p.433; locals believe Joe's Beechworth girlfriend being courted by Paddy, *Herald*, 1.7.1880, *Weekly Times*, 3.7.1880; Paddy's mare stabled during day, *Commission*, Q.1515, p.89.

Ward considers Anne Jane 'a secret, cunning, good girl', Q.14188, p.517; the second 'John Smith' letter of 30.4.1880, Kelly Papers.

Cookson, *op. cit.*, in his interview with Jim Kelly, quotes Aaron's 'bloodcurdling threat of unmentionable atrocity', (Sydney *Sun*, 5.9.1911). Kenneally, *op. cit.*, (p.124) doesn't quite mention the unmentionable, but McQuilton, *op. cit.* (Note 77, p.226) and Molony, *op. cit.*, (p.210) interpret the missing word as 'fuck'. The 'shadowy suggestion of a homosexual relationship between Aaron and Joe', is from Molony, who links Aaron's alleged threat with Enoch Downes' comment that Joe and Aaron had been 'more than a brother to each other', *(ibid.*, Note 17, p.286). This is hardly justified. Downes prefaced his remark by writing, 'You know the scripture phrase there is one that is more than a brother.' The reference is to the Book of Proverbs, 18:24, which contrasts true and false friendship, concluding 'there is a friend that sticketh closer than a brother'. (My thanks to Ernestine Lobb for identifying the Biblical reference.)

Joe's mention of threats supposedly reported via Belle, *Commission*, Q.13429, p.485; Joe's alleged death sentence on Aaron, Kenneally, *op. cit.*, p. 124.

Margret Byrne warns Anne Sherritt 'not to let Moses know', *Commission*, Appendix 5, p.695; Anne Jane sees whole Gang at Byrnes, Q.13207, p.477, cf. Appendix 5, p.695; Anne Sherritt describes the meeting with Joe at Murphy's hut, Q.13184, p.476; Ward puts Aaron on tracks, interview with Ward and Nicolson, Q.789–99, pp.34–5; Q.13858, p.503.

Nicolson fights for time, Q.977, p.44; Renwick called in, reports sighting of Joe, Nicolson's account of expedition, Q.799–801, p.35, and Q.16989–17011, p.640; Ward's version of the events, Q.13860, p.503; Stanhope O'Connor's, Q.1110, p.52. Batchelor sees Aaron with police, Q.15115, p.548; Aboriginal trooper aims at Batchelor, Q.17002, p.640; Aaron killed because of the encounter with Batchelor, Q.7308, p.282; Q.1110, p.397; Q.12098, p.431; Aaron thinks the incident doomed him, Q.13057, p.471.

'Renwick' claims that investigation of his report led to the shooting of Aaron, Reward Application, 24.8.1880; Nicolson rejects suggestion that he endangered Aaron, *Commission*, Q.17017, p.641; Aaron fearing for 'him and his connections', Q.1110, p.52; Nicolson's farewell gift to Aaron, Q.12212, p.437.

In their Second Progress Report, the Royal Commissioners cited the employment of Aaron 'as a guide during daylight—a proceeding that has induced many to attribute the murder of Aaron Sherritt to a want of discretion on the part of the Assistant Commissioner [Nicolson]'.

The Commissioners tended to reject this view because 'some time previously, Byrne had seen Mrs Sherritt at Sebastopol, and had threatened to shoot Aaron.' But, as noted in the text, the nature of the threat suggested that, at this stage, Joe intended merely to frighten Aaron. Nicolson's 'want of discretion' must be recognised as at least a significant factor in the chain of events which led to Joe's final decision to kill his mate.

Nicolson's instructions to Mullane, no further money to 'Tommy or his friends', etc., *Commission*, Q.1465, p.80.

Hare's discussion with Ward, the plan to station police in Aaron's hut, Q.13860–1, pp.503–4; Hare, *op. cit.*, pp.233–4; police in bizarre 'uniform', Q.13810, p.499, cf. Q.3637, p.180; Aaron's comment on Ward's instruction to post no sentry, Q.12207, p.437.

16 SHERRITT'S HAD HIS LAST SUPPER, page 171

Rumble of the coming storm from Chappells, *Commission*, Q.14112, p.514; Mrs Byrne's boast of the Gang astonishing the world, Hare, *op. cit.*, p.235.

Hare and Ward's meeting with Aaron, *Commission*, Q.13861, p.504; Aaron complains at Nicolson's distrust of him, nourishes Hare's ego, happy with the watch party in his hut, Q.1480, p.82.

Ward's greyhound-camouflaged visits to the hut, Q.13884, p.505; buys calico for bed-room door and windows, Q.13882, p.505; Q.14160, p.516; the police buy the hut from the 'foreigner', Q.12131 *et seq.*, p.432.

The arrival of Constables Duross and Dowling, Q.12127, p.432; their backgrounds, Q.4070–1, p.190; Q.3574, p.178; Q.4297–8, p.195; Duross *thinks* he could hit a haystack, Q.3631, p.179; warned against Aaron by Beechworth police, Q.3616, p.179; Armstrong's background, Q.12080, p.432; his courage praised, Q.3408–9, p.172; the new men briefed by Aaron, Q.4286–7, p.195.

Alexander agrees with Commission that Aaron 'false', describes use of towel as signal, Q.13053, p.471; obvious to the 'Melbourne men' that the Gang can arrive at the Byrne house via the back, while they watch only the front, Q.4397–402, p.197; Q.4722, p.205.

The encounter with the Chinese, Aaron delays the next night's departure, Q.12135, pp.432–3; changes story for Duross, Q.3771, p.183.

The 'firewood' incident, a bizarre example of Ward's deception of his superiors, was closely investigated by the Royal Commission. In essence it is described by Armstrong, Q.3771, p.183, by Hare, Q.1481–3, pp.82–3, and by Ward, Q.13861, p.504.

Hare's concern for Aaron lying out in 'the freezing bush', their discussion, etc., Q.1487, p.83; Alexander tells Hare of his doubts about Aaron, Q.13082, p.472.

Ward and Mullane fail to find a more suitable base for the police party, Q.13866, p.505; The Royal Commission considers Aaron's harbouring of police 'enough to seal his doom', Second Progress Report; Hare's 'astonishing' admission that police would remain in Aaron's hut 'till they were discovered', Q.16579, p.606.

Jack's letter to Hare, Q.5124, pp.213–14.

The police see Paddy ride off, Q.5107–113, p.213; Armstrong's report on the incident, Ward's memo describing his investigation of it (which includes the information from Anne Sherritt of a horseman passing her house), and Hare's rather laid back memo in response are all in Q.1516, p.89.

The visit of the 'Diseased Stock Agent' to Hare and his summary dismissal, are from Sadleir, *op. cit.*, p.222. His date of 24 June is disputed. The visit probably occurred on 25 June, the day before Aaron's murder. Nicolson (Letter to Royal Commission, 14.11.1881, Kelly Papers) claims that Hare gave the DSA a receipt bearing that date. Hare is predictably vague, if not totally misleading on the question. See *Commission*, Appendix 12, pp.700–1 for two letter to the Commission from Hare and an affidavit from Nicolson.

Aaron and 'a mounted constable' visiting the hotel where 'Maggie' worked, from 'How We Captured Ned Kelly' by 'Ex-Sergeant James O'Dwyer [*sic*]' in Fitchett, *op. cit.*

Local tradition placed Joe's 'barmaid' girl friend at the Vine Hotel in Sydney Road, a location which tallies with Dwyer's account (interview, Roy Harvey, June 1959). Miss C. Vandenberg, granddaughter of Jacob Vandenberg, original publican of the Vine, identified the girl as a general servant who sometimes helped in the bar. Her name was not 'Maggie' (interview, October, 1960). Miss Vandenberg also provided material about Jacob and gave a charming description of the hotel and its garden. Joe's last visit to his Beechworth girl friend, *Weekly Times*, 3.7.1880.

Much space has been devoted to stories of Aaron being 'sentenced to death' by the Gang. The version in Kenneally, *op. cit.* (p.124), is apparently from Tom Lloyd who was then married to Steve Hart's sister. This may explain Kenneally's contention that 'Steve Hart took no part in discussing this sentence of death'. In Kenneally's account Ned declares that 'he never went anywhere with the intention of shooting anyone; but in a fair fight he was prepared to shoot and shoot to kill', then adds, 'But in this case, Joe, you may do as you like.' In view of Ned's reluctance to believe in Aaron's betrayal ('Did you torture Aaron?' he asked Armstrong, *Commission*, Q.12214, p.437), he may well have tried to dissuade Joe. However, it is incredible that Joe would have shot Aaron without Ned's knowledge and approval. In the Benalla lock-up on the night of Ned's capture, a reporter asked him, 'Why did you shoot Aaron Sherritt in such a manner?' Ned is supposed to have replied, 'I did not do it. I knew nothing about it. Dan and Steve and Joe did it all together, unknown to me. I was bloody wild about it.' (*Weekly Times*, 3.7.1880; *Argus*, 3.7.1880.) The story must be taken on face value. The implication of Steve is patently ridiculous and elsewhere in the interview Ned makes the unlikely comments that accounts of Stringybark Creek were 'right enough in most particulars' and that at Glenrowan his plan was to 'get back into the Benalla barracks where I could hold out for a time'.

It should be noted that he told his prisoners at Glenrowan *before Joe and Dan's arrival*, 'I was in Beechworth last night, and I had a great contract with the police, I have shot a lot of them.' (*Commission*, Q.7607, p.276.) Ned knew there would be bloodshed at the Devil's Elbow and seems to have expected that members of the police party would also be killed. This was the nature of war.

Paddy's night expedition and surveillance of Aaron's hut, Q.4715–21, Q.4723, p.205. See Const. Dowling's view that Paddy was preparing for Aaron's murder, Q.4745–7, p.205.

Denny Byrne tracks the party, Q.12213, p.437, and spies on the hut the day of Aaron's murder; Aaron's warning to Armstrong, Q.12137, p.433.

Aaron's decision to turn Catholic, Q.13290, p.479; his exchange with Mrs Barry about her 'dream of bad', Q.13449, p.486.

The account of Aaron's death is drawn from the Royal Commission (the four police, Anton Wick, Mrs Barry and Belle all gave evidence) from *Charges Against Members of the Police Force, op. cit.*, from depositions at Aaron's Inquest, 28.6.1880 and 30.6.1880, VPRO, from an excellent interview with Belle in *O & M*, 2.4.1881 (arguably the best single account), and from interviews with two of Wick's grandsons, Bill Knowles (various, between 1959 and 1970) and Ron Wick (1989). Of these sources, only the Royal Commission evidence has been widely used in the past. However, my account of Aaron's murder broadly follows the generally accepted course of events and attribution of every detail would be tedious. The following seem worthy of note: Aaron's clothing, deposition by Dr Dobbyn at the inquest; the horses 'kept their heads up', Ron Wick; 'Aaron Sherritt's had his last supper', Bill Knowles; Joe speaks before firing, deposition by Belle at the inquest; 'I have a heart but it's cold as stone', and Dan Kelly looking at Aaron's body, Belle interview, *O & M*; Armstrong and Duross partly under the bed ten minutes after the first shot, Affidavit, Constable Alexander, 27.7.1881, Kelly

Papers; Belle thinks she is shot, *O & M* interview; voices outside the hut, Byrnes suspected, Commission, Q.13161, p.492; Armstrong's 'shivering with cold and greatly excited', Ward, q. in Cookson, *op. cit.,* Sydney *Sun,* 5.9.1911; police don't leave Beechworth until 3 p.m., *Weekly Times,* 3.7.1880.

17 ARMAGEDDON, page 183

Joe signals to sympathisers at the death hut, *Commission,* Q.3814, p.184, Q.13253, p.478.

The moon rises at midnight, Q.4386, p.197.

The contents of Joe's pockets, *Weekly Times,* 3.7.1880; the two rings are visible in a Burman photograph of his body. Scanlon's ring is described in *PG,* 4.12.1878 and *Weekly Times,* 3.7.1880. The second ring, also described in *Weekly Times,* identified as Lonigan's, Memo, Montfort to Secretan, 31.5.1881, and Ward to Secretan, 1.6.1881, both Kelly Papers.

The main source for this account of the Glenrowan hold-up, the gathering of prisoners, and the subsequent 'party', is the MS, 'Minutes of Evidence of the Board appointed to inquire into claim made by Mrs Jones for compensation for destruction of the Glenrowan Hotel', 18.11.1881, with a series of attached Letters from Mrs Jones, all VPRO.

Ned and Steve wearing armour under their coats for the Glenrowan hold-up, *Commission,* Q.7736–40, p.280.

The arrival of Joe and Dan at Glenrowan is usually put much later. Mrs Jones's letter, 1.8.1883, Jones Inquiry, makes it clear that they had arrived by the time Ned went to get Reardon and records that Joe had a drink at McDonnells on arrival. Mrs Reardon, Jones Inquiry, pp.130–2, describes the curious exchange between Joe and the women at the gate house, while Ned and Steve were breaking the line.

Curnow's role at Glenrowan is described in a letter to the Chief Commissioner, which was released to the press and became the basis of his reward application, and in a long statement to the Royal Commission, Q.17597, pp.663–6. See *Thomas Curnow* by L. J. Pryor, privately published, Melbourne, 1986. 'Checkmating the outlaws', Detective Report, A. Eason, 26.7.1880, Kelly Papers.

Mrs Jones's view of Joe quoted by Constable Bracken, Jones Inquiry, p.86, cf. Mrs Jones's evidence, p.35.

Plans to bail up a circus and kill a bullock, *Commission,* Q.7769, p.280; Jones Inquiry, p.135.

O'Connor 'humming and hawing', *Commission,* Q.7769, p.280.

The Inn 'a house of sport', Mrs Jones, letter, 5.12.1882, Jones Inquiry; dancing, card playing, etc., Jones Inquiry, p.53; bonfire, *Commission,* Q.17597, p.665; tired children, wives reluctant to leave without husbands, Jones Inquiry, pp.46–7.

'The Night Before Agincourt', from the *Fourth Book,* n.d., p.331; the train whistle mistaken for the crowing of a rooster, Commission, Q.7761, p.280.

The pressmen in Hare's first charge were Melvin and McWhirter, Q.10306, p.370; Ned describes firing at Hare, being wounded, Q.16317, p.595.

Joe's leg wound and the exchange between Ned and Joe, Affidavit sworn by Constable Phillips, 16.9.1881, *Commission,* Q.17786, p.674.

The firing of the rockets, etc., Man and Myth, *op. cit.,* pp.171–2; *Commission,* Q.11190, p.399; interview, Tom Lloyd jr, 4.1.1964.

Mrs Jones's demented tour of battlefield and hotel, *Commission,* Q.7378, p.284; Mortimer's picture of 'reckless' Joe, Age 30.6.1880; Dan's concern for prisoners, *Commission,* Q.7665, p.278.

Ned turns back the sympathisers, interview, Tom Lloyd jr, 4.1.1964, *Man and Myth, op. cit.*, pp.172–3. Descendants of sympathisers disagreed as to the precise location of this incident and the numbers involved, with estimates from 30 to 150. Subsequent events suggest that there would not have been more than 50. After his arrival in Melbourne, Ned told a fellow convict, 'I had plenty of mates in the neighbourhood ready to join us,' but claimed that he was unable to mount his horse (*Commission*, Q.16317, p.595). However, immediately after his capture, he said 'I...got on my mare and rode quietly up along the fence over the hill'. (*Weekly Times*, 3.7.1880).

The Royal Commission publishes Sadleir's *Return* (Q.2880, p. 154) supposedly showing the time each policeman arrived at Glenrowan (omitting Constables Cawsey and Bracken, who arrived with the Wangaratta mounted contingent). It is a deeply flawed document. It places the arrival of Hare's party almost 50 minutes too early (2.10 a.m. instead of nearly 3) and has Steele and his mounted men, Sadleir's party and the Wangaratta foot police arriving from 5 to 5.20 when they actually reached Glenrowan shortly before 6. See *Commission*, Q.11423, pp. 404–5; Q.11317, p. 402; Q.10321, p. 371 etc. My thanks to Marian Matta for encouraging me to tackle this mishmash and its causes—from deliberate distortion to unwound watches.

Ned's return to the hotel was described by Tom Lloyd jr, interview, 4.1.1964. Constable Dwyer reported that, after his capture, Ned Kelly knew of Joe's death and 'saw him drop', adding, 'Ned Kelly said, when he saw his best friend dead, he had no more faith in them; he left the house', *Commission*, Q.9483, p.343. This quotation bears a striking resemblance to the account given by 'a person who had an interview with the outlaw soon after he was captured', (Weekly Times, 3.7.1880) which has Ned saying, 'I saw Byrne drop dead', and quotes Ned's exchange with Dan in which he describes Joe as 'my best friend'. In Detective Report, 26.7.1880, Kelly Papers, Detective Eason reports, 'During the firing Byrne...called on McAuliffe to come and assist them but although the elder McAuliffe answered him he did not respond and Byrne was soon afterwards shot.' Joe's last words (a striking contrast to this recent call for assistance) and his death wound are reported by Stanhope O'Connor, *Commission*, Q.1141–2, p.55; Reardon hears him fall, blood gushing, Q.76723, p.278; falls across Delaney and Sandercook, Q.11427, p.405. Kate Reardon's memories of Joe's death are from her sister Bridget who, as a five-month-old baby, was also a prisoner at Glenrowan. Kate had died at 92 only a week before (interview, Mrs Bridget Griffiths, 7.8.1964).

Gascoigne's encounter with Ned, report, n.d., Kelly Papers. His verbal report to Sadleir and the superintendent's confirmation that the incident had virtually coincided with his arrival (shortly before 6 a.m.), Sadleir, *Recollections*, pp.229–30; cf. *Commission*, Q.9767, p. 353.

Ned Kelly's Last Stand was intensively documented in press reports, Royal Commission evidence, Police Reports, Reward Claims and later reminiscences. Of the latter, Steele's account, quoted in Fitchett, *op. cit.*, is enlightening. Ned's helmet ringing 'like a cracked bell', is from the 'plucky railway guard', Jesse Dowsett. (Report to Traffic Manager, 2.7.1880; q. in *La Trobe Library Journal*, April 1973, pp.60–1.)

Jack Sherritt, as a civilian, is not included in Sadleir's Return of Arrivals at Glenrowan but he was with the Beechworth contingent. He sleeps at the barracks, rides to get police from death hut, goes to Glenrowan with Beechworth police, 'to be revenged', *Commission*, Q.3885–92, p.186; rides 12 miles in 30 minutes, Q.14980, p.543; in action at Glenrowan, Q.4017, p.189.

Depositions and Jury List from Proceedings of Inquest on Aaron Sherritt, 28.6.1880 and 30.6.1880, VPRO.

Police pay for Aaron's funeral, Memo, Mullane to Sadleir, 2.7.1880, Kelly Papers; Rev.

Mackie conducts service, Death Certificate, Aaron Sherritt, 26.6.1880.

Gibney's description of Joe's body, *Commission*, Q.12314, p.442; Carrington follows to sketch it, Q.10113, p.365; Joe's body on the fence post, interview, Simon Hennessy with Will Sterling, 1959; Julian Ashton's 'most miserable assignment', *SMH*, 25.1.1934, q. in McMenomy, *op. cit.*, p.180; Henry H. Neary, *The Kellys*, Lakemba, n.d. but 1940s, p.33.

'Maggie' and Joe's body, Brown, op.cit., p.230, Age, 30.6.1880 and Diary of Supt Sadleir, 29.6.1880, (my thanks to John McQuilton for this reference); decision to pre-empt Inquest, *Commission*, Q.2249–55, p.130; depositions from Proceedings of Inquiry *(sic)* on Joseph Byrne, 29.6.1880, VPRO; Joe's burial, *Weekly Times*, 3.7.1880, Death Certificate, Joseph Byrne, 28.6.1880. Clune, *op.cit.*, p.317, assumes that the official witnesses at Joe's burial, W.H. Hoskin and J.P. Wilson, were policemen. Neither was a member of the force (Victoria Police Historical Unit). Hoskin was a Benalla blacksmith (*Bailliere's Victorian Post Office Directory 1880–1*) and Wilson appears later as a Beechworth draper (*Wise's Victoria Post Office Directory 1884–5*). The 'well-armed constable' accompanying the undertaker was probably Foot-Constable Thomas Reilly who had fought at Glenrowan, attended the inquest and was informant for Joe's death certificate. In the face of other evidence, Sadleir states that Joe's body was buried at 4 p.m. (Report, Sadleir to Standish, 1.7.1880; *Commission*, Q.2880, p.154).

18 AFTERWARDS, page 195

Belle miscarried. The baby's death was not registered but it was buried in Beechworth cemetery, suggesting that it was close to full term. Belle nearly dying, two doctors, etc., *Commission*, Q.13307, p.480; Q.13455, p.486; Q.13788, p.498.

Belle's accommodation, etc., Detective Report, Ward to Secretan, 20.5.1881, Kelly Papers; accounts attached to Memo, Montfort to Chomley, 24.6.1881, Kelly Papers.

Belle's marriage to Michael Murphy, Marriage Certificate, No. 6024, 1884. Three years later 'Mrs Murphy's' allowance was the subject of memos between Chomley, Montfort, Thomas and Flood, 4–8.7.1887, Kelly Papers. Bill Knowles, grandson of Anton Wick, went to school in the Woolshed with Belle's children (interview, 24.10.1970).

Hare's 'chilling valediction on Aaron', Hare, *op. cit.*, p.322.

Belle on Ward's fears of 'trouble' for 'allowing the camp to be stuck up and Aaron shot', *Commission*, Q.12223, p.438; Ward's Reward Application, 28.12.1880, inc. Detective Report, Ward to Sadleir, 14.8.1880, Kelly Reward Board Papers, VPRO.

John Sherritt goes to police, fears for lives of himself and his family, *Weekly Times*, 3.7.1880; Ward confirms the Sherritts in danger, Telegram, Ward to Standish, 5.7.1880; Sadleir urges help for them to leave district, Memo, Sadleir to Standish, 5.7.1880, both Kelly Papers.

Jack discussed the brief police careers of himself and Willie in his Royal Commission evidence. Date of discharge, 'got a fall from my horse', etc., *Commission*, Q.15196–7, p.550; Nicolson's hostility, Q.16896, p.631; Jack fears that Mrs Byrne would try to kill him, Q.14990, Q.15005 and Q.15014, p.543.

Nicolson's 'scathing condemnation' of the family and Jack, Memo, Nicolson to Standish, 25.8.1880, Kelly Papers; Jack suspected of 'thwarting if not betraying' Aaron, *Commission*, Q.16896, p.630.

Jack's share of the Kelly Reward, *Report of the Kelly Reward Board*, 1881, Schedule B.

Anne Jane spies on Byrnes, their threats to lives of Ward and Mullane, Memo, Ward to Sadleir, 24.7.1880; Ward clears Paddy on evidence of O'Donoghue, Memo, Ward to

Montfort, 10.7.1880, both Kelly Papers; Ward knows O'Donoghue a sympathiser, *Commission*, Q.14182–3, p.517; O'Donoghue running to see Mrs Byrne each day after school, interview, Elly Byrne, 4.8.1964.

Paddy takes a gold claim, Claims Register, op.cit., 11.2.1881; the Byrnes move to Albury, settle in Young Street, etc., interview, Elly Byrne, 4.8.1964; Death Certificate, Margret Byrne, 21.5.1921; Death Certificate, Ellen Byrne, 5.8.1964.

Fire of Christmas 1899, Sherritt family tradition and Harvey, *op. cit.*, p.51. Death Certificates, John Sherritt, 10.6.1900; Agnes Anne Sherritt, 3.3.1908; Robert Nesbitt, 14.10.1903.

Visit to Woolshed and Beechworth in 1906 by Paddy and Denny Byrne, interview, Bill Short, 8.7.1961; Bill Knowles and Jack McIntosh, 30.10.1962. The confrontation between Paddy and Jack was described by Bill Short.

Index